CRITICAL DISCOURSE ANALYSIS

SAGE BENCHMARKS IN LANGUAGE AND LINGUISTICS

CRITICAL DISCOURSE ANALYSIS

VOLUME IV

*Applications, Interdisciplinary Perspectives
and New Trends*

Edited by

Ruth Wodak

Los Angeles | London | New Delhi
Singapore | Washington DC

Los Angeles | London | New Delhi
Singapore | Washington DC

SAGE Publications Ltd
1 Oliver's Yard
55 City Road
London EC1Y 1SP

SAGE Publications Inc.
2455 Teller Road
Thousand Oaks, California 91320

SAGE Publications India Pvt Ltd
B 1/I 1, Mohan Cooperative Industrial Area
Mathura Road
New Delhi 110 044

SAGE Publications Asia-Pacific Pte Ltd
3 Church Street
#10-04 Samsung Hub
Singapore 049483.

© Introduction and editorial arrangement by
Ruth Wodak, 2013

First published 2013

Library of Congress Control Number: 2012936151

British Library Cataloguing in Publication data

A catalogue record for this book is available from
the British Library

Typeset by Zaza Eunice, Hosur, Tamilnadu,
India

Printed on paper from sustainable resources

Printed by MPG Books Group, Bodmin,
Cornwall

MIX
Paper from
responsible sources
FSC
www.fsc.org   FSC® C018575

ISBN: 978-1-4462-1058-1 (set of four volumes)

Contents

Volume IV: Applications, Interdisciplinary Perspectives and New Trends

Genetically Modified Food in the News: Media Representations of the GM Debate in the UK

Martha Augoustinos, Shona Crabb and Richard Shepherd

1. Introduction

Rapid developments in the biosciences and biotechnology have led to widespread public debates about the social, moral, and political implications of these scientific advances. The introduction of genetically modified (GM) food and crops has attracted considerable controversy, especially in Europe and the UK where to date, considerable quantitative and qualitative research has indicated that at best, public attitudes towards GM food and crops are ambivalent and at worst, resistant and hostile (Bauer, 2002; Durant et al., 1998; Gaskell, 1997; Gaskell and Bauer, 2001; Wagner et al., 2001).

This ambivalence and resistance to GM food and crops has posed significant dilemmas for the science/society relationship: the idea that science should provide an uncontested, objective basis for resolving public policy has been increasingly contested. In this context where the legitimacy and moral authority of scientific "facts" are being subject to challenge, there is widespread recognition of the need for new mechanisms of science communication, public consultation and for increased institutional accountability. Governments, in particular, have been faced with the challenge of negotiating and developing consensus policies that attend to the interests and

Source: *Public Understanding of Science*, 19(1) (2010): 98–113.

concerns of a range of stakeholders including industry, the scientific community, and the public at large. As Henderson et al. (2007) have recently demonstrated, debates over GM have become public "battlegrounds" where different stakeholders strategically compete with each other to set the contours of debate and to influence public policy decision making. Nowhere has this been more evident than in Britain with the government sponsored *GM Nation?* debate which took place in 2003 and which attracted significant media coverage and analysis (Heller, 2003; Horlick-Jones et al., 2007a).

Although some researchers have argued that the media is a significant site for gleaning the ways in which public understandings of contentious scientific issues are shaped by dominant and recurring representations, images and metaphors (Conrad, 1997, 1999, 2001; Petersen, 2001), others have been more circumspect about the media's influence arguing that the public processes messages about controversial scientific issues such as agri-food biotechnology in more complex and critical ways than has been previously assumed (Bates, 2005; Condit, 1999; Cook et al., 2006; Hornig Priest, 2006; Ten Eyck, 2005). Even those arguing against a direct link between the media and public opinion, however, have nonetheless emphasized the importance of examining media content in order to understand how controversial issues – such as the GM food debate in Britain – are framed and represented for public consumption. Recently, Hornig Priest (2006: 58, emphasis in original) has argued that the analysis of media is important,

> *not* because media directly determine (or ever fully reflect) public opinion, but because media accounts express relevant values and beliefs, help confer legitimacy to or discredit particular groups by treating them as part of the mainstream or as marginal, and therefore indirectly affect which perspectives do or do not ultimately come to dominate collective discourse and decision-making.

Although there is now a growing body of empirical work examining media coverage of GM foods, much of this analysis has been primarily content analytic identifying the frequency of broad thematic categories and their evaluative tone over designated periods of time (e.g., Bauer, 2002; Gaskell et al., 2003; Hornig Priest, 2006; Ten Eyck, 2005). In comparison, there have been fewer studies which explicitly use critical discursive methods of analysis to examine recurring linguistic patterns which function to construct specific versions or accounts of this highly contested issue. A notable exception is a recent analysis of British newspaper coverage of the GM food debate in the first half of 2003, conducted by Cook et al. (2006). Combining the methods of corpus linguistic analysis and critical discourse analysis, Cook et al. were able to characterize particular British newspapers as having either consistently pro or anti-GM positions. Specifically, *The Times* and *The Sun* were categorized as predominantly pro-GM, and *The Guardian* and *Daily Mail* as anti-GM. *The Times* largely constructed the issue of GM food and crops as a scientific and technological one, and attributed the public resistance and opposition to GM food to a lack of scientific understanding, or what is now typically referred to as the deficit model of the public's understanding (Irwin and Wynne, 2001; Sturgis and Allum, 2004). Opposition to GM food and concerns by critics over the possible environmental and health risks were commonly described as "irrational," "unscientific," "scaremongering," "ignorant," and "anti-science." In short, critics of GM food were positioned as "Luddites" who were responding to this issue with emotion rather than scientific reason. In contrast, the anti-GM broadsheet *The Guardian*, represented the national debate over GM food in a broader social and political context, which emphasized the stake and interest of various stakeholders on this issue, most notably the economic interests of biotechnology companies and the political interests of the British government. Like the pro-GM papers, emotion categories were also commonly deployed by the anti-GM papers, but this was to emphasize the "anxiety," "concern," and "worry" of critics concerning the potential long-term risks of the technology. Lastly, a common metaphor used by both anti and pro-GM papers to categorize the GM food debate in Britain was that of a "war" or "battle" between different stakeholders. Headlines such as "Blair loses GM Battle" and the "Battle of the Food Chain" depicted the issue as a struggle of competing interests (Cook et al., 2006).

This metaphor for the GM debate in the UK as a "battleground" of competing interests is the specific focus of this paper. The present study analyses a corpus of articles on GM crops and food which appeared in six UK newspapers in the first three months of 2004, the year following that analyzed by Cook et al. (2006). Unlike the Cook et al. analysis however, this paper specifically focuses on how the major stakeholders in the GM debate are represented in newspaper accounts and how these stakeholder identities are mobilized in particular argumentative contexts.

As we will demonstrate, the issue of GM food continued to receive extensive newspaper coverage during this period, equaling the attention it received during the *GM Nation?* debate in the previous year. Partly this can be attributed to the impending government decision which was announced in March 2004 to allow the first commercially grown GM crop, Bayer GM maize in Britain. This was anticipated to be a landmark decision which would open the way for GM farming in the UK. On 13 and 14 January all six newspapers contained articles pertaining to the "impending" government decision to approve the commercial growing of GM maize. This was followed by several articles on 19 and 20 February, on leaked minutes from a government cabinet meeting regarding the approval. This government decision was represented by *The Guardian* and the *Daily Mail* – both staunch GM critics – not only as "flying in the face" of widespread public opposition to GM foods among Britons, but also as contrary to the purported growing scientific evidence that cast doubt on the safety of GM farming practices. On 9 March, the long awaited announcement by Margaret Beckett on the commercial planting of GM maize was delivered to the House of Commons. As was widely anticipated there was "in principle" agreement to the commercial cultivation of GM herbicide-tolerant maize – Chardon LL by Bayer CropScience – to be used as cattle feed. However, this was subject to several conditions, most notably, that further scientific studies should be conducted comparing Chardon LL to conventional maize using an alternative and safer herbicide than that used in the government farm trials (atrazine). Furthermore separation distances between GM and non-GM crops had to comply with the European Union's thresholds, and a compensation scheme had to be established by the GM sector itself to compensate farmers who suffered financial loss. On 1 April, most newspapers reported that Bayer had withdrawn its application to grow GM maize claiming that the restrictions imposed on it by the British government had made it economically unviable.

Our analysis specifically focuses on how the major stakeholders in the debate were represented in six UK newspapers during this period. We will demonstrate how very specific and pervasive representations of the major stakeholders in the national debate on GM – the British public, the British government, the science of GM, and biotechnology companies – served significant rhetorical functions in the controversy.

2. The Newspaper Corpus and Analytic Method

The data examined in this paper come from a larger study analyzing genomics discourse in the UK press appearing over a 3-month monitoring period from 12 January 2004 to 11 April 2004, inclusive (Augoustinos et al., 2005). All newspaper articles containing the following keywords were selected for inclusion in the database: *genome, genomic, gene, genetic, hereditary, DNA, GM, clone, cloning*, and *stem cell(s)*. From this larger corpus, all articles pertaining to GM food and crops were extracted for the present analysis and included "standard" newspaper stories, editorials, commentaries, opinion pieces, and letters to the editor.

The six newspapers (including their Sunday editions) from which the data were drawn included the following: *The Times, The Guardian*, the *Daily Telegraph, The Sun, The Daily Mirror*, and *The Daily Mail*. These newspapers represented both the popular/tabloid and quality/broadsheet markets in the UK. The three widest circulation popular/tabloids (*Sun, Mail* and *Mirror*) were included, along with the three widest circulation quality/broadsheet newspapers within the UK (*Telegraph, Times* and *Guardian*).

Our analysis of these data is informed by social constructionist approaches that emphasize the socially constitutive nature of language. Using the methods of critical discourse analysis the corpus of newspaper data was systematically examined to identify central and recurring themes, constructions and understandings of GM crops and food, and more specifically, how various stakeholders in the national debate were represented and positioned in newspaper accounts.

Analysis of the texts involved a two-stage process. First, preliminary coding of the data was undertaken with the aid of the N6 (NUD*IST) software package to identify major themes and repertoires employed in the public presentation of GM crops and food. This involved the use of macro-level content analysis for the mapping of recurring descriptions, arguments and accounts. This level of analysis also provided a framework for sampling a representative subset of data for the purposes of detailed, in-depth discursive analysis. This micro-level discourse analysis was used to detail the types of argumentation and linguistic formulations that were regularly and repeatedly drawn upon to construct pervasive representations of the major stakeholders in the GM debate in the print media. We examine the fine detail of construction – how descriptions, versions, or accounts of these stakeholder identities are assembled and warranted as factual and as independent of their producers, and how these are mobilized in argumentation around these issues (Potter, 1996; Potter and Edwards, 2001; Wetherell, 1998).

3. Findings and Analysis

Our analysis of newspaper coverage of the GM debate in the UK is structured in two key parts. First, we briefly examine the dominant constructions of GM crops and food – both positive and negative. Second, our focus will turn to constructions of various stakeholders in the debate. Our aim is to show how each of these stakeholders was presented in ways that functioned to accomplish particular rhetorical purposes. Such constructions can be argued to frame the ways in which broader debates around scientific and technological developments can occur, and to mediate the public understandings of such developments.

Table 1 presents summary statistics of the newspaper data and indicates that approximately two thirds of articles came from the two broadsheet papers, *The Guardian* and *The Times*, the former contributing over 40 percent of articles in the database. Table 1 also compares the number of articles appearing over this 3-month period with the 6-month period in 2003, reported by Cook et al. (2006). For the four newspapers for which direct comparisons can be made, the number of articles appearing in 2004 ($N = 244$) was relatively proportional to the number appearing in twice the time period in 2003 ($N = 446$): 81.33 articles compared to 74.33 articles per month. Likewise, the proportional frequency of articles on GM crops and food appearing in each of the four newspapers was very similar. The controversy over GM crops and food therefore did not abate in early 2004 and continued to receive the similar levels of critical attention it had attracted during the *GM Nation?* debate in the previous year (Cook et al., 2006).

Table 1: Number (and frequencies) of articles on GM crops and food

Newspaper	12 January–11 April 2004	January–July 2003 (Cook, Robbins and Pieri, 2006)
The Guardian	101 (41.4%)	210 (47.0%)
The Times	61 (25.0%)	142 (31.8%)
The Daily Telegraph	31 (12.7%)	NA
Daily Mail	33 (13.5%)	82 (18.4%)
Daily Mirror	13 (5.3%)	NA
The Sun	5 (2.1%)	12 (2.7%)
Total	244 (100%)	446 (100%)

Constructions of GM Crops and Food

Negative Constructions

The following analysis will demonstrate how this debate was presented as highly controversial and divisive, which resulted in a pervasive and dominant negative construction of GM crops and food. The majority of articles, even those advocating GM crops, presented a range of critics who expressed concerns about actual, but more frequently *potential* risks to health and the environment associated with the growing of GM crops. These critics included government members, most notably, the previous Environment Minister, Michael Meacher, opposition MPs, and organizations such as Greenpeace, Genewatch UK, and Friends of the Earth (FOE). These criticisms can be collectively categorized as potential risks of GM crops and food. This risk discourse is consistent with earlier analyses of UK media coverage of GM and with wider discourses in the UK concerning GM foods (Frewer et al., 2002).

One negative story, which detailed the potential health risks associated with GM agriculture, received considerable attention by *The Guardian* (27 Feb) and, in particular, the *Daily Mail* (25 Feb). Both these papers reported that villagers living near a GM maize farm in the Philippines were experiencing physical ailments, claimed to be linked to the maize. Although both Monsanto and the Philippines government rejected this claim, the *Daily Mail* followed this story up with lengthy articles on 6 and 7 March, which likened GM crops and food to "poison." This negative portrayal is clearly evidenced in the headlines, which accompanied each of these articles:[1]

GM: Proof it <u>poisons</u>? (*Mail*, 6 Mar)

How I proved that GM crops <u>poisoned</u> an entire village. (*Mail*, 7 Mar)

During the monitoring period the highly graphic description of GM crops and foods as "Frankenstein crops/foods" was used on 33 occasions in 22 articles. The symbolism of Frankenstein in the context of GM crops and foods is seen by Scott (2000) as carrying a complex of meanings, including perceptions of risk, fears of the remixing of living identities and resentment at the spiritual nihilism of the reduction of life to a digital code. This category was most frequently deployed by the *Daily Mail* ($N = 18$), followed by *the Daily*

Mirror (*N* = 9), *The Times* (*N* = 4), and *The Guardian* and *The Daily Telegraph* (one occasion each). Unlike Cook et al. (2006) who found that this description was more likely to be used by proponents of GM food (than opponents) in argumentative contexts which questioned the validity of this characterization (e.g., "so-called Frankenstein foods"), our analysis found that just over 50 percent of uses could be categorized in this way, and just under half were deployed in highly negative and critical argumentative contexts. More significantly, all these negative uses of "Frankenstein foods/crops" (*N* = 15) appeared in the self-proclaimed anti-GM paper, the *Daily Mail*. The following headlines were especially graphic uses of this categorization:

> *If you ever had any doubts about FRANKENSTEIN FOODS read this litany of deceit, cynicism and manipulation.* (*Mail*, 20 Feb)
>
> *Frankenstein food? You'll be made to like it.* (*Mail*, 10 Mar)

Although this description was not uniformly deployed by the UK press, its use in particular contexts demonstrates how a tale originating in science fiction can be appropriated as a culturally available narrative to make sense of genetically modified foods and crops as artificial, dangerous, and monstrous. Arguably, a range of rhetorically powerful negative connotations and moral warnings are invoked whenever GM foods are categorized in this way.

Positive Constructions

Positive representations and opinion pieces on GM foods and crops were not as common during the monitoring period, but were nonetheless in evidence. On 14 March, *The Times* carried a feature article by Charles Pasternak, described as a "genetics expert" entitled *GM food could be good for you*. Pasternak's article emphasized the potential of GM technology to combat food shortages and hunger in the developing world. In this way, the development and application of GM farming by Western industrialized societies like Britain was constructed positively as a <u>moral obligation</u> for the alleviation of hunger in the Third World. As can be seen by the extracts below, this argument was also voiced in *The Guardian* in a lengthy opinion piece which cites an expert source (described as "an independent body"), and in an editorial from the *Daily Mirror*.

1. The strongest argument in favour of developing GM crops is the <u>contribution they can make to reducing world poverty, hunger and disease</u>. As the Nuffield Council of Bioethics, an independent body of experts and lay representatives, declared in 1999: "The moral imperative for making GM crops easily and economically available to developing countries who want them is compelling". (*Guardian*, 3 Mar)

2. But we should resist simply dismissing GM crops as Frankenstein food. They could also be a force for good. If the science shows they are safe,

they could help relieve famine and poverty in the developing world and save millions of lives. (*Mirror*, 5 Mar)

This argument in favor of GM crops and food, however, was not immune from detailed criticism from opponents of GM crops and food; even *The Times* carried an opinion piece challenging this argument by Camilla Cavendish (10 March). The most common criticism of the "feeding the world" argument was that GM agriculture would displace millions of agrarian farmers who could not afford the high prices required to purchase GM seeds and herbicides from multinational GM companies. Critics claimed that the argument was "disingenuous" and was primarily promulgated by the biotech industry in order to advance its own financial and economic interests (that is, the monopolization of the global food supply; see section below on Biotechnology Companies).

A closely related argument in favor of GM agriculture was that genetic modification is not a new technology but one that continues and extends thousands of years of "normal" farming practices in the selective breeding of healthier and better crops. This argument was mobilized to counter claims that GM farming was "unnatural," referenced in Extract 1 below by the formulation "fiddle with nature," and in Extract 2 "messed with nature." Both extracts thus work to construct genetic modification as a natural and normative practice in food production which has had a long and continuous history.

1. Why fiddle with nature? The answer is because Man has always fiddled with Nature. There is barely a foodstuff on supermarket shelves whose genes have not been manipulated through cross-breeding or selective breeding. (*Telegraph*, 7 Mar)
2. AS GOVERNMENT APPROVES "FRANKENSTEIN" CROP: GM FOOD ISN'T NEW, WE'VE MESSED WITH NATURE FOR CENTURIES. (*Mirror*, 10 Mar)

Constructions of Stakeholders

The British Public: Widespread Public Opposition to GM Crops and Foods

All newspaper articles presented the widely anticipated government decision on GM maize as highly contentious and contrary to widespread public opposition to GM crops. The most frequently cited study to support claims that the British public was opposed to GM crops and foods, was the government's own survey conducted in 2003 as part of the *GM Nation?* debate. This survey was reported to have found that over 90 percent of Britons were opposed to the growing of modified crops. This statistic was widely cited throughout the monitoring period, and was commonly used as an empirical warrant to construct the British public as uniformly opposed to GM farming. The following extracts demonstrate the pervasiveness of this representation of the British public's attitudes to GM crops:

1. The growing of genetically-modified crops will be approved today despite widespread public opposition ... A Government survey last year found that 90 per cent of Britons oppose growing modified crops and the sale of foods derived from them. (*Mail*, 13 Jan)
2. In the face of widespread opposition to GM food, they [ACRE] delivered a report giving the final verdict in the Government's assessment of the modified crops ... Last year a Government survey found 98 per cent of people opposed GM food. (*Telegraph*, 14 Jan)
3. The government is to go ahead with genetically modified crops despite what it acknowledges is considerable public resistance ... Last year the government attempted to test public attitudes [and] concluded that more than four out of five people were against GM crops and that just 2% would eat GM foods. (*Guardian*, 19 Feb)
4. Opinion polls show 85 per cent of people believe GM crops would have a negative impact on the environment, 86 per cent say the technology has been driven by profit rather than public interest, and only 4 per cent strongly agree that they would eat GM food. (*Times*, 5 Mar)

Although the actual statistics used to warrant this claim varied, all forms of quantification used above emphasize the extremity and strength of public opinion on this issue. The British public was therefore constructed as a homogeneous entity holding uniformly negative and consensual opinions on this issue.

This public resistance to GM crops was further consolidated by reports that many people were prepared to engage in direct action by destroying GM crops if they were to be grown. For example:

1. More than 2,500 people have already pledged to destroy GM crops if they are grown, or support those who do. (*Guardian*, 20 Feb)
2. AN ARMY of 3,000 men and women from all walks of life have vowed to rip up genetically-modified crops if they are planted commercially in Britain. (*Daily Mail*, 9 Mar)

As previously argued, this representation of the British public as uniformly opposed to GM crops and food was a powerful rhetorical warrant for various interest groups opposed to GM crops and food. At the same time it was also a rhetorical "stumbling block" for GM advocates, especially for the government which had sponsored the national debate. One way in which the government undermined this construction of widespread public opposition was to actually challenge the results of its own survey. On 18 February 2004, Environment Secretary, Margaret Beckett, cited a recent Mori poll which concluded that the government's own survey had:

> vastly overestimated the level of public opposition to GM. The [Mori] poll found that while 36% opposed GM food, 13% supported it and 39% had no strong feelings either way. (*Guardian*, 19 Feb)

On the basis of this new poll, Mrs. Beckett was indirectly reported to have claimed that "it was unclear whether the public actually wanted a complete ban [on the cultivation of GM crops] as commentators suggested" (*Guardian*, 19 Feb). The extremity of the formulation, "vastly overestimated," suggests that the government survey held in 2003 was an unreliable and inaccurate depiction of public attitudes. In contrast to previous figures that placed public opposition at "90 per cent," this opposition was now estimated to be merely 36 percent, with a similar percentage of people (39 percent) categorized as having "no strong feelings either way." The conclusions on public opposition derived from the *GM Nation?* debate have also been criticized in the literature, for among other things self-selection bias (e.g. Campbell and Townsend, 2003). Large scale surveys conducted around this time have also shown the British public to be much less negative than implied by the *GM Nation?* consultation process (Pidgeon et al., 2005; Sturgis et al., 2004).

As we will see further below, questioning the reliability and validity of empirical research was a common rhetorical strategy used by both proponents and opponents of GM crops and food to undermine and challenge their opponents' views and to substantiate their own position on this contentious issue. The existence of contradictory data, gathered from different samples and using different methods, makes this a ready avenue for seeking to discredit opposing views.

Another rhetorical strategy employed to undermine the public's opposition to GM crops and food was to represent the public opposition as irrational and based on the public's lack of scientific understanding. Consistent with the findings of Cook et al. (2006), the largely pro-GM broadsheet *The Times* framed the public opposition to GM crops and food as based on a deficit model of public understanding. This was evident in several articles and letters during this period which lamented what was perceived to be a retreat from scientific inquiry and reasoning (anti-science). This "Luddite mentality," as one letter writer described it, was represented as encouraging irrational fears and unnecessary anxieties in the British public. The following extract which comes from a feature article by Charles Pasternak, described as a "genetics expert," is a typical example:

> The widely held fears about "Frankenstein" food are <u>irrational</u> and <u>unscientific</u> ... For once the government has got it right. In sanctioning the

cultivation of genetically modified (GM) maize, it is allowing <u>fact</u> finally to triumph over <u>fantasy</u> … (*Times*, 14 Mar)

The Government

In direct contrast to the representation of the British public as uniformly opposed to GM crops, the British government was largely constructed by the UK press as determined to proceed with the introduction of GM farming in spite of widespread public opposition. The following headlines appearing on 13 and 14 January demonstrate how the impending government decision to approve the commercial growing of GM maize was constructed negatively as a decision that would be imposed on the British public.

1. *Blair will back GM "by stealth"* (*Mail*, 13 Jan)
2. *Britain braced for GM crops in spring* (*Telegraph*, 14 Jan)
3. *AMAIZED* (*Mirror*, 14 Jan)

Specific formulations such as "stealth," "braced" and the play on words "AMAIZED," together construct a picture of the government and the public engaged in an oppositional struggle over the GM issue.

On 19 and 20 February, several articles appeared in the UK press on leaked minutes from a government cabinet meeting regarding the government's intention to approve GM maize. The minutes, reported primarily in *The Guardian*, indicated that the government – although concerned about the public resistance to GM crops – viewed any decision to ban GM crops in Britain as "the easy way out," "irrational," "impractical," and inconsistent with the government's science policy. Note the use of the descriptive formulation "push ahead" in Extract 2 below, which works to construct the government as determined to proceed with GM crops despite a disapproving public.

1. … the government is equally clear in its view that any ban on the crops would be "<u>the easy way out</u>" and would be "<u>an irrational way for the government to proceed</u>" in the light of its desire to back and encourage UK science. (*Guardian*, 19 Feb, Paul Brown)
2. The government plans to <u>push ahead</u> with the commercial cultivation of GM crops and outlines a strategy. The minutes … claim that a GM free Britain is not feasible legally or in practice. (*Guardian*, 19 Feb, Ian Sample)

The *Daily Mail* and the *Daily Mirror* employed graphic headlines, which implied that the government had "betrayed" the public over this contentious issue. For example:

1. *THE GM CAVE-IN – Leaked papers show Blair's nod for "Frankenstein" crops.* (*Mirror*, 20 Feb)

2. *GM: The great betrayal.* (*Mail,* 20 Feb)
3. *Frankenstein food? You'll be made to like it.* (*Mail,* 10 Mar)

Moreover, as reported in *The Guardian* (19 Feb), aside from the decision to proceed with the commercial growing of GM maize, what attracted considerable attention in the press, was the government's extensive discussions at a cabinet meeting on strategies to shift public opinion in favor of GM crops and foods. The minutes recorded that "Opposition might eventually be worn down by solid, authoritative scientific argument" and that before the Parliament was informed of the GM maize decision, key MPs and pro-GM scientists would be encouraged to publicly support the decision.

This strategy of "preparing the ground" to promote more favorable and positive public attitudes to GM crops provoked moral outrage in some commentators who constructed the government as cynical, manipulative, and deploying political "spin" to win the public over. In Extract 1 below, the government is described as "arrogant" in assuming that it can undermine the public's opposition, and in Extract 2, the government is accused of ignoring both the scientific evidence and public concern over GM crops and basing its decision primarily on political and business interests. These constructions undermined the government's identity as a neutral and rational arbiter in the national debate over GM crops.

1. As revealed in this week's leaked minutes, <u>the government's commitment to GM crops is unswerving</u>. Revealed once more, too, is <u>its arrogance</u>; for it acknowledges public resistance but hopes that "opposition might eventually be worn down by solid, authoritative scientific arguments". (*Guardian*, 20 Feb, Colin Tudge)
2. The leaked cabinet minutes show this to be <u>an entirely political act</u>, taken in defiance of the scientific evidence and public concern, by <u>a Government desperate to curry favour with big business, appease President George Bush and, above all, to save the face of the Prime Minister</u>. (*Mail,* 20 Feb)

The *Daily Mail,* a vociferous critic of the government, on 20 February alone, published six lengthy articles devoted to the expected government decision to approve the growing of GM maize. The article headlined: "If you ever had any doubts about FRANKENSTEIN FOODS read this litany of deceit, cynicism and manipulation," provided a comprehensive list of significant events, findings, and decisions relating to GM foods dating from April 1997 ("PRIVATE biotech firms, including U.S. giant Monsanto, have begun testing GM crops at secret sites across UK, it is revealed") to January 2004 ("NO SCIENTIFIC evidence exists to support the growing of GM crops in the UK, says, the Economic & Social Research Council"). This list explicitly suggested that there was increasing and unequivocal scientific evidence and public consensus against the growing of GM foods and crops.

Margaret Beckett's announcement on 9 March approving the commercial planting of GM crops (which was described by Beckett in her speech as "precautionary" and "evidence-based"), not surprisingly, received a mixed response from the different stakeholders. Anti-GM groups such as Genewatch, accused the government of betraying public trust (*Guardian*, 10 March). Likewise, a spokesperson for FOE was quoted as saying: "In demonstrating its pro-GM credentials, the Government has ignored considerable scientific uncertainties, shown contempt to Parliament and utterly disregarded public opinion" (*Telegraph*, 10 March). One environmental commentator however, described the government's conditions as "major stumbling blocks" to the commercial farming of GM maize (Paul Brown, *Guardian*, 10 March). Even the self-proclaimed anti-GM paper, the *Daily Mail*, argued that Beckett's approval was tentative and unlikely to guarantee the growing of GM maize in Britain.

The then Prime Minister, Tony Blair, was typically constructed as a strong proponent of biotechnology, extolling the importance of the industry to Britain's economic and scientific development. But more importantly, he was frequently represented as being under considerable pressure from big business and the US (specifically President Bush) to approve the commercial farming of GM crops. Extracts 1 and 2 illustrate this construction of Blair, while extracts 3 and 4 depict the government, and Britain more generally, as being subject to such pressure.

1. Green groups yesterday <u>accused the PM of caving into big bussiness</u> and snubbing the public. (*Mirror*, 5 Mar)
2. Mr Blair brushes aside all objections. He seems <u>so in thrall to President Bush and America's GM conglomerates</u> that British public opinion no longer signifies. (*Mail*, 10 Mar)
3. Britain, along with the other EU member states, remains <u>under enormous pressure from the United States</u> to approve new GM products and imports. (*Guardian*, 20 Feb)
4. Mrs Beckett denied suggestions that Labour had been forced into lifting Britain's GM-free status as a result of <u>pressure from the United States</u>. (*Telegraph*, 10 Mar)

These extracts function to represent the Prime Minister and the government as beholden to powerful political and economic interests and as such, determined to proceed with the introduction of GM maize even in the face of public opposition. In this way, the government was depicted as undemocratic and failing to represent the views of the majority of Britons.

The Science of GM Farming

The use of scientific evidence to support the safety of the commercial growing of GM maize was represented in the UK press as highly problematic and
as generating empirical findings that were inconclusive and requiring further
scrutiny. ACRE's (the Advisory Committee on Releases to the Environment)
recommendation to government, based on an evaluation of the government's
3-year farm scale trials, that GM maize was less damaging to biodiversity
than conventional maize and was therefore safe to grow if "carefully managed", was disputed by a number of critics. Most notable was the previous
Environment Minister, Michael Meacher who claimed that the farm scale
trials were methodologically flawed because the ground in which conventional maize had been grown had been sprayed with a highly toxic herbicide
(atrazine) that had subsequently been banned by the EU. The following four
examples demonstrate the ways in which ACRE's recommendation was subject to challenge by a range of critics.

1. "To claim that everything is being done on the basis of full safety analysis
   both in terms of the environment and human health is a confidence trick",
   [Meacher] said. "Whenever proper testing is conducted, <u>real evidence of
   harm to the countryside is identified</u>" … A spokesman for the pressure
   group Greenpeace added: … "People who don't want GM are well
   informed and <u>base their opposition on science</u>." (*Mail*, 13 Jan)
2. Caroline Spelman, the shadow environment secretary, said "The queries
   and concerns surrounding GM crops have not yet been fully answered."
   The Soil Association, Genewatch UK, the Royal Society for the Protection
   of Birds, and Friends of the Earth <u>all said there were too many potential
   dangers</u>. (*Guardian*, 14 Jan)
3. Greenpeace [said] the decision was "<u>bad for farmers, bad for the organic
   food industry and bad for our countryside</u> … The only reason GM maize
   got through the tests was because its effect on the environment was compared to a <u>pesticide so toxic that it is now banned</u>." (*Telegraph*, 14 Jan)
4. <u>No scientific evidence exists to support the commercial growing of GM
   crops</u> … Yesterday's report, sponsored by the UK's largest research fund-
   ing agency, the <u>Economic & Social Research Council, warns that science
   "is not yet ready" to answer many important questions about GM crops</u>.
   (*Mail*, 28 Jan)

A common feature shared by these examples is the direct citing of expert
sources with entitlements to make authoritative claims about the scientific
validity of ACRE's recommendation to the government (Conrad, 1999).
Example 2 is most interesting in this regard as it lists a wide range of critics
including a parliamentarian and four environmental groups. The use of lists
in this way has been shown to be a common rhetorical device for claiming

the generality and completeness of an argument (Edwards and Potter, 1992). Moreover, it also conveys a strong sense that there is a wide consensus amongst experts in their views regarding the potential risks and dangers of GM farming.

At the same time however, most of the cited experts are spokespeople for environmental groups such as Greenpeace, FOE, and Genewatch UK, all of whom have a recognized stake and interest in the GM debate and are well-known for their strong opposition to GM crops and food. It is noteworthy therefore that all of these experts base their criticisms firmly on scientific grounds that challenge the validity and reliability of the government GM farm trials. In Extract 1, Meacher asserts that these trials produced "real evidence of harm to the countryside," and a Greenpeace spokesperson emphasizes that opponents of GM "are well informed and base their opposition on science." More credible, given its apparent neutrality, is the ESRC's finding that the scientific evidence for the commercial growing of GM crops is far from conclusive (Extract 4). Thus critics framed their opposition within the empiricist repertoire of science (Gilbert and Mulkay, 1984) to challenge and undermine the purported scientific "facts" and evidence produced by the farm trials, while simultaneously managing their own stake in the debate and thus heading off accusations of bias.

Of significance were the commonly occurring analogies that were drawn between the GM issue, the previous BSE (bovine spongiform encephalopathy) scare in Britain and Europe, and the disputed existence of "weapons of mass destruction," which was used as a primary justification by the US and Britain for the war in Iraq. In their analysis Cook et al. (2006: 6) also found that the war in Iraq was conflated with the GM debate and "provided a rich source of metaphor, allusion and comparison for commentators." As this letter writer in the extract below makes clear, central to these comparisons was the misplaced trust that the British people had placed on the government and, in particular, "experts" to provide accurate and reliable information.

> We went to war in Iraq because a government listened to the experts. Foot and mouth devastated the countryside because they listened to the experts … Experts told us BSE couldn't jump species. Experts tell us GM crops are safe. Feeling confident? (*Guardian,* 20 Feb)

These analogies were powerful rhetorical devices that were commonly used to warrant and justify people's concerns and anxieties about GM crops and food. Indeed, these particular warranting devices reflected a wider "crisis of confidence" in expert knowledge, scientific opinion, and, in particular, trust in the government to "tell the truth."

In stark contrast to *The Guardian* and the *Daily Mail*, which were both highly critical of the government's decision to approve GM maize, *The Times* welcomed Margaret Beckett's announcement. On 10 March, the leading article, entitled *First seeds: A cautious approval for a limited GM crop*, described the government's decision as "cautious" and "correct." In its editorial, the *Daily Mirror* was more equivocal but at the same time warned against the out right rejection of GM crops:

> Fear of the unknown is an understandable human reaction and environmentalists are correct to point out the potential dangers. But we should resist simply dismissing GM crops as Frankenstein food. They could also be a force for good. (*Mirror*, 5 Mar)

Biotechnology Companies

Biotechnology companies involved in the production of GM foods were commonly constructed in newspaper articles as a powerful "industry" and lobby group that was able to exert considerable political pressure on the government and Britain more generally. This categorization is evidenced in the three extracts below:

1. Britain has come under pressure from the US – which has a powerful GM lobby – for help in winning global backing for the science. (*Mail*, 13 Jan)
2. The European Union rejected the first application to grow a genetically modified crop in Europe since it imposed a moratorium on new approvals six years ago, dealing a blow to the biotechnology industry. (*Telegraph*, 3 Feb)
3. Representatives of the biotech industry welcomed the government's intention to approve GM maize. (*Guardian*, 20 Feb)

As well as depicting biotech companies as an "industry," a construction that emphasizes their size and power, GM critics used an even more extreme description by categorizing them as multinational "giants" who were primarily motivated by monopolizing the world food supply in order to make large profits. This construction was typically used by critics when countering claims that GM food would benefit developing countries by overcoming food shortages.

1. … campaigners yesterday branded it [government approval for the commercial farming of GM maize] a great tragedy for consumers and the environment – and a victory for profiteering biotech giants. (*Mirror*, 20 Feb)
2. "Why is the Government going ahead?" [Mr Meacher] asked. "It is not because of the science, it is because of the Bush Administration applying pressure and because big companies like Monsanto want to make a big profit out of cornering the world food supply. It has nothing to do with feeding the world". (*Times*, 20 Feb)
3. The question is as simple as this: do you want a few corporations to monopolise the global food supply? … The biotech companies are not

interested in whether science is flourishing or whether people are starving. <u>They simply want to make money</u>. (*Guardian*, 9 Mar)

In Extract 1 below, the use of the "trojan horse" metaphor constructs biotech companies as deceitful and cunning by trying to introduce GM foods into the EU surreptitiously through the "back-door." In Extract 2, they are represented by a Greenpeace spokesperson as "biopirates" who have stolen the collective knowledge of generations of Indian farmers.

1. Environmental groups accuse biotech companies such as Monsanto and Pioneer of using the former eastern bloc as a "<u>trojan horse</u>" to get GM products into the EU. (*Guardian,* 14 Feb)
2. Monsanto, the world's largest genetically modified seed company, has been awarded patents on the wheat used for making chapatti – the flat bread staple of northern India ... Greenpeace is attempting to block Monsanto's patent, accusing the company of "<u>biopiracy</u>". "It is theft of the results of the work in cultivation made by Indian farmers", said Dr Christoph Then. (*Guardian*, 31 Jan)

Finally, the biotechnology company Bayer CropScience's decision to withdraw its application to grow GM maize in Britain because the government's conditions and restrictions had made it uneconomic, was represented by critics as "evidence" that the biotechnology industry could not guarantee that GM crops would not contaminate conventional and organic crops. Bayer's refusal to agree to a compensation fund was seen as more evidence of the industry's deceit and dishonesty. Michael Meacher, in an article in *The Guardian* (7 April) said the following:

> The industry ... was invited to cover the costs of what it roundly declared to be a virtually non-existent problem, and it balked at it. <u>Its big lie was exposed</u>. Rather than taking the risk of having to compensate organic or conventional farmers driven out of business by GM contamination, it cut its losses and pulled out.

This interpretation of Bayer's decision worked further to represent biotechnology companies as primarily interested in profits rather than scientific progress and eradicating food shortages in the Third World.

4. Conclusions

Our analysis of newspaper coverage of the GM debate in Britain during the first three months of 2004 documents how this issue was constructed as highly problematic and divisive – a "battleground" of competing interests between the British public, the government, the scientific community and the biotechnology industry. In direct contrast to the representation of the British public as uniformly opposed to GM crops, the British government was largely constructed as determined to proceed with the introduction of GM farming in spite of widespread public opposition. The widespread representation of the "British public" as uniformly opposed to GM crops and food served rhetorically to position the British government as undemocratic and as being beholden to political and economic interests. In a Western liberal democracy where majority opinion is privileged over minority opinion, this purported "fact" about the British public was difficult to sidestep, especially by the government which had sponsored the *GM Nation?* debate, ostensibly in order to facilitate inclusive and deliberative processes in formulating science and technology policy. This representation arguably undermined the government's identity as a neutral sponsor of the *GM Nation?* debate and its desire to facilitate an inclusive, democratic, and consensual science policy on GM crops and food. Rather, it positioned the government as having a clear pro-GM bias consistent with the stake and interest of the scientific community and the biotechnology industry.

Horlick-Jones et al. (2007b) argue however that this representation by the media of the *GM Nation?* debate as being ostensibly a public referendum indicating widespread disapproval for GM crops and food was not only simplistic, but also a mistranslation of information and knowledge. Indeed, this dominant construction of the British public as a uniform and homogeneous entity with consensual views about GM is at odds with alternative constructions of the "public" as pluralistic and diverse and as holding a wide range of nuanced and complex views about GM – a construction which is being increasingly promoted by researchers in the field (Dietrich and Schibeci, 2003; Hornig Priest, 2006; Horlick-Jones et al., 2007a; Rowe et al., 2005; Sturgis et al., 2004).

Of significance also in our analysis is how the science of GM farming itself became a highly contested arena. Rather than providing objective data and clarity on any possible environmental risks and hazards, the results of the government's own GM farm trials were subjected to critical empirical scrutiny particularly in relation to their methodology and scientific design. As such, the debate over GM foods was inextricably linked to public confidence and trust in both the British government and expert scientific opinion. Consistent with previous focus group and survey research in both Britain and Europe, this mistrust was concretely anchored to previous health and food scares such as the BSE crisis, and to more recent political events, namely, the war in Iraq. Furthermore, mistrust and cynicism towards biotechnology companies were reinforced by Bayer CropScience's decision to withdraw its application to grow GM maize in Britain following the government's conditions and restrictions. This decision was represented by GM critics as concrete evidence that companies promoting GM technology were motivated by profits rather than scientific and technological progress.

In short, the GM debate in Britain was represented in newspaper accounts as a "political battleground," rather than a debate about science and technology per se. Indeed, the increasing politicization of science through controversial issues such as genomics, biotechnology, and more recently climate change, will only intensify the need for inclusive and democratic modes of decision-making in science policy. Whether the *GM Nation?* debate achieved its stated goals of "citizen engagement" is difficult to determine (Rowe et al., 2005). However, following our analysis of the ways in which the media represented the major stakeholders it is important to evaluate such processes of public engagement and deliberation within the political and argumentative contexts within which they take place. As Horlick-Jones et al. (2007a: 275) conclude, the GM debate in the UK must be understood within its "operating environment" including both "the influence of media coverage and political debate." Using critical discursive methods of analysis, we hope to have demonstrated how views and attitudes towards GM crops and food are articulated within argumentative and rhetorical contexts which emphasize the interests and views of competing stakeholder identities including the public, who is ultimately faced with negotiating and traversing a complex rhetorical arena of contested "facts" about GM crops and food.

Note

1. For space considerations extracts reproduced from newspaper articles do not retain their original formatting features, other than capitalisation. If headlines and bylines are included, these appear in italics at the beginning of each extract. Underlined text represents emphases for the purposes of analysis only. Three dots (…) represent omitted text from the article. The newspaper and date of publication from which extracts are sourced are cited in parentheses (e.g., *The Times*, 23 Jan) at the end of each extract. Authors of opinion pieces have been included.

References

Augoustinos, M., Crabb, S., and LeCouteur, A. (2005) "Representations of Genomics in the UK: Media, Interest Groups, and Government Texts," Unpublished manuscript, University of Adelaide.

Bates, B.R. (2005) "Public Culture and Public Understanding of Genetics," *Public Understanding of Science* 14: 47–65.

Bauer, M.W. (2002) "Controversial Medical and Agri-food Biotechnology: A Cultivation Analysis," *Public Understanding of Science* 11: 93–111.

Campbell, S. and Townsend, E. (2003) "Flaws Undermine Results of UK Biotech Debate," *Nature* 425(6958): 559.

Condit, C.M. (1999) "How the Public Understands Genetics: Non-deterministic and Non-discriminatory Interpretations of the 'Blueprint' Metaphor," *Public Understanding of Science* 8: 169–80.

Conrad, P. (1997) "Public Eyes and Private Genes: Historical Frames, News Constructions, and Social Problems," *Social Problems* 44: 139–54.

Conrad, P. (1999) "Uses of Expertise: Sources, Quotes and Voices," *Public Understanding of Science* 8: 285–302.

Conrad, P. (2001) "Genetic Optimism: Framing Genes and Mental Illness in the News," *Culture, Medicine and Psychiatry* 25: 225–47.

Cook, G., Robbins, P.T. and Pieri, E. (2006) "Words of Mass Destruction: British Newspaper Coverage of the Genetically Modified Food Debate, Expert and Non-expert Reactions," *Public Understanding of Science* 15: 5–29.

Dietrich, H. and Schibeci, R. (2003) "Beyond Public Perceptions of Gene Technology: Community Participation in Public Policy in Australia," *Public Understanding of Science* 12: 381–401.

Durant, J., Bauer, M.W. and Gaskell, G. (1998) *Biotechnology in the Public Sphere: A European Sourcebook.* London: Science Museum.

Edwards, D. and Potter, J. (1992) *Discursive Psychology.* London: SAGE.

Frewer, L.J., Miles, S. and Marsh, R. (2002) "The Media and Genetically Modified Foods: Evidence in Support of Social Amplification of Risk," *Risk Analysis* 22: 701–11.

Gaskell, G. (1997) "Europe Ambivalent on Biotechnology," *Nature* 387: 845–7.

Gaskell, G. and Bauer, M. (2001) *Biotechnology 1996–2001: The Years of Controversy.* London: Science Museum.

Gaskell, G., Allum, N., Bauer, M., Jackson, J., Howard, S. and Lindsey, N. (2003) "Climate Change for Biotechnology? UK Public Opinion 1991–2002," *AgBioForum* 6: 55–67.

Gilbert, G.N. and Mulkay, M. (1984) *Opening Pandora's Box: A Sociological Analysis of Scientists' Discourse.* Cambridge: Cambridge University Press.

Heller, R. (2003) *GM Nation? The Findings of the Public Debate.* London: Department of Trade and Industry.

Henderson, A., Weaver, C.K. and Cheney, G. (2007) "Talking 'Facts': Identity and Rationality in Industry Perspectives on Genetic Modification," *Discourse Studies* 9: 9–42.

Horlick-Jones, T., Rowe, G. and Walls, J. (2007a) "Citizen Engagement as Information Systems: The Role of Knowledge and the Concept of Translation Quality," *Public Understanding of Science* 16: 259–78.

Horlick-Jones, T., Walls, J., Rowe, G., Pidgeon, N., Poortinga, W., Murdock, G. and O'Riordan, T. (2007b) *The GM Debate: Risk, Politics and Public Engagement.* London: Routledge.

Hornig Priest, S. (2006) "The Public Opinion Climate for Gene Technologies in Canada and the United States: Competing Voices, Contrasting Frames," *Public Understanding of Science* 15: 55–71.

Irwin, A. and Wynne, B. (2001) *Misunderstanding Science: The Public Reconstruction of Science and Technology.* Cambridge: Cambridge University Press.

Petersen, A. (2001) "Biofantasies: Genetics and Medicine in the Print News Media," *Social Science and Medicine* 52: 1255–68.

Pidgeon, N.F., Poortinga, W., Rowe, G., Jones, T.H., Walls, J. and O'Riordan, T. (2005) "Using Surveys in Public Participation Processes for Risk Decision Making: The Case of the 2003 British GM Nation? Public Debate," *Risk Analysis* 25: 467–79.

Potter, J. (1996) *Representing Reality: Discourse, Rhetoric and Social Construction.* London: SAGE.

Potter, J. and Edwards, D. (2001) "Discursive Social Psychology," in W.P. Robinson and H. Giles (eds) *The New Handbook of Language and Social Psychology*, pp. 103–18. London: John Wiley & Sons.

Rowe, G., Horlick-Jones, T., Walls, J. and Pidgeon, N. (2005) "Difficulties in Evaluating Public Engagement Initiatives: Reflections on an Evaluation of the *UK GM Nation? Public Debate about Transgenic Crops," *Public Understanding of Science* 14: 331–52.

Scott, I.M. (2000) "Green Symbolism in the Genetic Modification Debate," *Journal of Agriculture* and *Environmental Ethics* 13: 293–311.

Sturgis, P. and Allum, N. (2004) "Science in Society: Re-evaluating the Deficit Model of Public Attitudes," *Public Understanding of Science* 13: 31–53.

Sturgis, P., Cooper, H., Fife-Schaw, C. and Shepherd, R. (2004) "Genomic Society: Emerging Public Opinion," in A. Park, J. Curtice, K. Thomson, C. Bromley and M. Philips (eds) *British Social Attitudes: The 21st Report*, pp. 119–45. London: SAGE.

Ten Eyck, T. (2005) "The Media and Public Opinion on Genetics and Biotechnology: Mirrors, Windows or Walls?," *Public Understanding of Science* 14: 305–16.

Wagner, W., Kronberger, N., Gaskell, G., Allum, N., Allansdottir, A., Cheveigne, S., Dahinder, U., Diego, C., Montali, L., Mortensen, A., Pfenning, U. and Rusanen, T. (2001) "Nature in Disorder: The Troubled Public of Biotechnology," in G. Gaskell and M. Bauer (eds) *Biotechnology 1996–2000: The Years of Controversy*, pp. 80–95. London: Science Museum.

Wetherell, M. (1998) "Positioning and Interpretive Repertoires: Conversation Analysis and Post-structuralism in Dialogue," *Discourse and Society* 9: 387–412.

51

The Language of Critical Discourse Analysis: The Case of Nominalization

Michael Billig

Ll discourse analysts face a paradoxical situation. We investigate language, yet at the same time we must use language in order to make our investigations. We have no separate tools to pursue our tasks. Discourse analysis does not, and cannot, exist outside of language: it comprises articles, books, talks, etc. We cannot, therefore, rigidly separate the objects of our analyses from the means by which we conduct our analyses. The problem is particularly acute for critical discourse analysts. We seek to analyse language critically, exposing the workings of power and ideology within the use of language. But how can we do this, if we have to use language in order to make our critical analyses? How can we be sure that our own use of language is not marked, even corrupted, by those ideological factors that we seek to identify in the language of others?

This is an inescapable problem which critical discourse analysts should bear in mind, particularly as critical discourse analysis (CDA) is becoming established as a successful, academic sub-speciality. With success there inevitably comes criticism. Of course, CDA's traditional critics continue with their attacks (Widdowson, 2004), but, as Beaugrande (2006) notes, some left-wing critics have recently been questioning the value of CDA. In addition, some critical discourse analysts have been engaging in self-critique. That is not surprising. If critical discourse analysts are to be fully 'critical', they should not be shy of critically examining the successful emergence of CDA

Source: *Discourse & Society*, 19(6) (2008): 783–799.

and other critical studies (Billig, 2000, 2003; and, more generally, Billig, 2008). Chilton (2005), who has contributed much to the development of CDA, questions what CDA has actually contributed to our understanding of the practice of language. As Wodak (2006) suggests, there is plenty of scope for fruitful, productive debate.

Accordingly, critical discourse analysts should be particularly concerned to examine their own use of language. How to write CDA is much more than an issue of style. It should be a major issue for analysts who stress the pivotal role of language in the reproduction of ideology, inequality and power. In discussing this, it is important to examine how critical analysts actually use language, rather than writing in general, theoretical terms. Therefore, in this article I try to identify and analyse a particular phenomenon: namely, critical analysts instantiating in their own writings the same linguistic forms that they criticize in the language of others.

This occurs when analysts are critically examining a particular form of discourse/syntax/semantics and they themselves use that particular form – not as an example, but as part of their analysis. In so doing, they provide an instance of the object of analysis within their own analysis of that object. This would not matter greatly if the analyst were providing the instance self-reflectively. It does matter if the analyst seems unaware that they are using the very linguistic forms that they are critically analysing. If critical analysts use the same forms of language whose ideological biases they are exposing in others, then they might be uncritically and unselfconsciously instantiating those very biases.

Nominalization and Passivization

In order to prevent the discussion about instantiating objects of analysis from becoming too diffuse, I concentrate on the ways that leading critical discourse analysts have discussed 'nominalization', and, to a lesser extent, 'passivization'. Both concepts have been enormously important in the development of critical discourse analysis, especially in the early work Roger Fowler and the East Anglian School. Teun van Dijk has recently identified *Language and Social Control* (Fowler et al., 1979) as the seminal book which really introduced CDA (Van Dijk, 2007: xxiv–xxv). In that work, Fowler and his co-workers built upon the linguistic ideas of Michael Halliday in order to demonstrate how the details of texts can serve to reproduce the workings of ideology. Although critical discourse analysts today are less reliant on the grammar of Halliday, the early work of Fowler and his colleagues has remained a major and continuing influence (Fairclough, 2005; Van Dijk, 2001b; Wodak, 2006, 2007).

The analysis of 'nominalization' was one of the most exciting features of the early work. By examining a series of examples, Fowler et al. (1979)

demonstrated that choosing noun phrases over verbs and the passive voice over the active voice was often ideologically charged. Their work, together with the classic work of Fowler (1991), transformed our understanding of common discursive phenomena such as newspaper headlines. Most readers of *Language and Social Control* would afterwards find it difficult to view headlines such as 'Attack on Protestors' as innocent summaries of reported stories. The East Anglian group pointed out that such headlines systematically omitted the agents of the action. In this case, the agents would be the people who were attacking the protestors. A headline writer could omit this information by using a noun such as 'attack', or by using a passive verb: 'Protestors Attacked'. A sentence, which used 'attack' as an active verb, would need to identify who was doing the attacking: e.g. 'Police Attack Protestors'. Fowler and his colleagues persuasively argued that in these contexts the choice of passive over active, or of noun over verb, was not ideologically random.

Fowler and colleagues bracketed together the producing of nouns/noun phrases, or nominalization, with the producing of passive constructions or 'passivization'. They took both concepts – nominalization and passivization – from linguistics. Significantly, Fowler and colleagues described both as processes or transformations. Nominalization was, for instance, 'turning verbs into nouns' (Fowler et al., 1979: 14). It was a 'process of *syntactic* reduction' (p. 41, emphasis added). They wrote: 'nominalization is a transformation which reduces a whole clause to its nucleus, the verb, and turns that into a noun' (p. 39). The significance of describing nominalization and passivization as processes or transformations will, it is hoped, become clearer later on.

The East Anglian group and subsequent analysts emphasized that there are several ideological features associated with nominalization and passivization: (i) deleting agency; (ii) reifying; (iii) positing reified concepts as agents; and (iv) maintaining unequal power relations.

(i) *Deleting agency.* As has been mentioned, the East Anglian group argued that if speakers/writers used nominalization or passivization, they can transform statements that identified agents of actions into agentless statements that convey less information. The linguist, Ronald Langacker (1999), has described nominalization as an asymmetric process. While a sentence that describes an agent performing an act can be easily transformed by nominalization into a statement about the act, the reverse is not true. 'Police attack protestors' can be easily transformed by anyone with a knowledge of the syntactic rules of English into 'An attack on protestors occurred'. However, knowledge of the linguistic rules of syntactic transformation does not enable the native speaker to construct the former sentence from the latter, because nominalization has ensured that the latter sentence contains less information than the former.

(ii) *Reifying*. By turning verbs into nouns, speakers/writers can convey that the entities, denoted by nominalization, have a real and necessary existence. Hallidayan grammar distinguishes processes and entities. In general terms, by means of nominalization speakers/writers turn processes into entities and typically assume the existence of such entities. Fowler (1991) writes that by means of nominalization 'processes and qualities assume the status of *things*: impersonal, inanimate, capable of being amassed and counted like capital, paraded like possessions' (p. 80). These linguistically created things have a privileged discursive status because of their presumed existence (see also, Moltmann, 2007). As Halliday and Martin (1993) have commented, the presuppositions that justify the existence of these entities are harder to contest because 'you can argue with a clause but you can't argue with a nominal group' (p. 39). Fowler et al. (1979) note that official discourse often uses nominalizations in this way, thereby conveying that present social arrangements are objective, unchangeable things. Muntigl (2002) and Mautner (2005) have examined how writers on economics can use nominalization to imply economic processes, such as 'market forces', are 'objective things' rather than the contingent results of human actions.

(iii) *Positing reified concepts as agents*. Speakers/writers can then use the abstract, reified concepts as agents of processes. Instead of talking about people buying and selling commodities for various prices, economists, administrators, journalists, etc. might talk about 'market-forces'. The nominal term 'market-forces' can then be used as the subject for verbs that denote agency: 'market-forces dictate/demand/forbid . . . ', etc. (see also Fairclough, 2003: 143ff; Stenvall, 2007). This completes the transformation of processes into entities: these nominalized entities then become posited as the agents of processes.

(iv) *Maintaining unequal power relations*. The East Anglian group claimed that it was no accident that the writers of formal documents tended to use nominalization and passivization. Fowler et al. wrote about the relations between 'nominalization' and 'lexicalization': new lexical terms can be created through nominalizing verbs. Technical and scientific writers often use nominalization in this way. The effect of creating new terms often 'is control through the one-way flow of knowledge' (Fowler et al., 1979: 33). Halliday and Martin (1993) make a similar point in their analysis of the language of science. Scientists use technical language which is filled with nominalizations rendering processes as entities. Those who create and use this specialized language act as the gatekeepers for the scientific community, ensuring that young researchers write in the appropriate way. As such, formal discourse belongs to, and helps reproduce, a social context of inequality.

Given these four properties, it is no surprise that Fowler et al. (1979) warned that nominalization and passivization, especially when used by official speakers/writers, lent themselves to ideological uses. Fowler (1991), referring to the argument of *Language and Social Control*, commented that 'we claimed nominalization was inherently potentially mystificatory; and that it permitted habits of concealment' (p. 80).

Problems with the Ideological Analysis of Nominalization

Although the work of the East Anglian group has had a decisive impact on CDA, some analysts have found problems with their work on nominalization. For example, some critics have suggested that in certain contexts it is by no means mystificatory to use nominalization (Malrieu, 1999). Instead of listing all possible problems, I focus on two themes, which are relevant to the issue of instantiating the objects of analysis.

The first theme is the assumption that some forms of description are more congruent than others. Points (i) and (ii) suggest that there are more and less 'natural' syntactic forms for particular sorts of description. Halliday's *Introduction to Functional Grammar* claimed that some descriptions were 'congruent' as compared with others that were 'metaphorical' (see, for example, Halliday, 1985: 321ff). Fairclough (2003), who criticizes the notion of congruency, succinctly summarizes what it means in relation to describing entities and processes: 'Entities, things (as well as persons) are congruently represented linguistically as nouns, whereas processes are congruently represented linguistically as verbs with associated subjects, objects and so forth' (p. 143). According to Halliday and Martin (1993) modern sciences and social sciences often fail to use congruent language, because scientific writers use nominalization routinely to treat processes as if they were entities (but see Goatly, 2007, for an important, extended critique of the notion of congruency).

There is a second line of possible criticism – although critical discourse analysts have tended not to develop it in great detail. Fowler et al. (1979) and subsequent analysts describe nominalization as a process – although, as I will suggest, they do not use the concept consistently. However, they do not specify what sort of process nominalization is. If verbs are said to be transformed into nouns, then how, when and by whom is this transformation accomplished? There are several very different transformations which the concept 'nominalization' can describe:

1. *Linguistic nominalization*. Linguists have often examined the syntactic rules by which competent speakers of a particular language regularly transform verbs into nouns and noun phrases (Maynard, 1999).
2. *Etymological nominalization*. Over time a new noun might be derived from a verb and become established as a standard lexical item in the language. Fowler et al. are describing this process when they offer as examples of nominalization 'reporting' from 'to report', and 'reference' from 'to refer' (see Fowler et al., 1979: 14).

3. *Psychological nominalization.* This would be a supposed cognitive process, which would occur if speakers/writers spontaneously (and congruently) were to think in terms of noun/active-verb sentences, and then transform these thoughts by nominalization when they come to express them.
4. *Between-text nominalization.* This occurs when one text uses noun/active-verb descriptions but the writer of a second text repeats these descriptions, but transforms them through nominalization (see, e.g., the study by Kuo and Nakamura, 2005).
5. *Within-text nominalization.* This occurs when a text describes a process in terms of noun/active-verb, but then introduces a noun as a name for such a description and henceforth uses this noun as a way of referring to the process. According to Halliday and Martin (1993) this is a common feature of scientific writing (see also Halliday, 2003: 42ff).

Many critical analysts have retained the general concept of nominalization (and that of passivization) within their critical armoury, despite not distinguishing between the different possible processes for nominalizing verbs. Like the East Anglian group, such analysts convey an ideological distrust of nominalization. Recent analysts continue to quote approvingly Fowler's comment about nominalization being potentially mystificatory (Kuo and Nakamura, 2005; Stenvall, 2007). Likewise, Schroder (2002: 105) claims that 'syntactic transformations, particularly those labelled "passivization" and "nominalization", can be considered ideologically problematic'.

Describing and Instantiating Nominalization

Readers with a background in CDA will probably have read the quotation from Schroder as a familiar description that scarcely merits examination. But look at it carefully. It warns against 'passivization', calling it problematic. The sentence contains two verbs. Both are in the passive tense: 'labelled' and 'can be considered'. In using them, the writer omits agency – leaving unspecified who does the labelling or who might consider passivization as problematic. By the omission, the writer conveys that everyone might do so. The sentence also warns against 'nominalization'. It uses three words that, at least etymologically, are the products of nominalization: namely, 'transformation', 'passivization' and 'nominalization'. Again agency is omitted. We are not told whose syntactic transformations are problematic; nor are we told how the activity of transforming was accomplished. In short, this familiar type of description seems to instantiate the very linguistic features that it warns against.

Of course, one quotation proves little. It is necessary to show a pattern. To this end, I will look at some of the classic writings on nominalization by Roger Fowler and his colleagues. I will also examine how one of the most respected figures in CDA, Norman Fairclough, discusses 'nominalization'. My aim is not to subvert their important work; quite the reverse, by taking their ideas of nominalization seriously, I intend to examine how these authors can instantiate the very syntactic forms that they are analytically putting under suspicion.

First, I will give a couple of examples to show that the Schroder quotation is not exceptional. Fowler et al. (1979) write that 'in most styles that people find "formal" and "impersonal" two syntactic constructions are almost invariably found to be prevalent: *nominalization* and *passivization*' (p. 39). The verb 'find' is used twice, once in the active tense. The second use is passive – 'are almost invariably found'. The sentence, like Schroder's, uses three nouns that prima facie may have etymologically emerged through nominalization: construction, nominalization and passivization.

Fairclough (1992: 27), in introducing the concepts of nominalization, writes that 'nominalization is the conversion of a clause into a nominal or noun'. He goes on to say that nominalization, along with 'passivization', 'may be associated with ideologically significant features of texts such as the systematic mystification of agency; both allow the agent of a clause to be deleted'. He uses the passive tense: passivization 'may be associated'. In using the passive tense, he does not specify the agents who might associate nominalization and passivization with ideologically significant features of the text. When he says that these features 'allow the agent of a clause to be deleted', again he uses a passive – 'to be deleted' – which in its turn permits him to delete who might be the agent who is deleting agents. He presents nominalization as a 'conversion'. By using the noun 'conversion', rather than the active tense of the verb 'convert', he need not specify who does the converting or how and when they do it. Fairclough, Fowler and Schroder do not comment that they are using the sort of terms that they are analysing. The indications are that they are instantiating their objects of analysis unselfconsciously.

To give a further example from Fowler et al. (1979), they suggest that nominalization can involve the creation of new specialized words or 'relexicalization'. They write:

> Many derived nominals can be spotted by their ending in *-ion, -ition, -ation, -ience, -ness, -ment*, etc. . . . We have already seen that nominalization facilitates *relexicalization*, the coding of a new, specialised, set of concepts in a new set of lexical terms. (p. 40)

Fowler et al. then do not note that the terms they are using to make their analysis – 'relexicalization', 'passivization', 'nominalization' – are precisely the sort of terms that they are discussing: derived nominals ending in '-ation'. Their own theoretical terms, to use their own phrase, comprise a specialized set of concepts in a new set of lexical terms. Yet this is just the sort of language that the authors suggest might be ideologically problematic.

Nominalization as Process: Fowler

If Fowler and his colleagues are correct, then nominalization and passivization can function to conceal and this would include their own use of nominalizations. Examples, however, need to be examined in detail. Here is a section from Fowler's *Language in the News*, in which he discusses nominalization:

> Nominalization is a radical syntactic transformation of a clause, which has extensive structural consequences, and offers substantial ideological opportunities. To understand this, reflect on how much information goes unexpressed in a derived nominal, compared with a full clause: compare, for example, 'allegations' with the fully spelt-out proposition 'X has alleged that Y did A and that Y did B (etc.)'. Deleted in the nominal form are the participants (who did what to whom?), and indication of time – because there is no verb to be tensed – and any indication of modality – the writer's views as the truth or the desirability of the proposition (see pp. 85–7). In *Language and Control*, we claimed that nominalization was, inherently potentially mystificatory; that it permitted habits of concealment, particularly in the areas of power-relations and writers' attitudes . . . If *mystification* is one potential with nominalization, another is *reification*. Processes and qualities assume the status of *things*: impersonal, inanimate, capable of being amassed and counted like capital, paraded like possessions.
>
> (Fowler, 1991: 80)

The passage describes a number of aspects of nominalization, and, in describing them, it instantiates them. First, Fowler describes nominalization as a process – 'a radical syntactic transformation of a clause'. This characterization is self-referential. A process – namely transforming a clause from verb forms into a nominal – is itself described by a nominal ('nominalization'), not a verb form. Fowler is treating nominalization as if it were an entity, rather than an activity. He is not referring to individual speakers/writers engaging in the activity of nominalizing. The verb 'nominalize' does not appear in the quoted passage.

Fowler (1991) writes that nominalization offers opportunities for deleting information, such as information about the participants, time and modality. When speakers/writers use active verb clauses, they typically include such information. In describing this, Fowler also uses phrases that delete the sort of information that would have been included had he used active verbs. Fowler gives the example of a text referring to 'allegations', rather than stating X alleged that Y did A. He claims that 'deleted in the nominal form' is information about the participants, etc. The phrase 'deleted in the nominal form' is itself a passive. It too deletes: in this case, it contains no information about how the writer in question went about the activity (or process) of deleting information nor when the activity took place.

This goes to the heart of the matter. Critical discourse analysts typically describe nominalization as a process, but they tend to be vague about how the process occurs. Do individual speakers/writers engage in nominalization as a psychological process when they use nominal forms? Fowler et al. (1979) discuss the example of a writer of regulations who uses the nominal phrase 'take responsibility', rather than the verb 'be responsible for'. They write: 'The effect of this nominalization is to present a complex relation as a simple lexical item, and to introduce the process verb "take"' (p. 30). Fowler et al. add the comment: 'We are not suggesting that the writer of these rules went through this sequence of syntactic changes; "responsibility" is after all a word which is listed in any dictionary of English' (p. 30).

The comment is revealing. Fowler et al. are denying that the nominalization within the text indicates that the producer of the text actually engaged in the activity of nominalization, thinking first in the active tense and then syntactically transforming the active into a nominal form. They are stating that 'nominalization' does not necessarily refer to a mental process, but they do not indicate what sort of process it might be. Instead, there is a gap. They are claiming that verbs have somehow been transformed into nouns with a loss of information along the way. They describe this process with a noun – 'nominalization'. In so doing, they reproduce the process, which they are describing, by avoiding specifying exactly what this process is; how and when it occurs; and most importantly who does it.

In practice, Fowler et al., along with other critical discourse analysts, often use 'nominalization' (and 'passivization') not to describe the process that produces the syntactic forms in a given text, but as a description of the textual entities themselves. When Fowler et al. write that in most formal styles, 'two syntactic constructions are almost invariably found to be prevalent: *nominalization* and *passivization*' (p. 39, emphasis in original), they are not using 'nominalization' to describe the process of turning of verbs into nouns; they are using 'nominalization' (and 'passivization') to describe particular syntactic forms. In this sense, nominalizations include nouns that have been historically derived from verbs, as in the case of 'allegation' from 'to allege', or 'reference' from 'to refer'. However, the analysts are not examining the historical, or etymological, processes of derivation, or any of the other possible sorts of transformation. Instead, the analyst is examining the semantic effects of these linguistic forms that are taken as completed entities.

The consequence is that analysts, despite defining 'nominalization' as a process, frequently treat it methodologically as a syntactic or grammatical entity, which can be identified alongside linguistic entities, such as nouns, verbs, gerunds, actives, etc. For example, Van Dijk (2001a) discusses the meaning of various syntactical forms. He includes nominalization in a list of such forms: 'ordering, primacy, pronominal relations, active–passive voice, nominalizations, and a host of other formal properties of sentences and sequences' (p. 107). Typically discourse analysts, including critical analysts, examine the discursive and linguistic features of given texts, rather than examining the processes of producing and consuming texts (see, for instance, the criticisms of Chilton, 2005). In so doing, they treat nominalization as a fixed textual feature. When Biber (1992) examined the number of nominalizations in particular corpuses, he was not studying processes of transformation, but the grammatical properties of those texts (see also Bratlinger, 1997; Clark, 2003; Muntigl and Horvath, 2005; Van Leeuwen and Wodak, 1999; Yeung, 2007 for more research that treats 'nominalization' as a textual/grammatical entity). In this syntactic sense, the word 'nominalization' is most certainly a nominalization.

In the passage quoted earlier, Fowler (1991) writes that nominalization facilitates 'reification' because processes assume the status of things. Here Fowler is using a nominalization (at least in the sense of a syntactic entity) because he uses the noun form ('reification') rather than saying that speakers/writers are reifying when they nominalize. When Fowler and other analysts write in this way, then, according to the force of their own arguments, they are engaged in the activity of reifying. This happens also when they use 'nominalization', which ostensibly describes a process, as the name of a linguistic entity. By using the word 'nominalization' as a nominalization, denoting an entity whose existence is taken for granted, they avoid specifying what sort of process 'nominalization' also seems to name.

Nominalization as Process: Fairclough

At this point, someone might object: 'You have concentrated on the classic work of Fowler et al., but there is little reason for supposing that current work in CDA contains the same features.' In order to deal with such criticism, I will briefly consider how Norman Fairclough treats the concept of nominalization. I will suggest that Fairclough, when he discusses nominalization, like Fowler, instantiates the forms he writes about.

As has been mentioned, Fairclough (1992) describes nominalization as a process of 'conversion', which permits the deletion of agency. When he describes nominalization, he too deletes agency and uses passive forms. For example, Fairclough (2003) refers to nominalization as involving 'the exclusion of Participants in clauses' (p. 144). He uses a nominal 'exclusion', rather than writing of a writer/speaker 'excluding participants' from clauses. If nominalization is a process, then it is a process that tends linguistically to conceal processes. Thus, Fairclough describes nominalization as 'the conversion of processes into nominals, which has the effect of backgrounding the process itself – its tense and modality are not indicated – and usually not specifying its participants, so that who is doing what to whom is left implicit' (1992: 179).

By using nominal terms such as 'conversion', 'transformation' and 'deletion' in this context, Fairclough avoids using phrases that draw attention to the activities that language users must accomplish when they nominalize. He does not say that 'when writers/speakers nominalize, they convert clauses into nouns'. If Fairclough had written that, then a reader might ask how exactly do speakers/writers engage in the activity of converting? What is that they must do? And when must they do it? Instead, it is said that there is a 'conversion of processes into nominals' which, as Fairclough suggests, has the effect of backgrounding the process. The conversion is presented as an existing entity: it has what Wodak (2007) describes as an 'existential presupposition'. Therefore, when Fairclough talks about backgrounding processes, he uses a form of language that itself backgrounds the process by which he has defined the nominal 'nominalization' in terms of another nominal, namely 'conversion'. As such, he backgrounds the very process of nominalizing, which ostensibly his statement is foregrounding.

According to Fairclough, 'nominalization turns processes and activities into states and objects, and concretes into abstracts' (1992: 181). The statement could be read as a description of the way that critical analysts have used 'nominalization' as a concept. They have linguistically turned the process of nominalizing into an object – 'nominalization'. They are vague about the ways speakers/writers accomplish this transformation. They do not typically distinguish between the different forms of transformation that were presented earlier. Analysts then treat nominalization as a syntactic entity that exists in the words of a text, rather than as a process that produces, and thereby stands behind, the syntax of the text.

In this spirit, Fairclough (2003) identifies the word 'destruction' as a nominalization, comparing it with 'is destroyed' or 'was destroyed' (p. 143). The full sentence in which Fairclough (2003) describes the 'exclusion of Participants' is revealing:

> It (nominalization) also may involve the exclusion of Participants in clauses – so in this case none of the process nouns or nominalizations has an agent (what would most commonly be the grammatical subject in a clause). (pp. 143–4)

'Nominalization' here refers to an entity rather than a process. The phrase 'process nouns or nominalizations' suggests that the two terms are equivalent: a nominalization is a noun denoting a process. In other words, the writer is indicating that a nominalization is a lexical entity, rather than an unspecified process that results in the use or creation of a particular sort of noun. This is what Fowler describes as 'reification' or the linguistic creation of a thing. In this case, analysts of nominalization are reifying nominalization as a thing.

The Return of the Agent

The language of analysts examining nominalization shares a further feature with the characteristics that they identify in ideological language. They claim that ideological language not only deletes the agents of processes through the use of nominalization, but it then ascribes these nominalized processes with agency. Accordingly, nominalized forms become the subjects of active sentences, appearing as the agents who do things. This is reified language: things and abstract entities, not people, perform actions. According to Hallidayan grammar, this is an incongruent use of language. Yet, at the same time, critical discourse analysts sometimes depict language (rather than language-users) as doing things, as if the language, or particular forms of language, is the agent of action. For example, Fairclough (2003), in his discussion of nominalization, writes that nominalization, through generalization and abstraction, 'can obfuscate agency, and therefore responsibility' (p. 144). Here the writer attributes the action of obfuscating to nominalization. Similarly Fairclough (1992: 182) claims: 'Nominalization turns processes and activities into states and objects, and concretes into abstracts.' Nominalization is presented as the actor that transforms processes into objects. The agents, having been deleted, return but they return as linguistic concepts.

Analysts of language often use active verbs that normally attribute agency to humans. We are accustomed to reading about the things that language, discourses and syntactic forms can do – as if they were capable of agency. Critical analysts can use this way of writing even when warning of the ideological dangers of attributing agency to non-agentic entities. Fowler et al. (1979), analysing the phrasing of regulations concerning university applications, write that 'the passive structure, allowing agent-deletion, permits a discreet silence about who if anyone might refuse to admit the applicant' (p. 41). Fowler (1991) writes that nominalization was potentially mystificatory because 'it permitted habits of concealment' (p. 80). 'Allowing' and 'permitting' are usually activities ascribed to human agents. Here, a grammatical structure is said to permit actions to occur or not occur. The form of wording not only 'permits' agent-deletion but then it ascribes agency for the deleting, not to speakers/writers but to forms of wording.

Jay Lemke (1995) has described this move in his book *Textual Politics*. He discusses critically the abstract language of scientific reports, which linguistically delete human agents and then present processes as agents or participants in actions:

> Other types of Processes tend to be expressed as Participants, in these relations (nominalization). Animate agents, especially the human researchers, tend not to appear. This often results from using agentless passive clause structures. The nominalized processes on the other hand are frequently reified and used as agents in the place of human agents . . .

> Nominalization allows an entire activity, a process complete with its typical Participants and Circumstances, to be understood merely by naming it with the process noun. (p. 60)

Lemke is instantiating the very linguistic constructions that are the objects of critical analysis. He uses passives, as he writes about the role of passives ('to be expressed'; 'are frequently reified'; 'to be understood', etc). His own words do not indicate the agents of the processes that he describes. Who is doing the understanding, the nominalizing, the using passive structures, etc? Nominalizations, it is said, are 'used as agents in the place of human agents'. This sentence is phrased in the passive with 'nominalizations' as the grammatical subject. The writer's own choice of phrasing exemplifies the way that writers can delete agency.

Lemke, having written that nominalized processes are used as agents in the place of human agents, instantiates this unselfconsciously in his very next sentence. He writes that 'nominalization allows an entire activity . . . to be understood'. Here he uses an agentive word 'allows'. Who is allowing an entire activity to be understood? No-one, it appears. 'Nominalization' is grammatically the subject that performs the action of allowing a nominalized process – the very term 'nominalization' – is said to allow this to happen. The author does not specify how nominalization might be able to allow or permit occurrences. Nor does the author give any sign that his readers should understand the use of the agentive verb 'allow' metaphorically: there is no additional 'so to speak', or other rhetorical device to convey the use of figurative language. Instead, the author presents his words as a straightforward, or literal, description. In this way, Lemke instantiates the very grammatical features of reification as he is describing them.

Edifice of Nouns

When critical discourse analysts use nominalizations (in the sense of syntactic entities) and passive constructions that do not mention human agents, they are not writing in a particularly unique manner. They are following styles of writing that are common in the sciences and social sciences. Halliday and Martin (1993) argue that nominalization is a perennial feature of contemporary scientific writing, as scientists constantly name processes through nominalizing verbs. Halliday and Martin also point out that the vast majority of technical terms in the sciences are nouns. Nouns are the key terms in this writing, with the interconnecting verbs semantically downgraded. The resulting prose is an 'edifice of words and phrases' (p. 39).

We can see these features in CDA. Authors use technical nouns to describe processes – nominalization, passivization, perspectivation, genericization, personalization, etc. The verbs that link these technical nouns are often comparatively vague: 'involves', 'allows', 'permits'. It is as if the verbs are the humble servants who lead out their important, nominalized masters in a parade of technical prose.

The question is not whether critical discourse analysts use technical nouns more than other social scientists, but whether they should be attempting to use them less. Social scientists often justify their use of technical concepts by saying that clearly defined specialist words are more precise than those of ordinary language. To judge by the example of 'nominalization', this justification is not entirely convincing. There is a frequent gap between the way analysts define 'nominalization' as a process of syntactic change and their use the term to denote a syntactic entity. Moreover, the definition is imprecise: analysts do not specify what sort of process they are describing. They then use this technical term in ways that ensure that they do not need to specify the process. Far from using the technical term to explore underlying processes more precisely, they can use the term to give an appearance of precision while skirting over what the processes are.

For a number of reasons, critical analysts should be concerned about their use of technical language. The work of Halliday and others has indicated that technical jargon tends to emerge within, and to sustain, social conditions of inequality. High status scientists ensure that lower status scientists use technical terms appropriately. Writing specifically about nominalization, Lemke (1995: 60) comments:

> Discourse types that rely heavily on this strategy divide the world of potential readers into initiates and the uninitiated to a much greater degree than do other kinds of written expository texts . . . The world of technical discourse is a closed world which admits no criteria of validity outside its own.

If critical analysts are to take heed of their own analyses, they should worry lest their own use of technical jargon, such as 'nominalization' and 'passivization', belongs to a closed world of the initiated.

Critical discourse analysts should also worry that they might be using the same sort of reifying language that they criticize other social scientists for using. Using this language, writers avoid identifying human agents of actions, transform processes into entities, and then treat these process–entities as if they were the agents of actions. Historically, the analysis of ideology began with the assertion that social analysts should explain social life in terms of the actions of actual people, rather than seeing social actions as determined by theoretical concepts. In *The German Ideology*, the first book that uses 'ideology' in its modern critical sense, Marx and Engels (1846/1970) declared that, in contrast to the German idealists, they 'set out from real, active men, and on the basis of their real life-process we demonstrate the development of the ideological reflexes and echoes of this life-process' (p. 40). The implication is that it is real humans (men and women) who do things and who produce the illusions and evasions of ideology. If social analysts fail to base their analyses on the study of human actions and life-processes, then they will produce 'ideological echoes' of social life.

The work of critical discourse analysts has suggested that the language of much contemporary social science is poorly equipped for the task of exploring life-processes. It is weighted towards nominals, with nouns having priority over verbs, entities over processes. Critical discourse analysts have shown how writers, by nominalizing descriptions of processes, can describe human life as if it were agentless. Conservative analysts might not be bothered about their use of such technical jargon. Critical analysts, on the other hand, should be concerned, lest their desire to explore the linguistic processes of ideology results in their instantiating those very processes.

There is a political implication. Critical analysis, if it is to be critical, should have political targets. These targets should not be abstract entities but the actions of actual people or classes of people. It is not language as a system (or discourses or grammar) that we should be seeking to change, but the ways that people use language and the circumstances in which they do so. The problem is not what language does or does not do: it is what people do with language. The demand to start with actual people is as pertinent today as it was over a century and a half ago.

Implications of Unconscious Instantiation

In the previous sections, I have presented examples showing how critical analysts can instantiate those features of discourse that they are revealing as problematic. I hope to have presented sufficient examples to suggest that this is not the stylistic habit of an individual author, but that it is more general. Of course, the case would be strengthened were there a greater range of examples. Hopefully, other analysts will take up these points.

For now, one key question remains: do the examples, discussed earlier, refute or support the East Anglian group's ideas on nominalization? The case that they refute the East Anglian group might run as follows: critical writers have argued that nominalization conceals and distorts. Their argument is made through the use of nominalization. Because it uses forms that are said to distort, the argument must itself be distorted. Thus, the critical argument either destroys itself – or reduces itself to a self-referential paradox. Either way, it is seriously compromised. Long-term opponents of critical discourse analysis might pounce gleefully upon the preceding analyses.

There is, however, another way of looking at the matter. We can accept the basic analyses of Fowler et al. about the inherent dangers of nominalization and passivization – about how such forms enable writers/speakers to express less information than using active forms. Indeed, such analyses represent some of the most exciting and provocative work in critical discourse analysis. Having accepted these analyses in general terms, we might then draw conclusions about the ways that we should aspire to write. The examples of authors instantiating what they warn against do not undermine the basic analyses. Rather, they show that writers are not heeding their own warnings, even as they are writing those warnings.

One of the most attractive features of Halliday's approach to language is that he stresses that the users of language have to make choices. 'Discourses', 'grammars', 'lexicalizations', or whatever, do not determine what speakers say or writers write. Language users have to select between options. This is one reason why a critical analysis of language-use needs to be based on a psychology of language users (Billig, 1996; Chilton, 2005; Edwards, 2006; Edwards and Potter, 1993; Potter, 2006). On occasions speakers/writers may find it easier not to consider the range of options that are available to them, but to go along with familiar, linguistic habits. This might be happening with discourse analysts. We have been long accustomed to using standard, academic ways of writing, formulating complex passive sentences and linguistic edifices of technical nouns. In so doing, we have not appreciated that the message of Fowler et al., if taken seriously, should have profound consequences for the ways that we write our critical analyses.

If Halliday is correct, then we do not have to nominalize processes and use passives: there are always other possible options. With effort, we can try to avoid the standard habits of academic writing. This will not be easy. As I know from drafting this article, at each point passive impersonal clauses seem readily available; it is so easy to mobilize unthinkingly the available technical words, which, like 'nominalization', often end in '-ization'. It requires extra effort to turn the passives into actives, or to resist the technical vocabulary. When writers do so, they must fill in blanks, supply extra information and consider more carefully the social relations that they are describing.

Of course, it would be possible to go through this present article and point out all the passives that have been used (including this one) and so on. I could easily be accused of perpetrating the faults that I have accused others of committing. However, the tu quoque (literally: 'you also') argument is not necessarily fatal (Walton, 1992). Failing to live up to one's own standards is not, in itself, a refutation of those standards, just as one need not jettison all moral values because one has not lived a perfectly moral life. George Orwell stressed this in his essay 'Politics and the English Language'. He proposed six rules for writing that would help to avoid the lazy habits that were threatening, in his view, independent political thinking. The rules included avoiding jargon and passive sentences. Orwell admitted that he had probably failed to keep all his own rules, but that made the rules all the more, not less, necessary. Orwell commented that his rules might sound elementary; yet they 'demand a deep change of attitude in anyone who has grown used to writing in the style now fashionable' (Orwell, 1946/1962: 156).

Given the influence of Orwell on Roger Fowler, it is appropriate that, in our own small way as critical analysts of language, we should aspire to change deeply our styles of writing. As the critical perspective becomes academically successful, so we need to become self-critically vigilant, lest by default we slip into the very discursive habits that we criticize in others. The message of critical analysis is that when speakers/writers start defending their own established ways of using language, they are often defending established social positions. One might predict, therefore, that as critical discourse analysis becomes established in the academic world, so its practitioners will be increasingly tempted to write in ways that are socially and intellectually problematic.

In the preceding analysis, I have stressed the dangers of 'nominalization'. One might, then, conclude that the argument expresses the need for 'De-Nominalization' and 'De-Technologization', in order to combat 'Rhetorical Instantiation'. That, however, would exemplify just the sort of language to be avoided. We should not seek to create new linguistic entities, which, to paraphrase Fowler, we can parade like possessions. Perhaps, however, the argument could be reduced to something snappier and more widely understood: 'Power to the Verb.' It seems to encapsulate the underlying thought. But the slogan contains no verbs. Besides, we should be wary of slogans. Critical analysis requires clear thinking and clear writing. It will not be easy. Nor should it be.

References

Beaugrande, R. de (2006) 'Critical Discourse Analysis: History, Ideology, Methodology', *Studies in Language & Capitalism* 1: 29–56.

Biber, D. (1992) 'On the Complexity of Discourse Complexity: A Multidimensional Analysis', *Discourse Processes* 15: 133–63.

Billig, M. (1996) *Arguing and Thinking*. Cambridge: Cambridge University Press.

Billig, M. (2000) 'Towards a Critique of the Critical', *Discourse & Society* 11: 291–2.

Billig, M. (2003) 'Critical Discourse Analysis and the Rhetoric of Critique', in G. Weiss and R. Wodak (eds) *Critical Discourse Analysis*, pp. 35–46. London: Palgrave Macmillan.

Billig, M. (2008) *The Hidden Roots of Critical Psychology*. London: SAGE.

Bratlinger, E. (1997) 'Using Ideology: Cases of Nonrecognition of the Politics of Research and Practice in Special Education', *Review of Educational Research* 4: 425–59.

Chilton, P. (2005) 'Missing Links in Mainstream CDA: Modules, Blends and the Critical Instinct', in R. Wodak and P. Chilton (eds) *A New Agenda in (Critical) Discourse Analysis*. Amsterdam: John Benjamins.

Clark, J.T. (2003) 'Abstract Inquiry and the Patrolling of Black/White Borders Through Linguistic Stylization', in R. Harris and B. Rampton (eds) *Language, Race and Ethnicity*. London: Routledge.

Edwards, D. (2006) 'Discourse, Cognition and Social Practices: The Rich Surface of Language and Social Interaction', *Discourse Studies* 8: 41–50.

Edwards, D. and Potter, J. (1993) *Discursive Psychology*. London: SAGE.

Fairclough, N. (1992) *Discourse and Social Change*. Cambridge: Polity Press.

Fairclough, N. (2003) *Analyzing Discourse*. London: Routledge.

Fairclough, N. (2005) 'Critical Discourse Analysis', *Marges Linguistiques* 9: 76–94.

Fowler, R. (1991) *Language in the News*. London: Routledge.

Fowler, R., Hodge, B., Kress, G. and Trew, T. (1979) *Language and Social Control*. London: Routledge.

Goatly, A. (2007) *Washing the Brain*. Amsterdam: John Benjamins.

Halliday, M.A.K. (1985) *An Introduction to Functional Grammar*. London: Arnold.

Halliday, M.A.K. (2003) *On Language and Linguistics*. London: Continuum.

Halliday, M.A.K. and Martin, J.R. (1993) *Writing Science*. London: Falmer Press.

Kuo, S.-H. and Nakamura, M. (2005) 'Translation or Transformation? A Case Study of Language and Ideology in the Taiwanese Press', *Discourse & Society* 16: 393–418.

Langacker, R.W. (1999) *Foundations of Cognitive Grammar*. Stanford, CA: Stanford University Press.

Lemke, J.L. (1995) *Textual Politics*. London: Taylor and Francis.

Malrieu, J.P. (1999) *Evaluative Semantics*. London: Routledge.

Marx, K. and Engels, F. (1846/1970) *The German Ideology*. London: Lawrence and Wishart.

Mautner, G. (2005) 'For-profit Discourse in the Nonprofit and Public Sectors', in G. Erreygers and G. Jacobs (eds) *Language, Communication and the Economy*, pp. 25–44. Amsterdam: John Benjamins.

Maynard, S.K. (1999) 'On Rhetorical Ricochet: Expressivity of Nominalization and da in Japanese Discourse', *Discourse Studies* 1: 57–81.

Moltmann, F. (2007) 'Events, Tropes and Truthmaking' *Philosophical Studies* 134: 363–403.

Muntigl, P. (2002) 'Politicization and Depoliticization: Employment Policy in the European Union', in P. Chilton and C. Schäffner (eds) *Politics as Talk and Text*. Amsterdam: John Benjamins.

Muntigl, P. and Horvath, A. (2005) 'Language, Psychotherapy and Client Change: An Interdisciplinary Perspective', in R. Wodak and P.A. Chilton (eds) *A New Agenda in (Critical) Discourse Analysis*. Amsterdam: John Benjamins.

Orwell, G. (1946/1962) 'Politics and the English Language', in *Inside the Whale and Other Essays*, pp. 143–57. Harmondsworth: Penguin.

Potter, J. (2006) 'Cognition and Conversation', *Discourse Studies* 8: 131–40.

Schroder, K.C. (2002) 'Discourses of Fact', in K.B. Jensen (ed.) *Handbook of Media and Communication Research*. London: Routledge.

Stenvall, M. (2007) 'The Politics of Fear: A Critical Inquiry into the Role of Violence in 21st Century Politics', in A. Hodges and C. Nilep (eds) *Discourse, War and Terrorism*. Amsterdam: John Benjamins.

Van Dijk, T.A. (2001a) 'Multidisciplinary CDA: A Plea for Diversity', in R. Wodak and M. Meyer (eds) *Methods of Critical Discourse Analysis*. London: SAGE.

Van Dijk, T.A. (2001b) 'Critical Discourse Analysis', in D. Schiffrin, D. Tannen and H.E. Hamilton (eds) *Handbook of Discourse Analysis*. Oxford: Blackwell.

Van Dijk, T.A. (2007) 'Editor's Introduction', in T.A. van Dijk (ed.) *Discourse Studies*. London: SAGE.

Van Leeuwen, T. and Wodak, R. (1999) 'Legitimating Immigration Control: A Discourse–Historical Analysis', *Discourse Studies* 1: 83–118.

Walton, D. (1992) *The Place of Emotion in Argument*. University Park, PA: Penn State University Press.

Widdowson, H.G. (2004) *Text, Context, Pretext*. Oxford: Blackwell.

Wodak, R. (2006) 'Critical Linguistics and Critical Discourse Analysis', in J.-O. Östman and J. Verschueren (eds) *Handbook of Pragmatics*, pp. 1–24. Amsterdam: John Benjamins.

Wodak, R. (2007) 'Pragmatics and Critical Discourse Analysis: A Cross-disciplinary Inquiry', *Pragmatics & Cognition* 19: 203–25.

Yeung, L. (2007) 'In Search of Commonalities: Some Linguistic and Rhetorical Features of Business Reports as a Genre', *English for Specific Purposes* 26: 156–79.

Reflections on Discourse and Critique in China and the West

Paul Chilton, Hailong Tian and Ruth Wodak

China is now experiencing a wide-spread and profound social transformation. This phenomenon has been and is being studied by scholars in a wide range of disciplines, principally economics, politics,
sociology and international relation. However, the study of socio-political
transformation in Chinese society, we believe, also requires research into *discourses* in contemporary China. By 'discourse' we understand primarily the
ways in which a language is used in diverse systematic ways, in a society as
a whole, but also in many specific sub-domains, social fields, national,
regional, and local contexts. When we talk of discourses in this sense, we
mean not just the jargon used in diverse fields of activity (such as the government, education, law, and so forth), but the way complex kinds of verbal
exchange are institutionalized around specific macro-topics and realized in
genres and texts (cf. Reisigl and Wodak 2009) as well as the conceptual representations carried by discourse (Chilton 2004). To research discourses in
China is then to examine how discourses change in context-dependent ways,
and to relate the changes to the social factors that lead to these changes or
are the effects of them. Discourse research also examines how social identities are constructed through language use and how discourse facilitates
change in society. Further, this kind of research may include the investigation
of the ways in which agents or agencies manipulate meanings. In the context
of Chinese society, a discourse approach has its focus on the role of the

Source: *Journal of Language and Politics*, 9(4) (2010): 489–506.

Chinese language, or more precisely its use, in the socio-political transformation that is currently unfolding.

For many western scholars the analysis of discourse is not only a matter of technical description – though of course it certainly can be that – but also a way of understanding human beings, their behaviour and activities in society. This means that, in a certain sense of the term, discourse analysis can be "critical" – hence Critical Discourse Analysis (CDA). But the term "critical", especially when translated into another language and another culture, is a term that gives rise to many interpretations. As Shi-xu has often argued, it is essential that scholars from different cultural traditions seek to understand one another's methods, concepts and values (Shi-xu 2005, 2007, 2009). This article seeks to begin a theoretical discussion around culturally varying concepts of the critical.

Being "Critical" in the West

In the West, and in various European languages, the term "critical" (or its translation equivalents) has a complex history but it is clear that for proponents of CDA the aim of using discourse analysis to challenge and expose what they regard as undesirable social and political practices is central. Western CDA scholars generally see their roots in (post-)Marxist "critical theory" and this perspective has developed in a political and cultural environment in which it is possible for Western scholars to be "critical" vis à vis all political regimes, including that of the country of which they are citizens or subjects.

The term "critical" is associated with currents of thought whose recent sources are in the eighteenth-century European Enlightenment but whose roots are in ancient Greek philosophy. Etymologically, the verb "criticize" derives from a Greek word *krinein* "to separate, decide", in the sense of making a judgement or a distinction. In the European philosophical tradition of the eighteenth century, "critique" further implies not accepting arguments or states of affairs as given and unchangeable but analyzing them on the basis of rational judgement. Criticism in this sense is assumed to be value-free, except in so far as high value is given to rationality itself. More specifically, to be critical in the European Enlightenment meant, in many cases, rejecting metaphysics, denouncing religion and challenging political abuse. In the work of Immanuel Kant, "critique" (*Kritik*) has an anti-metaphysical meaning to some degree, but not a denunciatory meaning. Rather "Kantian critique" has to do with the use of rational analysis to explore the bounds of concepts and theories, including, the human use of reason itself and its relationship to the physical structure of the world. Later philosophers radically extended the reach of Kant's notion of *Kritik*. Marx applied it to political economy. The *Frankfurt School of Critical Theory* in the twentieth century (e.g., Theodor W. Adorno, Walter Benjamin, Jürgen Habermas, and Max Horkheimer) extended it to include rational analysis of cultural forms of various kinds. Another philosophical development of the Kantian outlook is *Critical Realism*, the British version (e.g. Roy Bhaskar's [1989] work) being a case that is relevant to the socio-political domain. In the second half of the twentieth century, this broad "critical" tendency produced studies that linked cultural forms with some prominent social issues, notably genderism/ sexism and racism. *Critical Discourse Analysis* can certainly be seen in this tradition, as claimed by its early exponents (e.g. Roger Fowler, Bob Hodge and Gunther Kress, who referred to their endeavours as *Critical Linguistics*). Among the "critical" academic disciplines in the West (cultural studies, critical international relations theory, critical legal studies, gender studies, and the like) Critical Discourse Analysis has perhaps tried the hardest both to theorize its approaches and to apply technical tools often imported from linguistics.

It is of course the case that the meanings of the word "critical" in English include non-technical meanings that might be glossed as "censorious" and in some contexts "denunciatory". It is arguable that there are two senses in English and European languages. The first and more specialised sense might be called "cognitive": to "criticise" is to engage in "critique", to engage in a rational conceptual activity. The second and everyday meaning is primarily interactive. In this sense, to "criticise" denotes an interactive social activity that somehow incorporates a normative ethical or quasi-ethical standpoint. The verb "criticise" is thus a particular kind of speech act verb. Below we shall consider how the Chinese translation equivalents of "criticise" ("criticism", "critique", "critic", etc.) compare with these senses.

Within Western CDA, there are varied and sometimes vague understandings of terms such as "critical", "criticism" and "critique". One can distinguish at least three interrelated concepts. First, critical analysis of discourse can mean to make the implicit explicit. More specifically, it means making explicit the implicit relationship between discourse, power and ideology, challenging surface meanings, and not taking anything for granted. In societies where people, especially those in dominant or influential positions, tend to convey their propositions in a rather opaque manner, it is by being "critical" in this sense that one can "make more visible these opaque aspects of discourse" (Fairclough and Wodak 1997: 258). And to be "critical" requires analysis. As Fairclough put it twenty years ago:

> *Critical* is used in the special sense of aiming to show up connections which may be hidden from people – such as the connections between language, power and ideology. [Italics in original] (Fairclough [1989] 2001a: 4)

Second, for advocates of CDA, being "critical" has an additional element – putting theory into action. On one level, this follows from the view that all discourse is a form of action, not "mere words". Thus, critical analysis which is of course a form of discourse (or rather "metadiscourse") is also a form of social action. For instance, Wodak (1996, 2001: 9, 2003, 2007) speaks of the "application of the results" to communication problems in, for example, schools and hospitals, as well as to guidelines for non-discriminatory language behaviour which should make prejudicial, sexist, and racist "coded" utterances explicit (e.g., expert opinions at court). Chilton's early work on the discourse of nuclear deterrence arose from peace movement interests during the Cold War period (cf. Chilton 1982, 1983, 1985, 1988, 1996). Van Dijk has on numerous occasions stated the view that critical discourse studies should be engaged in the "critique of social inequality" (cf. van Dijk 1993, 1995, 1998, 1999, 2001). Fairclough makes specific proposals for critical discourse analysts: working with activists in designing and carrying out research, linking it, for instance, to the campaigns of disabled people over welfare reform, seeking to publish pamphlets, articles in newspapers and magazines, or on the web, and developing ways of writing which are accessible to many people without being superficial (Fairclough 2001b: 264–265). The implication appears to be that critical discourse analysts have some obligation to be (i) politically committed, (ii) to seek to apply practical results of analysis to communication problems, or (iii) both of these activities combined. Kress summarises the political project of CDA as follows:

> Critical studies of language, Critical linguistics (CL) and Critical Discourse Analysis (CDA) have from the beginning had a political project: broadly speaking that of altering inequitable distributions of economic, cultural and political goods in contemporary societies. The intention has been to bring a system of excessive inequalities of power into crisis by uncovering its workings and its effects through the analysis of potent cultural objects – texts – and thereby to help in achieving a more equitable social order. (Kress 1996: 15)

This line of thinking is question-provoking if compared to some of the features that we will note later with respect to the Chinese context – in particular the close linkage between "criticism" and ethical or socio-political principles, according to which the social order can be improved if public language is rid of undesirable elements.

CDA itself is subject to critique. For example, Billig (2003) challenges the CDA community by asking if their institutionalisation might have led to being less critical and self-reflective; recently, Billig (2008) has illustrated how some CDA scholars employ certain linguistic features frequently in their writing which they tend to criticise in the writing of others such as the use of nominalisations.

However, the desirability of a political "mission" (or practical "application") in CDA is not acceptable to certain linguists and discourse analysts in the West. There is also an argument based on methodological considerations to the effect that the research of CDA is not scientifically "objective" enough. Widdowson (2004), for example, is well known for criticism of the CDA approach to discourse. It is not so much the "mission" of CDA that Widdowson objects to, as what he regards as a methodological problem (but see Wodak 2006 in response to this and for an argument that Widdowson's critique is unjustified). One of his specific points is that critical discourse analysts sample text selectively and analyse linguistic features selectively in order to confirm their own political values. Similar kinds of objection to the CDA paradigm have been made by Stubbs (1997) and Schegloff (1997). Several kinds of arguments have been made in response. One is that CDA analysts do in fact acknowledge their normative position, while this frequently stays implicit in other social science research. Moreover, many studies in CDA have not only selected a few texts to illustrate their assumptions but have, indeed, analysed huge data sets in quantitative and qualitative ways (e.g., Krzyżanowski & Wodak 2008; Wodak & van Dijk 2000) – a fact rarely or not acknowledged by the above mentioned critics. Another response is to argue that no research is objective, all scientific research is always subservient to interests. This line of argument often cites Kuhn (1962) on the shift of scientific paradigms and Habermas (e.g. Habermas 1968, 1971) on science, normativity, knowledge, and interests.

It is worth considering another type of claim to scientific objectivity in discourse analysis. The claim runs roughly as follows and can easily be found for lexical items and (with more difficulty) for grammatical constructions. Texts can be processed automatically, without the intervention of a human brain in a process of text understanding, thus eliminating subjective bias. The techniques of quantitative corpus linguistics are now well known: relative frequencies, collocations and correlations with context and co-text can. For selecting texts for analysis, statistical sampling techniques are available and well known in the social sciences. The problem here, however, is that meanings cannot be found this way. Assuming you have an object text sample and some statistically significant lexical or grammatical patterns, the discourse analyst still wants to investigate first the meaning and second the social significance of these findings. There is no objective method for these two interpretative stages (but see Baker et al. 2008 and Mautner 2008, 2009 for attempts of integrating CDA with corpus linguistics in innovative ways).

Since objectivist defences are difficult to sustain some, CDA scholars have elaborated a different response to reproaches of subjective bias. One such response (cf. Chilton 2004) might be: "Analysts are also socialised members of a speech community. They are concerned with the meanings of texts and they can only know those meanings via their socialised membership in a society. Therefore any and all discourse analysis concerned with meanings must involve analysts' existing knowledge about potential meanings that different readers will arrive at in processing texts under consideration; otherwise they would be unable to make sense of the text at all." This response does not address the selection of texts for analysis; nor does it guarantee that the analyst will spot all potential meanings. But it may be that there is in fact no other route than to produce analyses and allow open critical discussion about alternative analyses and readings. Critical researchers emphasise "*retroduct-ability*" in their studies: this implies that the analysis must be explicit and transparent enough so that other researchers are able to understand and replicate it, possibly with different goals and results.

This approach can be elaborated further. "Being critical" in CDA includes being reflexively self-critical. For CDA, discourse is a form of social practice and, consequently, the discourse produced by the critical analysis of discourse is also a form of social practice among free intellectuals. In this sense, critical discourse analysis does not only mean to criticise others. It also means to criticise the "critical" itself, a point that is in line with Habermas, and was made in 1989 (Wodak 1989) and again ten years later:

> CDA, like other critical social sciences, needs to be reflexive and self-critical about its own institutional position and all that goes with it. (Chouliaraki and Fairclough 1999: 9).

A similar point about self-reflection is made strongly in Reisigl and Wodak (2001: 32ff.) with respect to the sampling and analysis of texts. These authors also make useful distinctions between text-immanent critique, socio-diagnostic critique, and prospective (retrospective) critique. Whether these levels can really be separated remains of course a matter for debate.

Their view of *text-immanent critique* is not focussed first and foremost on the linguistic description of texts. Rather it is, based on hermeneutics (the study of possible meanings in texts) and pursues one of the early ideas of Critical Theory, namely, the unearthing of inherent contradictions (a method also, incidentally, incorporated in versions of literary postmodernist deconstruction à la Derrida) via linguistic means; these are thus selected depending on the research questions and should be adequate to operationalise these in systematic ways. To this end descriptive methods sometimes seem to be taken from linguistics *ad hoc*.

While *text-immanent critique* is claimed to be inherently text-oriented, *socio-diagnostic critique* is avowedly based on the analyst's social and political commitments, i.e. integrating context. At this level, also, the aim is to reveal multiple interests and contradictions in the text producers, on the basis of the evidence of the text and its *contexts*. Utterances in a text, or the text as a whole, may belie or be belied by other utterances and texts. This is described by Reisigl and Wodak (2001) as a process of "demystifying". They are careful to note that mystificatory or manipulative intentions cannot be detected in any simply manner, and insist that contextual understanding by speakers and hearers is the basis for the production and processing of meaning.

Prospective critique builds on these two levels in order to identify areas of social concern that can be addressed by direct social and political engagement. In many Western polities, this is possible to a large degree if we make comparisons with many other nation states around the globe, even if there are also limitations on action that many citizens, including discourse analysts, would also criticise. What is important, when we come to think in terms of a cross-cultural and indeed globalised critique of discourse, is that authors like Reisigl and Wodak, whatever view one may take of the technicalities of their theories, are open about the *ethical* basis of their criticism:

> ...an engaged social critique is nurtured ethically by a sense of justice based on the normative and universalist conviction of the unrestricted validity of human rights and by the awareness of suffering, which both takes sides *against* social discrimination, repression, domination, exclusion and exploitation and *for* emancipation, self-determination and social recognition ... (Reisigl & Wodak 2001: 34)

Such statements are not remarkable in Western political culture, but in a global context they are highly controversial, and Western CDA writers need to be aware of the fact and begin to address the problem. But this is not all that is globally significant in the critical approach outlined by Reisigl and Wodak (ibid.), and shared by other writers (including, for example, Chilton 2004, Chapter 2 on 'language and freedom'). For Reisigl and Wodak make clear what their preferred political model is – and it is not of course simply an endorsement of the current political regime in their own country.

From a theoretical standpoint the ideas of Habermas are of fundamental importance, especially as found in Habermas (Habermas 1971, 1979, 1984/1987, 1996; see also Wright 2005 or Koller & Wodak 2008 for criticism of Habermas' ideas and recent developments of these). The key concepts are: public sphere and a "deliberative democracy" in which free and equal participation in debate, critique and decision-making is guaranteed by the rule of law. Drawing on these principles, Reisigl and Wodak (2001: 34) give what is perhaps the most detailed statement in CDA of the grounds that underly the critical analysis of public discourse. In this perspective language itself is crucial:

> ... language is the central medium of democratic organisation and free public exchange of different interests, wishes, viewpoints, opinions and arguments is vital for a pluralistic democracy in a modern decentred society, since it is essential for deliberatively and justly organising the different preferences, and since it can also have a critical influence on the relationship between legality and administrative power changes.

Ultimately, it is the individual citizen who engages in free critique, not just the scholar-analyst. The above quotation is an example of a discourse type yet to emerge in the Chinese context. But there is one further point to note in relation to the Reisigl and Wodak approach to critique – and again, it is one already shared among many critical discourse analysts. Time present and time past are both perhaps co-present in discourse practices and discourse practices in social and political practices. What Reisigl and Wodak mean by *retrospective critique* is that past events in a society's history (in Europe the slave trade and the Holocaust, for example, in China the Cultural Revolution, among many other episodes of history) are interpreted and perspectivised in narratives re-told and re-constructed in the present (see also Heer et al, 2008). In the present issue of *JLP*, we see this kind of critical approach in Cao's paper, which looks at the transformation of historical narratives about Western imperialism in the Chinese media.

Being "critical" in Western CDA does, then, imply ethical value judgments concerning what is "the good life", and these fundamental premises in all CDA work are not always overt. What this implies is a rather open-ended need to incorporate philosophical reflection on the underlying social, political and ethical premises of CDA, which may actually be independent of language and discourse.

Let us now turn to the question of what it could mean to transpose such issues into the Chinese context: self-critique is advocated in the writings of Confucius.[1] This is not a private matter: the Confucian text appears to imply that self-criticism is a *public* duty. Moreover, public political discourse in modern China can be seen to incorporate such a "self-criticism" element, perhaps as a form of self-legitimation. Self-critique is thus historically embedded in Chinese discourse culture in a way that is not the case (except perhaps for some religious discourses) in the West. The implications of this observation need to be explored further as scholars work together to deepen Western and Chinese understandings of the "critical".

Being "Critical" in China

While the concept of critique has developed rich technical meanings in the West, being "critical" in Chinese is generally associated with unfavourable meanings in daily life. This may also be the case for English, but in the Chinese context, if one is said to be "critical", one is most likely to be considered a person who is not considerate, not friendly, and who finds fault with everyone and everything. This meaning may be traced back to the early recorded meanings of the word *pi* (批), the first syllable of the word *piping* (批评), which is the usual translation equivalent of the English "criticism" or "being critical".

The etymology of the Chinese word *piping* is conceptually different from that of *criticise* and its cognates in European languages. According to *Cihai*, a Chinese encyclopaedic dictionary that provides earlier meanings of individual Chinese characters, *pi* in the ancient Chinese language mainly meant (i) "to hit with the hand, especially on the face" or (ii) "to remove by beating and sharpening" (Xia 1999: 1906).[2] In (ii) the meaning involves a material object as affected participant; in (i) the affected participant is human. It is not clear which of these meanings comes first historically. It is worth noting, however, that in the case of *pi* with material object, a change of state appears to be involved in the semantics, a change of state brought about by hitting or beating. In the case where the grammatical object of *pi* is semantically human,[3] we have to envisage a change of state in some different sense, perhaps a change of mind or a change of heart. It is significant that the end result brought about by beating is the removal of something (considered by the speaker to be) undesirable. Such semantic transfers between domains are not uncommon in language change and would account for the emergence of a sense of *pi* that is translated as "criticise". However, it remains a matter of speculation how much this historical association with physical beating and its effects remain a significant factor in its modern meaning. It is also worth noting that *Cihai* gives meaning of *piping* (批评) as "to rectify, to comment and to evaluate by causing physical pain". In addition, another word, sometimes used to translate "criticise", is *pipan* (批判) and an earlier meaning of *pipan* is "to differentiate by sharpening and cutting".[4] These cases are of interest because *piping* appears to denote a primarily physical act in a social context, while the etymology of *pipan* suggests how a concept of physical refinement or division could lead to the intellectual act of "criticising", in the same way as the etymology of "criticise" in the European languages.

Let us briefly consider the modern meanings of *pi*. This morpheme is rarely, if ever, found alone in modern Chinese usage but is frequently found in two-morpheme compounds with other single morphemes, such as *ping* (评) and *pan* (判). In *Cihai*, *ping* (评) is defined as "to comment and to evaluate" (Xia 1999: 1711), and *pan* (判) is defined as "to differentiate and distinguish, often in public" (Xia 1999: 521). While the combined two-morpheme compounds (*piping* and *pipan*) have a meaning in themselves, they nonetheless have some associations with the earlier meanings of the separate Chinese characters/morphemes (*pi*, *ping*, and *pan*). For modern Chinese, the *Grand Chinese Dictionary* (汉语大辞典), a Chinese dictionary that provides meanings of modern Chinese characters, gives the following two meanings for *piping* (批评): (i) "to point out the strong points and weak points; to comment on these" and (ii) "esp. to point out the errors and mistakes" (Editorial Board 2006: 367). The word *pipan* (批判) is defined as "to make systematic analysis of wrong ideas" (Editorial Board 2006: 366). If this is an accurate reflection of the contemporary meanings of these two words, then it appears that there is a shift to a more abstract conceptual domain, with a lessening of the conceptual difference between the two words. It appears that in this abstract domain, concepts of rational comment may be involved. However, *pipan* may include more clearly a concept of social censure, reflecting perhaps the earlier link between *pi* and physical punishment. Some bilingual dictionaries give "sentence, condemn" (in the judicial sense) as equivalents of *pipan*. In both words, there is a clear implication that the object of the verb denotes something regarded by the speaker as in some sense "wrong". These are words deeply embedded in normative cultural practices. Clearly, "errors", "mistakes" and "wrong ideas" imply some basis of judgement, possibly ideo-logical. Dictionaries can incorporate, and even seek to impose, ideological conceptions, but we shall not pursue this particular issue here.

Of course, most word meanings are not a matter of stipulation by dic-tionaries. Rather, meanings are conceptual frames (often complex ones) associated with a phonological form. Such conceptual frames can include knowledge of the situations in which the words are typically used or have been used. In the case of *pipan* and *piping* associations of this kind, given the historical context of China, might be expected to include the discourse practice of public denunciation and private self-criticism enforced under Mao Zedong (Ji 2004). At least, this may be the case for a certain gener-ation of the contemporary Chinese population. The practice of "criticism", conducted in large meetings and small groups, was not left to the reasoning of individuals. From its systematic establishment in the "rectification" (*zheng feng* 整风) campaign of 1942–44 at the Communist base in Yan'an (self-) criticism was closely directed by supervisors who ensured conformity with the Party line. Such practices included what is in effect the discourse com-plement of denunciation, namely confession (Ji 2004: 48–50). The princi-pal psycho-social tool of directed mass criticism is exclusion from the group. Physical violence was of course also used, notably in the Cultural Revolution, and it is of some interest to note in this connection the earlier meaning of *pi*, discussed above, "to change, or to remove something undesirable by beating".

The goal of the kind of critical discursive practice instituted at Yan'an is conformity with a specific public vocabulary of political terminology approved by the Party, on the assumption that politically correct language causes pol-itically correct thinking and behaviour. But the purpose of the discourse prac-tice of criticism meetings was also to influence the masses by a public display in which an individual was humiliated by verbal denunciation. During the Cultural Revolution this kind of mass public meeting – the *pipan hui* (批判会) – was formalized and ritualized. It was in this kind of practice that *pipan* acquires its specific set of associations rooted in a specific phase of Chinese history (Ji 2004: 161ff.). Today Chinese political discourse does not go to these extremes. Nonetheless, there remains an expectation of conformity to central government policy and this can be enforced in part by the tradition of self-critical discussion accompanied by the rectificatory guidance of the local Party secretary in small groups of Party members in work units. Being "critical" in the Chinese context thus carries a heavy ideological load, in the sense that many members of the population will have cognitive frames that include the kind of knowledge just outlined. Moreover, the conceptual frame of *pipan* is not one in which the individual criticises a central authority, as it is in the European Enlightenment tradition but rather the reverse. That is to say, it is individuals who are picked out for "criticism" by officials or by the masses incited by ideologically motivated elites.

There may be other cultural reasons why the words *piping* and *pipan* carry unfavourable connotations. It is often claimed that the Chinese tradition is more oriented to the concept of *harmony* than it is oriented to what might be termed critique. This is a complex area, especially if one bears in mind the historical context outlined in the last paragraph. For the notion of "harmony" may be bound up with ideological concepts of mass "unity", that is of political and social conformity with an ideology. In which case, "harmony" can be seen not simply as a benign ethical or aesthetic principle but as part of a power structure. The recent re-assimilation of the notion of "harmony" in Chinese Communist Party discourse is open to the same kind of consideration – indeed "critical" consideration in the sense of the Western tradition, which is precisely the concern of CDA.

However, it is also important to bear in mind that the manipulation of public language for reasons that can be regarded as socio-political may be deeply embedded in pre-Communist culture. One of the key themes in Confucian thinking – we may call it Confucian *discourse*, since "Confucian thinking" is constituted in a social *practice* of verbal and other behaviours transmitted from generation to generation by educational and other channels – is the "rectification of names" (*zheng ming* 正名). The following passage from Confucius (1979) is well known, but gains a particular relevance when considered in the present context:

Tzu-lu said, 'If the Lord of Wei left the administration [*zheng* 政] of his state to you, what would you put first?'

The Master said, 'If something has to be put first, it is perhaps the rectification [*zheng* 正] of names.'

Tzu-lu said, 'Is that so? What a roundabout way you take! Why bring rectification in at all?'

The Master said, 'Yu, how boorish you are. Where a gentleman is ignorant, one would expect him not to offer any opinion. When names are not correct, what is said will not sound reasonable, affairs will not culminate in success; when affairs do not culminate in success, rites and music will not flourish; when rites and music do not flourish, punishment will not fit the crimes; when punishments do not fit the crimes, the common people will not know where to put hand and foot.'...

(子路曰: "卫君待子而为政, 子将奚先?" 子曰: "必也正名乎。" 子路 曰: "有是哉, 子之迂也。奚其正?" 子曰: "野哉由也。君子于其所不知, 盖阙 如也。名不正则言不顺, 言不顺则事不成, 事不成则礼乐不兴, 礼乐 不兴 则刑罚不中, 刑罚不中则民无所措手足。故君子名之必可言也, 言之 必可 行也。君子于其言, 无所苟而已矣。")

(*Analects*, XIII, 3, translated by D.C. Lau)

What can this tell us about present-day political discourse and indeed about language ideology and language policy? It seems that Confucius is outlining, however sketchily, a view of language according to which words determine thoughts. The language philosophy involved here is not, it seems, like the Platonic doctrine (or the doctrine of Cratylus) that words naturally denote their real-world referents (see Plato's (1996) dialogue *Cratylus*). Rather, it seems clear from the use of the word *zheng* (正) that Confucian means that words should be chosen by the ruler in the belief that they determine the way people think about reality, in line with the policies espoused by some such ruler.

The appeal to traditional Chinese values, or simply the transmission of the ideas in family and pedagogic discourse, may direct ruling elites to think about language in this way. In modern terms we could say that a traditional language ideology makes it appear natural for a regime to seek to control terminology in the perceived interests of society as a whole. Moreover, anyone familiar with the Western cultural tradition is bound to be reminded of George Orwell's (1949) novel *Nineteen Eighty-four*, in which an artificial language called "newspeak" is imposed by a totalitarian regime in the interests of "thought control".

Despite the historical tendencies just outlined, there have been indications of a different kind of "critical" spirit in Chinese scholarship in the past. Interestingly, these resemble those of the early Western "critical" spirit in some respects. The period from the middle of the seventeenth century to the middle of the eighteenth was a period in China that was "a period of free thought and of radical criticism of the authoritarian empire" (Gernet 1999: 497). Such attitudes had their roots in the late sixteenth century, as was the case, *mutatis mutandis*, in the West. What is interesting is that the critical frame of mind was linked to researches into the previous ages of Chinese culture and, in the work of for instance, Wang Fuzhi, into the nature and evolution of human societies. Significantly, thinkers like Wang Fuzhi were associated with textual criticism, the re-analysis of classical texts. The questioning of the authenticity and accuracy of texts by the use of rational methods is most famously associated with Gu Yanwu. This rich history cannot be pursued further here, but it is worth noting that it was also the tradition of textual criticism in the West, reaching back into the sixteenth century, that eventually merged textual criticism with political critique in the European Enlightenment.

A "Colonising" Recontextualization?

"Recontextualisation" has become a key term in much CDA writing. A piece of language (written or spoken) produced by one speaker may under certain conditions be repeated later by other speakers: the piece of repeated language is "text". Each utterance, new or repeated, derives its meaning from its context; that is, in broad terms, the speech situation (participants, location, and medium) and genre combined with varying degrees of socio-cultural knowledge shared among the participants. A text may be "re-cycled" into a context that is different in kind and historical circumstances from its initial production.

An example is the use in the previous section of the quotation from Confucius. If Confucius and Tzu-lu ever held a conversation along these lines it was first "entextualised" orally and only many years later scribally (for this approach to text, cf. Blommaert 2005). Generations of scholars contributed to its continuous transmission in discourse over time. One can assume that it was recontextualised countless times for various purposes, including political purposes. Translation into English is a kind of recontextualisation. In our text above, we have in turn inserted this translation, recontextualised, for our own argumentation purposes, in a new context, a recontextualisation with which readers may or may not agree.

CDA authors have argued that recontextualisation can play a crucial role in discourse-mediated power structures (see Iedema 1997; van Leeuwen & Wodak 1999; Wodak 2000a, b, 2008; Wodak & Fairclough 2010). Recontextualization is linked to *intertextuality*. This latter term can be defined as referring to the linkage of all texts to other texts, both in the past and in the present. Such links can be established in different ways: through continued reference to a topic or to its main actors; through reference to the same events as the other texts; or through the reappearance of a text's main arguments in another text. Precisely the latter process is also labeled *recontextualization*. By taking an argument out of context and restating it in a new context, we first observe the process of de-contextualization, and then, when the respective element is implemented in a new context, of recontextualization. The element then acquires a new meaning, because, as Wittgenstein (1953) famously argued, meanings are forged in use. To take an example relevant to the present collection, the traditional discourse of education has in the West begun to include commercial vocabulary – indeed commercial text in the sense outlined above. A similar phenomenon is happening in China. One may ask: is it the universities that are "appropriating" the language of commerce and managerialism for their own strategic goals? Or is it business that is somehow "colonising" the territory of the scholar? And one may ask, self-critically, à propos of our recontextualisation of Confucius above: are we appropriating Confucius? Or is Chinese culture colonising the discourse of CDA? Or, in an even more complicated dialectic, are we appropriating Confucian discourse, colonising it with a selective Western interpretation, and using it to colonise CDA discourse, or, even to colonise an emergent Chinese discourse on CDA?

Why are such convoluted points worth making? The reason, within the perspective of the present special issue of *JLP*, is that the dialogue between Chinese and Western scholars in the field of CDA is indeed dialectic, as indeed is the entire historical process of "opening up", intensified in the contexts of globalization and glocalization. It is dialectic in which Chinese and Western intellectual perspectives and traditions meet one another, in various local, regional, and national contexts, at differing points in time.

Concluding Note

The papers that we have included in this special issue of the *Journal of Language and Politics* are necessarily limited in scope. The aim, however, is much wider – to call the attention of discourse and language analysts to the challenging research tasks that the development of social, political and intellectual life in China is opening up. These tasks are both theoretical and empirical. As we have hoped to make clear in these reflections, there are some major and quite urgent theoretical – actually, philosophical – problems that are emerging as the analysis of political discourse becomes global and cross-cultural. On the empirical front, we are facing a very diverse, complex and dynamic culture which it is not even desirable to try to grasp as a stable totality. In any case, the concept of "discourse" is itself fluid and multiplex, so we can never be sure, nor do we need to try to be, that we have some sort of definitive inventory of a society's discourses at some moment in time.

Nonetheless, the Leverhulme-funded project, *New Discourses in Contemporary China* (NDCC), which is the source for the selected papers in this issue of *JLP*, has enabled us to envisage further research topics, among which the dynamics of emergent discourses is one. For example, many new discourses gestate at the oral level, among circles of acquaintances, in notebooks, diaries, mobile phone messages and blogs; even later when they become sufficiently stable to be recognizable as "discourses", they are originally recognised as marginal and alternative discourses, in contrast to mainstream discourses conveyed via mainstream media. Between these discourses are dialogues, and sometimes tensions and even struggles, resulting in a change of status, with marginal turning to mainstream or mainstream to marginal. Something essential in this dynamics of discourses is "critique", be it a perspective or a discursive act.

In researching the complexity of discourses, CDA has made its contribution in the past few decades. However, scholarly discourse analysis may be said to be itself a discourse, one that consciously engages with its sociopolitical context. In this sense, CDA's critical perspective can be characterised as having "narrow focus" on specific socio-political issues. Tian (2008, 2009) therefore proposes a "wider angle" perspective, one which focuses research on the roles of discourse in contemporary Chinese society, for example, how discourse represents social events, constitutes identity, and hence participates in social practice. This way of doing CDA in China is an outcome of dialogue between reflections on discourse and critique in China and the West, and also of a recontextualisation of CDA in the Chinese context. We do not yet know where the collaboration of Chinese and Western scholars in understanding communication in different societies will lead. The entire environment for discourse studies in China, and indeed world-wide, could change.

Notes

1. For example, Tseng Tzu, one of Confucius' students, said: "Each day I examine myself in three ways: in doing things for others, have I been disloyal? In my interactions with friends, have I been untrustworthy? Have not practiced what I have preached?" 曾子曰：「吾日三省吾身–爲人謀而不忠乎? 與朋友交而不信乎? 傳不習乎? 」
2. Translations from the cited dictionaries are by Tian.
3. Strictly speaking, a human body part, the face. The metaphorical significance of "face" is culturally relevant.
4. *Cihai* is not explicit about dates or chronological sequence.

References

Baker, Paul et al. 2008. A useful methodological synergy? Combining critical discourse analysis and corpus linguistics to examine discourses of refugees and asylum seekers in the UK press. *Discourse & Society* 19/3, 273–306.

Bhaskar, Roy A. 1989. *Reclaiming Reality: A Critical Introduction to Contemporary Philosophy*. London: Verso.

Billig, Michael. 2003. Critical discourse analysis and the rhetoric of critique. In: Gilbert Weiss and Ruth Wodak (eds). *Critical Discourse Analysis: Theory and Interdisciplinarity*. London: Palgrave, 35–46.

———— 2008. The language of critical discourse analysis: The case of nominalisation. *Discourse and Society*, 19(6), 783–800.

Blommaert, Jan. 2005. *Discourse: A Critical Introduction*. Cambridge: Cambridge University Press.

Chilton, Paul. 1982. Nukespeak: Nuclear language, culture and propaganda. In: Crispin Aubrey (ed.). *Nukespeak: The Media and the Bomb*. London: Comedia Publishing Group, 94–112.

———— 1983. Newspeak. In: Crispin Aubrey and Paul Chilton (eds). *Nineteen eighty-four in 1984: Autonomy, Control and Communication*. London: Comedia Publishing Group, 33–44.

———— 1985. *Language and the Nuclear Arms Debate*. London: Pinter.

———— 1988. *Orwellian Language and the Media*. London: Pluto Press.

———— 1996. *Security Metaphors: Cold War Discourse from Containment to Common European Home*. Berne: Peter Lang.

———— 2004. *Analysing Political Discourse: Theory and Practice*. London: Routledge.

———— 2009. Critical discourse analysis. *The Cambridge Encyclopedia of the Language Sciences*. Cambridge: Cambridge University Press.

Chouliaraki, Lilie and Fairclough, Norman. 1999. *Discourse in Late Modernity: Rethinking Critical Discourse Analysis*. Edinburgh: Edinburgh University Press.

Confucius. 1979. *Analects*, translated by D. C. Lau, London: Penguin Books.

Editorial Board. 2006. *Grand Chinese Dictionary*. Shanghai: Century Publisher.

Fairclough, Norman. 2001a (1989). *Language and Power* (2nd Edition). London: Longman.

Fairclough, Norman. 2001b. The discourse of new Labour: Critical discourse analysis. In: Margaret Wetherell, Stephanie Taylor, and Simeon Yates (eds). *Discourse as Data*. London: Sage in association with The Open University, 229–266.

Fairclough, Norman and Wodak, Ruth. 1997. Critical discourse analysis. In: Teun A. van Dijk (ed). *Discourse as Social Interaction*. London: Sage, 258–84.

Gernet, Jacques. 1999. *A History of Chinese Civilization* (2nd edition). Cambridge: Cambridge University Press.

Habermas, Jürgen. 1968. Science and technology as ideology. In: Barry Barnes (ed.). *Sociology of Science*. Harmondsworth: Penguin, 74–85.

—— 1971. *Knowledge and Human Interests*, translated by Jeremy Shapiro, Boston: Beacon Press.

—— 1979. *Communicaiton and the Evolution of Society*, translated by Thomas McCarthy, Boston: Beacon Press.

—— 1984/1987. *The Theory of Communicative Action*, 2 vols. Translated by Thomas McCarthy, Boston: Beacon Press.

—— 1996 (2nd edition). *The Structural Transformation of the Public Sphere*. Cambridge: MIT Press.

Heer, Hannes, Manoschek, Walter, Pollak, Alexander, and Wodak, Ruth. (eds). 2008. *The Discursive Construction of History. Remembering the Wehrmacht's War of Annihilation*. Basingstoke: Palgrave.

Iedema, Rick. 1997. The language of administration: Organizing human activity in formal institutions. In: Frances Christie and James Martin (eds). *Genre and Institutions: Social Processes in the Workplace and School*. London and Washington: Cassell, 73–100.

Ji, Fengyuan. 2004. *Linguistic Engineering: Language and Politics in Mao's China*. Honolulu: University of Hawaii Press.

Koller, Veronika and Wodak, Ruth. 2008. Introduction: Shifting boundaries and emergent public spheres. In: Ruth Wodak and Veronika Koller (eds). *Communication in the Public Sphere*. Berlin: De Gruyter, 1–21.

Kress, Gunther. 1996. Representational resources and the production of subjectivity: Questions for the theoretical development of critical discourse analysis in a multicultural society. In: Carmen Rosa Caldas-Coulthard and Malcolm Coulthard (eds). *Texts and Practices: Readings in Critical Discourse Analysis*. London and New York: Routledge, 15–31.

Krzyżanowski, Michał and Wodak, Ruth. 2008. *The Politics of Exclusion. Debating Migration in Austria*. New Orleans: Transaction Press.

Kuhn, Thomas. S. 1962. *The Structure of Scientific Revolutions*. Chicago: University of Chicago Press.

Mautner, Gerlinde. 2008. Analyzing newspapers, magazines and other print media. In: Ruth Wodak and Michał Krzyżanowski (eds). *Qualitative Discourse Analysis in the Social Sciences*. Basingstoke: Palgrave, 30–53.

Mautner, Gerlinde. 2009. Checks and balances: How corpus linguistics can contribute to CDA. In: Ruth Wodak and Michael Meyer (eds). *Methods of CDA*. London: Sage (2nd revised edition), 122–141.

Orwell, George. 1949. *Nineteen Eighty-Four*. London: Secker and Warburg.

Plato.1996. *Plato: Cratylus. Parmenides. Greater Hippias. Lesser Hippias*. Translated by Harold N. Fowler (Loeb Classical Library No. 167) St Edmunds, Suffolk, UK: St Edmundsbury Press.

Reisigl, Martin and Wodak, Ruth. 2001. *Discourse and Discrimination*. London: Routledge.

————— 2009. The discourse-historical Approach. In: Ruth Wodak and Michael Meyer (eds). *Methods of CDA*. London: Sage (2nd revised edition), 87–121.

Schegloff, Emanuel. 1997. Whose text? Whose context? *Discourse and Society* 8, 165–187.

Shi-xu. 2005. *A Cultural Approach to Discourse*. New York: Palgrave.

————— (ed.). 2007. *Discourse as Cultural Struggle*. Hong Kong: Hong Kong University Press.

————— 2009. Reconstructing eastern paradigms of discourse studies. *Journal of Multicultural Discourses* 4 (1), 29–48.

Stubbs, Michael. 1997. Whorf's children: critical comments on CDA. In: Ryan, A. & Wray, A. (eds). *Evolving Models of Language*. Milton Keynes: Multilingual Matters.

Tian, Hailong. 2008. Critical perspectives on discourse studies. *Foreign Language Teaching and Research* 40(5), 339–344.

————— 2009. *Discourse Studies: Categories, Perspectives and Methodologies*. Shanghai: Shanghai Foreign Language Education Press.

Van Dijk, Teun A. 1993. Principles of critical discourse analysis. *Discourse & Society*, 4(2), 249–283.

————— 1995. Discourse semantics and ideology. *Discourse & Society* 6(2), 243–289.

————— 1998. Opinions and ideologies in the press. In A. Bell & P. Garrett (eds). *Approaches to Media Discourse*. Oxford: Blackwell, 21–63.

————— 1999. Discourse analysis as ideology analysis. In C. Schäffner & A. Wenden (eds). *Language and Peace*. Amsterdam: Harwood Academic Publishers, 17–33.

————— 2001. Critical discourse analysis. In: Deborah Schiffrin et al. (eds). *The Handbook of Discourse Analysis*. Oxford: Blackwell, 352–371.

Van Leeuwen, Theo and Wodak, Ruth. 1999. Legitimizing immigration control: A Discourse-historical analysis. *Discourse Studies* 1(1), 83–118.

Widdowson, Henry. 2004. *Text, Context, Pretext: Critical Issues in Discourse Analysis*. Oxford: Blackwell.

Wittgenstein, Ludwig. 1953. *Philosophische Untersuchungen./Philosophical Investigations*. Translated by G.E.M. Anscombe. Oxford: Blackwell.

Wodak, Ruth. (ed.). 1989. *Language, Ideology, and Power: Studies in Political Discourse*. Amsterdam: Benjamins.

————— 1996. *Disorders of Discourse*. London: Longman.

————— 2000a. From conflict to consensus? The co-construction of a policy paper. In: Peter Muntigl, Gilbert Weiss, and Ruth Wodak (eds). *European Union Discourses on Unemployment*. Amsterdam: Benjamins, 73–114.

————— 2000b. Recontextualization and the transformation of meaning: A critical discourse analysis of decision making in EU-meetings about employment policies. In: Srikant Sarangi and Malcolm Coulthard (eds). *Discourse and Social Life*. Harlow: Pearson Education, 185–206.

————— 2001. The discourse-historical approach. In: Ruth Wodak and Michael Meyer (eds). *Methods of CDA*. London: Sage, 63–94.

————— 2003. Populist discourses. The rhetoric of exclusion in written genres. *Document Design* 4:2, 133–148.

————— 2006. Dilemmas of discourse (analysis). *Language in Society* 35, 595–611.

————— 2007. Pragmatics and critical discourse analysis. A cross-disciplinary analysis. *Pragmatics and Cognition* 15:1, 203–225.

————— 2008. Introduction: discourse studies – Important concepts and terms. In: Ruth Wodak and Michał Krzyżanowskis (eds). *Qualitative Discourse Analysis in the Social Sciences*. Basingstoke: Palgrave, 1–29.

————— 2009. *The Discourse of Politics in Action: Politics as Usual*. Basingstoke: Palgrave.

Wodak, Ruth and van Dijk, Teun A. (eds). 2000. *Racism at the Top*. Klagenfurt: Drava.

Wodak, Ruth and Chilton, Paul. (eds). 2007. *A New Agenda in (Critical) Discourse Analysis.* Amsterdam: Benjamins.

Wodak, Ruth and Koller, Veronika. (eds) 2008. *Communication in the Public Sphere.* (Handbook of Applied Linguistics, Vol. IV) Berlin: de Gruyter.

Wodak, Ruth and Fairclough, Norman. 2010. Recontextualising the Bologna process in Austria and Romania, *Critical Discourse Studies* (in press).

Wright, Scott. 2005. Design matters: The political efficacy of government-run online discussion forums. In: Sarah Oates, Diana Owen, and Rachel K. Gibson (eds). *The Internet and Politics: Citizens, voters, and activists.* London: Routledge, 80–99.

Xia, Zhengnong (editor-in-chief). 1999. *Cihai.* Shanghai: Shanghai Dictionary Publisher.

53

Critique, the Discourse–Historical Approach, and the Frankfurt School

Bernhard Forchtner

Introduction

Over the last two decades, critical discourse analysis (CDA) has become an established academic tradition – a development which has not challenged CDA's pluralistic character (Wodak, 2001a, p. 11, 2001b, p. 64; Wodak & Weiss, 2005, p. 124). Thus, despite many overlaps, Teun van Dijk (2008, p. 822) suggests that CDA should not be understood as a uniform school but as a heterogeneous 'movement'. Of course, CDA shares a focus on the embeddedness of semiosis in social contexts, on discourse as the social activity of meaning-making through (written/spoken) language, bodily expressions and/or sounds. Therefore, discourses are seen as crucial in the (re)production of the social – although being both enabled and constrained by other, material, factors. It is the role of discourse in the (re)production of unjustified discrimination and inequalities, the way discourses obscure (but can also denaturalise) such power relations, which forms the common interest of CDA (cf. Fairclough & Wodak, 1997). However, at the same time CDA, as a diverse 'movement', entails various methodologies and epistemological positions. In particular with regards to the latter, attempts to ground a critical stance thus rest on *different* giants. That is, CDA's different approaches are orientated towards different epistemological underpinnings ranging from Foucauldian poststructuralism to normatively rich theories like the Frankfurt School (cf. Wodak & Meyer, 2009).[1]

Source: *Critical Discourse Studies*, 8(1) (2011): 1–14.

How CDA validates and grounds its own critical standards is therefore not easy to answer. Its pluralism in theoretically justifying critique is, however, held together by a few basic convictions: hidden power structures should be revealed, unjustified discrimination and inequality have to be fought, and the analyst has to reflect on her/his own position and make her/his standpoint transparent. Having said that, van Dijk (2008, p. 823) has recently nevertheless pointed to 'the lack of theory about the norms and principals of its [CDA's] own critical activity'. A detailed account of these principles and their theoretical grounding which goes beyond a self-reflective stance and the aim of making power structures transparent is indeed necessary as a lack of justification causes problems. For example, academic communities are often based on a progressive consensus and committed to a seemingly self-evident (more or less) humanist agenda. However, can or should such conventions define what has to be critiqued, our notions of critique and emancipation, our moral position? I assume that this alone is not convincing enough to ground a 'socially transformative teleology' (McKenna, 2004, p. 9). Without an extensive elaboration of why one's critique is particularly reliable, one encourages accusations of being unprincipled and biased (cf. Hammersley, 1997, or – more polemical – Widdowson, 2004 and Stubbs, 1997). Furthermore, clarifying one's own grounds helps to avoid self-righteous blaming of other approaches as uncritical (Billig, 2003). Thus, a progressive consensus which is 'biased – and proud of' (van Dijk, 2001, p. 96) taking a standpoint has to justify theoretically why its understanding of particular social circumstances should (and could) be rejected.

In this article I argue that, *in the case of the discourse–historical approach* (DHA), what is needed when approaching this issue is rather a matter of clarification and explicitness. While the DHA shares CDA's core orientation, among the various strands in CDA, it has most consistently referred to the Frankfurt School as the foundation of its critical stance. Thus, it takes on an explicitly modern standpoint, claiming what ought and ought not to be on the basis of emancipatory reasoning. However, indeed, such a moral stance has to be theoretically justified.

I start by reviewing how the DHA has justified its critique by referring to the Frankfurt School. I then review works of the Frankfurt School, in particular *The dialectic of enlightenment, Negative dialectics* and Jürgen Habermas's language-philosophy. This double review enables me in a third step to make explicit those theoretical assumptions which underlie CDA's critical standard, as well as evaluating the benefits and problems for the DHA resulting from this. Finally, I summarise my findings.

The Discourse–Historical Approach and the Frankfurt School

The DHA bases its critique on a foundational notion of emancipation. Although not unique to the DHA, its core orientation as an interdisciplinary, socially transformative force echoes Horkheimer's opening speech as director of the Institute for Social Research in 1931.[2] However, with regards to the grounding of its critical stance, and it is only this aspect which is of relevance to this article, the DHA differs from other approaches to CDA as it 'adheres' to the Frankfurt School (Reisigl & Wodak, 2001, p. 32, cf. also Fairclough & Wodak, 1997, p. 261; Reisigl, 2003, pp. 82ff, 147ff; Reisigl & Wodak, 2009, p. 88; Wodak, 1996, pp. 28–31, 2001a, pp. 2, 9f; Wodak & Meyer, 2009, p. 6f). Locating itself in this tradition leads the DHA to formulate its call

> *for* emancipation, self-determination and social recognition . . . [which] is motivated by the perhaps utopian conviction that unsatisfactory social conditions can, and therefore must, be subject to methodological trans- formation towards fewer social dysfunctional and unjustifiable inequali- ties. (Reisigl & Wodak, 2001, p. 34)

On the one hand, the DHA's general understanding of critique remains in line with other approaches to CDA. Critical interventions aim to reveal and demystify power structures from the 'perspective of those who suffer' (Fairclough & Wodak, 1997, p. 258; Wodak, 2001a, p. 10). Enabling informed choices through a self-reflective stance (Reisigl & Wodak, 2001, p. 265; Wodak, 2001b, p. 65) and a rejection of a 'know-that-all or know-it-better attitude' (Reisigl & Wodak, 2001, p. 265) also remain shared goals. However, the particularity of the DHA already becomes visible in its three-dimensional conceptualisation of critique (Reisigl & Wodak, 2001, pp. 32f, 268; Wodak, 2001b, p. 65):

- Immanent critique – problematises contradictions in the text/discourse internal structure. This kind of critique can be 'objective' as logical contra- dictions are perceivable by every competent language user.
- Sociodiagnostic critique – intends to demystify propagandist, populist, etc. discursive practices. This kind of critique takes a normative stand- point insofar as the critic refutes such positions and has thus to justify its point of view.
- Prognostic/retrospective critique – at this level, the DHA tries to trans- form the current state of affairs via direct engagement by referring to guiding principles such as human rights or the rejection of suffering. Here too, a justification of one's own standpoint is needed.

On the other hand, a closer reading of the seminal works of the DHA demon- strates a series of specific propositions concerning its understanding of cri- tique which are linked to the Frankfurt School. Although we find references to Horkheimer and Adorno, in particular *The dialectic of enlightenment,* in the DHA (Reisigl & Wodak, 2001, p. 32ff., 2009, p. 88), and Fairclough & Wodak (1997, p. 261) mention their insistence on 'the role of culture' in the repro- duction of the capitalist social order, the only detailed comments refer to the work of Habermas. For example, Ruth Wodak (2001a, p. 2) quotes Habermas as saying that 'language is also a medium of domination and social force. It serves to legitimize relations of organized power'. Not surprisingly, references to Habermas's ideal speech situation (ISS) can be found too (Wodak, 1996, pp. 28–31) which Fairclough and Wodak (1997, p. 261) see as a 'utopian vision of interaction'. In her more detailed account of Habermas, Wodak (1996, p. 30) mentions the 'utopia of an ideal speech situation' which is characterised by the 'absence of any constraints'. Following Habermas, Wodak also rejects the idealisation of an ISS in saying that communication always presupposes an ISS – otherwise communication would be impossible (see below). In what follows, she claims that distorted communication is to be identified by comparing an ISS with the situation being analysed. According to Wodak (1996, p. 28), this enables 'emancipation through self-reflection'.

As CDA critiques real life, so the DHA is concerned with language-in-use and perceives discourse as 'a form of "social practice"' (Fairclough & Wodak, 1997, p. 258). In other words: discourse is action. Here, Martin Reisigl (2003, p. 90) identifies a problem for the implementation of Habermas in his politolinguistic framework as he interprets Habermas as setting discourse 'in strict opposition' to action. Thus, Habermas would even fall behind the insights of the linguistic turn. Connected to this issue, Reisigl (2003, p. 82f) stresses that for Habermas there is a difference between discourse and critique: while discourse is necessarily reciprocal – and thus related to issues of truth and rightness – critique is rather unidirectional and related to therapeutic or aesthetic questions. Reisigl's own conceptualisation (2003, p. 89) seeks to avoid this by understanding discourse as an empirical concept. However, he stresses that he does not misunderstand the Habermasian notion of discourse as idealist, but accepts the idea that discourses are necessary regulative and normative frames of interaction. This leads Reisigl and Wodak (2001, pp. 263–271; cf. also Koller & Wodak, 2008; Wodak, 2009, p. 196f) to argue strongly in favour of Habermas's inclusive, deliberative concept of democracy as an emancipatory way of integrating plural societies.

Based on the outline above, it is not surprising that Reisigl and Wodak (2001, p. 265) claim that the DHA is able to:

> contribute greatly to answering the question of what are 'good reasons' because such an approach provides criteria, which enable one to distinguish between manipulative and suggestive procedures of persuasion and discursive procedures of convincing argumentation.

Consequently, contesting manipulation is the central aim of the DHA. In order to help answer the question of what 'good reasons' are, Reisigl and Wodak (2001, p. 70ff) refer to Franz van Eemeren and Rob Grootendorst's rules for rational arguing. For Reisigl and Wodak (2001, p. 71), these rules 'should form the basis of a discourse ethics on which a political model of discourse, deliberative democracy . . . can be grounded'. According to van Eemeren and Grootendorst (2004, pp. 158–186), violations of these rules, i.e. fallacies, mark manipulative practices which can be identified and critiqued. In order to support their empirical analysis, Reisigl and Wodak (2009, p. 100ff) have more recently linked this concept of fallacies with the Habermasian concept of validity claims in order to analyse an actors' claims and their potentially fallacious use (see below).

Before I evaluate these claims made by the DHA, let me turn to proponents of the Frankfurt School and review their different groundings of critique.

The Frankfurt School: From *The Dialectic of Enlightenment* to *Negative Dialectics*

Although the *The dialectic of enlightenment* (Horkheimer and Adorno, 1973) is not quoted, Reisigl and Wodak (2001, p. 32ff, 2009, p. 88) refer at least twice to the book as a point of reference for the DHA. I start by briefly recapitulating the main theses of the book. I will then turn to Adorno's (1973) *Negative dialectics* which – although not mentioned in the DHA's canon so far – will further help to illustrate the problems of grounding a critical position in the work of Horkheimer and Adorno.

The Dialectic of Enlightenment

Exploring why humanity – instead of realising its potential for good – produces Nazism, Fascism, Stalinism and mass culture, Horkheimer and Adorno aim to critique not just capitalism. Instead, they investigate the primal history of the human species itself, that is, its violent stepping out of its entanglement in nature. For Horkheimer and Adorno (1973, pp. 54–56), in order to survive, the species had to, from the very beginning, master both its inward and outward natures via (self-)restriction, cunning and renunciation. According to them (1973, p. 54; Adorno, 1973, p. 149), domination and reification are thus not primarily products of capitalist socialisation but constitute the 'nucleus of all civilizing rationality'. Instrumental reason thus emerged which, Horkheimer and Adorno (1973, p. xiv) claim, has created a new iron cage in which individuals are 'wholly devalued [annulliert]' and public opinion, as well as language, become simple commodities (1973, p. xif., cf. also p. 147). However, their *petitio principii* remains that a rational socialisation is possible (Horkheimer & Adorno, 1973, p. xiii).

From this emerges an aporia: how is rational, emancipatory critique possible if our reasoning takes place within such a totally, bureaucratically administered world system? Such a *verwaltete Welt* must, by definition, make immanent transcendence impossible.

Negative Dialectics

Continuing on from *The dialectic of enlightenment*, Adorno's *Negative dialectics* aims to enlighten society and lift reason to a higher level by critiquing its instrumental aspects. However, this is radicalised by linking domination to thinking itself. According to Adorno, every act of dealing with an object does harm to this object by not acknowledging its full richness. Adorno's (1973, p. 146) key claim is that 'identifying thought', that is, to identify something, is necessarily a violent act as it reduces an object to only one or a few of its ontological characteristics. What cannot be rationalised in this process of identification is excluded. Consequently, Adorno (1973, p. 146) states that: 'Identity is the primal form of ideology' and strives for a method 'designed to forgo the need for argument' (Adorno, 1982, p. 1). What makes rationality indeed rational in Adorno's eyes (1973, p. 18) is not the cognitive act of thinking but philosophical contemplation and non-conceptual mimesis, e.g. in moments of deep affection for a piece of art, that is, an intuitive act which holds opportunity for reconciliation with the object. At the same time, Adorno (1973, p. 15) claims that it is only 'by way of the concept to transcend the concept' as '[t]hinking without a concept is not thinking at all' (p. 98). In order to bring together the unavoidable necessity of conceptual thinking and the rejection of 'identifying thought', Adorno proposes a methodical tool: constellations. These are arrangements of concepts around the central one, thereby expressing 'what that concept aims at, not to circumscribe it to operative ends' (Adorno, 1973, p. 166). Elaborating this tool further, Adorno (1973, p. 163) employs the metaphor of a lock which is not to be opened by 'a single key, but a constellation of numbers'. The critical analyst is thus supposed to present ensembles of models, e.g. in aphoristic form (cf. Adorno, 1974), which circulate around the concept, thereby throwing light on it instead of providing an analytic definition.

However, even if the aporia between a need for conceptual thinking and the unavoidable violence it does could be overcome and emancipation thus became possible via constellations and mimetic moments, Adorno (1973, p. 145) himself remains doubtful about grounding his critical position and about the possibility of immanent transcendence: 'What would be different has not begun yet'.

Jürgen Habermas's Continuation of the Frankfurt School: Language and Emancipation

In reaction to what Habermas perceives to be theoretical dead-ends in the work of Horkheimer and Adorno, he develops a language-philosophy which claims to be able to 'validate[s] its own critical standards' (Habermas, 1984, p. xxxix). As I focus on the theoretical justification of an emancipatory position, I concentrate on his understanding of language and the concepts of validity claims, discourse and social learning.

Language and Validity Claims

Habermas's point of departure lies not in the concept of labour, as in previous forms of Marxist thought, but in another question: what happens as soon as we start to communicate? Following Wittgenstein's *Philosophical Investigations* (1968), he is interested in the deep patterns which underlie communication – a theory he calls *formal pragmatics*. Habermas (1976, p. 9) therefore re-establishes hermeneutics as a science based on '*the intuitive knowledge of competent subjects*'. From here, Habermas elaborates a theory of intersubjectivity by uncovering pragmatic universals which are not based on first principles but, nevertheless, provide a normative and cognitive foundation for emancipatory critique.

Habermas (1987, p. 77) starts by observing 'the linguistification of the sacred' through which 'the *spellbinding* power of the holy is sublimated into the binding/bonding force of criticisable validity claims'. That is, in modern societies, traditional norms and sacred authorities are no longer unquestionable but become evaluated in everyday talk. According to Habermas (1984, p. 99), this became possible due to the evolutionary development of three differentiated perspectives towards the world: the *objective world*, i.e. the 'real' world of objects; the *social world*, i.e. becoming aware of norms as being societal products; and the *subjective world*, i.e. subjects which can view themselves from the perspective of a third person.

For Habermas, this leads to different ways of how agents relate to these worlds in either an instrumental/strategic or a communicative manner. Instrumental action refers to the non-social objective world. Far more relevant here is action which is based on agents' calculation of success, taking into account a second agent's decisions. Here, Habermas (1984, pp. 85, 87f) speaks of *strategic action*. Strategic action is purposive-rational by aiming to influence the other in order to fulfil the speaker's perlocutionary intentions. However, as such a mode cannot integrate societies, Habermas (1984, p. 101) proposes a second, prior mode of social action, *communicative action*, which is orientated towards understanding (but not to be equated with communication in general). Although communicative action does not dispense with goal-oriented action as something, i.e. agreement on something, which is still to be achieved, it is only via communicative action that subjects coordinate their interaction and create lasting, shared definitions and meaning.

Communicative action is only possible due to the formal pragmatic properties of every conversation. Habermas (1984, p. 99) calls these properties *validity claims*: whenever we say something meaningful, we implicitly or explicitly raise the claim that our utterance is true, right and/or truthful. These claims commit the participants by creating a social bond. Here,

Habermas relies on John Austin's (1975) speech-act theory. For Habermas, the binding or illocutionary force of performative clauses can rest on three different validity claims: (a) a truth claim, Austin's constative element, e.g. 'I hereby say that he is there'; (b) a rightness claim as normative utterances have a force too and can be right or wrong, e.g. 'I hereby claim that killing is bad'; (c) a truthfulness claim, referring to the degree of honesty in our daily self-representation, e.g. 'I hereby promise to come back'. By raising such claims, we might get caught up in an argument, have to justify the claim and, thereby, accept the 'peculiar constraint-free force of the better argument' (Habermas, 1984, p. 28) in order to coordinate action. Habermas sees that this 'force of the better argument' will always be restricted to a certain degree, e.g. exchanges of arguments cannot last forever. Habermas (1976, p. 3) thus speaks of 'gray areas' between the extremes of pure strategic and communicative action, an aspect he (1996) has recently further developed. Habermas (1976, p. 1) also acknowledges the strategic use of validity claims in order to deceive the listener but insists that strategic action is only a 'derivate of action oriented to reaching understanding'. For example, lying only succeeds because, under normal circumstances, we expect the other's claims to be true, right and/or truthful. Otherwise, the idea of lying would not work. To that extent, communicative action precedes strategic action.[3]

For example, a teacher might suggest that, because the day will be hot, the remaining classes should take place outside. She could simply force the pupils to do so by way of her professional authority. However, she could also tell the class that she listened to the weather forecast and thus knows the day will be hot (truth claim). She could add that the rooms will soon be stuffy and that some pupils might thus be unfairly disadvantaged due to declining concentration (rightness claim). By pointing out, linguistically and/or via her body language, that she really thinks classes would not be enjoyable if they were to be held inside (truthfulness claim), a communicative act would be performed. After a brief discussion, the pupils might agree and move outside. Alternatively, some could reject her suggestions by pointing to widespread hay-fever among them and that classes outside would worsen their condition. In both cases, a binding, shared definition would be established – not through constraint (or relatively little) but the 'force of the better argument'. Habermas therefore understands rationality not in terms of the capacity of a monologically working mind, i.e. *self*-reflection, but as a property of intersubjectivity where validity claims can be raised and refuted freely.

Habermasian Discourse and the Ideal Speech Situation

In most cases, misunderstandings and open questions can be resolved on the basis of a common *lifeworld*, the totality of the groups' knowledge and symbolic understanding from which we can never step outside. However, as soon as participants discuss contested issues which are not covered by such an intuitive, common understanding, they have to justify their acceptance or rejection of the validity claim in question. Thus, they enter a *discourse*. In Habermas's concept of discourse, validity claims become virtualised, which enables a reflective, i.e. critical, attitude towards them. In other words: they had been naively carried on with communicative action but are now tested. Hence, for Habermas (1983b, pp. 125, 158f, 1997, p. 323), discourses are still forms of social practice in which it is only the 'attitude' or 'perspective' towards raised claims which changes. Consequently, Habermas (1997, p. 109, cf. also 1983b, p. 125, 130) speaks of discourse as 'a reflective form of communicative action'.

It is in this context that Habermas (1972, p. 177f) initially presented the idea of an *ideal-speech situation* (ISS) which consists of four main aspects: publicness, absence of coercion, sincerity on the part of the participants, and inclusivity/the same rights for all participants. The concept of an ISS has evoked widespread criticism as being idealistic and out of touch with factual conditions. Critics seem to assume that Habermas is suggesting such a condition will be realised at some point – and that it is just from such a position that one would be able to justify one's emancipatory critique. Although Habermas's earlier explanation (1971, p. 103, 1972, p. 181) has tempted such misinterpretations, he (1997, p. 322) clarified that

> [w]e would misunderstand the discursive character of public opinion- and will-formation if we thought we could hypostatize the normative content of general presuppositions of rational discourse into an ideal model of purely communicative social relations.

According to Habermas, the ISS cannot be seen as a deviation from an ideal, the blueprint of a concrete form of life to come but as a counterfactually anticipated, pragmatically necessary presupposition of every meaningful interaction (2008, p. 27). Habermas (1997, p. 332) describes an *idealistic* understanding of the ISS as an 'essentialist misunderstanding' which does not understand that we already always have to adopt such *idealising* assumptions. Following Habermas, we have to assume, often counterfactually, that the other is not manipulating us, that the other raises claims which are true, right and truthful. And even if such experiences are, as Habermas (1982, p. 235) himself suggests, like 'islands in the sea of practice', claims of truth, rightness and truthfulness are necessary, reciprocally anticipated conditions of social life, an 'inevitable fiction' (1971, p. 102). To that extent, the ISS captures what validity claims already imply. The necessary implicitness of these validity claims in speech acts is a condition we are not able to reject. And although communication is obviously not always driven by communicative action, a social fabric not based on such counterfactual assumptions would ultimately collapse.

Therein rests Habermas's foundation for social transformation. Formal pragmatics illustrates that we interact on the basis of a weak idealisation, that inclusive and egalitarian interaction is immanent in our social practice. Emancipatory critique is thus grounded in the species' intersubjective condition. Consequently, Habermas (1983a, p. 92) argues for institutional measures which 'sufficiently neutralise empirical limitations and avoidable internal and external interference so that the idealised conditions pragmatically presupposed by participants in argumentation can at least be adequately approximated'. This also justifies Habermas's (1996, p. 299) broader claim for deliberative democracy which 'reckons with the higher-level intersubjectivity of processes of reaching understanding that take place through democratic procedures or in the communicative network of public spheres'. Deliberative democracy is thus to be understood as the further development of formal pragmatics on the macro-political level, aiming for more inclusive and egalitarian (political) institutions and social structure.

Although this weak idealisation is often betrayed, it points to potentials for immanent transcendence. And although settings which partly realise this immanent transcendence, e.g. deliberative democracy, do not lead to a utopia, they certainly favour self-determination and social recognition. Emancipatory critique can and should therefore support such more inclusive and egalitarian social structures.

Social Learning and Pathological Communication

For Habermas, critique must thus reveal what *distorts* communication and enables *learning processes*. In the course of the latter, societal world views evolve, allowing for the solution of problems and wrongs societies face. However, learning processes themselves depend on rather unrestricted communication.

> Whereas the openness of rational expression to criticism and the grounding merely *points* to the possibility of argumentation, learning processes – through which we acquire theoretical knowledge and moral insight, extend and renew our evaluative language, and overcome self-deceptions and difficulties in comprehension – themselves *rely on* argumentation. (Habermas, 1984, p. 22)[4]

Splitting learning processes into cognitive–theoretical learning processes and moral–practical learning processes has consequences for the specification of critique: the former aim at improving our instrumental capacity in order to manipulate the objective world, e.g. through the invention of new technologies. They have to be balanced by the latter which are based on communicative action in order to enable successful social integration. According to Habermas (1987, p. 142ff), an instrumentally biased rationalisation leads to deformations of the lifeworld and hampers what communicative action should achieve: the reproduction of shared meaning. Drawing on Freudian thinking in general and Alfred Lorenzer (1975) in particular, Habermas describes such conditions as pathological, as the unrestricted exchange of arguments is (unconsciously) hampered. For example, the colonisation of the lifeworld works against the free development of a strong Ego through pressure generated by capitalism on families (Habermas, 1987, pp. 318, 386ff). In the case of the individual, pathologies might lead to distortions of the structure of communication itself due to, e.g. repression (Habermas, 1974a, p. 169, 1984, p. 21). On a collective level, societal orders might experience legitimation-crises to various degrees. Thus, Habermas (1987, p. 378) states: 'deception and self-deception can gain objective power in an everyday practice on the facticity of validity claims'. However, while the rationalisation of the lifeworld can create new pathologies, it can also enable opportunities for our well-being (Habermas, 1987, p. 313f). As society is the product of struggles, the direction rationalisation can take is open. Empirical critical social sciences aim to influence these struggles by illuminating emancipatory directions. I now turn to the DHA as one of its representatives.

The Frankfurt School Supporting the DHA?

Having reviewed the DHA's claims as well as the grounding of critique in some of the main strands of the Frankfurt School, it seems hard to imagine how Horkheimer and Adorno's approach can provide such a grounding. The aporias of their writings, in particular the anti-argumentative bias of Adorno, prevent a systematic adoption and reflect a loss of the political in their work. This does not signify a rejection of their writings in general, quite the contrary.[5] However, the above review illustrates the particular importance of Habermas's theory in and for the DHA – a significance which is, to my knowledge, not yet outlined explicitly enough.

Reviewing Habermas's work illustrates that he perceives discourse as still being a form of action, language-in-use (although a very specific form of action, different from the general understanding of discourse in CDA and the DHA), involving validity claims to be raised and/or rejected. Beyond this, Habermasian discourse implies a change in perspective, so that these claims become questioned and virtualised. It operates on often counterfactual assumptions of the ISS – which is not to be understood as a utopian ideal but a presupposition that we have to anticipate. Rationality, for Habermas, thus has a dialogical foundation, going beyond a monological notion of rationality in terms of self-reflection. In sum, both the DHA and Habermas conceive language as 'a medium of domination and social force'. However, as Habermas (1974c, p. 17) indicates, such 'distorted communication is not ultimate; it has its basis in the logic of undistorted language communication'. Emphasising this counterfactual double role of language (or rather of *semiotic* forms as they too have a propositional content), that is, the *possibility* of undamaged intersubjectivity, of emancipation built into every meaningful communication, seems crucial to me. Not because this conceptualisation is not already inherent in the writings of the DHA, but because only through its explicit elaboration does this grounding become transparent.

Empirical research inspired by the DHA has addressed issues like anti-Semitism and racism, gender and institutions. The latter, e.g. interaction in courts (Leodolter, 1975), doctor–patient communication, school committees and therapy sessions (Wodak, 1996, pp. 35–62, 63–99, 131–169), or the European Union (Wodak & Weiss, 2005), can also benefit from a Habermasian justification of critique. Although the object of research might sometimes suggest that an emancipatory vocabulary is not in place, research into, for example, the European Union need in no way be less emancipatory than research into, for example, issues of right-wing propaganda. Quite the contrary, institutions are able to neutralise or enforce constraints of arguments. An emancipatory critique of them is thus not only necessary but requires a justification as well.

What can link this theoretical level of justification with the DHA's key interest in the detailed analysis of language-in-use is the concept of validity claims. This started recently by including the concept of validity claims in the DHA's empirical analysis and is a way to further enrich the DHA. As outlined above, the idea of the ISS as a hypostatised ideal cannot serve as a point of departure – and Habermas himself has rejected such an 'essentialist misunderstanding'. A better way is indeed to draw on the concept of validity claims. That is, speakers perceive their arguments as being true, right or truthful while hearers have other beliefs and must be convinced (with better arguments) by the first person. Here, it is the interaction between the first and second person, and their claims and justifications, which generates an always fallible dynamic towards truth, rightness and truthfulness (Habermas, 2003, p. 45).

A Habermasian approach concentrates on exactly this dynamic, thus, on procedures which enable the exchange of arguments to be as inclusive and egalitarian as possible. Applying the concept of validity claims in an analysis of texts cannot therefore simply focus on the content of raised claims. Instead, analyses which include the concept of validity claims have to focus on the *form* of arguments, in particular the *form of their justification*. That is: does the text enable an undistorted exploration of differences; does it allow an open and critical discussion? Or does it serve the construction of boundaries which lead to closed worldviews? I suggest understanding a text's clarity and accessibility as an alternative way to make sense of validity claims in written texts (this is particularly relevant in the evaluation of the author's truthfulness which is otherwise impossible as readers of written texts generally have no access to gestures or the mimic of the author). This might, for example, lead to a criticism of the heavy use of metaphors which tend to create extremely coherent and suggestive text-structures, thereby counteracting a transparent exchange of arguments. In consequence, it becomes much harder for the audience to reflect on arguments given in the text and to raise critical questions. To that extent, such texts are tendentially non-rational while rational, as defined above, is the raising of validity claims which can be critically questioned in an open, inclusive way.

As the DHA is particularly interested in the historical context of text-production and thus takes the *longue durée* into account, the concepts of successful and failed learning processes, i.e. social change as normatively directed, provide a further, yet ignored, resource. By looking at discourses concerning one topic over a long period, the ways in which forms of arguing change and become more open or closed can reveal developmental tendencies. Similarly, do institutions and societal structures become more or less inclusive and egalitarian? Is a particular historical period or place characterised by higher degrees of systematically distorted communication, e.g. through the colonisation of the lifeworld? Hence, discourse analysis becomes a necessary, even inevitable tool to analyse the evolution of society and criticise distorted communication.

As outlined, the DHA's toolkit can undoubtedly contribute to an understanding of *how* discrimination and inequality are linguistically/semiotically realised. However, I cannot see how the DHA itself should be able to define the dividing line between manipulative procedures (what is distorted communication) and emancipatory ones (what is undistorted communication). In *Discourse and Discrimination*, Reisigl and Wodak (2001) claim that van Eemeren and Grootendorst's rules of discussion would ground the DHA's discourse ethics (see above). This would ultimately mean that critical rationalism forms the basic theoretical point of reference for the DHA. While van Eemeren and Grootendorst's pragma-dialectical theory (e.g. 2004, p. 16f) has always referred to Karl Popper and Hans Albert's critical rationalism as its theoretical point of departure, this has never been the case for the DHA. Pragma-dialectics might contribute to an analysis by describing fallacious forms of argumentation which hamper a free debate, the *how* of manipulation. However, it seems impossible, in my view, for any approach based on critical rationalism to ground an emancipatory position on which a critical discourse analysis relies when identifying their object of criticism, as well as the conditions it strives for. However, it is, for example, Habermas's language-philosophy which gives an account of *why* fallacious arguments are fallacious at all and should therefore be criticised in order to reach more inclusive and egalitarian conditions (for a detailed discussion of this argument, see Forchtner & Tominc, under review).

I now relate the previous findings to the DHA's three-dimensional model of critique:

- *Immanent critique* refers to text-internal contradictions and is more or less independent of the investigator's point of view. For example, an argument is contradictory if the speaker brings forward two logically opposing opinions. To that extent, Habermasian grounding does not necessarily affect this kind of critique. However, Habermas has outlined elements which could benefit an immanent critique of texts. For example, inconsistency as well as ignoring others' arguments might signal individual or societal communication pathologies.
- *Sociodiagnostic critique* intends to demystify discourses, e.g. right-wing populism. Arguing on the basis of a progressive consensus, critiquing such populism might seem unproblematic and comprehensible in some groups but could be perceived as biased from another position. An explicit reference to Habermas's formal pragmatics grounds the judgements possible while particular texts, e.g. a speech by a politician, can be checked with regards to the claims made. Are these claims true, right and/or truthful? To what extent do they support or prevent rational understanding and undamaged intersubjectivity?
- In the case of *prognostic/retrospective critique*, critique aims to transform conditions. The DHA has already pointed to Habermas's concept of deliberative democracy which rests on inclusive and egalitarian communication. However, such a goal has to be theoretically justified as the merits of deliberative democracy are not necessarily self-evident. Tendencies pointing in this direction illustrate a process of successful learning. Thus far, current conditions and the development of discourses can be criticised prognostically against the backdrop of such a concept of democracy. At the same time, prognostic critique is linked to retrospective critique which asks: what should we remember (in order to achieve a more deliberative community)? Consequently, studies inspired by the DHA (e.g. Heer, Manoschek, Pollak, & Wodak, 2008) can draw on Habermas's insights (1974b, p. 121) that critique has to promote an inclusive self-critical reference to one's own tradition, e.g. the recognition of one's own past wrong-doings, instead of exclusionary, chauvinistic narratives.

Concluding Remarks

Departing from van Dijk's acknowledgement of a lack of theoretical justification of CDA's critical stance, I have outlined the DHA's continuous reference to the Frankfurt School whose evolution of thought provides resources to address his objection. I have claimed that the DHA should discuss and relate to this tradition explicitly and in even greater detail in order to ground its critique of unjustified discrimination and inequality theoretically, its moral position. In other words: I have clarified why the object of criticism should actually be rejected – which might seem self-evident within a given community but not necessarily outside it – by providing a theoretical basis for the DHA's emancipatory stance. In contrast to Horkheimer and Adorno, Habermas provides such a foundation which is able to 'validate its own critical standards' by reconstructing unavoidable, pragmatic presuppositions of interaction. Because Habermas is able to show that living together demands an often counterintuitive idealisation of interaction, we can rationally, i.e. not only in terms of subjective preferences, ground the move from 'is' to 'ought'. Critique which strengthens universal and egalitarian aspects and enables rather unrestricted debate, e.g. through reforming institutions accordingly, is thus theoretically justified. No doubt, there are more theories which aim for emancipation but formulate alternative foundations (and have not been addressed here due to the particular aim of this article). However, the DHA's consistent reference to Habermas's programme makes it well suited to critique discourses in increasingly pluralist societies while anticipating

> the claim to reason announced in the teleological and intersubjective structure of social reproduction themselves . . . [which again and again] is silenced; and yet in fantasies and deeds it develops a stubbornly transcending power, because it is renewed with each act of unconstrained understanding, with each moment of living together in solidarity, of successful individuation, and of saving emancipation. (Habermas, 1982, p. 221)

Notes

1. The Frankfurt School denotes a heterogeneous tradition of neo-Marxist thought more or less connected with the Institute for Social Research (Frankfurt, Germany), which originated during the 1920s and early 1930s. Within this tradition, many strands have emerged, among others, Horkheimer and Adorno's primal history of the species, Jürgen Habermas's language-philosophy and Axel Honneth's recognition paradigm. Despite profound differences, its strands are bound together by the conviction that (a) society can be structured in a reasonable way, that this is (b) currently not the case, and that (c) societal transformation rests on reason already immanent in social praxis. For a comprehensive account of its history, strands and ideas, see Wiggershaus (1995).
2. Although it might seem strange not to refer to Marx in this context (given the influence of his critical method in general, as well as on the Frankfurt School), I do so as the DHA rarely even mentions his name (cf. also Wodak & Meyer, 2009, p. 20). For an evaluation of Marx's method and its relevance for (the dialectical–relational approach to) CDA, see Fairclough and Graham (2002).
3. On the related issue of claims made by poststructuralist theory, e.g. Foucault's radical anti-naturalism and the concept of performative contradiction, see Habermas, 1990.

4. Following Jean Piaget's late theory of cognitive development (1970), Habermas (1975, p. 162) initially perceived individual learning processes as running ahead of social learning, as 'pacemakers of social evolution'. Since then, Habermas (1995, see also Strydom, 1992) has altered his focus, emphasising intersubjectivity as the medium of development and learning.

5. For example, a comprehensive analysis of cultural phenomena, such as the recent analysis of the fictionalisation of politics in American soaps (Wodak, 2009, pp. 156–186) might benefit from observations made in *The dialectic of enlightenment* and similar works by Herbert Marcuse (e.g. 1991) on the cultural industry. These observations on the infantilisation of the political and/or aesthetical through its mixing with (commercial) entertainment (and vice versa) are rich enough to inspire research. However, a discussion of this goes beyond the scope of this article and it remains to be seen if such research is pursued further within the frame of the DHA.

References

Adorno, T.W. (1973). *Negative dialectics* (E.B. Ashton, Trans.). London: Routledge.

Adorno, T.W. (1974). *Minima moralia: Reflections from damaged life* (E. F. N. Jephcott, Trans.). London: New Left Books.

Adorno, T.W. (1982). *Against epistemology: A metacritique. Studies in Husserl and the phenomenological antinomies* (W. Domingo, Trans.). Oxford: Blackwell.

Austin, J.L. (1975). *How to do things with words*. Oxford: Oxford UP.

Billig, M. (2003). Critical Discourse Analysis and the rhetoric of critique. In G. Weiss & R. Wodak (Eds.), *Critical discourse analysis: Theory and interdisciplinary* (pp. 35–46). London: Palgrave.

Fairclough, N., & Graham, P. (2002). Marx as a critical discourse analyst: The genesis of a critical method and its relevance to the critique of global capital, In N. Fairclough (2010), *Critical discourse analysis. The critical study of language*, 2nd edn (pp. 301–346). London: Longman.

Fairclough, N., & Wodak, R. (1997). Critical discourse analysis. In T. van DijkA. (Ed.), *Discourse as social interaction* (pp. 258–284). London: Sage.

Forchtner, B., & Tominc, A. (under review). Critique in the discourse-historical approach – Between Critical Rationalist pragma-dialectics and the Critical Theory of Jürgen Habermas. *Journal of Language and Politics*.

Habermas, J. (1971). Reflections on the linguistic foundation of sociology: The Christian Gauss lecture. In (2001). *On the pragmatics of social interaction. Preliminary studies in the theory of communicative action* (B. Fultner, Trans.) (pp. 3–103). Cambdrige: Polity Press.

Habermas, J. (1972). Wahrheitstheorien. In (1984) *Vorstudien und Ergänzungen zur Theorie des kommunikativen Handelns* (pp. 127–183). Frankfurt/Main: Suhrkamp.

Habermas, J. (1974a). Reflections on communicative pathology. In (2001) *On the pragmatics of social interaction. Preliminary studies in the theory of communicative action* (B. Fultner, Trans.) (pp. 131–170). Cambridge: Polity Press.

Habermas, J. (1974b). Können komplexe Gesellschaften eine vernünftige Identität ausbilden? In (1976) *Zur Rekonstruktion des Historischen Materialismus* (pp. 92–126). Frankfurt/Main: Suhrkamp.

Habermas, J. (1974c). Introduction: Some difficulties in the attempt to link theory and praxis. In *Theory and practice* (J. Viertel, Trans.) (pp. 1–40). London: Heinemann.

Habermas, J. (1975). Towards a reconstruction of Historical Materialism. In (1979) *Communication and the evolution of society* (T. McCarthy, Trans.) (pp. 130–177). London: Heinemann.

Habermas, J. (1976). What is universal pragmatics? In (1979) *Communication and the evolution of society* (T. McCarthy, Trans.) (pp. 1–68). London: Heinemann.

Habermas, J. (1982). A reply to my critics. In J.B. Thompson & D. Held (Eds.), *Habermas. Critical debates* (pp. 219–283). London: MacMillian Press.

Habermas, J. (1983a). Discourse ethics: Notes on a program of philosophical justification. In (1990) *Moral consciousness and communicative action* (C. Lenhardt & S. W. Nicholson, Trans.) (pp. 43–115). Cambridge, MA: MIT Press.

Habermas, J. (1983b). Moral consciousness and communicative action. In (1990) *Moral consciousness and communicative action* (C. Lenhardt & S. W. Nicholson, Trans.) (pp. 119–194). Cambridge, MA: MIT Press.

Habermas, J. (1984). *The theory of communicative action. Volume I. Reason and the rationalization of society* (T. McCarthy, Trans.). London: Heinemann.

Habermas, J. (1987). *The theory of communicative action. Volume II. Lifeworld and system* (T. McCarthy, Trans.). Cambridge: Polity Press.

Habermas, J. (1990). *The philosophical discourse of modernity: Twelve lectures* (F. Lawrence, Trans.). Cambridge: Polity Press.

Habermas, J. (1995). Individuation through socialization: George Herbert Mead's theory of subjectivity. *Postmetaphysical thinking* (W. M. Hohengarten, Trans.) (pp. 149–204). Cambridge: Polity Press.

Habermas, J. (1996). Some further clarifications of the concept of communicative rationality. In (1998) *On the pragmatics of communication* (pp. 307–342). Cambridge, MA: MIT Press.

Habermas, J. (1997). *Between facts and norms: Contributions to a discourse theory of law and democracy* (W. Rehg, Trans.). Cambridge: Polity Press.

Habermas, J. (2003). Introduction: Realism after the linguistic turn. In *Truth and justification* (B. Fuller, Trans.) (pp. 1–49). Cambridge, MA: MIT Press.

Habermas, J. (2008). Communicative reason and the detranscendentalized 'Use of Reason'. In *Between naturalism and religion* (C. Cronin, Trans.) (pp. 24–76). Cambridge: Polity Press.

Hammersley, M. (1997). On the foundations of Critical Discourse Analysis. *Language & Communication, 17*(3), 237–248.

Heer, H., Manoschek, W., Pollak, A., & Wodak, R. (Eds.). (2008). *The discursive construction of history: Remembering the Wehrmacht's war of annihilation.* Basingstoke: Palgrave.

Horkheimer, M. (1931). The present situation of social philosophy and the task of an Institute for Social Research. In (1995) *Between philosophy and social science. Selected early writings* (G. F. Hunter, M. S. Kramer & J. Torpey, Trans.) (pp. 1–14). Cambridge: MIT Press.

Horkheimer, M., & Adorno, T.W. (1973). *The dialectic of enlightenment* (J. Cumming, Trans.). London: Penguin.

Koller, V., & Wodak, R. (2008). Introduction: Shifting boundaries and emergent public spheres. In R. Wodak & V. Koller (Eds.), *Communication in the public sphere* (pp. 1–21). Berlin: De Gruyter.

Leodolter, R. (1975). *Das Sprachverhalten von Angeklagten vor Gericht.* Kronberg: Scriptor.

Lorenzer, A. (1975). *Sprachzerstörung und Rekonstruktion.* Frankfurt/Main: Surhkamp.

Marcuse, H. (1991). *One dimensional man: Studies in the ideology of advanced industrial society.* London: Routledge.

McKenna, B. (2004). Critical Discourse Studies: Where to from here? *Critical Discourse Studies, 1*(1), 1–31.

Piaget, J. (1970). *Genetic epistemology* (E. Duckworth, Trans.). New York: Columbia University Press.

Reisigl, M. (2003). *Wie man eine Nation herbeiredet. Eine diskursanalytische Untersuchung zur sprachlichen Konstruktion der österreichischen Nation und österreichischen Identität in politischen Fest-und Gedenkreden.* Wien: Dissertation an der Universität Wien.

Reisigl, M., & Wodak, R. (2001). *Discourse and discrimination. Rhethorics of racism and anti-Semitism*. London: Routledge.

Reisigl, M., & Wodak, R. (2009). The Discourse–Historical Approach. In R. Wodak & M. Meyer (Eds.), *Methods of critical discourse analysis*, 2nd edn (pp. 87–121). London: Sage.

Strydom, P. (1992). The ontogenetic fallacy: The immanent critique of Habermas's developmental logical theory of evolution. *Theory, Culture and Society*, 9, 65–93.

Stubbs, M. (1997). Whorf's children: Critical comments on Critical Discourse Analysis (CDA). In A. Ryan & A. Wray (Eds.), *Evolving models of language* (pp. 100–116). Clevedon: British Association of Applied Linguistics.

van Dijk, T.A. (2001). Multidisciplinary CDA: A plea for diversity. In R. Wodak & M. Meyer (Eds.), *Methods of critical discourse analysis* (pp. 95–120). London: Sage.

van Dijk, T.A. (2008). Critical Discourse Analysis and nominalization. *Discourse & Society*, 19(6), 821–828.

van Eemeren, F.H., & Grootendorst, R. (2004). *A systematic theory of argumentation. The pragma-dialectical approach*. Cambridge: Cambridge UP.

Widdowson, H.G. (2004). *Text, context, pretext. Critical issues in discourse analysis*. Oxford: Blackwell.

Wiggershaus, R. (1995). *The Frankfurt School: Its history, ideas and political significance* (M. Robertson, Trans.). Cambridge, MA: MIT Press.

Wittgenstein, L. (1968). *Philosophical investigations*. Oxford: Blackwell.

Wodak, R. (1996). *Disorders of discourse*. London: Longman.

Wodak, R. (2001a). What CDA is about – a summary of its history, important concepts and its developments. In R. Wodak & M. Meyer (Eds.), *Methods of critical discourse analysis* (pp. 1–13). London: Sage.

Wodak, R. (2001b). The Discourse–Historical Approach. In R. Wodak & M. Meyer (Eds.), *Methods of critical discourse analysis* (pp. 63–94). London: Sage.

Wodak, R. (2009). *The discourse of politics in action: Politics as unusual*. London: Palgrave.

Wodak, R., & Meyer, M. (2009). Critical Discourse Analysis: History, agenda, theory and methodology. *Methods of critical discourse analysis*, 2nd edn (pp. 1–33). London: Sage.

Wodak, R., & Weiss, G. (2005). Analyzing European Union discourses: Theories and applications. In R. Wodak & P. Chilton (Eds.), *A new agenda in (critical) discourse analysis. Theory, methodology and interdisciplinarity* (pp. 121–135). Amsterdam: John Benjamins.

Critique and Argumentation: On the Relation between the Discourse-Historical Approach and Pragma-Dialectics

Bernhard Forchtner and Ana Tominc

1. Introduction: Potential Conflicts in the Paradigm-Core of the Discourse-Historical Approach[1]

In a recent article, van Dijk (2008: 823) has pointed to "the lack of theory about the norms and principles of its [= critical discourse analysis] own critical activity". For one part of this movement, the discourse-historical approach (DHA), van Dijk's observation is less valid as its adherents extensively refer to the critical theory of the Frankfurt School (cf. Forchtner 2011). However, we argue that there remains incoherence at the paradigm-core of DHA concerning the theoretical justification of its "norms and principles". In order to ground their "critical activity", Reisigl and Wodak have frequently pointed to the Frankfurt School, in particular Habermas' language-philosophy. Here, the reconstruction of unavoidable presuppositions of argumentative speech serves as a criterion in order to identify manipulative and regressive practices. Apart from this, their seminal work *Discourse and Discrimination* also refers to van Eemeren and Grootendorst's rules for a critical discussion (a key notion already in the writings of Popper and Albert) which "should form the basis of a discourse ethics on which a political model of discourse, deliberative democracy (…) can be grounded" (Reisigl and Wodak 2001: 71f). Here, it is the violation of these rules which should be identified and, subsequently, critiqued. In consequence, it appears as if van Eemeren and Grootendorst's Pragma-Dialectical[2] theory of argumentation plays a role in justifying DHA's notion of critique "*for* emancipation, self-determination and social recognition" (Reisigl and Wodak 2001: 34).

Source: *Journal of Language and Politics*, 11(1) (2012): 31–50.

At first glance, this move seems plausible as Pragma-Dialectics provides an elaborated framework of reasonable argumentation through which "two parties (...) try to resolve a difference of opinion by means of a methodological exchange of discussion moves" (van Eemeren and Grootendorst 2004: 22). In this paper, however, we argue that the status of Pragma-Dialectics within DHA contradicts the central epistemological and normative positions at the paradigm core of DHA. Van Eemeren and Grootendorst's version of pragma-dialectics is influenced by Popper and Albert's critical rationalism, i.e. methodological scepticism, which is hardly compatible with Habermas' normatively rich, emancipatory critical theory (for earlier differences between critical rationalism and the Frankfurt School theorists, cf. Adorno 1976). Critical rationalism has always rejected grounded principles via which critique can be theoretically justified. Instead, it proposes an evolutionary understanding of the growth of knowledge through steady falsification, an estimation which is transferred to other societal dimensions such as moral reasoning and politics. This latter dimension of critical rationalism's methodological scepticism was conclusively formulated in Albert's (1968: 11–15) Münchausen-Trilemma which refutes *any* attempt to ground one's judgement finally. But does not Popper's approval of steady falsification, anti-dogmatism and open discussions, as well as his hope in the critical function of reason, ask for a theoretically grounding as well (we take this point from Apel 1980: 262–270 and Habermas 1983: 78–83)? Popper (1962b: 231) recognises this but refuses to provide a justification and, consequently, acknowledges an "irrational *faith in reason*" underlying his method of critical testing.

In contrast, we argue that a theoretical justification of DHA's emancipatory notion of critique and reason, i.e. to argue for deliberative democracy, self-determination and social recognition, does not have to rest on such an irrational act of faith. Quite the contrary, as Habermas (2008: 27) points out: "the rational structure of action oriented towards reaching understanding is reflected in the presuppositions [inclusivity, absence of external constraints, freedom to agree or disagree, and truthfulness] that actors must make if they are to engage in this practice at all". As such, the aim of critical rationalist Pragma-Dialectics – open debate through which a difference of opinion is resolved reasonably, i.e. a critical discussion (see below) – is always already grounded in the intersubjective nature of human existence. Due to this, DHA is able to advocate a stronger and theoretically justified notion of emancipation and rationality while Pragma-Dialectics, in line with critical rationalism's methodological scepticism, attempts to separate the analysis of sound argumentation from the latter's ethico-moral evaluation.

This article does not primarily provide a critique of Pragma-Dialectics but aims rather to clarify and explicate possible contradictions at the paradigm-core of DHA.[3] Thus, our objective is threefold: we start by reviewing the concept of critique in both Popper and Albert's critical rationalism as well as in the critical theory of Habermas in section two. This enables us to outline the meaning of critique in Pragma-Dialectics and DHA in section three.

Consequently, in section four, we argue, from a position of great sympathy for DHA, that Pragma-Dialectics' philosophical and dialectical orientation conflicts with the emancipatory underpinnings of DHA. Although acknowledging the benefits of Pragma-Dialectics for DHA, we thus lay bare the resulting contradiction at the paradigm-core of DHA, i.e. in its notion of critique.

2. Reviewing Epistemological and Normative Positions

2.1 Critique, Critical Rationalism and the Münchausen Trilemma

We have already indicated that the critical rationalist view of reasonableness as used by Pragma-Dialectitians "is in fact an extended version of the Popperian critical perspective" (van Eemeren and Grootendorst 2004: 17). In this section we sketch this perspective in order to be able to elaborate on Pragma-Dialectics' notion of critique in section three.

Popper's basic epistemological concept of 'falsification' is a reaction to the way the growth in scientific knowledge was understood by the positivists of his time, in particular the Viennese Circle (for more information on Popper's formative years, cf. Hacohen 2002). Similar to them, Popper's starting point is the problem of how to demarcate science from pseudo-science. The prevailing answer of the time was that science follows an inductive method, meaning that knowledge can be accumulated through experimentation or observation. Insisting that natural laws can never be known for certain, Popper argues that a different perspective is needed in order to understand the growth of knowledge. Studying the history of science, in particular the developments in physics, Popper (2008: 154, 204) realises that, e.g., the Galilean claim that the Sun, not the Earth is in the centre of the Solar System and that the Earth is not flat, was initially a guess and only later supported and, ultimately, confirmed by additional astronomical observations. He thus concludes that positivist verificationism is not convincing and that something beyond experience is involved in the growth of science: critical examination, i.e. falsification.

Falsification aims for the steady improvement of scientific knowledge and the approximation of objective truth through continued criticism of existing theories and modification as well as the elimination of mistakes (Popper 2008: 6, 38, 311). According to Popper, this is the only rational approach towards knowledge and (solving) the problems of the world, hence the name 'critical rationalism'. Consequently, Popper (2008: 293) argues that "among the real dangers to the progress of science is not its likelihood of being completed, but such things as lack of imagination (…) or a misplaced faith in formalisation and precision (…) or authoritarianism in one or another of its many forms".

What is important here is that Popper's decision in favour of trial and error is a *subjective* choice based on an "irrational *faith in reason*", a subjective preference for the Greek Pre-Socratic tradition of reasoning, initiated by Thales. Contrary to the Pythagorean School which, according to Popper (2008: 201), had "the character of a religious order", Thales encouraged critical debate among pupils as well as between pupils and their teachers. In the tradition of this school, any idea, regardless of the authority of its author, can and ought to be criticised. In other words, "the other fellow has a right to be heard, and to defend his arguments" (Popper 1962b: 238). But listening to the other is a subjective decision for which rightness cannot be proven and can thus not be based on arguments alone as they "cannot determine such a fundamental moral decision" (ibid.: 232). Therefore, critical rationalism has to admit "its origin in an irrational decision" and recognise "the fact that the fundamental rationalist attitude results from an (at least tentative) act of faith – from faith in reason. Accordingly, our choice is open" (ibid.: 231).

The ethico-moral and political implications of this position are concisely formulated in Albert's Münchausen-Trilemma. To that extent, the Münchausen-Trilemma is at the core of critical rationalism itself and a direct consequence of Popper's falsificationism. Accordingly (Albert 1968: 13), any justification which claims to be based on first principles (Albert refers to the *principle of sufficient reason*) must lead to either:

a. an *infinite regress* of new justifications,
b. a *logical circle* of mutually supporting arguments, or
c. a breaking off from the justificatory process at an *arbitrary* point.

Instead of fleeing into the security of dogmatic certainty, e.g. first principles, critical rationalists draw the conclusion that building hypotheses and discussing them rationally is the only reliable way through which knowledge can grow and societies are able to learn (ibid.: 182). Consequently, Albert (ibid.: 35), following Popper, defends the "*idea of critical examination*, the critical discussion of all possible statements with the help of rational arguments". And like Popper (1962a: 3), Albert (1968: 97, 100, 105f) stresses that such a methodological scepticism should be applied to all statements, i.e. societal areas, as neither scientific claims nor political or moral positions can ever be ultimately justified.

The ethico-moral and political consequence of such a "consistent *fallibilism*" (ibid.: 36), i.e. "critical testing" (ibid.: 35) as a "methodical principle[s]" (ibid.: 33), is the putting forward of hypotheses instead of dogmatic standpoints, including the notion of dialogical or negative (instead of Hegelian or positive) dialectics (ibid.: 41–47; Popper 2008: 435). Such a method would, Popper (1962a: 3) states, offer social science space for critical "awareness of its limitations" rather than try to "offer proofs where nothing can be proven" and "pretend to be scientific where it cannot give more than a personal point of view". But this has consequences for critical rationalists as well: they cannot justify their decision in favour of a critical and rational debate because it is itself just a pragmatic hypothesis. In other words, decision-making based on critical debates cannot claim to be theoretically more rational but rests ultimately in a subjective and irrational act of faith in reason. Critical rationalists' preference for a rational debate is thus a far-reaching subjective choice as not even reason serves as a first principle (Albert 1968: 92f).

2.2 Critique, Habermas' Critical Theory and Emancipation

We now move to the critical theory of Habermas, i.e. the main point of reference for DHA. We introduce Habermas' reconstruction of a deep structure in argumentative speech, the often misunderstood concept of the ideal speech situation, and discuss its meaning and significance.

Habermas' point of departure is the question: what happens as soon as we communicate? He subsequently identifies a justification of rationality in the act of every language game by reconstructing the universal intuitive knowledge shared by every competent speaker, i.e. "*the intuitive knowledge of competent subjects*" (Habermas 1976: 9). Here, Habermas (1998) builds upon the late Wittgenstein's (1968: e.g. §202, §204, §380, §398) concept of intuitively known rules of language games and the German philosopher and linguist Wilhelm von Humboldt who identified three related functions of language: the cognitive function (representation of the objective world), the expressive function (manifesting emotions and feelings) and the communicative function (being able to exchange views, object and agree). Language is thus not reduced to an instrumental tool but a holistic ability through which societies reproduce the meaning that their existence relies on. This, Habermas claims, provides a foundation for emancipatory critique.

Habermas (1984: 99) roots this shared intuitive knowledge in the basic human condition of social interaction and intersubjective meaning making. He does so by pointing to Austin's (1975) speech-act theory and subsequently identifies three validity claims and their binding force: whenever we mean what we say, we raise the claim that our utterance is true, right and/or truthful. An example for a truth claim, Austin's constative element, is "I hereby say that he is there". Rightness claims are about normative utterances which can be right or wrong, e.g. "I hereby claim that killing is bad". The idea of truthfulness concerns the degree of honesty in our daily self-representation, e.g. when saying that "I hereby promise to come back". We raise these claims (naively) *every time we say something we mean* and thereby (re-)produce shared definitions and coordinate action. In course of raising such claims, irritations or even conflicts might emerge which may end the process of communicating or lead to the justification (and negotiation) of these claims vis-à-vis an interlocutor, thereby accepting the "peculiar constraint-free force of the better argument" (Habermas 1984: 28).

This leads to Habermas' often misunderstood idea of the ideal speech situation. From the time when Habermas (1972: 177f) initially presented the concept, resting on inclusivity, absence of external constraints, freedom to agree or disagree, and truthfulness, it has evoked widespread criticism. Critics assume that Habermas idealistically believes that the ideal speech situation will be realised at some point – and/or that legitimate critique is possible only from such a point. Although Habermas' earlier explanation (e.g. 1972: 181) has tempted such misinterpretations, he (1997: 322) has since clarified that the concept would be misunderstood "if we thought we could hypostatize the normative content of general presuppositions of rational discourse into an ideal model of purely communicative social relations". Accordingly, the ideal speech situation is not a realisable ideal, the blueprint of a concrete form of life which is to come. Rather, it is a counterfactually anticipated presupposition of every meaningful debate (cf. also Wodak 1996: 28–31).

Habermas (1997: 332) describes the former interpretation as an "essentialist misunderstanding" which does not take into consideration that we already have to adopt such idealising assumptions whenever we start to communicate (for support from evolutionary psychology for this strong proposition, cf. Tomasello 2010). The concept of the ideal speech situation is thus not an ideal but must be understood in terms of the presuppositions of every meaningful interaction, rooted in the very nature of human interaction. Following Habermas, whenever we mean what we say, we presuppose that the raised claims are true, right and truthful, the absence of external constraints, the freedom to agree or disagree, as well as the inclusivity of the debate. And even if such experiences might be rare, claims of truth, rightness and/or truthfulness are still necessary reciprocally-anticipated conditions of social life. *To that extent, a universal moral of reciprocal recognition is implied in the very act of arguing.* In Habermas' (1991: 50) own words, the "ideas of justice and solidarity are already *implicit* in the idealizing presuppositions of communicative action, above all in the reciprocal recognition of persons capable of orienting their actions to validity claims". Thus, these presuppositions capture what validity claims already imply and the weak moral constraint of these validity claims – in contrast to what Popper argues for – is a condition we cannot simply reject. Habermas (1991: 57) therefore grounds ethics in "a logic of moral argumentation".

Although this logic of idealised presuppositions underlying argumentation is rooted in interaction between discussants, it goes beyond the reciprocal recognition of participants in a particular argumentation. Thus, what Habermas calls the "principle of universalisation" implies that those exchanging validity claims do not only (implicitly or explicitly) recognise each other as equals. If participants hold their claims to be true, right and/or truthful, these claims transcend the specific argumentation. This is the "logic of moral argumentation" which ultimately implies that "*[a]ll* affected can accept the consequences and the side effects its *general* observance can be anticipated to have for the satisfaction of *everyone's* interests (and these consequences are preferred to those of known alternative possibilities for regulation)" (Habermas 1983: 65).

Certainly, the "force of the better argument" will always be restricted, e.g. exchanges of arguments cannot last forever and the raising of validity claims can also be deceiving – intentionally or not. However, Habermas (1976: 1) insists that such strategic action is only a "derivate of action oriented to reaching understanding" as the social fabric would otherwise have to collapse. Take the example of 'lying' which only 'works' because we counter-factually expect the other's claims to be true, right and/or truthful. For example, we might be suspicious of a friend's promise. However, we cannot doubt all the time as this would render impossible any social bond (indeed, friendship), i.e. the social fabric. Moreover, engaging in a truthful argument without assuming that truth and rightness are key means performing a self-contradiction as such argumentation "denies or fails to credit itself with its own truth" (Apel 1980: 265), "its own truth" being the aforementioned pre-suppositions of every truthful dialogue.

Habermas' uncovering of (communicative) rationality enables a theoretical grounding of emancipatory critique. That is, only those (institutional) settings which approximate to and realise as many as possible of the emancipatory potentials rooted in unavoidable presuppositions of human interaction are legitimate. Racist attitudes, e.g., contradict these presuppositions – and their rejection is consequently grounded. Reason and critique are not dependent on acts of faith as in the case of Popperian critique. However, Habermas' proposal for grounding an emancipatory agenda does not represent a dogmatic act which prevents open debate. Instead, he reconstructs a strong but *procedural* rationality via insights into the intersubjective nature of human lives.

3. Reviewing the Notion of Critique in Pragma-Dialectics and DHA

3.1 Critique and Critical Rationalism in Pragma-Dialectics

We now move from reviewing relevant theories to their application. We start with van Eemeren and Grootendorst whose Pragma-Dialectical approach is influenced by Popper and Albert (van Eemeren and Grootendorst 1988: 279f, 1992: 192f, 208–220, 1994: 274, 281, 2004: 16–7, 51, 57, 188; van Eemeren 2010: 5, 31–36, 221; van Eemeren et al. 1993: 45, 48, 170f), asking: what do 'critical' and 'rational' in Pragma-Dialectics refer to?

Pragma-Dialecticians view human thought as fundamentally fallible, stating that "we cannot be certain of anything" (van Eemeren and Grootendorst

2004: 16) – an idea clearly originating in critical rationalism. In line with this, van Eemeren (2010: 5, cf. also 32) states that:

> a critical conception of reasonableness (...) replaces self-defeating 'justificationism' with a critical testing procedure (...) associated with the (Popperian) "critical rationalist" philosophy of reasonableness, which claims that, ultimately, nothing is a certainty, and takes, as its guiding principle the idea of critical testing as claims that are made to acceptability.[4]

This link between Pragma-Dialectics and critical rationalism is not superficial but substantial as van Eemeren et al. (1993: 170f) define their position explicitly as a critical rationalist one which locates "reasonableness in publicly negotiated procedures for discussion (intersubjective validity), while maintaining a pragmatist standard for successful resolution of a dispute (...) (problem validity)". In line with this, reasonableness denotes the capacity to resolve a difference in opinion (*problem validity*) and its acceptability to all parties involved (*intersubjective validity*) (van Eemeren and Grootendorst 2004: 132, 1994: 131f). This points to a central aspect of Pragma-Dialectics: its dialectical character. That is, Pragma-Dialectics is defined to be "premised on two parties who try to resolve a difference of opinion by means of a methodical exchange of discussion moves" (van Eemeren and Grootendorst 2004: 22). This notion of dialectics resembles Albert and Popper's understanding (see above) and, accordingly, builds on Socratic dialectics where everything should be subject to scrutiny between two discussion parties exchanging their views (ibid.: 57). The basis for the 'pragmatic' part of this "amalgam" (Blair 2006: 11) of different theories is the work of Searle, Grice and Austin according to which "discussion moves" are understood as speech acts which depend on the situation and the context of the exchange (van Eemeren and Grootendorst 2004: 22). Blair (2006: 11) identifies these two features – the dialectical and the pragmatic – as well as the fact that the theory is normative, aiming at "the improvement of the practice of discussion" (van Eemeren and Grootendorst 1994: 2), as the essentials of a "*pragma-dialectical* approach".

Like Popperian theory, Pragma-Dialectics allows steady progression by means of critical testing of claims in and through, what they describe as, a critical discussion (see below). Here, standpoints have to be examined with as much scepticism as possible because the "optimal satisfaction" of the parties, as van Eemeren and Grootendorst (2004: 188) concede, does not automatically mean that discussants agree on everything. A 'critical' attitude is thus inclined towards as severe criticism of proposed standpoints as possible and their subsequent acceptance/refutation. A difference of opinion is resolved "when the arguments advanced lead the antagonist to accept the standpoint defended, or when the protagonist retracts his standpoint as a consequence of the critical reactions of the antagonist" (ibid.: 133).

It is particularly its normative aspect, founded upon the concept of a critical discussion (cf. van Eemeren et al. 1993: 1–19 for details of this integration of descriptive and normative interpretation), which has attracted interest in Pragma-Dialectics. Van Eemeren and Grootendorst (2004: 52) describe a critical discussion "as an exchange of views in which parties involved in a difference of opinion systematically try to determine whether the standpoint or standpoints at issue are defendable in the light of critical doubt or objection". The model of a critical discussion is an ideal model, serving both a critical-normative function as well as a heuristic purpose and it is in relation to this model that the aforementioned rules, which should guide an exchange of standpoints, become central.

These rules are intended to facilitate the reasonable resolution of a difference of opinion between the discussants whereby an argument is acceptable only if it follows the rules the discussants specified before the argumentation itself takes place (for a definition of 'argumentation' cf. van Eemeren and Grootendorst 1994: 18). And while falsification is important for testing the opponent's standpoint, these rules do ultimately derive from the aim to avoid impediments of resolving differences of opinion. Concerning the violation of these rules, Pragma-Dialectics draws on the concept of fallacy, defined as "every violation of any of the rules of the discussion procedure" (van Eemeren and Grootendorst 2004: 175, cf. also van Eemeren et al. 2002: 182f). Both parties, the protagonist and the antagonist, should accept the general norm of reasonableness (given shape by the rules) and, consequently, "only speech acts which accord with a system of rules acceptable to all discussants (…) which can lead to a resolution of the dispute at the centre of the discussion" count as reasonable (van Eemeren and Grootendorst 1994: 18). These rules alone, however, by no means guarantee that the discussion will be successful because other factors, such as the state of mind of the participants, also influence the process. For practical use, the fifteen rules formulated by van Eemeren and Grootendorst (2004: 190ff) as guidelines for a critical discussion are reformulated into "ten commandments" which consist of (1) the freedom rule, (2) the obligation-to-defend rule, (3) the standpoint rule, (4) the relevance rule, (5) the unexpressed-premise rule, (6) the starting-point rule, (7) the validity rule, (8) the argument scheme rule, (9) the concluding rule and (10) the general language use rule. A critical discussion is violated if *the discussants* do not abide by the rules. That is, effects on third parties, i.e. people affected by the discussion of the protagonist and the antagonist, are not considered (third parties only enter the framework in case of mediation, cf. van Eemeren et al. 1993: 117–141). The 'true' and/or 'good' are thus not central to Pragma-Dialectics as a procedural and dialectical theory (see above, cf. also Garssen and van Laar 2010, van Eemeren 2010: 55, 213–223).

3.2 Critique and Habermas' Critical Theory in DHA

The concept of critique in DHA is an intrinsically emancipatory one. And although the approach remains open and refers to a variety of social theories, it is fair to say that its most fundamental intellectual ancestor is the critical theory of the Frankfurt School, in particular Habermas' language-philosophy (cf. Fairclough and Wodak 1997: 261; Reisigl and Wodak 2001: 32ff, 2009: 88; Wodak 1996: 28–31, 2001: 2, 9f; Wodak and Meyer 2009: 6f). We cannot do justice to the full scale of references made by proponents of DHA to this intellectual tradition, but will give an outline of how the normative positions of DHA are justified by referring to Habermas' social-philosophy (for an extensive review, cf. Forchtner 2011).

In general terms, critical discourse analysis argues against inequality and discrimination and aims to reveal hidden power structures. Similarly, the analyst is supposed to reflect on her/his own position and make her/his standpoint transparent, taking the "perspective of those who suffer" (Fairclough and Wodak 1997: 258). Consequently, DHA aims to enable informed choices through a self-reflective stance (Reisigl and Wodak 2001: 265) and rejects a "know-that-all or know-it-better attitude" (ibid.). This stance "adheres to the sociophilosophical orientation of critical theory" and is at the bottom of their three-dimensional concept of critique (ibid.: 32f):

- Immanent critique
- Sociodiagnostic critique
- Prognostic/ retrospective critique

To that extent, critique in DHA goes beyond a 'negative being against it' attitude. Quite the contrary, its notion of critique carries strong positive elements. In particular, the second and third dimensions of critique indicates DHA's social and political commitment, formulating a distinctively progressive agenda

> *for* emancipation, self-determination and social recognition (…) [which] is motivated by the perhaps utopian conviction that unsatisfactory social conditions can, and therefore must, be subject to methodological transformation towards fewer social dysfunctional and unjustifiable inequalities. (ibid.: 34)

In doing so, DHA goes beyond a thin notion of critique. It is not just about intellectually honest self-reflection and the denaturalisation of apparent facts but rests rather upon a strong emancipatory programme of critique. DHA, however, does not simply claim this position but introduces its stance as grounded. This enables DHA to claim that it can differentiate between *überzeugen* and *überreden*. While the former is about rational acts of deliberation and convincing argumentation, i.e. a discursively generated consensus based on the unavoidable presupposition of human interaction, the latter refers to persuasion and even manipulation, i.e. speech acts solely orientated towards one's own success (ibid.: 70). Therefore, Reisigl and Wodak (ibid.: 265) claim that

> [a] critical discourse analysis orientated towards argumentation theory and rhetoric (…) can contribute greatly to answering the question of what are 'good reasons', because such an approach provides criteria, which enable one to distinguish between manipulative and suggestive procedures of persuasion and discursive procedures of convincing argumentation.

However, as we have pointed out above, in a crucial part of their book, the authors (ibid.: 70f) do not explain this contribution by pointing to Habermas' social theory, in particular his outline of deliberative democracy, but refer to van Eemeren and Grootendorst's Pragma-Dialectical approach and their rules for a critical discussion. Accordingly, Reisigl and Wodak (ibid: 71) claim that the "ten rules for rational arguing should form the basis of a discourse ethics on which a political model of discursive, deliberative democracy (…) can be grounded".

This passage raises the possibility that not only critical theory but also critical rationalism – the philosophical ancestor of van Eemeren and Grootendorst's Pragma-Dialectics – can be seen as part of DHA's paradigm-core, causing a contradiction in its notion of critique. This, in turn, would imply that DHA could no longer theoretically justify its emancipatory position as being grounded but only of being a subjective moral choice. According to such a view, not even argumentation deemed immoral is necessarily critiqued as argumentation theory and ethico-moral stances become a different pair of shoes. Habermas' critical theory, in contrast, theoretically grounds DHA's emancipatory agenda and does exactly reject such a division. We acknowledge that problematising this issue on the basis of a short passage might seem to be exaggerated and we are not claiming that Pragma-Dialectics is already fully integrated into the interdisciplinary programme of DHA. However, given the seminal character of Reisigl and Wodak's book, the strong claims made by them, the consequences for DHA's core category of critique, and the significant benefits of Pragma-Dialectics for DHA's empirical work, this potential theoretical conflict should be considered.

4. Discussion

In the above sections, we have outlined the epistemological and normative position of critical rationalism and Habermas' language-philosophy as well as their implementation in Pragma-Dialectics and DHA. We have seen that the approaches differ significantly on what critique means and if/how it is grounded. This strikes us as being an issue for DHA which draws – to different degrees – on both traditions. In this section, we elaborate on this problem.

The key argument we make in this article is that Reisigl and Wodak link their critical aims to van Eemeren and Grootendorst's critical rationalist interpretation of a pragma-dialectical theory which causes incoherence at the paradigm-core of DHA. After all, Reisigl and Wodak claim that "a discourse ethics (...) can be grounded" in van Eemeren and Grootendorst's rules for a critical discussion. A critical rationalist may well accept Reisigl and Wodak's call "*for* emancipation, self-determination and social recognition" and even welcome Reisigl and Wodak's position as a subjective choice based on their "irrational faith in reason". The question would then be whether reason is indeed just something we have to believe in – or if a non-dogmatic foundation for emancipatory critique can be provided. As Reisigl and Wodak explicitly commit DHA's emancipatory agenda "to the sociophilosophical orientation of critical theory", they seem to have opted for the latter. Thus, a conflict emerges between reason as not being theoretically justifiable (critical rationalism) and reason as being grounded in the structure of human interaction (Habermas' language-philosophy).

Recapitulating the origin of this problem, one has to emphasise that the aim to separate *überreden* from *überzeugen* refers to DHA's aspiration to separate good, i.e. emancipatory, reasons from bad, i.e. regressive, ones. Within Pragma-Dialectics, *überzeugen* can be understood as the acceptance of a standpoint based on a discussion procedure which follows the rules for a critical discussion while *überreden* might rest on the acceptance of such a standpoint due to fallacious discussion moves. As critical rationalists and Pragma-Dialecticians, Reisigl and Wodak could thus indentify bad reasons by saying that this or that reason impedes an open debate and resolving a difference of opinion. If this could be accepted by Reisigl and Wodak, then Pragma-Dialectical rules of a critical discussion could indeed form the basis of the DHA's agenda. However, this raises two questions concerning the possibility of a more critical rationalist and pragma-dialectical DHA: (a) is this lack of theoretical justification convincing, and (b) do the consequences of this lack correspond with the emancipatory claims made by DHA itself?

Regarding (a), i.e. the lack of theoretical justification for Pragma-Dialectics' ideal model of a critical discussion and its rules, scholars have problematised critical rationalism's underpinning of Pragma-Dialectics. Most comprehensibly, Biro and Siegel (2006: 7) criticise Pragma-Dialectics for its dialectical model of argumentation instead of aiming for truth as the outcome of arguing, what they call "epistemic normativity". More recently, Siegel and Biro (2008) linked this point to an explicit criticism of critical rationalist dimensions of Pragma-Dialectics. We partly agree with this criticism; however, throughout this article, we have introduced Habermas' reconstruction of non-metaphysical non-dogmatic presuppositions of meaningful argumentation as the most promising way to address this issue – at least in the context of DHA.

Following a Habermasian approach does imply that we do not see Pragma-Dialectics' orientation towards resolving a difference in opinion as problematic per se. We only object to the consequences of Pragma-Dialectics' view of reasonableness for DHA. As a consequence of their critical rationalism, van Eemeren and Grootendorst (2004: 3, 187f) focus on argumentation in terms of its problem and intersubjective validity. The latter does actually point beyond an understanding of argumentation which is concerned with (or restricted to) the actual process of arguing between discussants and can be related to Habermas' insights into the deep structures underlying interaction. However, it seems as if neither epistemological nor normative fundamental consequences are drawn from the fact that these rules have empirical validity, as illustrated by van Eemeren et al. (2009). The sheer fact that intersubjective validity has been empirically verified does not, however, justify a strong notion of rationality (Alexy 2010: 182f) – even if it points to and indeed supports Habermas' theoretical considerations concerning unavoidable presupposition. In other words, while an empirical 'justification' as provided by Pragma-Dialectics is indicative, it requires theoretical modes of justification in order to provide a grounding that is solid enough for to support emancipatory claims made by DHA.

Habermas' approach provides such theoretical justification by insisting on a deep structure underlying human interaction. This deep structure provides a theoretical foundation for emancipatory critique, i.e. it provides grounds for criticising arguments as well as their starting points and wider consequences. To that extent, Habermas' own proceduralist striving for rational consensus is rooted in weak but "pragmatically unavoidable presuppositions" (Rehg 2001: 119), which circumvent the Münchausen-Trilemma. These presuppositions are *pragmatically* held because the possibility for radical emancipation is not to be sought in an ultimate external justification, e.g. a holy book. They are nevertheless *unavoidable* because whenever we say what we mean, we necessarily raise validity claims which rest on (often) idealised assumptions. Finally, these presuppositions are *weak*: although they are rooted in human interaction, nothing forces the speaker not to capitalise on the trust of her/his counterpart in order to deceive her/him.[5] That is, acting morally does not follow automatically from the existence of these presuppositions. Like in critical rationalism, "our choice is open" and it is the agent who ultimately decides. However, within a Habermasian frame, we are not entirely free to reject these presuppositions. Thus, although both approaches accept that *decisions* have to be taken, they differ on the character of what is *moral*. After all, Habermas' (1984: 10)

> concept of communicative rationality carries with it connotations based ultimately on the central experience of the unconstrained unifying consensus-bringing force of argumentative speech, in which different participants overcome their merely subjective views and, owing to the mutuality of rationally motivated conviction, assure themselves of both the unity of the objective world and the inter-subjectivity of their lifeworld.

This has fundamental consequences for the notion of critique as Habermas does not only circumvent the Münchausen-Trilemma and the apparent need for an irrational belief in reason, but provides a theoretical foundation for emancipatory critique. Similar to Pragma-Dialectics, this agenda, in its rejection of telling what 'the good' is, is procedural but is, nevertheless, able to provide immanently justified criteria in order to evaluate the quality of argumentation. This concerns (b). After all, what makes an argument rational for DHA is not only its effectiveness in problem solving or its acceptability to both parties but, given Habermas' "principle of universalisation", also the effects of such a consensus for third parties which have not necessarily had a say in the argument itself. In other words, given DHA's socio-political orientation, arguments are not (primarily) emancipatory/regressive because they help/impinge in resolving a difference in opinion but because of their consequences in reproducing unjustified discrimination, power relations, etc. Consider the following example.

A Young Earth creationist believes in the time frame of biblical genealogies, i.e. that God created Earth within the last several thousand years.[6] As a true believer, (s)he also defends the position that the universe must be of a similar age to Earth. In this case, the rules formulated within Pragma-Dialectics might help to evaluate the claims made by our creationist and, consequently, enable the analyst to reject them on the grounds that they are fallacious. Among others, the creationist might violate commandment one (the freedom rule, i.e. *the right to challenge the other's standpoint*) as God's word cannot, supposedly, be doubted. Thereby, it would be impossible to criticise arguments which are justified through reference to God. Similarly, commandment two (*the obligation-to-defend rule*) might be violated if the creationist refused to react to propositions made regarding fossil-discoveries which indicate that Earth is much older than acknowledged by Young Earth creationists in general. In consequence, it could be argued that, solely on the basis of Pragma-Dialectic's rules, the evaluation of reasons as being good or bad is possible. However, two issues remain. Firstly, even in this example concerning the material world, arguing necessarily presupposes the often counter-factual recognition of the other as equal. Thus, critical rationalism and Pragma-Dialectics, although insisting on the Münchausen-Trilemma, are always already operating within a normative frame: whenever they mean what they say, e.g. that their method is the most adequate one, they raise validity claims linked to these unavoidable presuppositions. Secondly, and more crucial in this section, the example above refers to the material world, i.e. claims which can ultimately draw on hard evidence. But for Pragma-Dialectics, the rules for a critical discussion should be equally applicable to issues of normative rightness, such as discrimination against 'others' which are, arguably, central to most critical discourse analyses.

Let us therefore consider a second example: a group of neo-Nazis discusses an assault on a Jew (for a similar example, cf. Siegel and Biro

2008: 194). Within a Pragma-Dialectical frame, the outcome of their discussion would be reasonable if they could agree on how to conduct the attack in accordance with the rules for a critical discussion. As Pragma-Dialectics makes clear, the procedure proposed (and thus their understanding of reasonableness) is 'only' concerned with "people who want to resolve their difference of opinion" (van Eemeren and Grootendorst 2004: 135, cf. also the formulation of the rules and commandments which always address "discussants", "protagonist" and/or "antagonist"). Thus, third parties are not considered and Pragma-Dialectical reasonableness does not cover their standpoints. The focus is on the dialectical exchange between discussants, i.e. the validity of their exchange. That is, Pragma-Dialectics, in accordance with critical rationalism, does not adopt a strong emancipatory notion of rationality and, as such, what is immoral to DHA can be acceptable to Pragma-Dialectics if put forward as a logically valid argument. An argument by a group of neo-Nazis might thus be unproblematic from a purely Pragma-Dialectical perspective as long as their 'reasoning' follows the rules. As such, Pragma-Dialectics cannot criticise in a theoretically justified way the extra-argumentative unjust treatment of 'others', a Jew in the example mentioned above, which would require a stronger concept of rationality. Indeed, Pragma-Dialectics does not aim to do so. However, such a position contradicts DHA's entire agenda.

At one point, van Eemeren (2010: 74) rightly identifies common ground with Habermas' ideal speech situation and notes that the latter should not, similar to critical discussion, "be taken as anything but an ideal model". However, while Habermas has indeed warned against any hypostatization of the ideal speech situation, he has equally made it clear that, to some degree, this model is always in place through weak but unavoidable presuppositions. Via reconstructing the latter, Habermas and DHA are able to validate their critical standards, enabling an emancipatory critique which goes beyond a dialectical analysis of the very process of arguing between discussants. Instead, the wider personal and societal consequences of argumentation, an aim simply not shared by Pragma-Dialectics, becomes addressable. Following Habermas' language-philosophy, the hallmark of rationality, and thus the driving force of social criticism, is the degree of undamaged intersubjectivity which is enabled in and through argumentation. Consequently, Habermas and DHA are both concerned with the issue of including not only the standpoints of those who are already part of the discussion but also those who are affected by the outcome of an argument. The voices and well-being of third parties, so often ignored, violated and robbed of any chance to self-determination, are at the heart of DHA. The strong claims to be found in DHA's emancipatory agenda thus demand a coherent and explicit position based on a critical theory of argumentation, being different from the critical rationalist' underpinning of Pragma-Dialectics.

5. Conclusion

Our concern in this article was a potential inconsistency at the paradigm-core of DHA concerning its notion of critique. While DHA's adherents draw extensively on Habermas' language-philosoply, whose concept of critique is a grounded and emancipatory one, they also refer to van Eemeren and Grootendorst's Pragma-Dialectical approach to argumentation. Here, the notion of critique rests in the Popperian tradition which is directed against justification and in favour of critical testing. However, we have argued that Habermas' notion of critique provides a non-dogmatic validation of one's own critical standards by reconstructing *uncircumventable* presuppositions of human interaction. Only through such a strong justification of DHA's notion of critique can DHA claim legitimacy for its muscular agenda.

In our discussion, we have aimed at making the normative core of DHA explicit and argued for a more coherent notion of critique. Here, we follow Popper and Thales in their celebration of open debate, welcoming the benefits of Pragma-Dialectics for DHA but criticising the theoretical inconsistency caused if (critical rationalist) Pragma-Dialectics is unwittingly transferred into a DHA-frame. Thus, it could be said that we even argue for a Habermasian pragma-dialectical theory. Not only would it do justice to presuppositions we always already hold when entering an argument, but it would also provide a way to evaluate arguments – not just with regards to argumentation's internal rules but a broad emancipatory agenda.

Notes

1. We are thankful to Ruth Wodak, Andrew Sayer and two anonymous reviewers for their detailed comments on an earlier version of this article. All mistakes remain of course our own. Both authors are recipients of an ESRC studentship at the Department of Linguistics and English Language at Lancaster University. Bernhard Forchtner is also the recipient of a DOC-fellowship from the Austrian Academy of Sciences.
2. Following Anthony Blair (2006: 12) we use initial capital letters (Pragma-Dialectics) when referring to the pragma-dialectical theory of van Eemeren and Grootendorst and lower-case initial letters (pragma-dialactics) when referring to a wider understanding of a particular argumentation theory.
3. We have no doubt about the fruitfulness of Pragma-Dialectical tools for the empirical analysis of argumentation – an aspect neglected in Habermas' elaborations. Indeed, there are similarities between these two which should not be overlooked. Although Habermas is fundamentally concerned with the properties of language use, he, like Pragma-Dialectics, draws heavily on pragmatics and is interested in reconstructing what happens during the process of arguing. Indeed, what Pragma-Dialectics defines as intersubjective validity seems to resemble Habermas' idea of pragmatically unavoidable presuppositions (cf. van Eemeren et al. 2009 and section five) – even if these concepts lead to radically different conclusions (see below). Moreover, both approaches are concerned with practical reason and are in favour of open debate in order to increase knowledge and understanding. They both agree that progress can only be secured if structures which enable open argumentation are institutionalised.

In our view, the Pragma-Dialectical rules should thus be seen as a possible opera-tionalisation of Habermas' pragmatically unavoidable presuppositions, providing what his approach does not provide: tools for *empirical* analysis. This, however, requires a reflection on theoretical differences in the first place – something we hope to provide in the following.

4. Van Eemeren (2010: 29) separates *reasonableness* from *rational*. While the former has a "normative dimension" and concerns "*interpersonal* reasoning", the latter is about calculating, egoistic behaviour. In contrast, Habermas retains a strong notion of rationality, separating communicative rationality (interpersonal, emancipatory) from strategic rationality (monological, purely oriented towards success) (see below).

5. This can be understood as being similar to the Pragma-Dialectical notion of strategic manoeuvring according to which discussants balance the dialectical ideal of reason-ableness with their own personal goals which might require deception (van Eemeren 2010).

6. We thank Martin Reisigl for suggesting this example.

References

Adorno, Theodor W. 1976. *The Positivist Dispute in German Sociology*. London: Heinemann.

Albert, Hans. 1968. *Traktat über kritische Vernunft*. Tübingen: J.C.B. Mohr.

Alexy, Robert. 2010. *A Theory of Legal Argumentation: The Theory of Rational Discourse as Theory of Legal Justification*. Oxford: Oxford University Press.

Apel, Karl-Otto. 1980. The a priori of the communication community and the founda-tion of ethics: the problem of a rational foundation of ethics in the scientific age. In: *Towards a Transformation of Philosophy*. London/Boston: Routledge & Kegan Paul, 225–300.

Austin, John L. 1975. *How to Do Things with Words*. Oxford: Oxford University Press.

Biro, John and Siegel, Harvey. 2006. Pragma-Dialectics versus epistemological theories of arguing and arguments: rivals or partners. In: Peter Houtlosser and Agnes van Rees (eds). *Considering Pragma-Dialectics. A Festschrift for Frans H. Eemeren on the Occasion of his 60th Birthday*. Mahwahl/New Jersey/London: Lawrence Erlbaum Association, 1–10.

Blair, Anthony J. 2006. Pragma-Dialectics and pragma-dialectics. In: Peter Houtlosser and Agnes van Rees (eds). *Considering Pragma-Dialectics. A Festschrift for Frans H. Eemeren on the Occasion of his 60th Birthday*. Mahwahl/New Jersey/London: Lawrence Erlbaum Association, 11–22.

Corvi, Roberta. 1997. *An Introduction to the Thought of Karl Popper*. London: Routledge.

Fairclough, Norman and Wodak, Ruth. 1997. Critical Discourse Analysis. In: Teun A. van Dijk (ed.). *Discourse as Social Interaction*. London: Sage, 258–284.

Forchtner, Bernhard. 2011. Critique, the discourse-historical approach, and the Frankfurt School. *Critical Discourse Studies* 8(1), 1–14.

Garssen, Bart and van Laar, Jan Albert. 2010. A Pragma-Dialectical response to objectivist epistemic challenges. *Informal Logic* 30(2), 122–141.

Habermas, Jürgen. 1972. Wahrheitstheorien. In: 1984. *Vorstudien und Ergänzungen zur Theorie des kommunikativen Handelns*. Frankfurt/Main: Suhrkamp, 127–183.

Habermas, Jürgen. 1976. What is universal pragmatics? In: 1979. *Communication and the Evolution of Society*. London: Heinemann, 1–68.

Habermas, Jürgen. 1983. Discourse ethics: notes on a program of philosophical justifica-tion. In: 1990. *Moral Consciousness and Communicative Action*. Cambridge: MIT Press, 43–115.

Habermas, Jürgen. 1984. *The Theory of Communicative Action. Volume I. Reason and the Rationalization of Society.* London: Heinemann.

Habermas, Jürgen. 1991. Remarks on discourse ethics. In: 1993. *Justification and Application. Remarks on Discourse Ethics.* Cambridge: MIT Press, 19–111.

Habermas, Jürgen. 1997. *Between Facts and Norms: Contributions to a Discourse Theory of Law and Democracy.* Cambridge: Polity Press.

Habermas, Jürgen. 1998. Hermeneutic and analytic philosophy: two complementary versions of the linguistic turn. In: 2005. *Truth and Justification.* Cambridge: MIT Press, 51–81.

Habermas, Jürgen. 2008. Communicative reason and the detranscendentalized "Use of Reason". In: *Between Naturalism and Religion.* Cambridge: Polity Press. 24–76.

Hacohen, Malachi Haim. 2002. *Karl Popper. The Formative Years, 1902–1945. Politics and Philosophy in Interwar Vienna.* Cambridge: Cambridge University Press.

Popper, Karl. 1962a. *The Open Society and Its Enemies. Volume I.* London: Routledge.

Popper, Karl. 1962b. *The Open Society and Its Enemies. Volume II.* London: Routledge.

Popper, Karl. 2008. *Conjectures and Refutations. The Growth of Scientific Knowledge.* London/New York: Routledge.

Rehg, William. 2001. Adjusting the pragmatic turn: ethnomethodology and critical argumentation theory. In: William Rehg and James Bohman (eds). *Pluralism and the Pragmatic Turn. The Transformation of Critical Theory. Essays in Honour of Thomas McCarthy.* Cambridge: MIT Press, 115–143.

Reisigl, Martin and Wodak, Ruth. 2001. *Discourse and Discrimination. Rhetorics of Racism and Antisemitism.* London: Routledge.

Reisigl, Martin and Wodak, Ruth. 2009. The discourse-historical approach. In: Ruth Wodak and Michael Meyer (eds). *Methods of Critical Discourse Analysis.* London: Sage, 87–121.

Siegel, Harvey and Biro, John. 2008. Rationality, reasonabless, and critical rationalism: problems with the pragma-dialectical view. *Argumentation* 22, 191–203.

Tomasello, Michael. 2010. *Origins of Human Communication.* Cambridge: MIT Press.

van Dijk, Teun A. 2008. Critical Discourse Analysis and nominalization. *Discourse & Society* 19(6), 821–828.

van Eemeren, Frans H. 2010. *Strategic Maneuvering in Argumentative Discourse. Extending the Pragma-Dialectical Theory of Argumentation.* Amsterdam: John Benjamins.

van Eemeren, Frans H. and Grootendorst, Rob. 1988. Rationale for a pragma-dialectical perspective. *Argumentation* 2(2), 271–291.

van Eemeren, Frans H. and Grootendorst, Rob. 1992. *Argumentation, Communication and Fallacies: A Pragma-Dialectical Perspective.* London: Routledge.

van Eemeren, Frans H. and Grootendorst, Rob. 1994. *Speech Acts in Argumentative Discussions. A Theoretical Model for the Analysis of Discussions Directed towards Solving Conflicts of Opinion.* Dordrecht/Cinnaminson: Foris Publications.

van Eemeren, Frans H. and Grootendorst, Rob. 2004. *A Systematic Theory of Argumentation. The Pragma-Dialectical Approach.* Cambridge: Cambridge University Press.

van Eemeren, Frans H., Garssen, Bart and Meuffels, Bert. 2009. *Fallacies and Judgments of Reasonableness: Empirical Research Concerning the Pragma-Dialectical Discussion Rules.* Dordrecht/Heidelberg/London/New York: Springer.

van Eemeren, Frans H., Grootendorst, Rob and Snoeck Henkemans, Francisca A. 2002. *Argumentation. Analysis, evaluation, presentation.* Mahwah/New York/London: Lawrence Erlbaum Association.

van Eemeren, Frans H., Grootendorst, Rob, Jackson, Sally and Jacobs, Scott. 1993. *Reconstructing Argumentative Discourse.* The University of Alabama Press.

Wittgenstein, Ludwig. 1968. *Philosophical Investigations.* Oxford: Blackwell.

Wodak, Ruth and Meyer, Michael. 2009. Critical discourse analysis. History, agenda, theory and methodology. In: Ruth Wodak and Michael Meyer (eds). *Methods of Critical Discourse Analysis*. London: Sage, 1–33.

Wodak, Ruth. 1996. *Disorders of Discourse*. London: Longman.

Wodak, Ruth. 2001. What CDA is about – a summary of its history, important concepts and its developments. In: Ruth Wodak and Michael Meyer (eds). *Methods of Critical Discourse Analysis*. London. Sage, 1–13.

55

Conversation Analysis and Discourse Analysis: Methods or Paradigms?

Martyn Hammersley

Thereare many different approaches to the study of discourse. Here I want to focus on just two: ethnomethodological conversation analysis (CA) and Potter and Wetherell's discourse analysis (DA).[1] In my view, both of these make important contributions towards understanding human social life. CA, in particular, represents one of the few examples in the social sciences of a genuinely cumulative empirical research programme. However, my particular interest is in whether these forms of analysis should be treated as *methods* – to be used by social scientists when appropriate for the problem being investigated, perhaps in combination with other methods – or as *paradigms* – as exclusive and self-sufficient approaches to investigating the social world.

The proponents of both kinds of analysis treat them as paradigms rather than as methods, and as superior to available alternatives. CA seems to be viewed this way by most of its practitioners; even though there are occasional suggestions from even the most radical exponents that it might provide the foundation for other kinds of work (see, for example, Schegloff, 1997, 1998). Similarly, although in some places Potter and Wetherell explicitly deny that they see DA as replacing other forms of social psychology, they introduce it as breaking with traditional approaches, and as avoiding what they regard as the fundamental problems these face. Furthermore, in practice, they have employed it largely on its own, and they do not appear to have selected it as the most appropriate method for studying particular topics, but rather on the basis of what they take to be its general advantages.[2]

Source: *Discourse & Society*, 14(6) (2003): 751–780.

My specific focus here will be on two basic methodological commitments shared by CA and DA that are central to their presentation as self-sufficient approaches. These commitments are negative in character:

1. A refusal to attribute to particular categories of actor distinctive, substantive psychosocial features – ones that are relatively stable across time and/or social context – as a basis for explaining their behaviour.
2. A refusal to treat what the people studied say about the social world as a source of information about it.

What I mean by the first of these commitments is an unwillingness to view actors as controlled, or even as guided in their behaviour, by substantive, distinctive and stable mental characteristics such as 'attitudes', 'personalities', 'perspectives', or 'strategic orientations'. Rather, actors are treated as *employing* cultural resources that are *publicly available*, and doing so in *contextually variable* ways. As a result, what they do is not seen as relying on anything specific about *them*: what they do is what any 'member' could or would do.[3]

The meaning of the second commitment is more obvious: it rules out the content of what people say about the world as a source of analytically usable information. This is not a technical matter, it is not simply a denial that what this source produces can ever reach an appropriate level of likely validity. Rather, it is insisted that everyday accounts must be included within the analytic focus, treated as topic not resource. They must be examined for the ways they are *constructed*, and the social phenomena they portray thereby *constituted*; and for what this can tell us about the cultural resources available to members and/or about the practices in which members participate.

I will begin by exploring the rationales which underpin these two commitments – as will become clear I believe that the rationale is different for each approach. I will then assess the cogency of those rationales. Finally, I will consider whether CA and DA abide by these commitments in practice.

Conversation Analysis

In the case of CA, I take it that the justification for these two negative commitments arises out of Garfinkel's ethnomethodology.[4] He started from a problem which he detected in efforts to create a theoretically informed scientific sociology in America in the late 1940s and early 1950s. The dominant theoretical framework at this time was Parsons' social theory, and Garfinkel has often expressed his respect for, and debt to, it. As is well known, Parsons' focus was on 'the problem of order', and he explained the orderliness of social action in terms of the socialization of actors into the values and norms characteristic of their society. However, Garfinkel raised questions about this theory by arguing that every application of a norm requires *interpretation*; in the sense that it involves identifying a situation as being of a kind that is relevant to a norm, or to one norm rather than another, and recognizing what the implications of the norm are for action in that situation.[5] The implication of this is that particular values and norms, being members' constructs, which they *use* in making sense of and acting in the world, cannot be taken as adequate descriptions of behaviour or treated as analytic devices for explaining behaviour, because they do not include instructions for their own interpretation. Moreover, this is not just a problem of a missing element in Parsons' theory, it is a basic flaw. This is because there is no scientific or general way of remedying the indexicality of any formulation of a value or norm: how it is to be applied has to be 'determined' on each and every occasion. In other words, the process of interpretation involved in applying norms, or rules of any kind, depends on practical rather than scientific rationality (see Sharrock,1977: 568–9, and passim).

Garfinkel treats this difficulty as pointing to a more fundamental one about the very way in which Parsons had formulated the problem of social order. Parsons took this problem over from Hobbes, even while rejecting the Hobbesian solution to it. And implicit in Parsons' approach is the idea that social order is something whose existence (and non-existence) can be scientifically explained. However, in setting out to do this, he conflates two quite different conceptions of order: Hobbes' political sense of order, which refers to the absence, or minimization, of conflict and violence; and the kind of order whose existence is required if scientific understanding is even to be possible. The latter refers to intelligibility or explainability; and, of course, social conflicts are not disorderly in this sense. Although they may involve much uncertainty, their causation, temporal course and consequences can be understood to the same extent and in much the same ways as can social harmony. By contrast, if human social life were disorderly in a fundamental *scientific* sense, we could have no knowledge or understanding of it. This conflation of two different meanings of 'order' arises because Parsons' conception of social order is a pragmatic or political one, yet also claims to be scientific. In this way, Garfinkel's critique suggests, his project of a scientific sociology is vitiated.

Contrary to the way in which ethnomethodology is sometimes understood, Garfinkel's response to this problem was to try to find a more rigorous, scientific basis for the study of human social life. He did this by respecifying the focus of the sociological project, drawing on phenomenology. The work of Husserl, Schutz, and other phenomenologists emphasizes that we inhabit a lifeworld which is experienced as orderly *in the sense of being intelligible*: any problems in understanding particular events or actions are framed in terms of, indeed are only problems *in the light of,* our general sense of orderliness. Moreover, these authors see this orderliness as something that is a product of the constitutive activity of human beings. Phenomenological philosophy treats our experience of the world not as a passive matter of sense *impression*, but as constituted through prepredicative activity. Thus, to use one of Husserl's examples, our perception of a cube involves going beyond immediate appearances, anticipating other features of this object, including what we would see if we were to look at it from other points of view. We experience it, in other words, not simply as a collection of edges and planes, but as an object of a particular kind; and in doing so we draw on memories of previous encounters with similar objects, and anticipations of how it might appear or behave in the future. Husserl regarded these memories and antici- pations as based upon our access to an essential notion of a cube; and he saw such essences as underlying all perception and cognition.

Garfinkel follows Schutz and many later phenomenological philosophers, rather than Husserl, in keeping his focus on the lifeworld rather than on underlying essences; and this is also in line with his commitment to doing sociology rather than philosophy.[6] He argues that the orderliness of social life must be a product of collective human activity: of our ability to interpret situ- ations and act on those interpretations. However, this is not a matter of everyone automatically understanding a situation in the same way. There are always many different ways of interpreting any scene. Rather, what is involved is that we have the ability to understand how others are defining a situation, not just (or so much) from their explicit communications about it but primarily from what they *do*. We 'read' the behaviour of others for what it tells us about how they understand a situation, and we act on the basis of those 'readings'. Furthermore, in acting we indicate to them *our* understand- ings, and they will in turn act on the basis of *their* understanding of *us*; and so on.

In this way, social situations are self-organizing: their character is created ongoingly in and through the actions that make them up. But how is it pos- sible for actors to read one another's behaviour in this way and thereby to coordinate their actions? Garfinkel's answer to this question is that, in making sense of the situations they face, ordinary people engage in practical reason- ing that is *methodical* (or *accountable*) in character. If it were not, others would not be able to follow it. He was drawn to this conclusion through empirical work: in particular, as a result of looking at how jury members went about determining 'the facts' in legal cases. Thus, he argues that it is the availability of shared methods for sense-making, rather than the existence of stable substantive meanings, which makes social coordination and commu- nication possible. It follows from this that what we should be focusing on as social scientists, if we are interested in the problem of social order, are the methods employed by actors in the practical reasoning through which they continuously constitute, and thereby display the orderliness of, the social world. This is his respecified focus for sociological inquiry. Like Parsons, he sees the problem of order as central, but he reformulates the problem and provides a different methodological strategy for addressing it. For Garfinkel what is to be explained is not why there is order rather than conflict, but how it is that social processes are orderly in the sense of being intelligible. Moreover, he takes over from Schutz the insight that the social world's intelligible orderliness is reflexive: it is produced in and through social action, and is recognizable to those involved in such action. In this crucial respect, it contrasts with the intelligible orderliness of the natural world.

Going back to the two negative commitments I identified, conversation analysts reject them because they breach the analytic orientation which ethnomethodology suggests is necessary for a science of social life. Both the attribution of substantive, distinctive and stable psychosocial characteristics to actors, and the use of what people say as a source of information about the world, treat common sense methods and understandings as a *resource* rather than as a *topic*. By contrast, what is demanded of social *science*, ethnomethodology and CA argue, is that it documents the processes by which social life is constituted; rather than treating social phenomena as given objects in the world. This does not amount to denying the independent existence of social phenomena (in relation to the researcher), only to arguing that they are constituted in and through the ordinary actions of the people involved in them.[7] But if documentation of the methods by which social phenomena are constituted is to be scientific, it must not itself rely on those methods in an unexplicated way. Thus, for conversation analysts, all the data must be presented in research reports, and the analysis should only appeal for evidence to what is observable in those data. If these requirements are not met, the conclusions will be a *product of* the methods that constitute the human social world, rather than a scientific *analysis of* them.[8]

So, the problem with attributing substantive and distinctive orientations to actors is that it relies on common sense methods of interpretation in an unexplicated way. Furthermore, it implies a causal analysis of human behaviour rather than one focusing on constitutive, methodical practices. Thus, it cannot deal with the contingent and reflexive relationship between the ascription of orientation (of commitment to norms and values, or to goals, interests, etc.) and the behaviour this is used to explain. Even more obviously, relying on informants' accounts of the world trades on the informants' exercise of members' methods in making sense of this world, so that those methods remain unexplicated; and it implies a focus on the substantive features of the world rather than on the way in which such features are constituted in and through social interaction.[9]

In other words, values, norms, rules, etc. cannot be employed as explanatory factors in accounting for human behaviour because they are actually resources that are used by participants and must be interpreted in particular contexts in order to lead to any course of action. In short, they cannot form the first part of stable law-like statements which can then be employed to explain people's behaviour. They must be treated as part of the social world, and as matters for study, rather than being taken into the analytic machinery of sociology.[10] As actors in the world we rely on a great deal of knowledge-at-hand about how things generally go, organized to a large extent around our recurrent interests. And this involves trusting things as they appear to us from within that framework, until further notice.[11] Moreover, this involves trusting other people: assuming that, generally speaking, they are not manipulating appearances to fool us. Of course, in some circumstances we may suspect this; indeed, there are contexts in which suspicion is the normal orientation, albeit directed towards particular possibilities of deception. However, for the most part we treat our environment in a more routine way, only pausing occasionally to consider the possibility that we might be mistaken, whether as a result of others' deception or for 'naturally occurring' reasons, if evidence emerges that this may be likely. Furthermore, this is not a matter of personal confidence, but a matter of normative sanction: trusting in appearances is enforced. To question appearances is, potentially, to be seen to impugn the integrity of those with whom one is engaging in action. This reflects the collective character of the way the social world comes to be, and continues to be, constituted over time.

Discourse Analysis

Let me turn now to Potter and Wetherell's approach to discourse analysis (Potter and Wetherell, 1987). This draws considerably on conversation analysis, and ethnomethodology. From these sources are derived a primary reliance on transcribed audio-recordings as data and a central concern with discourse as action. However, other influences have also been important, including the ethnography of communication, the philosophy of language, semiology and post-structuralism (Potter, 1996b; Potter and Wetherell, 1987). And these have contributed to the adoption of a 'constructionist' orientation which is significantly different from the ethnomethodological approach of conversation analysis.[12]

Like conversation analysts, Potter and Wetherell are particularly impressed by the fact that language-use is a form of action, and on this basis they specifically reject the representational model of language, whereby statements are held to correspond to phenomena that exist independently of them. However, whereas ethnomethodologists and conversation analysts adopt the Husserlian position that the objects to which language-use refers exist in correlation with it, constructionists place most emphasis on the generative power of discursive acts. In other words, the constructed character of social phenomena is taken to indicate that those phenomena do not have the kind of objective reality normally ascribed to them by everyday social actors and by most social scientists. In other words, a distinction is drawn between how social phenomena appear to people, as objective things existing in the world, and their true nature, which is that they are discursively constructed – and constructed precisely in such a way as to appear to be objective features of the world. Central here, then, is the notion of reification: the question of how social phenomena are discursively constructed to appear as non-discursively *given*.

Also distinctive is that discourse analysts see their approach as opening up a new way of studying issues that have long preoccupied social psychologists and sociologists, one which avoids the problems that other approaches face; rather than as radically respecifying the very focus of inquiry in the way that ethnomethodology does. A clear indication of this is discourse analytic work on racism and sexism (for example, Edley and Wetherell, 1995, 1997; Wetherell and Potter, 1992). However, it is also true of a more recent development out of DA: 'discursive social psychology' (see, for example, D. Edwards, 1997). Potter and Edwards describe this as 'an approach to social psychology that takes the actionorientated and reality-constructing features of discourse as fundamental', rather than being 'a social psychology of language' (Potter and Edwards, 2001: 2). Thus, attitudes are treated not as 'inner entities that drive behaviour', but as evaluations that are part of discourse practices; in other words, they are seen as constituted in and through participants' ways of talking.

What is involved here is a change in view about the ontological status of social phenomena: they are now to be treated as discursive products, and the focus of inquiry becomes how and why they are constructed in the way they are. Moreover, in some DA, this is done against the background of a view of social life in which individuals and groups employ discursive strategies in pursuit of various interests, and this is held to explain why the world is currently constructed in the ways that it is. Here the discursive constitution of the world comes to be located within a wider social philosophy or social theory, often largely implicit, that provides the background in terms of which discursive strategies gain their significance. Following on from this, there is a concern with how reifying accounts can be undermined; and this forms a link with 'critical' approaches to social research. It is argued that the world can always be constructed differently. Thus, the mission of some discourse analysts is constantly to remind readers of this fact, and thereby to facilitate the process of change. At this point, DA comes close to critical discourse analysis.[13]

Although the sources of constructionism include phenomenology – which, as we saw, was a key influence on ethnomethodology – they extend well beyond this.[14] One way to understand it is as a linguistic transformation of Kantianism. Kant argued that our experience of the world does not simply reflect its nature. Rather, mind plays an active role in constituting 'the world as it appears' in our experience. Thus, some features of experience – notably spatial, temporal and causal relations – derive from the constitutive activity of the mind rather than from things-in-themselves. Post-Kantian philosophy, in its various forms, involved several moves away from Kant's position, while accepting his starting point. In line with this, discourse analysts first of all abandon Kant's distinction between reality and appearances; so that it is reality that is constituted, not appearances. Second, where the constituting mind for Kant was transcendental in character, though modelled on the individual ego, for social constructionists it is the individual-as-social-actor, or social interaction as a process, or Discourse, or even Power, which is the constituting agent. In other words, the constitution of reality is a social process. Third, the range of what is constituted is greatly expanded: it is not just space, time and causality, but the whole of the world as given to us in experience; though usually, of course, the focus of inquiry is on some particular aspect of that world.

DA also differs from CA in placing less emphasis on the distinction between an analytic and a practical orientation; in other words, they disagree about what is involved in a commitment to science. Whereas CA can be seen as relying on phenomenology in this respect, as in many others, or even on a form of 'primitive empiricism' (Lynch, 1993; Lynch and Bogen, 1994), Potter and Wetherell appeal to recent developments in the philosophy and sociology of science to justify their approach. These developments question not only older views about scientific method, but also any claim that there is a fundamental difference in orientation between science and other social activities.[15] This move is reinforced by the influence of post-structuralism, which is taken to undermine any claim to scientific authority; such authority being treated as a strategy used in the exercise of power, one that is of especial significance in contemporary societies.

A further difference from CA is that sometimes discourse analysts' arguments for their focus on discourse are ethical or political in character. For constructionists, the attribution of substantive psychosocial characteristics to people must be avoided because those characteristics are discursive products rather than ontologically given properties of the people concerned. To ignore this, it is suggested, is to collude in essentialism: to take as fixed and beyond human control what is actually a product of human activity. Similarly, constructionists believe that reliance on people's accounts about themselves, or about social situations they have experienced, ignores the fact that these accounts are themselves constructs; and that quite different versions could have been provided. Behind this is a commitment to recognizing, and perhaps even celebrating, the diversity or creativity of interpretation.[16] So, from the constructionist point of view, discourse analysis not only captures something important about the social world, but also plays a key ethical and political role in showing how social phenomena are discursively constituted: it demonstrates *how* things come to be as they are, that they could be *different*, and thereby that they can be *changed*.

DA, like CA, involves a reflective turning back on our experience of the world; but in the case of DA this is not done from a separate analytic standpoint, it is done as a participant rather than as a spectator.[17] Implicit here is a notion of ethical or political authenticity: we must always remain aware that the world is a discursive construction, that we are ourselves constantly engaged in constituting it, and of the ethical obligations which are held to follow from this. In some ways, we might say that constructionism is existentialism to ethnomethodology's phenomenology.[18]

Assessing the Two Rationales

In my view, the rationales for treating CA or DA as self-sufficient and superior paradigms are not convincing. I will discuss each of them in turn.

Ethnomethodology and CA

The problems with ethnomethodology as a rationale for CA can be highlighted by comparing it with phenomenology. One problem concerns the nature of the data CA employs. The slogan of phenomenology was 'Back to the Phenomena!'. And what was meant by 'phenomena' here were the mundane appearances of things as they are 'given' in our experience. These were the data from which investigation was to start. It is less clear, however, what the phenomena or data are in the case of CA. There are four possibilities: the features of the *particular conversational interactions* under study; *audio- or video-recordings* of those interactions; *transcripts* of those recordings; or the analyst-as-member's *interpretations* of the transcripts and/or recordings.[19]

If the first position is taken, a problem that arises – at least in terms of the parallel with phenomenology – is that the details of conversational interactions are not directly accessible to us in the way that it might be claimed experiential phenomena are. Furthermore, Sacks and other conversation analysts specifically reject any reliance on intuitive or remembered data, insisting on the use of recording and transcription; because these provide for detailed, extended study, and the presentation of the data as evidence for readers of research reports.

If the second answer is given, we must note that recordings are not the same as the social interaction they record. They are selective. Much went on before they started and after they stopped. Furthermore, what is 'picked up' or 'in shot' is only part of a much wider realm of happenings. Sacks recognizes this, but claims that 'other things, to be sure, happened, but at least what was on the tape had happened' (Sacks, 1984: 26). But this is to assume that what is on the tape is analytically separable from what is not; an assumption that would be difficult to justify. Moreover, we do not relate to recordings in the same way that we orient to social interaction when we are participants in it. In analysing recordings, we listen or watch as spectators (or, at most, in vicarious participation). This is heightened by the fact that we can slow down the recording, stop and replay it.

Next, if it is the transcripts that are treated as the data (and we should remember that the recordings are not usually available to readers of CA research reports), this neglects the fact that transcripts are themselves constructions (see Atkinson, 1992; J.A. Edwards and Lampert, 1993; Lapadat, 2000; Ochs, 1979). Decisions have to be made about what to include and how to represent the talk; and these can affect readers' interpretations. Specific issues are: how to identify speakers (are they given numbers or names; and if names, real names, pseudonyms or role names; titles and surnames, or just first names; is gender indicated; is any other information provided about speakers?); how is the speech to be represented (so as to match the sound or so as to capture as clearly as possible what is taken to be the message?); and how is the talk to be laid out on the page (in the form of a playscript, in separate columns for each speaker, or in some other manner)? In specific respects, different decisions about these and other matters will produce different data.

Finally, if the data are the analyst-as-member's interpretations of what was going on in the interaction, questions arise about the status of those interpretations. On what grounds can we take them to be *members'* interpretations? And this links to the deeper problem of what a 'member' is a member of.[20] The very nature of ethnomethodology appears to prevent any analytic specification of the boundaries of membership (see Moerman, 1968; Sharrock, 1974), and thereby of what would (and would not) count as a member's interpretation of a recording or transcript. To try to specify this would be to rely on commonsense understandings as a resource, and to attribute substantive and distinctive psychosocial characteristics to members. After all, membershipping is itself an everyday practice (see, for example, Payne, 1976). Furthermore, treating analysts-as-members' interpretations as the data involves a reliance on intuitions, not unlike that of some conventional linguists – even though these are interpretations of careful and detailed transcriptions.

A related problem concerns the very possibility of an analytic approach that is without presuppositions; in ethnomethodological terms, an approach that does not trade on unexplicated common sense assumptions and methods as resources. Husserl never managed to solve this problem. What he proposes in his later writings is that, although there can be no presuppositionless starting point, the outcome of phenomenological analysis will be a full explication of the presuppositions of the phenomenological project: a demonstration of their apodictic character (Elveton, 1970: Introduction). And a presuppositionless starting point looks no more possible in the case of ethnomethodology and CA than it was with phenomenology. Yet the claim that this is possible sometimes appears to underly CA's restriction of evidence to what is 'observable' in the data. Garfinkel's argument is that people construct-and-display social order in the course of interaction. If they did not do this, then there would be no order to find. So, the fact that they do this not only makes society possible, it simultaneously makes a *science* of society possible. But the question that arises is: by whom are the constitutive practices that generate order observable? Or alternatively, though it probably amounts to the same thing, *how* are they observable? Is what is observable only observable to 'members'; in other words does it rely on 'members' methods'? Or is it observable in some more direct sense, so that analysts (and readers) can see the evidence without relying on those methods? If the first answer is given, it is clear that there cannot be a presuppositionless starting point. If the second answer is given, some justification needs to be provided for what is an implausible claim in the light of twentieth-century philosophical criticism of direct perception, and of foundationalism more generally.

The argument that the process of conversation analysis can be self-explicating is no more convincing. Here, in doing the analysis, the researcher is simultaneously engaged in constituting the social order that he or she is claiming to document. The threat of circularity looms. At best, CA could only be self-explicating if there were a finite and fixed set of members' methods. But it is not clear whether conversation analysts believe this, or what grounds they could have for doing so. Furthermore, CA is not directed towards explicating its own rationale in the way that phenomenological philosophy is: it is intended to be a science rather than a philosophy; though, as will become clear in the next paragraphs, there are questions about its status in this respect.

A third issue is the question of the nature of the methods which ethnomethodology and CA claim to document. There have been attempts to clarify this, but these raise more problems than they solve (see, for instance, Coulter, 1983; Heap, 1979). For example, Coulter claims that some of the sequential structures that conversation analysts have identified, such as adjacency pairs, are synthetic a priori in epistemological status. He notes that no amount of evidence of unanswered questions could reasonably persuade us that answers do not follow questions, or that they follow some other kind of speech act. Rather than treating as counter-evidence cases that do not display this structure, at least those that are clearly not intended as snubs, we rightly judge them to be the product of incompetence on the part of participants, or the result of interactional accident or misunderstanding.

However, Coulter argues that while these structures are a priori – not susceptible to disproof by empirical evidence – this does not mean that they are immediately intuitable; and on this basis he claims that empirical data can play a role in their discovery. Coulter uses parallels with chess and mathematics to try to establish this point. He cites Vendler (1971: 255–6), who points out that when, in a game of chess, we see two pawns of the same colour standing in the same column we can conclude that one of them must have taken an opposing piece in a previous move. And we know this not inductively, on the basis of observing what happens in many chess games, but because (given the rules of chess, and the assumption that these have been followed in this particular game) this is the only way in which this arrangement of pieces could have happened. However, while the empirical evidence cannot confirm this conclusion, since it is true a priori, the evidence may bring it to our attention. Without observing a game in which this arrangement of pieces occurred we might never have recognized the possibility. Vendler also offers an example from mathematics. There is a theorem that, for any n, the sum of the first n odd integers is equal to n squared. However, recognition of this fact, and the logical proof of it, were stimulated by a great deal of study of integers and their properties, rather than being deduced from the premisses of mathematics.

Now, the existence of a priori synthetic truths has been a controversial matter ever since Kant formulated the distinctions between a priori and a posteriori, and between analytic and synthetic, knowledge.[21] Furthermore, Coulter's position has some important implications for the practice of CA. As he makes clear, it runs against the notion of proof employed by Sacks, Schegloff and Jefferson (1974), which implicitly treats sequential structures in conversation as a posteriori in epistemological terms, appealing to the evidence of participants' understandings displayed in the data and/or to the capacity of an analysis to explain all of the data (Schegloff, 1968). Indeed, in a much more recent article, Schegloff specifically contrasts CA with approaches that rely on a priori knowledge (Schegloff, 1997). As already noted, Coulter's argument implies that close analysis of empirical materials may not be *essential* in order to discover sequential structures, suggests that those materials cannot establish the existence of such structures, and proposes that any contradictory data can be dismissed as the product of snub, incompetence or accident. Furthermore, it follows from this that these sequential structures are normative in character. As a result, insofar as it is primarily concerned with these a priori sequential structures, CA is not an empirical science. It is perhaps closer in character to a form of philosophy.

This argument raises a question about the relationship of CA to Garfinkel's original project because, as we saw, this was designed to produce a rigorous empirical science of social life. Coulter's interpretation reintroduces a normative conception of social order, such that any failure of what actually happens to match the analysis can be treated as a case in which the world failed to be orderly. In other words, it breaches the scientific presupposition that the world is orderly in a factual way, and that the task is to discover the details of that orderliness.

A further issue concerns how use of the conversational rules which CA identifies to explain the form that any particular conversation takes can escape Garfinkel's original point: that the application of rules always involves interpretation or judgement.[22] And if the argument is that CA involves not explanation of social interaction but explication of its constitution, what exactly does that mean? After all, Husserl did not see his constitutive phenomenology of natural science as *replacing* the causal explanations for physical phenomena generated by physicists and chemists. Yet, as noted earlier, as a rationale for conversation analysts ethnomethodology *does* seem to imply the impossibility of a science of social life concerned with causal analysis.[23]

Finally, there is the question of what the *product* of CA is intended to be. There are at least two possible answers to this. First, the goal could be knowledge of the universal, though context-sensitive, methods through which social life, or at least orderly conversation, is constituted (with examples used solely for evidence and illustration). Or, second, the intended product could be explications of particular stretches of talk. The first answer is justifiable in principle, but runs into the various problems I have outlined. The second, idiographic, interpretation of the goal of CA may escape some of those criticisms, but it raises a question about what the *point* of this form of analysis is. Why would such explications be of interest and value to readers? Schegloff (1997) draws a parallel with literary criticism;[24] but the reason why readers are interested in literary criticism is because this deals with important works of art that are taken to have intrinsic value. The same is not obviously true of extracts from mundane conversations that have not been selected on value relevant grounds.

Constructionism and DA

Rather different problems face the constructionist rationale that underlies DA. In many respects, these result precisely from the fact that it does not respecify the topic of analysis in the radical way that ethnomethodology does. Whereas, for the latter, the focus is on the methods through which social phenomena are constituted, for constructionists it is the constructed character of particular social phenomena that is highlighted. More than this, as noted earlier, there is often a concern with the sociohistorical purposes and interests underlying the ways in which accounts are constructed, and the social consequences of those constructions. In this respect, it is an up-dated version of ideology-critique. Thus, the discursive construction of realities is located in a larger social theory or philosophy which supplies knowledge of the motivating forces that lead to the world being discursively constructed one way rather than another. As a result, the topics for analysis are the same as, and as diverse as, those of other kinds of social inquiry. In Potter and Wetherell's own work, for example, these include natural science as a form of practice, the nature of racism, and forms of masculinity.

What is distinctive about constructionist analyses of these and other topics, as compared with conventional accounts, is that the phenomena concerned are treated as discursive products, rather than as features of the social world that are caused by psychological or social forces; although, as already noted, such forces may be appealed to in order to explain the character of discursive productions. By contrast with ethnomethodology, interest is not confined to the identification of 'members' methods'. This probably reflects the influence of post-Husserlian forms of phenomenology; and of the post-structuralism that was inspired, in part, by one of these, that of Heidegger.[25] At the same time, the intended product of DA does not seem to be simply explications of what is going on in particular texts. Rather, discourse analysts make claims on the basis of such explications about discursive practices that are available to various categories of actor in particular societies, and about the functions and effects of specific discursive strategies.

There are several problems with this rationale. One is that a particular theoretical model of the actor is treated as if it were exhaustive, or sufficient for all purposes. In the case of DA, this is what we might call *Homo rhetoricus* – where the actor is primarily concerned with formulating accounts that are as persuasive as possible, in order to serve his or her interests. As Crossley and others have pointed out, this is a very thin and partial model, one which leaves out much of the person and of social life that we might reasonably think is important (see Crossley, 2000: 30–2). There is no problem with using such a model to learn what it can teach us about human behaviour. But there *is* a problem if discourse analysis based on such a model is treated as a self-sufficient way of understanding such behaviour. Furthermore, while the model of the actor is a thin one, the model of the social context in which he or she operates is, by comparison with CA, quite 'thick'. For example, in Wetherell and Potter's analysis of racist discourse in New Zealand, the discursive strategies that are the focus of inquiry, through which racism operates, are presented against the background of a society in which Maoris are an indigenous group that is exploited by the predominantly white settler community (Wetherell and Potter, 1992). Here questions arise not just about the adequacy of this background account, and about the justification for its evaluative slant, but also about the legitimacy within DA of such claims about social phenomena *as they are*, rather than as social constructions. If *these* social phenomena – for instance, the positions of different groups within New Zealand society – are not to be studied as discursive products, why should other phenomena be treated solely in this way? It is difficult to see what grounds there could be for differential treatment of this kind within DA. It parallels the kind of 'ontological gerrymandering' that Woolgar and Pawluch (1985) have identified in the constructionist literature on social problems.

There is also a fundamental *methodological* problem involved in DA. It assumes the possibility of a process of generalization that is by no means easy to validate. Much discourse analysis depends on the following argument: that, in the instance studied, one or more participants employed discursive practice X; that we can conclude from this that X was part of their repertoire; and, finally, that this can be taken as evidence that X is available to all participants who belong to some category or set of categories to which the people studied belong. Once again, Wetherell and Potter's account of the discursive strategies by which white New Zealanders construct a racist society is a case in point.[26] This argument raises various questions.

One is about the category of actor to which the discursive practice should be ascribed. Given that any participant is describable in terms of a large number of social categories, there are many alternative possibilities here. Yet, as already noted, discourse analysts are not concerned simply with documenting members' methods in the manner of CA. They seek to locate discursive acts in terms of the concerns of particular types of actor, for example, those of white New Zealanders.

A second question concerns why it can be concluded that the availability of this discursive practice to one or a few members of a category means that it is available to, or used by, most or all of them. This is the standard problem of generalization from sample to population, but it is not addressed by discourse analysts. Indeed, Potter and Wetherell emphatically deny that sampling issues are relevant to the validity of discourse analysis accounts (Potter and Wetherell, 1987: 161–2). Yet they are not interested simply in what goes on in the data extracts they discuss, they want to make wider claims about the way particular discursive strategies function, for example, to sustain a sexist or a racist social order (Edley and Wetherell, 1995; Wetherell and Potter, 1992).[27]

A more general problem with DA and its constructionist rationale is that discursive practices are treated as having an ontological status that is different from that of the phenomena they are taken to construct. While most social phenomena are presented as occasioned constructions, the practices which generate them are treated as real and stable objects in the world. Yet, we must ask, are these practices themselves not also discursive constructions? Potter and Wetherell insist in a number of places that their own writing can itself be subjected to discourse analysis, but they do not address the implications of this effectively.

The central message of DA is that phenomena could always be constructed differently; and that how they are constructed has consequences, or fulfils certain social functions. But this raises questions about the appeal to data, and to consistency of argument, which discourse analysts make in supporting their own analyses. Why is their analysis itself not to be treated simply as a series of rhetorical moves designed to have particular effects on readers? If, as Potter and Wetherell insist, we should not be concerned with the correspondence between accounts and the world, does this mean that no correspondence is being claimed between *their* accounts and the discursive practices those accounts identify? As noted earlier, in pragmatic terms, what they write is suffused with a commitment to documenting the reality of discursive practices. Although they note that some authors have employed 'new literary forms', they do not usually do so themselves.[28] But, even if they did employ these, thereby reminding readers that their own writing constructs the phenomena to which it refers, this would not escape the problem. Indeed, it leaves open the question of what possible justification there could be for discourse analysis research. It seems that it could only be justified in ethical or aesthetic terms, given that epistemic justification is taken to be no longer legitimate. But on what grounds can it be assumed that ethical and aesthetic criteria are any less 'constructed' than epistemic ones?

In short, constructionism seems logically to imply the reflexive application of DA to itself: having documented the discursive production of some phenomenon, it apparently then requires a reflexive analysis of how that documentation was itself discursively constructed; and so on, ad infinitum. And, given that this process of self-explication can never be completed, we might conclude that no progress toward self-explication is ever made. This suggests that the moral or political authenticity to which constructionists appeal is unattainable. Furthermore, this endless reflexivity undermines any claim for research as an activity distinct from fictional writing.[29]

Conversation and Discourse Analysis in Practice

CA and DA are both going enterprises, in the sense that they often produce interesting and convincing empirical findings; unlike some other social research paradigms. Should we conclude from this that the problems raised earlier have been solved or avoided? I think not. It seems to me that the viability of these two forms of analysis stems, to a considerable extent, from the ways in which they deviate from the two theoretical rationales I have outlined; and that this is associated with a partial, pragmatic abandonment of the two negative commitments I outlined at the beginning.

So, I want to look briefly at the actual practice of these two forms of analysis, in order to determine how far they live up to those commitments. To do this, I will use as a resource the recent debate between Schegloff, Wetherell and others in the pages of *Discourse & Society* (see, especially, Schegloff, 1997, 1998; Wetherell, 1998). Both the two main protagonists include some analysis of data within their articles, so I will focus on this.

Although neither Schegloff nor Wetherell engage in the attribution of substantive distinctive psychosocial features to actors in the way that conventional research does, in practice they both do this in a more limited way. At the very least, they attribute occasioned orientations; and, as already indicated, DA often goes some way beyond this. Similarly, although neither relies on information from informants in the way that much social research would, they do both make some use of such information as background.

Conversation Analysis in Practice

In analysing the data extract in his article, Schegloff makes explicit that he is focusing on 'the overtly displayed concerns of the participants themselves, the terms in which they relate to one another, the relevancies to which they show themselves to be oriented'. Indeed, he emphasizes that what he is interested in is 'what was going on in [this exchange] for the participants, in its course' (Schegloff, 1997: 174). This formulation of his purposes plays a central role in the rationale he presents for CA, as against any kind of critical discourse analysis, which he treats as (at best) premature. He comments: 'if the parties are hearing that way and responding that way – that is, with an orientation to this level of turn design – we are virtually mandated to analyze it that way' (p. 175). Thus, he objects to critical discourse analysis because it begins by imposing the analyst's own concerns on what is happening, rather than attending (at least first of all) to what are the participants' concerns.

For my purposes here, the questions that arise about Schegloff's mode of analysis are: Why is the attribution of occasioned orientations legitimate, whereas that of stable and distinctive perspectives, attitudes, worldviews, etc. is not? On what basis is it assumed, as it seems to be, that the kind of orientation to what is going on in the talk on which Schegloff concentrates exhausts available participant orientations? In other words, why should we assume, even for the purposes of analysis, that people engage in interaction solely on the basis of resources available to 'anyone', and that they are primarily (even if unwittingly) concerned with displaying what they are doing to one another? One answer to this question would appeal to a theoretical model of human behaviour: one which assumes a very thin and standardized actor. And this is a model whose application in CA is illuminating. However, it is no more exhaustive of the character of human behaviour than is, say, *Homo economicus*, or the model of human behaviour that I suggested was built into discourse analysis. The problem is not the adoption of this theoretical model, but the implied claim that it is the only scientific basis for understanding human social life, or that it provides the essential foundation for other kinds of analysis.

A rather different answer to the question of why the attribution of occasioned orientations is legitimate is that they are observable. I will put aside here the problem I noted earlier about what is observable to whom and how, as this aspect of Schegloff's argument does not necessarily rely on ethnomethodology. Instead, it can be formulated in methodological terms. In effect, the claim is that the ascriptions made in CA are much less open to reasonable doubt than are those of conventional sociologists. And this is very often true. But we must then ask: what is the appropriate threshold above which ascriptions are too speculative to be acceptable? After all, while Schegloff's ascriptions of occasioned orientation may be less open to question than conventional sociological attributions of perspectives and attitudes, some of the latter could also be beyond reasonable doubt. Why draw the line below these rather than above them? Schegloff does not address this issue; yet it raises questions about the sharp, and questionable, distinction he makes between what is observable and what is not.

My argument here is similar in some respects to Lynch and Bogen's criticism of CA's primitive empiricism (Lynch and Bogen, 1994); even though it comes from a different direction. I am suggesting that what distinguishes CA from other kinds of analysis of social interaction, such as that of ethnographers, may be not so much a commitment to ethnomethodology as to what we might call methodological severity: a refusal to put forward claims about the orientations of participants that cannot meet a very strict threshold, and one that demands reliance on transcribed talk.[30] If this is correct, what becomes crucial for any defence of CA as a self-sufficient approach to understanding the social world is a justification for the adoption of such a strict threshold. But this is not supplied.

Turning to the other issue – the rejection of what people say as a source of information about the world – we can note that here too, in practice, Schegloff does not abide by the principle completely. Thus, he begins by providing us with information about the two participants in the data extract that he analyses: that one is male and the other female, that they are in a strained relationship, that they are 'the parents – now separated or divorced – of the teenaged Joey, who lives with his father in northern California, but has just spent a period of vacation from school with his mother in southern California'; that the day of the telephone call was when he was 'scheduled to drive back up north'. This information is not available in the transcript which is provided. But, even if it were, Schegloff would still be using these data as a source of information about the world rather than as a topic for analysis.

The first point to be made about the use of such data, even to provide context, is that it surely undermines any argument that this sort of information is in principle illegitimate or of no value. So, the questions arise: Why not use it more extensively and systematically? Why is only *this* information provided? And, what would be the effect on our interpretation of the data extract if we were given *more* contextual information? Perhaps, if that had been done, we would have been able to move a little further up the methodological gradient, in terms of what aspects of the orientations of conversational participants we could produce convincing knowledge claims about. In a sense, it is by *not* providing more information about the people and the situations from which their data come that conversation analysts render those data largely immune to conventional sociological investigation.

Discourse Analysis in Practice

DA also attributes occasioned orientations; but it goes beyond this, for example, in seeking to 'map' the discursive or interpretative repertoires drawn on by particular categories of actor, and also in identifying the functions of discursive strategies. Wetherell defines an interpretative repertoire as: 'a culturally familiar and habitual line of argument comprised of recognizable themes, commonplaces and tropes (doxa)' (Wetherell, 1998: 400). In her analysis of the range of discursive strategies employed by a group of male students involved in a discussion about relations with the opposite sex, she identifies a number of such repertoires: 'male sexuality as performance and achievement, a repertoire around alcohol and disinhibition, [and] an ethics of sexuality as legitimated by relationships and reciprocity [. . .]' (p. 400). Moreover, she indirectly links these to the concept of ideology by suggesting that the young men's discursive strategies can be seen as seeking to deal with 'ideological dilemmas' (see Billig et al., 1988).

This amounts to the ascription of relatively stable sets of resources that are held to be constantly available to the young men. And it arises, in part, from Wetherell's attempt to integrate CA with elements drawn from post-structuralism. She summarizes the argument of Mouffe: that 'subject positions, and thus the identities of participants in social life, are determined by discourses and in this sense are prior, already constituted, and could be read off or predicted from knowledge of the relevant discourse'. She denies that discourses should be treated as the agent here, but she seems nevertheless to accept that interpretative repertoires exist prior to the interaction in which they are used, which implies that they must be relatively stable features of the orientations of the participants.

Furthermore, she argues that there should also be a focus on discursive resources that are *not* drawn on. She suggests that, in relation to her data:

> We should also be interested in the 'heteronormativity' (Kitzinger, personal communication) evident throughout this discussion which supplies a further taken for granted discursive back-cloth organizing these young men's participant orientations and their members' methods for making sense. A more adequate analysis of 'why this utterance here?' would also explore the silences and absences in this material – the argumentative threads which are hearably not part of these participants' orientations and everyday sense-making. Crucially, it would be concerned with the ideological dilemmas [. . .] evident in the struggle and collaboration over how to formulate Aaron [one of the young men interviewed] and his actions.

Thus, she notes that:

> It is important and interesting from a feminist perspective that these young men only appeal to some notion of autonomous female sexuality at this point in their conversation [that is, where they are trying to justify the promiscuity of one of their number]. (p. 404).

Wetherell presents her work as part of critical discursive social psychology, which 'is concerned with members' methods and the logic of accountability

while describing also the collective and social patterning of background normative conceptions (their forms of articulation and the social and psychological consequences)'. She describes critical discursive social psychology as
'a discipline concerned with the practices which produce persons, notably
discursive practices, but seeks to put these in a genealogical context'
(p. 405).[31] Here there is the suggestion that which discursive strategies are
used reflects, in part, stable features of the actors, and also that those features have been shaped by discursive practices in the past. Earlier on in the
article, she quotes Antaki to the effect that the ascription of a tendency to
drunkenness in the course of a conversation 'gives a person their (portfolio
of) identities' (Antaki et al., 1996: 488). The argument here seems to be that,
as a result of the discursive practices employed by others, people gain particular, stable reputations and that these shape how they will be treated in
the future; and perhaps even how they come to view themselves and therefore their mode of orientation. There is a hint here of some version of the
labelling theory of deviance.[32]

So, even more obviously than with CA, what is involved in DA is not a
rejection of all attributions of psychological or social attributes to people, but
rather an insistence that only *certain kinds* of attributes be applied. In effect,
DA treats attribution of those orientations deriving from recent processes of
discursive interaction as legitimate, while rejecting any produced by genetic
constitution or by early upbringing. In other words, rather than no
psychological theory being involved in DA, one kind of theory is being promoted against another. Yet this is done by methodological, epistemological
or even ethical fiat; rather than on the basis of empirical evidence.

Turning to the second negative commitment, we find that Wetherell also
provides some contextual information about her data, though no more than
Schegloff. She tells us that the interviewees were 17–18-year-old male students attending the sixth form of a single sex boys' independent school in the
United Kingdom. And she describes her data as arising from a 'relatively
large scale project on the construction of masculine identities', and indicates
that this involved 'an intensive reflexive ethnography' (Wetherell, 1998:
389).[33] The information about the young men and their context must have
come from descriptions provided by the boys themselves, by some representative of the school or from documents. And, whatever its origin, this
information is being used as resource rather than as a topic for analysis.

In addition, in analysing the data Wetherell tells us that the data refer to
'Aaron's behaviour at a pub on the Friday night and at a party on the Saturday
night and the nature of his involvement with four different young women'
(Wetherell, 1998: 389). Here too it seems clear that the data are not being
treated as a focus for analysis but rather as a source of, albeit minimal, information about the events to which the young men's discussion refers.

As with Schegloff, the fact that Wetherell breaches this second commitment not only indicates that this kind of data can be useful, but also that

rejection of it is not part of a consistent stand on the part of those who engage in DA. Again, the question arises: why is there not more of this kind of information? Indeed, such data would be of even greater significance for Wetherell's analysis than for Schegloff's, precisely because the latter stays so close to the interactional ground. Wetherell's claims about discursive repertoires and their consequences might have been supported much more effectively by drawing on information about the social situations in which these students participate. Data sources such as observation of their activities in a wide range of contexts, interviews with their peers, with parents, and with the women concerned, etc., could be of considerable value in seeking to understand why they behave as they do, including what they say in interviews.

Here my argument parallels Wetherell's own criticism of Schegloff and CA. She argues that

> it is the conversation analyst in selecting for analysis part of a conversation or continuing interaction who defines [. . .] relevance for the participant. In restricting the analyst's gaze to [a] fragment, previous conversations, even previous turns in the same continuing conversation, become irrelevant for the analyst but also, by dictat, for the participants. We do not seem to have escaped, therefore, from the imposition of theorists' categories and concerns. (p. 403)

My argument is that by restricting the primary data to discursive acts in taperecorded interviews, discourse analysts may also fail to provide adequate context for their analyses.

Conclusion

In this article I began from the question of whether CA and DA should be treated as self-sufficient paradigms, in the way that their proponents tend to treat them, or whether they ought to be viewed, instead, as useful methods that are valuable for particular purposes, and may be combined with other approaches.[34] I identified two negative methodological commitments which serve as defensive barriers around CA and DA, leading them to be treated as self-sufficient paradigms rather than as methods. I looked at the rationales for these commitments, which I suggested were different in each case. I argued that the ethnomethodological rationale that CA often seems to rely on, although distinctive and challenging, involves some fundamental problems. And, in my view, these are at least as serious as those which ethnomethodologists ascribe to conventional sociology.

This is not necessarily damaging for CA, because it is unclear how heavily it depends on the ethnomethodological rationale. I hinted that it could rely on a different, *methodological*, one. In these terms, CA succeeds in documenting important features of human social interaction that had hith-erto been overlooked. And it does this relatively uncontentiously, for the most part, because its claims are descriptive and of a kind that, generally speaking, can be established by the sort of data it uses. Nevertheless, there are problems with this methodological rationale. In some ways, it amounts to a new form of behaviourism, and suffers from the same weaknesses as the older kind.[35] One of these is that it relies on a notion of observability that is indefensible. What we are faced with in our experience of the world, surely, is not a sharp contrast between the observable and the unobservable, but a gradient of credibility. And, once that is recognized, we need to ask about where on that gradient we should draw the line between what is sufficiently credible to be accepted as true, until further notice, and what is not. That we should draw the line where conversation analysts draw it is by no means self-evident.

The second weakness shared with psychological behaviourism is a ten-dency to treat anything that is not observable in the defined sense as having a different ontological status from that which is. At the very least, it is treated as constituted rather than constituting; and, therefore, even if it is not pre-sented as less real, it is treated as less fundamental and determinate in char-acter. The effect of this is to operate on the basis of a very thin model of the human actor, one whose concerns are exhausted by what is 'observable' and is therefore preoccupied with achieving interactional coordination. This may be a useful theoretical model for understanding an important aspect of human social relations, but it is unlikely to be the only useful one. Furthermore, while knowledge of what Goffman referred to as 'the interaction order' may force us to rethink various features of our accounts of other aspects of social life, it is yet to be established that those accounts must always start from the interaction order, any more than that they should always end with it.[36]

The constructionist rationale to which DA appeals is also problematic. Ironically, this is partly because it does not respecify the focus of inquiry in the fundamental way that ethnomethodology does. Instead, it displays an ambiguity about the ontological status of social phenomena. It sometimes implies that those phenomena are constituted by, rather than independent of, the accounting practices we use to talk about them; but it exempts some phenomena from such treatment, such as racism and sexism, as well as the accounting practices that are its focus. Here it is open to the charge of onto-logical gerrymandering.[37]

If, however, we interpret DA as not denying the independence of social phenomena from accounts of them, then it is open to methodological quetion about the sufficiency of the evidence it puts forward, and is able to present on the basis of the kind of analysis and data it uses. What can we infer from the fact that a particular participant or set of participants used one discursive repertoire on a particular occasion? What discourse analysts *want* to be able to conclude, it seems, is that this person or these people use this repertoire on other occasions, that there are reasons or causes for why just this repertoire and not others was used, and that this usage is widespread and has determinate and systematic effects. In other words, they are claiming to document a pattern or regularity. But they do not set out to validate this in the way that is necessary. This would require showing, first of all, that the use of this repertoire on this occasion was indicative of a general tendency on the part of the participant(s) concerned; and/or on the part of other members of the designated category. The second task would be to try to show *why* this particular interpretative repertoire is employed by that category of person. This is a complicated issue since discourse analysts wish to take account of the local reasons for the way the repertoires are used, but at the same time to explain why particular repertoires are available for use within a setting and why they are likely to be used by the relevant categories of actor. In order to test such interpretations we would need data about those types of actor from across situations that involve variation in the candidate explanatory factors. This would be necessary to provide evidence that it is these factors rather than others which play the key role. That discourse analysts do not do this renders much of their analyses speculative.

Furthermore, like CA, DA also relies on a very partial model of the human actor. This is that of *Homo rhetoricus*, an actor who is preoccupied with persuading others to accept his or her point of view in order to further particular goals or to protect particular interests.[38] Again, this theoretical model may give us considerable insight into an aspect of human social action in many spheres, but it is not exhaustive. It involves a very limited vocabulary of motives. So, when it is presented as if it gives a full account, or in a way that implies its sufficiency, it is systematically misleading.

There is no doubt about the value of conversation and discourse analysts' work, nor that their methodological and philosophical arguments point to significant problems with conventional social science. What I am questioning here is whether they offer a solution to those problems, in the sense of an approach that does not involve other difficulties that are at least as severe. Furthermore, the drift of my argument is towards suggesting that both these forms of analysis could be usefully combined with other qualitative and even quantitative approaches. My inclination is towards trying to draw together the diverse methodological approaches that currently make up social research, in the belief that fragmentation – especially when 'paradigmized' – is a barrier against progress towards more effective scientific study of social life.[39]

In specific terms, I am suggesting that conversation analysis can and should be detached from ethnomethodology; and that discourse analysis can and should be detached from constructionism. This does not mean that I believe that nothing is to be learned from those two lines of theoretical argument. But it seems to me that, in so far as they propose a radical respecification of sociological topic, or a radical change in view about the ontological status of social phenomena, they lead us in the wrong directions: away from the search for general knowledge of the social forces and institutions that structure human social life. It may be that the only justification for the possibility of such general knowledge is that all of us in the course of our lives act as if we have it or could have it. That would be a sad reflection on the considerable work of many generations of social scientists – and an unfair one too, in my judgement, given what has been achieved – but it would still be sufficient. One of the oddest features of both ethnomethodology and constructionism is that, while they insist that they respect the orientations of the people they study, rather than judging those orientations from some scientistic vantage point, both effectively deny what seems to be a near universal feature of human experience, and one which has been the driving concern behind much conventional social science: that we are part of a causal nexus of physical and social events which shapes how we think and act, and what we are able to accomplish. CA and DA have shown that to focus instead on how the social world is 'constituted' or 'constructed' through our actions can be illuminating. However, this focus cannot tell us all there is to know about human social life. As a result, these approaches cannot be replacements for more conventional forms of social scientific research. They offer important supplements and correctives. Nothing less, but nothing more.

Notes

1. For an attempt at a bibliographical 'map' of the diverse forms of discourse analysis, see Hammersley (2001). There is a huge literature on CA, but Hutchby and Wooffitt (1998) and ten Have (1999) provide useful recent introductions. On DA, Potter and Wetherell (1987) is the key source. Some more recent developments in this field have been under the heading of 'discursive psychology'; on which see, for example, D. Edwards (1997). A recent debate among Wetherell, Schegloff, and others about how discourse should be studied was one of the stimuli for this article: see Billig (1999a, 1999b), Schegloff (1997, 1998, 1999a, 1999b), Wetherell (1998). See also Edley (2001) and Speer (2001a, 2001b).
2. In one place, Potter describes it as 'not just a method but a whole perspective on social life and research into it [. . .]' (Potter, 1996b: 130). Furthermore, in their work on racism, Wetherell and Potter suggest that other kinds of social psychology have often sustained 'some of the ideological practices of racist discourse' (Wetherell and Potter, 1992: 2). This suggests political as well as methodological grounds for rejection of at least some other approaches.
3. I will suggest later that the term 'member' has different meanings in the contexts of CA and DA.
4. It is worth noting that the relationship between CA and ethnomethodology, and the nature of both, are contested matters. On the relationship between the two, see the discussion and references in G. Watson and Seiler (1992): introduction, and in Clayman and Maynard (1995). D.R. Watson (2000) documents the influence of Wittgenstein, Ryle and Austin on British forms of ethnomethodologically informed conversation analysis. Another important influence on the development of CA was the work of Erving Goffman, who like Garfinkel was one of Harvey

Sacks' teachers at the University of California. Goffman's central focus throughout his life was on features of what he called 'the interaction order' (Goffman, 1983). His work not only drew attention to talk as an important part of human social life, but also displayed a concern with the formal properties of social interaction and the role of careful observation of mundane interpersonal conduct in discovering such properties. However, Goffman's work involves neither of the negative commitments I have outlined, nor did he present it as the only legitimate approach to studying the social world. On Goffman, see Manning (1992) and Williams (1988).

5. This argument was not new, it is to be found for instance in Kant and Aristotle. However, Garfinkel has explored its implications for sociological analysis further than anyone else: see Heritage (1984). Note that I am using the term 'interpretation' in a broad sense that not all ethnomethodologists and phenomenologists would approve of: some would restrict the term to those circumstances in which the meaning of a rule for a situation is uncertain. This is in line with the approach to interpretation taken within hermeneutics prior to the work of Schleiermacher. Others object to the term on the grounds that its logical grammar in English implies ironic downgrading – 'that's your interpretation' – and/or that it implies a residual cognitivism which is at odds with the praxiological approach of ethnomethodology: see D.R. Watson (2000). My usage here is not intended to carry either of these implications, and it is difficult to know what alternative could be used that is not open to similar complaints. One alternative would be 'judgement'; but, if anything, this seems likely to be interpreted even more readily in a cognitivist manner.

6. According to Lynch (1993: ch. 4), there are other respects in which Garfinkel was closer to Husserl than to Schutz.

7. The relation between account and object for ethnomethodology is much the same as that between the act of experiencing and what is experienced (noesis and noema) for phenomenology. On the role of this distinction in Husserl, see Hammond et al. (1991: ch. 2).

8. Ethnomethodologists and conversation analysts sometimes deny that their work is based on, or implies, criticism of conventional sociology. What *is* implied, though, is criticism of any claim to scientific status on the part of that sociology. Later, I will raise some questions about the conception of science involved here.

9. Not all those expressly committed to ethnomethodology and conversation analysis adopt these two negative principles. For example, Moerman (1988) argues for 'culturally contexted conversation analysis' which draws on conventional ethnographic work. For general discussions of the issue, see Button (1978), Nelson (1994) and G. Watson and Seiler (1992). The question of the role of 'ethnographic context' has arisen in a particularly sharp form in debates about the study of 'institutional talk' and about the relationship between CA and feminism. On the first, see Boden and Zimmerman (1991), Drew and Heritage (1992), Hak (1995) and Psathas (1995); on the second, see Edley (2001), Kitzinger (2000), Speer (1999, 2001a, 2001b) and Stokoe and Smithson (2001). The relationship between CA and Garfinkel et al.'s 'studies of work' programme also touches on this issue, though the way it is dealt with there is distinctive: see Lynch (1985: ch. 1) and the discussion in Psathas (1995). For an argument from outside ethnomethodology about the fruitfulness of incorporating conversation analysis into ethnography, see Atkinson (1988). The line I take in this article in relation to CA is similar in key respects to that of Atkinson. For an ethnomethodological response to Atkinson's argument, see D.R. Watson and Sharrock (1991). See also Pollner and Emerson's (2001) discussion of the relationship between ethnomethodology and ethnography.

10. As Sharrock points out, the use of concepts like values and norms as explanatory devices in accounting for human behaviour suffers from an analogous problem to that

which Durkheim identified in criticizing use of the concept of contract to explain social order: the establishment and operation of a contract relies on mutual understanding, which the notion of a social contract was itself introduced to explain: see Sharrock (1977).

11. Time is a crucial element here, indicating that what is involved is not some one-off constitution of the social world but its continuing unfolding over time in and through the process of human activity.

12. Of course the term 'constructionism' can carry a wide range of different meanings. For accounts of the contrast between constructionism and ethnomethodology see Button and Sharrock (1993) and G. Watson (1994). For an account of constructionism from the point of view of DA, see Potter (1996a). Note that there is variation within DA about what constructionism entails, arising from differential emphasis on the disparate sources on which it has drawn, notably between ethnomethodology and post-structuralism: see Wetherell (1998).

13. Originally, the philosophy that provided the basis for critical discourse analysis was a form of Marxist critical theory, whereas discourse analysts like Wetherell have drawn more on feminism, anti-racism and post-structuralism. However, with a recent shift on the part of some critical discourse analysts towards a reliance on Foucault (see Chouliaraki and Fairclough, 1999), the differences have narrowed; although there remain important divergences in the approach to analysing data between the two traditions – for example, Fairclough relies much more on the techniques of mainstream linguistics than do Potter and Wetherell. For an assessment of critical discourse analysis, see Hammersley (1997).

14. There is a form of constructionism emerging out of ethnomethodology which is quite close to that of DA, in some respects: see Pollner (1987). The gist of Pollner's argument is provided on the inside of the back cover of his book in a commentary on Magritte's picture *Le Chateau des Pyrénées*, which is to be found on the front: 'The painting depicts a stone castle resting on a huge rock. Despite their size and weight, the castle and rock float in mid-air suspended over the sea. When the inhabitants of the castle look down, they see that it is built on solid foundations. If they were to gain perspective, however, they would see that their world is not as secure as they believe. *Mundane Reason* examines the castle of assumptions in which people enact their daily lives, showing that despite their apparent naturalness, these assumptions are interactionally, culturally, and historically created and sustained, and their seemingly solid foundations are in fact precarious.'

15. This is also questioned by some ethnomethodologists, see Lynch (1988, 1993).

16. Not all interpretations are celebrated, of course; in particular, not those deemed racist or sexist: see, for example, Wetherell (1998) and Wetherell and Potter (1992).

17. In practice, though, Potter and Wetherell do not write up their analyses in this way, for example by using 'new literary forms'. Instead, they adopt a mode of writing that has a fairly standard academic character, while yet seeking to distance themselves at various points from the implications that they take to be built into that mode of writing.

18. This is not entirely accurate, however. The ethical value of phenomenological philosophy was central for Husserl, especially in his later writings. By contrast, Garfinkel's interest in phenomenology is methodological, in the sense that he uses it to find a way to study social life scientifically (see Anderson et al., 1985).

19. In a popular introduction to conversation analysis, Hutchby and Wooffitt claim that 'for CA, transcripts are *not* thought of as "the data". The data consist of tape recordings of naturally occurring interactions'. They state that '[transcripts] are not intended as "objective" representations of social reality [. . .]'. These are 'necessarily impressionistic: they represent the analyst/transcriber's hearing of what is on the tape'. At the same time, indeed on the same page, these authors argue that 'transcripts play a key role in the claim of CA to be a rigorous empirical discipline. An important aspect of

this is that analyses produced by one researcher do not amount merely to idiosyncratic and untestable assertions about what is going on in a stretch of talk' (Hutchby and Wooffitt, 1998: 92). There is some ambiguity here; and this is not unrepresentative of discussions of this issue by conversation analysts.

20. This is a question raised, but not answered, by G. Watson (1994). Lynch (1993: 253) provides an answer, although not one, it seems to me, that solves the problem.

21. For a useful discussion of these distinctions, see Bennett (1966).

22. For one attempt to respond to this criticism, see Clayman and Maynard (1995: 17).

23. There is a dispute about whether Schutz's work implies a radical respecification of conventional sociology or is simply an attempt to explicate its foundations: see Helling (1984). The attitude of ethnomethodologists and conversation analysts towards what they often refer to as 'constructive analysis' seems to oscillate between 'indifference', whereby conventional sociological work simply becomes more grist for the analytic mill, and radical methodological critique.

24. Moerman (1988: ch. 1) does the same. Of course, neither argues that literary criticism and CA are identical in character.

25. Some ethnomethodologists draw on these sources, and also reject the search for universal methods, in favour of documenting heterogeneous fields of local orderliness, see Lynch (1993). For an assessment of the possibility of a Heideggerian ethnomethodology, see McHoul (1998).

26. Jonathan Potter (personal communication) has argued that the concept of interpretive repertoire has been dropped by many discourse analysts, especially those involved in discursive psychology. However, the same problems arise with the ascription of discursive strategies, and identification of the functions and consequences of these; which is central, for example, to his *Representing Reality* (Potter, 1996a).

27. Elsewhere, Potter explicitly argues that DA provides a basis for generalizations about discursive strategies: see Potter (1996b). Similarly, in a later article, Wetherell and Edley (1999: 339) claim that the 'broad methods of self-accounting' they identify in interviews with male Open University students 'have a generality outside the interview context and in this sense are robust phenomena'. In neither case is it explained how such generalizations are to be validated.

28. For an exception, see Ashmore et al. (1995). The phrase 'new literary forms' is, in any case, rather misleading: most of the forms are far from new. Some of them are not even novel in the context of scholarly writing, witness the considerable use that has been made of dialogues and fictions in philosophy since Plato.

29. Some will embrace this, but in my view those who do so ought to make their literary ambitions clear in claiming a livelihood as researchers and in bidding for research funds.

30. 'Methodological severity' is a reformulation of 'methodological purism', in one of its meanings. The latter term emerged in a rather different context: see Troyna (1995). For a discussion, see Hammersley (2000: ch. 5).

31. It also implies an evaluative stance. Thus at one point she judges the interpretative resources used by the young men she studied from a feminist perspective; describing them as of a 'crass and highly offensive nature' (Wetherell, 1998: 403).

32. The epistemological ambiguity of that theory is significant in this context, see Hammersley (2000: ch. 3).

33. It is clear from other publications relating to this research that observational data were collected, and also data from interviews with school staff. However, while more use is made of these data in those other publications than here, they are still employed as a source of background information. The main focus remains detailed analysis of the discourse of the young men in interviews. See, for example, Edley and Wetherell (1997). See also Edley and Wetherell (1995). In later work on a similar theme, reliance is placed entirely on the interview data: see Wetherell and Edley (1999).

34. It is perhaps necessary to emphasize that combining approaches might require some modification on both sides. In particular, the kind of analysis that many qualitative researchers engage in may need to be refined substantially if it is to be compatible with the detailed textual work of CA and DA.
35. On the methodological character of psychological behaviourism, see Mackenzie (1977).
36. The relation between CA and Goffman's analysis of 'forms of talk' is, of course, a contested one. See Schegloff (1988) and Watson (1992). And, in fact, it seems to me that Goffman alerts us to some of the explanatory resources, for example, notions of civility and politeness, that are necessary even if we limit our focus to the character of conversation in western societies. For a historical account of the development of conversation in this context, see Burke (1993).
37. Woolgar and Pawluch (1985), who invented the term 'ontological gerrymandering', see the phenomenon it refers to as unavoidable, as a constituent feature of all accounts. If discourse analysts were to follow this line they would have to abandon the 'realist' mode of writing most of them currently adopt.
38. This model is especially obvious in Potter (1996a).
39. In that sense I am another example of what D.R. Watson and Sharrock (1991), in replying to Atkinson's critique, referred to as the 'incorporationist tendency'. I make no apologies for that, but I hope that it does not lead to my arguments being dismissed as 'misguided to the point of prejudice'.

References

Anderson, R.J., Hughes, J.A. and Sharrock, W.W. (1985) 'The Relationship Between Ethnomethodology and Phenomenology', *Journal of the British Society for Phenomenology* 16: 221–35.

Antaki, C., Condor, S. and Levine, M. (1996) 'Social Identities in Talk: Speakers' Own Orientations', *British Journal of Social Psychology* 35: 473–92.

Ashmore, M., Myers, G. and Potter, J. (1995) 'Discourse, Rhetoric, Reflexivity: Seven Days in the Library', in S. Jasanoff, G.E. Markle, J.C. Petersen and T. Pinch (eds) *Handbook of Science and Technology Studies*. Thousand Oaks, CA: Sage.

Atkinson, P. (1988) 'Ethnomethodology: A Critical Review', *Annual Review of Sociology* 14: 441–65.

Atkinson, P. (1992) *Understanding Ethnographic Texts*. Newbury Park, CA: Sage.

Bennett, J. (1966) *Kant's Analytic*. Cambridge: Cambridge University Press.

Billig, M. (1999a) 'Conversation Analysis and the Claims of Naivety', *Discourse & Society* 10: 572–6.

Billig, M. (1999b) 'Whose Terms? Whose Ordinariness? Rhetoric and Ordinariness in Conversation Analysis', *Discourse & Society* 10: 543–58.

Billig, M., Condor, S., Edwards, D., Gane, M., Middleton, D. and Radley, A.R. (1988) *Ideological Dilemmas*. London: Sage.

Boden, D. and Zimmerman, D.H. (eds) (1991) *Talk and Social Structure*. Cambridge: Polity Press.

Burke, P. (1993) *The Art of Conversation*. Ithaca, NY: Cornell University Press.

Button, G. (1978) 'Comments on Conversation Analysis', *Analytic Sociology* 1: 2.

Button, G. and Sharrock, W. (1993) 'A Disagreement Over Agreement and Consensus in Constructionist Sociology', *Journal for the Theory of Social Behaviour* 23: 1–25.

Chouliaraki, L. and Fairclough, N. (1999) *Discourse in Late Modernity: Rethinking Critical Discourse Analysis*. Edinburgh: Edinburgh University Press.

Clayman, S.E. and Maynard, D.W. (1995) 'Ethnomethodology and Conversation Analysis', in P. ten Have and G. Psathas (eds) *Situated Order: Studies in the Social Organization of Talk and Embodied Activities*. Lanham, MD: University Press of America.

Coulter, J. (1983) 'Contingent and a priori Structures in Sequential Analysis', *Human Studies* 6: 361–76.

Crossley, M. (2000) *Introducing Narrative Psychology*. Buckingham: Open University Press.

Drew, P. and Heritage, J. (eds) (1992) *Talk at Work*. Cambridge: Cambridge University Press.

Edley, N. (2001) 'Conversation Analysis, Discursive Psychology and the Study of Ideology: A Response to Susan Speer', *Feminism and Psychology* 11(1): 136–40.

Edley, N. and Wetherell, M. (1995) *Men in Perspective: Practice, Power and Identity*. London: Harvester-Wheatsheaf.

Edley, N. and Wetherell, M. (1997) 'Jockeying for Position: The Construction of Masculine Identities', *Discourse & Society* 8: 203–17.

Edwards, D. (1997) *Discourse and Cognition*. London: Sage.

Edwards, J.A. and Lampert, M.D. (1993) *Talking Data: Transcription and Coding in Discourse Research*. Hillsdale, NJ: Erlbaum.

Elveton, R.O. (1970) *The Phenomenology of Husserl: Selected Critical Readings*. Chicago: Quadrangle Books.

Goffman, E. (1983) 'The Interaction Order', *American Sociological Review*, 48: 1–17.

Hak, T. (1995) 'Ethnomethodology and the Institutional Context'. *Human Studies* 18: 109–37.

Hammersley, M. (1997) 'On the Foundations of Critical Discourse Analysis', *Language and Communication* 17(3): 237–48.

Hammersley, M. (2000) *Taking Sides in Social Research: Essays on Bias and Partisanship*. London: Routledge.

Hammersley, M. (2001) 'Discourse Analysis: An Introductory Bibliographical Guide', http://www.cf.ac.uk/socsi/capacity/Activities/Themes/In-depth/guide.pdf.

Hammond, M., Howarth, J. and Keat, R. (1991) *Understanding Phenomenology*. Oxford: Blackwell.

ten Have, P. (1999) *Doing Conversation Analysis: A Practical Guide*. London: Sage.

Heap, J. (1979) 'What are Sense-Making Practices?', *Sociological Inquiry* 46: 107–15.

Helling, I.K. (1984) 'A. Schutz and F. Kaufmann: Sociology Between Science and Interpretation', *Human Studies* 7: 141–61.

Heritage, J. (1984) *Garfinkel and Ethnomethodology*. Cambridge: Polity Press.

Hutchby, I. and Wooffitt, R. (1998) *Conversation Analysis: Principles, Practices and Applications.* Cambridge: Polity Press.

Kitzinger, C. (2000) 'Doing Feminist Conversation Analysis', *Feminism and Psychology* 10(2): 163–93.

Lapadat, J.C. (2000) 'Problematising Transcription: Purpose, Paradigm, and Quality', *International Journal of Social Research Methodology* 3(3): 203–19.

Lynch, M. (1985) *Art and Artifact in Laboratory Science*. London: Routledge and Kegan Paul.

Lynch, M. (1988) 'Alfred Schutz and the Sociology of Science', in L. Embree (ed.) *Worldly Phenomenology: The Continuing Influence of Alfred Schutz on North American Human Science*. Washington, DC: Center for Advanced Research in Phenomenology and University Press of America.

Lynch, M. (1993) *Scientific Practice and Ordinary Action*. Cambridge: Cambridge University Press.

Lynch, M. and Bogen, D. (1994) 'Harvey Sacks's Primitive Natural Science'. *Theory, Culture and Society* 11: 65–104.

McHoul, A. (1998) 'How Can Ethnomethodology be Heideggerian?'. *Human Studies* 21: 13–26.

Mackenzie, B.D. (1977) *Behaviourism and the Limits of Scientific Method*. London: Routledge and Kegan Paul.

Manning, P. (1992) *Erving Goffman and Modern Sociology*. Cambridge: Polity Press.

Moerman, M. (1968) 'Being Lue: Uses and Abuses of Ethnic Identification', in J. Helm (ed.) *Essays on the Problem of the Tribe*. Seattle: University of Washington Press.

Moerman, M. (1988) *Talking Culture: Ethnography and Conversation Analysis*. Philadelphia: University of Pennsylvania Press.

Nelson, C.K. (1994) 'Ethnomethodological Positions on the Use of Ethnographic Data in Conversation Analytic Research', *Journal of Contemporary Ethnography* 23: 307–29.

Ochs, E. (1979) 'Transcription as Theory', in E. Ochs (ed.) *Developmental Pragmatics*. New York: Academic Press.

Payne, G.C.F. (1976) 'Making a Lesson Happen: An Ethnomethodological Analysis', in M. Hammersley and P. Woods (eds.) *The Process of Schooling: A Sociological Reader*. London: Routledge and Kegan Paul.

Pollner, M. (1987) *Mundane Reason: Reality in Everyday and Sociological Discourse*. Cambridge: Cambridge University Press.

Pollner, M. and Emerson, R.M. (2001) 'Ethnomethodology and Ethnography', in P. Atkinson, A. Coffey, S. Delamont, J. Lofland and L. Lofland (eds) *Handbook of Ethnography*. London: Sage.

Potter, J. (1996a) *Representing Reality: Discourse, Rhetoric and Social Construction*. London: Sage.

Potter, J. (1996b) 'Discourse Analysis: Theoretical Background', in J.E.T. Richardson (ed.) *Handbook of Qualitative Research Methods*. Leicester: British Psychological Association.

Potter, J. and Edwards, D. (2001) 'Discursive Social Psychology', in W.P. Robinson and H. Giles (eds) *The New Handbook of Language and Social Psychology*. London: Wiley.

Potter, J. and Wetherell, M. (1987) *Discourse and Social Psychology: Beyond Attitudes and Behaviour*. London: Sage.

Psathas, G. (1995) '"Talk and social structure" and "Studies at work"', *Human Studies* 18: 139–55.

Sacks, H. (1984) 'Notes on Methodology', in J.M. Atkinson and J. Heritage (eds) *Structures of Social Action: Studies in Conversation Analysis*, pp. 21–7. Cambridge: Cambridge University Press.

Sacks, H., Schegloff, E. and Jefferson, G. (1974) 'A Simplest Systematics for the Organization of Turn-Taking in Conversation', *Language* 50(4): 696–735.

Schegloff, E.A. (1968) 'Sequencing in Conversational Openings', *American Anthropologist* 70: 1075–95.

Schegloff, E.A. (1988) 'Goffman and the Analysis of Conversation', in P. Drew and A. Wootton (eds) *Erving Goffman: Exploring the Interaction Order*. Cambridge: Polity Press.

Schegloff, E.A. (1997) 'Whose Text? Whose Context?', *Discourse & Society* 8: 165–87.

Schegloff, E.A. (1998) 'Reply to Wetherell', *Discourse & Society* 9: 413–16.

Schegloff, E.A. (1999a) 'Naïveté vs Sophistication or Discipline vs Self-Indulgence: A Rejoinder to Billig', *Discourse & Society* 10: 577–82.

Schegloff, E.A. (1999b) '"Schegloff's Texts" as "Billig's Data": A Critical Reply', *Discourse & Society* 10: 558–72.

Sharrock, W.W. (1974) 'On Owning Knowledge', in R. Turner (ed.) *Ethnomethodology*. Harmondsworth: Penguin.

Sharrock, W.W. (1977) 'The Problem of Order', in P. Worsley (ed.) *Introducing Sociology*. Harmondsworth, Penguin.

Speer, S. (1999) 'Feminism and Conversation Analysis: An Oxymoron?', *Feminism and Psychology* 9(4): 471–8.

Speer, S. (2001a) 'Reconsidering the Concept of Hegemonic Masculinity: Discursive Psychology, Conversation Analysis and Participants' Orientations', *Feminism and Psychology* 11(1): 107–35.

Speer, S. (2001b) 'Participants' Orientations, Ideology and the Ontological Status of Hegemonic Masculinity: A Rejoinder to Nigel Edley', *Feminism and Psychology* 11(1): 141–4.

Stokoe, E.H. and Smithson, J. (2001) 'Making Gender Relevant: Conversation Analysis and Gender Categories in Interaction', *Discourse & Society* 12: 217–44.

Troyna, B. (1995) 'Beyond Reasonable Doubt? Researching "race" in Educational Settings', *Oxford Review of Education* 21: 395–408.

Vendler, Z. (1971) 'Summary: Linguistics and the A Priori', in C. Lyas (ed.) *Philosophy and Linguistics*. London: Macmillan.

Watson, D.R. (1992) 'The Understanding of Language Use in Everyday Life: Is There a Common Ground?', in G. Watson and R.M. Seiler (eds) *Text in Context*. Newbury Park, CA: Sage.

Watson, D.R. (2000) ' "Interpretive" Sociology in Great Britain: The State of the Art', *Swiss Journal of Sociology* 26(3): 507–29.

Watson, D.R. and Sharrock, W.W. (1991) 'On the Provision of "Ethnographic Context" in Ethnomethodological and Conversation-Analytic Research', Paper presented at the International Conference on Current Work in Ethnomethodology and Conversation Analysis, University of Amsterdam, 15–19 July.

Watson, G. (1994) 'A Comparison of Social Constructionist and Ethnomethodological Descriptions of How a Judge Distinguished Between the Erotic and the Obscene', *Philosophy of the Social Sciences* 24: 405–25.

Watson, G. and Seiler, R.M. (eds) (1992) *Text in Context: Contributions to Ethnomethodology*. Newbury Park CA: Sage.

Wetherell, M. (1998) 'Positioning and Interpretative Repertoires: Conversation Analysis and Post-Structuralism in Dialogue', *Discourse & Society* 9: 387–412.

Wetherell, M. and Edley, N. (1999) 'Negotiating Hegemonic Masculinity: Imaginary Positions and Psycho-Discursive Practices', *Feminism and Psychology* 9(3): 335–56.

Wetherell, M. and Potter, J. (1992) *Mapping the Language of Racism*. New York: Harvester Wheatsheaf.

Williams, R. (1988) 'Understanding Goffman's Methods', in P. Drew and A. Wootton (eds) *Erving Goffman: Exploring the Interaction Order*. Cambridge: Polity Press.

Woolgar, S. and Pawluch, D. (1985) 'Ontological Gerrymandering: The Anatomy of Social Problems Explanations', *Social Problems* 32: 314–27.

56

Force-Interactive Patterns in Immigration Discourse: A Cognitive Linguistic Approach to CDA

Christopher Hart

Introduction

Cognitive Linguistics has recently gained significant ground in critical discourse analysis (see Hart, in press b; Hart and Lukeš, 2007). Indeed, a dedicated Cognitive Linguistic approach, which has largely found its niche in Critical Metaphor Analysis, can now be identified (e.g. Charteris-Black, 2004; Koller, 2004; Musolff, 2004). The key claim of Critical Metaphor Analysis is that metaphorical expressions in text reflect and effect underlying construal operations which are ideological in nature. However, metaphor is just one kind of construal operation identified in Cognitive Linguistics (see Croft and Cruse, 2004). Several others may also be ideologically significant and contribute to the realization of discursive strategies of the kind identified in CDA (see Hart, in press a). In this article, I analyse the role that one construal system, force-dynamics, plays in anti-immigration discourse. I then introduce the Cognitive Linguistic approach and present a typology of relevant construal systems. In the following section, I introduce the theory of Force-Dynamics and show how it can be applied to uncover expressions of force. I then describe the various force-dynamic schemas which seem to underlie many representations in discourse on immigration.[1] Finally, I conclude with some summary remarks.

Source: *Discourse & Society*, 22(3) (2011): 269–286.

The Cognitive Linguistic Approach to CDA

Within Fairclough's (1995) tripartite model of discourse and discourse analysis, it is description-stage analysis which has received the most attention. Here, Halliday's systemic functional linguistics (1973) has provided the methodology for ideological research in text analysis. Insufficient attention, however, has been paid to interpretation-stage analysis. As Fowler (1996: 7) puts it, 'the reader simply is not theorised'. In particular, according to O'Halloran (2003: 14), 'much of CDA suffers from a paucity of appreciation of language cognition'. This gap in the research is striking, since the successful communication of ideology depends on cognitive processes reproduced in the minds of text-consumers.[2] Ideological discursive strategies of the kind identified in CDA (e.g. Reisigl and Wodak, 2001) can only be brought into effect when the structures realizing them receive cognitive representation. It is curious, then, that Cognitive Linguistics, which developed at around the same time as Critical Linguistics and explicitly addresses the relation between structures in language and cognition, has not until recently been a major framework called upon in critical discourse research.[3]

While Van Dijk adopts a cognitive perspective in CDA (e.g. 2001, 2002), Cognitive Linguistics is not a feature of his approach. Cognitive Linguistics is a specific school associated with Lakoff, Langacker, Talmy, Taylor, Fillmore and Fauconnier, for example. It is not a single discipline but a paradigm of cognitive science and linguistics which comprises a number of research programmes related by a common set of assumptions. These assumptions include, for example, the idea that grammar and semantics are both based on the same general processes as other domains of cognition, that linguistic knowledge is conceptual in nature and cannot be separated from non-linguistic knowledge, that meaning is based in experience, and that language serves to construe experience.[4] Although Cognitive Linguistics sees no fundamental distinction between grammar and semantics, then, research still falls at two loci: Cognitive Grammar and cognitive lexical semantics. Programmes of research across these two areas include Conceptual Metaphor Theory (Lakoff and Johnson, 1980), Frame Semantics (Fillmore, 1982), Mental Spaces (Fauconnier, 1994), Cognitive Grammar (Langacker, 1987, 1991) and Force-Dynamics (Talmy, 1988).

The Cognitive Linguistic approach to CDA can be characterized as investigating ideological patterns in text *and conceptualization*. The so far fruitful synergy between Cognitive Linguistics and CDA has largely been confined to critical metaphor studies, with Conceptual Metaphor Theory providing the theoretical framework. However, Cognitive Linguistics in CDA may extend beyond Critical Metaphor Analysis to create a broader but coherent Cognitive Linguistic approach which incorporates aspects of Cognitive Grammar, Mental Spaces, Frame Semantics and Force-Dynamics (see Hart, 2010).

Cognitive Linguistics is primarily concerned with conceptualization – a dynamic, online cognitive process through which meaning is constructed. Unlike functional linguistics which is 'speaker-oriented' and 'process-focused', Cognitive Linguistics is 'hearer-oriented' and 'pattern-focused'. As such, it is well placed to address interpretation-stage analysis in CDA. Cognitive Linguistics can model ideological mental representations that text-consumers are prompted to construct in response to particular structures in text and which constitute their experience of the phenomena described. Moreover, Cognitive Linguistics is concerned with the very same phenomena that are of interest in CDA. For example, Cognitive Linguistics addresses within language and cognition the structuring of basic categories such as space and time, situations and events, entities, actions and processes, motion and location, force and causation, and intention and volition (Fauconnier, 2006).

The key claim of Cognitive Linguistics for CDA is that the structuring of these categories always involves 'construal'. The notion of construal refers to the fact that the same phenomenon is potentially conceptualized in any number of different ways but that alternative language structures impose particular conceptualizations on the scene at hand (Langacker, 1991). Linguistic structures in text therefore reflect the text-producer's own conception of reality (or at least one they wish to promote in order to effect ideological discursive strategies). The concept of construal in Cognitive Linguistics, then, is consistent with the relativism of CDA, according to which, representation in text is 'always representation from some ideological point of view, as managed through the inevitable structuring force of transitivity' (Fowler, 1991: 85).

For Cognitive Linguistics, the relevant structuring system is not transitivity but a number of 'construal systems' or 'operations', including metaphor and force-dynamics, which are responsible for conceptualization (Croft and Cruse, 2004). These conceptstructuring systems offer 'a range of alternative structural characterizations, among which a speaker chooses so as to convey a particular conceptualization of a scene' (Talmy, 2000: 214). Construal operations, then, are indexed in text and invited in textconsumers to engender ideological cognitive representations realizing discursive strategies.

Several typologies of construal systems have been proposed and different labels applied. For example, Langacker (1987) surveys a number of systems under the rubric of 'focal adjustments'. However, Langacker's classification includes only systems based on general cognitive processes of attention and perspective. His classification does not include the construal operations identified in cognitive lexical semantics such as categorization and metaphor, both of which rely on the general cognitive process of comparison. Neither does it include force-dynamics. Hart (in press a) therefore presents a typology of construal operations drawn from Croft and Cruse (2004) and shows how they serve to realize three types of discursive strategy which he calls 'identification', 'framing' and 'positioning'.[5] This typology is reproduced in Table 1.

Table 1: Construal operations and discursive strategies

Strategy	Process	Attention	Comparison	Perspective
Identification/ Framing	Construal operations	Profiling/backgrounding Metonymy Scalar adjustment		
			Categorization Metaphor	
Positioning				Deixis Modality

Identification strategies concern which social actors are represented (explicitly or implicitly), in which roles, and to what degree of salience or 'granularity'. For example, those construal operations based in attention can de-focus or de-individuate certain social actors. Identification strategies, then, include those that fall under the general rubric of 'mystification' in Critical Linguistics (Fowler et al., 1979; Kress and Hodge, 1979). They also include what we can call 'scope of reference', as categorization (including metonymic categorization and scalar adjustments) can be used to identify a certain set of social actors while precluding others as the subject of a predication. Framing strategies concern how an entity, action, event, process or relation, through categorization and metaphor, is attributed particular evaluative qualities or structural properties. Framing strategies therefore include negative-Other presentation (Van Dijk, 1997), often through metaphorical strategies such as militarization, naturalization or biologization (Reisigl and Wodak, 2001), as well as a strategy we can call 'structural configuration'. Identification and framing appear in the same box because wherever there is explicit identification, the choice of referring expression necessarily frames the actor(s) in some particular way by evoking associated evaluative scripts – and because identifying participants in particular roles ascribes to them particular qualities or statuses. Positioning strategies can be deictic, epistemic or deontic, and concern the positioning of social actors/events in relation to one another (deictic) and the positioning of propositions in relation to one's conception of reality (epistemic) or morality (deontic).[6] Positioning strategies, then, include proximization and legitimization as outlined by Cap (2006) and Chilton (2004) respectively.

One major contribution of the Cognitive Linguistic approach is to offer new perspectives on semantic and grammatical structures which are staple objects of analysis in CDA but whose real impact has recently been called into question (cf. Widdowson, 2004). For example, Hart (in press a) shows that identification strategies like agent-deletion or agent-substitution, through profiling/backgrounding and metonymy, do carry some conceptual import at the interpretation stage. These analyses therefore give credence to the claim in CDA that grammatical metaphor can keep responsible actors 'in the semantic background' (Reisigl and Wodak, 2001: 58). Another major advantage of the Cognitive Linguistic approach is that it reveals very subtle ideological features of text and conceptualization not previously recognized in CDA, and so can add to the inventory of linguistic/conceptual categories to be targeted. For example, metaphor has not been a typical object of analysis in mainstream CDA but has recently received significant attention from a Cognitive Linguistic perspective where it has been shown to be an important device in covertly ideological or persuasive communication (Charteris-Black, 2004; Chilton, 2004; Koller, 2004; Musolff, 2004). Force-dynamics, however, has not been addressed anywhere in CDA, including in the Cognitive Linguistic approach.

In the following sections, I introduce the theory of Force-Dynamics and show how this concept-structuring system operates ideologically in discourse on immigration. Examples are all taken from a corpus of newspaper articles on immigration and asylum published in the UK between 2000 and 2006.[7]

Force-Dynamics

In relation to the typology in Table 1, force-dynamics is based on a fourth general cognitive process, Gestalt psychology, and serves in the realization of identification, framing and positioning strategies. Gestalt construal operations impose image-schematic representations on the entity, relation or event cognized in order to constitute our experience of its basic structural configuration (Croft and Cruse, 2004: 63). Image schemas are abstract, holistic knowledge structures which emerge as distillations from repeated patterns of experience in our earliest interactions/observations within basic domains like SPACE, GEOMETRY, ACTION and FORCE (Johnson, 1987: 29). They come to form the foundations of our conceptual system and can be called upon in conceptualization. Image schemas serve to both connect and demarcate phenomena so that we can construe the world, and crucially can reason about it, in terms of whole, discrete schematic constructs. Image schemas are not specific images, then, but idealized, schematic structures, which represent the bare essence of their instantiations. They include, for example, a DISTANCE/PROXIMITY schema, a CONTAINER schema, various ACTION-CHAIN schemas and a whole set of FORCE-DYNAMIC schemas.[8]

Force-dynamic schemas arise from the experience of pressure and motion. Unlike other construal operations, which are grounded in the visual modality, the force-dynamic system is grounded in somesthesia and kinaesthesia. Experience of force is ubiquitous. For example, all causal interaction requires the exertion of force, either as we act upon other objects or as we are acted upon by other objects (Johnson, 1987: 42). It is not surprising, therefore, that patterns in experiences of physical interaction should 'work their way up into our system of meaning' (1987: 42).

Force-dynamic schemas come to play a structuring role in our conceptualizations of physical interactions but, also, by metaphorical extension, social, psychological, political, legal and linguistic interactions. The force-dynamic system is a generalization that operates over concepts of 'causing', 'letting', 'helping' and 'hindering' (Talmy, 2000: 409). It concerns the way in which objects are conceived to interact with respect to the exertion of force, resistance to force, the overcoming of such resistance, barriers to the exertion of force and the removal of such barriers (Talmy, 2000: 219). It ought to be apparent, then, that the force-dynamic system might function in discourse surrounding immigration. And, indeed, as reflected in and reified by particular representations in text, the force-dynamic system does seem to be constitutive of conceptualizations of immigration, both of the physical process of migration itself and also legal and political processes like amnesty, application and appeal. Immigration issues, however, need not necessarily be construed in terms of force interactions. That is, the force-dynamic system need not be invoked in their conceptualization.[9] Any force-dynamic representation in discourse on immigration is therefore inherently ideological. To illustrate this, consider the contrast between (1) and (2):

(1) The *Mirror*, 10 May 2002

It's estimated that between 1,000 and 1,200 asylum seekers are coming into the country every month.

(2) *Sunday Telegraph*, 28 July 2002

As asylum seekers **continue to** arrive in Britain at the rate of 1,500 a week, the number of camps may eventually rise to 20.

In (1) immigration is construed as force-dynamically neutral. The process of migration is represented as one of straightforward motion. There is no hindrance to the motion and no causation behind it. Hence, there is only one participant, the grammatical subject 'between 1,000 and 1,200 asylum seekers', and no force interaction. By contrast, in (2) there is a second, implicit participant. The use of *continue to* suggests the presence either of some causative force compelling the subject participant to migrate to Britain or some barrier to the process of migration, in spite of which asylum seekers are still able to arrive in Britain. The two different construals are made explicit in (3) and (4) respectively. In (3) desperation, conceived of as a psychological 'pressure', acts as a force compelling refugees to migrate to Britain. In (4) a raft of reforms presents a barrier to the process of immigration but asylum numbers nevertheless continue to increase.

(3) The *Express*, 6 November 2002

Critics believe they [refugees] will **continue to** attempt the journey even now, **because** they are desperate to enter the UK.

(4) *Daily Telegraph*, 8 October 2002

But after watching asylum numbers **continue to** rise **despite** a raft of reforms, Mr Blunkett yesterday resurrected the idea . . .

There are various other adverbial 'indicators' or 'facilitators' of force-interactive conceptualizations. For example, consider *keep on* in (5) and *still* in (6):

(5) *Daily Mail*, 11 November 2002

Calais crisis as asylum seekers **keep on** coming.

(6) *Daily Mail*, 1 March 2003

And from Calais, of course, they [asylum seekers] are **still** coming.

Force-interactive construals, then, are prompted by closed class elements like conjunctions (e.g. *because, despite*) which specify the role and relative strength of an opposing participant to the one encoded as subject, and semi-closed class elements such as certain adverbials which indicate force-dynamic opposition in general (Talmy, 2000: 416).[10] Force-interactive construals are also expressed by open class lexical elements, which, as a result, are brought into systematic relationships with one another inside an order of discourse. These 'force-dynamic indicators', then, when they appear in text, reflect the text-producer's construal of the scene as a force interaction and prompt for the textconsumer to conceptualize the scene in the same way, with various ideological consequences. They can therefore usefully add to the inventory of linguistic categories analysed in CDA.

In Talmy's (2000) terminology, the two participants or 'force-interacting entities' in force-dynamic construals are referred to as Agonist (Ago) and Antagonist (Ant).[11] In the force-dynamics system, the Agonist is 'the entity whose circumstance is at issue' (Talmy, 2000: 415). In (3) the Agonists are the asylum seekers. Agonists have an 'intrinsic force tendency' toward action (including motion) or rest and are subject to force interactions of various kinds with the Antagonist. In (3) the Antagonist is a raft of reforms which acts upon the Agonist to hinder the process of immigration.[12] Depending on the perceived relative strengths of Ant and Ago, the Agonist is represented as either realizing its intrinsic force tendency or not in a 'resultant of force inter-action'. Talmy uses the diagrammatic notation in Figure 1 to represent the various elements which make up the force-dynamic system.[13]

This 'grammar' gives rise to various force-dynamic schemas which, alongside other idealized cognitive models, can be called upon to structure

(a)	Force entities	(b)	Intrinsic force tendency
	Agonist (Ago): ◯		toward action: >
	Antagonist (Ant): ⌐|		toward rest: ●
(c)	Balance of strengths	(d)	Resultant of force interaction
	stronger entity: +		action: ⟶⟩⟶
	weaker entity: –		rest: ⟶●⟶

Figure 1: Elements of force-dynamics

our conceptualization of situations and events. Conceptualizing immigration as a force interaction is in the first place ideological since, as demonstrated in the contrast between (1) and (2), a force-dynamic representation is only one available construal. The same material process can be represented either as a force interaction or as force-dynamically neutral. Imposing a forceinteractive construal is further ideological, because in doing so a set of 'entailments' are carried forward which can serve to realize particular discursive strategies. Entailments in this sense are defined as 'implications of the internal structure of image schemata' (Johnson, 1987: 22). Image schemas are especially important ideologically, then, because they 'constrain and limit meaning as well as patterns of inference in our reasoning' (1987: 42).

Recall that image schemas are holistic. They have an 'internal logic' which is imparted as a whole when they are apprehended to conceptualize a given scene. The structural configuration strategy of force-dynamics in immigration discourse entails that (i) immigration is framed as a physical, perhaps violent, interaction invoking a 'struggle', and (ii) that the actors encoded as Ant and Ago are positioned in opposition to one and other. Within the force-dynamics system, there is then a further 'ideological dimension in the text-producer's decision as to which participant a role is assigned' (Wolf and Polzenhagen, 2003: 265). Realizing an identification strategy of role assignment, immigrants and asylum seekers are, of course, routinely cast in the role of Agonist. This has the consequent effect of framing immigrants and asylum seekers as instigators of force interactions.

We now turn to the force-interactive schemas invoked in anti-immigration discourse. Following Talmy (2000), force schemas can be organized into two categories: 'steady-state opposition' schemas and 'shift-in-state of opposition' schemas.

Force-Interactive Patterns in Immigration Discourse

Steady-State Opposition Schemas

The steady-state schemas are given in Figure 2. These constitute a natural set in so far as they involve an 'extended' force relation between Ant and Ago. Within the set, as Talmy points out, relations between pairs can be seen. For example, the patterns in (a) and (b) are of a 'despite' type in which the Ago realizes its intrinsic force tendency in spite of some force enacted upon it: either by continuing to move (a) or by continuing to stay in place (b). In contrast, (c) and (d) are both of a 'causative' kind in which the Ago is unable to realize its intrinsic force tendency: either because it is caused to come to a halt (c) or because it is caused to move (d).

Perhaps the most ubiquitous schemas to be found in anti-immigration discourse are the 'despite' types modelled in Figure 2(a) and (b). The schema in 2(a), which arises from our experience of overcoming obstacles, is of a

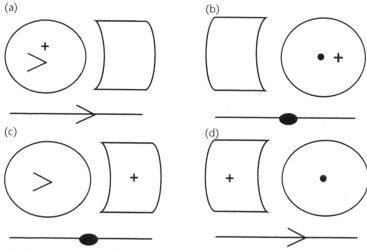

Figure 2: Steady-state opposition schemas

'hindrance' relation between Ant and Ago. This is the schema invoked to conceptualize the scene in (4). However, consider two further examples:

(7) *Daily Telegraph*, 21 May 2000

Downing Street acknowledge that illegal immigration was an issue because of growing frustrations over [the stream of people $_{AGO}$] **getting into Britain** from France through the channel tunnel.

(8) *Sunday Times*, 4 September 2005

[Illegal immigrants $_{AGO}$] are **getting into Britain** by enrolling on university degrees, obtaining visas to stay for the length of their courses and then failing to turn up to study.

Although *getting* appears relatively neutral in comparison to more emotive verbs often analysed in the same construction, such as 'flooding' (Gabrielatos and Baker, 2008), a force-dynamic analysis reveals the ideological properties of this verb. *Getting* implies the presence of some physical or legal barrier which the Ago is able to negotiate in order to realize its intrinsic force tendency. In (7) this is an implied physical barrier in the form of border control. In (8) this is an implied legal hurdle which immigrants overcome by exploiting some 'loop-hole' in the law. The construal encoded in (7) and (8) therefore also involves the force-dynamic schema given in Figure 2(a).[14] The Ago has an intrinsic force tendency toward action which is hindered by the Ant. However, the Ago is the stronger of the two entities and the resultant of force interaction is still action. The schema in Figure 2(a) entails that immigration is construed as a process not currently under control and that immigrants are presented as persistent beings able to penetrate our 'protective' barriers, thus realizing a spatial deictic positioning strategy of proximization. In proximization (see Cap, 2006), an entity construed as negative-Other is presented as 'closing in' on the entity, which includes the text-consumer, construed as positive-Self.

The 'despite' type in Figure 2(b) is of a 'resistance' relation held between Ago and Ant. The Ago has an intrinsic tendency toward rest but is subject to a compelling force toward motion enacted upon it by the Ant. In this conceptualization, the Ago is again presented as the stronger of the two entities and therefore able to realize its intrinsic force tendency, this time toward rest. The Ago remains in place in spite of the force exerted upon it by the Ant. The representations in (9) and (10) both activate this schema.

(9) The *Sun*, 31 June 2001

[About 20,000 illegal immigrants $_{AGO}$] **remain** in Britain **despite** [a Government pledge to crack down on them $_{ANT}$].

(10) *Daily Telegraph*, 1 February 2001

. . . it seems likely that [most $_{AGO}$] **stay on** indefinitely **despite** having been [told to go $_{ANT}$] – thus making a comprehensive mockery of the whole sorry business.

Verb choices *remain* and *stay on* in the main clause mark a force-interactive construal with the role of the Ant as the weaker entity expressed by the conjunction *despite*. The current location of the Ago is in spite of some force from an Ant attempting unsuccessfully to move (or remove) it. In both cases, the Ant is explicitly spelled out in the subordinate clause as the illocutionary force of a speech act. Imposing this schema on the scene entails that immigrants are conceptualized as stubborn, irremovable objects.

The schema in 2(a) is counterposed by the schema in 2(c) which is constitutive of our concept of prevention and is thus clearly integral to anti-immigration discourse. In contrast to 2(a), the schema in 2(c) involves an Ant as the stronger of the two entities able to prevent the Ago from realizing its intrinsic force tendency toward motion. The schema is invoked in examples such as (11) and (12).

(11) *Sunday Mirror*, 7 July 2002

The spokesman said [two GNIB members based in Amsterdam's Schiphol Airport for a month $_{ANT}$] had resulted in . . . [a significant number of illegal immigrants $_{AGO}$] being **blocked**.

(12) *Mail on Sunday*, 22 September 2002

[About 200 people $_{AGO}$] have been **stopped** by [French police $_{ANT}$] at the Channel Tunnel in the past 18 months . . .

The verbs *block* and *stop* indicate a physical force encounter between the two entities encoded as Ant and Ago. The semantics of the verbs specify the role of a stronger Ant, which in both examples is made explicit. This is in contrast to *get* in (7) and (8), the semantics of which specify the role of a weaker Ant. Crucially, though, in apprehending both schemas 2(a) and 2(c) immigrants are construed in a negative way as inherently forceful actors. Immigration is conceptualized in terms of a 'force vector' whose 'terminal point', where the impact of the force will be felt, unless otherwise abated, is Britain (the 'landmark' in Cognitive Grammar).

Conceptualizations of immigration based on the three schemas discussed so far fail to take into account the causes or motivations of migration. By not representing the causal nature of immigration, the text-producer presents immigrants as the source of the force vector and ignores the motives for migration in the first place. There is therefore an ideological dimension in choosing whether or not to designate the antecedent in a chain of causal interaction.

The schema invoked in conceptualizing the causes of immigration is the one depicted in 2(d). This schema counterposes the one in Figure 2(b). Like the schema in 2(b), it involves an Ago with an intrinsic tendency toward rest. And the Ago is similarly subject to a compelling force enacted upon it by an Ant. However, the schema in 2(d) captures an extended causative relation which is manifested in the fact that the Ago is unable to realize its intrinsic tendency and is instead compelled toward movement. The embodied basis of this schema lies in our experience of things (including ourselves) being driven or drawn by some external physical force.

As we have suggested, though, force-interactive construals are not restricted to the physical domain but extend to the intra-psychological domain incorporating drives and desires as metaphorical force interactions. Representations which recognize the causes compelling individuals toward migration can focus on either 'push' or 'pull' factors.[15]

Push factors include the desire to escape poverty or persecution. Representations which distinguish push factors tend to be more sympathetic toward the plight of immigrants and asylum seekers. Anti-immigration discourse more typically focuses on pull factors such as work or welfare which supposedly act as 'magnetic' forces on immigrants/asylum seekers. Consider (13) and (14), in which the force-interactive construal is indicated by *drawn* and *lure* and the role of the stronger Ant is indicated by *because*.

(13) *Daily Mail*, 21 May 2003

[Asylum seekers ᴀɢᴏ] are **drawn** to the UK **because** [it is so easy to work here illegally ᴀɴᴛ], the head of a Leftwing think-tank warned yesterday.

(14) *Mail on Sunday*, 25 March 2001

There have been claims that [the Romanians ᴀɢᴏ] had travelled to Britain again **because** of the **lure** of [free housing and benefits given to their relatives in Britain ᴀɴᴛ].

The construal in (13) and (14) is of an Ago with an intrinsic tendency toward rest but which is acted upon by the stronger Ant whose compelling force the Ago is unable to resist, and the resultant of force interaction is action. Note, then, that although the Ago is not construed as intrinsically forceful, as in 2(a) and 2(c) its caused action is still construed in terms of a force vector with a trajectory toward Britain.

Shift-in-State of Opposition Schemas

In addition to the four steady-state schemas, there are four shift-in-state of opposition schemas invoked in anti-immigration discourse. These schemas capture changes in time to the condition of the Ant which effect a change in the force tendency of the Ago. In contrast to the steady-state schemas, shift-in-state of opposition schemas are dynamic and involve 'onset' causation or letting. The four shift-in-state of opposition schemas are represented in Figure 3. Of these, (e) and (f) are of an onset 'letting' type where a stronger Ant previously in place leaves its state of impingement, thus allowing the weaker Ago to realize its intrinsic tendency either toward action (e) or rest (f). The patterns in (g) and (h) are both of an onset 'causation' type, in which a stronger Ant not previously in place comes into position against a weaker Ago to prevent it from realizing its intrinsic tendency: either by causing it to move (g) or by causing it to come to a halt (h).

Perhaps the most common shift-in-state of opposition schemas to be found in antiimmigration discourse are the ones depicted in (e) and (f),

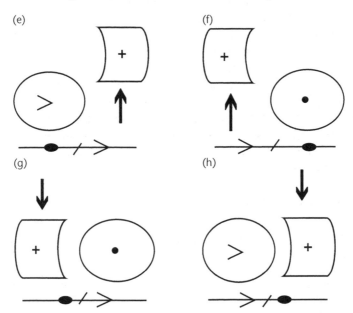

Figure 3: Shift-in-state of opposition schemas

which underpin the concept of permission in general. The schema in (e) constitutes the prototypical concept of permission, onset letting of motion, and is invoked in (15) and (16):

(15) The *Express*, 26 July 2001

Meanwhile, experts predict an appeal court ruling will **let** [hundreds more people $_{AGO}$] into Britain.

(16) *Daily Mail*, April 10 2003

The low-skilled migration programme, starting in May with a quota of 10,000 migrants each for the food processing and hospitality sectors, will **allow** [many who might otherwise try to come to the UK as asylum seekers $_{AGO}$] to enter legally with work permits.

In both examples, notice that the Ago now appears as the direct object of the relevant verb, the force-dynamic indicator, the semantics of which suggest the role of a stronger Ant previously in place preventing the Ago from realizing its intrinsic tendency toward motion. However, the Ant disengages, thereby releasing the Ago to manifest its tendency. In each example, the Ant is left implicit. But it can be taken as a change in law brought about by precedent in (15) or policy in (16). The image invoked in these examples, then, is one in which a forceful entity previously kept in check is allowed through as the barrier is removed. Such a conceptualization invites the inference that the force behind the barrier will have been building in pressure and its release will therefore result in a force of increased intensity. The available inference is made explicit in (17) and (18):

(17) *Daily Mail*, 28 December 2005

Asylum crisis as amnesty deal for 15,000 turns into **stampede** (headline).

(18) The *Express*, 22 May 2004

The ruling **opens the floodgates** for 666 asylum seekers to claim they have been treated inhumanely.

The schema in Figure 3(f) constitutes the less prototypical concept of permission, onset letting of rest. Although more peripheral in most contexts, this schema is frequently invoked in anti-immigration discourse. Consider (19) and (20) by way of example:

(19) The *Express*, 9 December 2005

Any day now the Government will decide that, with the numbers of failed asylum seekers still here continuing to rise, the only way to solve the problem is to give yet another 'final' amnesty. This will **enable** [every one of them $_{AGO}$] to **stay . . .**

(20) *Sunday Mirror*, 21 May 2006

A Crown Court judge has **allowed** [Ling Cheng, 34 $_{AGO}$], to **stay** in Britain indefinitely. Ling was ordered to leave the country by magistrates in Redhill, Surrey, eight months ago when they jailed him for selling pirate DVDs.

In these examples, the verbs *enable* and *allow* again encode the role of a stronger Ant previously in place, preventing the Ago in the object from realizing its intrinsic force tendency but which disengages, thereby allowing the Ago to manifest its 'natural' tendency. Indicated by *stay* in both (19) and (20), however, the Ago's intrinsic tendency is this time toward rest rather than motion. The stronger Ant is once again left implicit, but can be taken as a previous legal 'force' which would have resulted in the Ago's removal but which has been suspended or superseded, allowing the Ago to remain in Britain.

The schemas in Figure 3(g) and 3(h) counterpose those given as 3(f) and 3(e) respectively. In 3(g) and 3(h), a stronger Ant not previously in place comes into position against an Ago and thereby prevents it from realizing its intrinsic force tendency. Thus, in both 3(f) and 3(g), the Ago has an intrinsic tendency toward rest, but in 3(g) the Ago becomes blocked from realizing this tendency whereas in 3(f) it is released and so able to manifest its intrinsic tendency. In 3(e) and 3(h), the Ago has an intrinsic force tendency toward motion which is blocked in 3(h) but is allowed to manifest itself in 3(e). These two schemas (3g and 3h) operate over concepts of prevention rather than permission, then, and tend to be invoked in immigration discourse by statements concerning the deportation of immigrants or the prevention of entrance in the first place. In (21) and (22), for example, we see a stronger Ant coming into place, causing the Ago with an intrinsic tendency toward rest to go from a stationary state to one of movement. The force-interactive construal in both examples is prompted by the verb *remove,* which codes the role of an Ant as the stronger of two force entities and suggests resistance on the part of the Ago.[16]

(21) *The Guardian*, 13 August 2001

In the last financial year only 8,000 asylum seekers were removed, but [a change in resources $_{ANT}$] is now feeding through, meaning [large numbers of asylum seekers $_{AGO}$] will start to be **removed** by late autumn.

(22) The *Mirror*, 19 April 2000

'[The policy $_{ANT}$] will allow [people who are refused $_{AGO}$] to be **removed** quickly from this country' (quoting Opposition Leader William Hague).

In (23) and (24), by contrast, we see a stronger Ant coming into place (through a tightening of security in [23] and a tightening of the law in [24]) to block the Ago, which is construed as having an intrinsic tendency toward motion, from continuing on its intended trajectory. The force-interactive

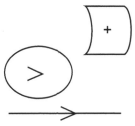

Figure 4: Secondary steady-state schema

construal and the role of the Ant as the stronger entity is marked by *stop* in (23) and *prevent* in (24).

(23) *Daily Mail*, 28 November 2003

(The Home Secretary) pointed to [tighter security at French ports-ₐₙₜ] which has **stopped** [6,300 illegal immigrants_AGO] from crossing the Channel so far this year.

(24) *The Independent*, 14 January 2000

It (the Home Office) says [the law _ANT_] has been tightened to **prevent** [bogus asylum claims _AGO_]

There is one final schema worth discussing in relation to the shift-in-state of opposition schema depicted in Figure 3(h). This is the 'secondary' steady-state schema modelled in Figure 4.

From Figure 3, it is possible to characterize the concept of permission as involving the cessation of impingement and the concept of prevention as involving its implementation. The schema in Figure 4 represents the non-occurrence of impingement but its presupposed potential. That is, the schema in Figure 4 presupposes the possibility for the event schematized in Figure 3(h) resulting in the state of affairs schematized in Figure 2(c). The pattern in Figure 4 is considered as 'secondary', then, because according to Talmy (2000: 421) it is conceptually derived from the negation of the schema in Figure 2(c). A force-dynamic construal inherently involves an Ant and an Ago engaged in a force interaction. Any reference (implicit or explicit) to an Ant and Ago not so engaged depends on their potential to be so engaged (2000: 421). And if the schema in Figure 4 presupposes those in 3(h) and 2(c), then it is also *presupposed by* the event schematized in 3(e). The schema in 3(e) represents 'onset' letting of motion. The schema in Figure 4, however, represents 'extended' letting of motion and is invoked in (25) and (26):

(25) The *Sun*, 20 February 2004

BNP chief Mr Griffin later accused Mr Howard of playing the 'typical Tory con trick' by talking tough on asylum while **still letting** [immigrants _AGO_] in.

(26) The *Express*, 30 August 2005

I find it absurd that, given the security fears since 9/11, we are **still let-ting** [immigrants ₐₒₒ] into this country without interviewing them.

In both examples, the force interaction is indicated by *let* and the extended nature of the force-dynamic relation is marked by the adverbial particle *still*, which carries the implicature 'despite some compelling reason not to'.

Concluding Remarks

Hopefully, I have been able to demonstrate that, and how, force-interactive patterns feature in discourse on immigration to structure our conceptualizations of both physical and political/legal interactions in this domain. These schemas are invoked in *discourse on immigration*, then, and through repeated patterns of representation and processes of entrenchment can come to constitute, alongside other idealized cognitive models, *the discourse of immigration* (see Hart, 2010). Force-interactive patterns are prompted by elements in text including certain adverbials, prepositions and various open class elements which seem to have inherent in their conceptual representation a force-dynamic component.

The force-dynamic analyses we have presented reveal the ideological potential of force-dynamic conceptualizations in immigration discourse. The Cognitive Linguistic approach we have taken can therefore add to the armoury of CDA with force-dynamic indicators one further target on the analyst's hit list.

As will be clear from the analyses above, the force-dynamics system is in many respects similar to transitivity. For example, force-dynamics concerns the kind of process designated in the clause, i.e. whether or not a process is conceived as a force interaction, and in which interactional roles particular actors are cast. Force-dynamic conceptualizations therefore realize strategies of identification and framing, as well as positioning. As with transitivity, the force-dynamic system has the facility to analyse the same situation from one perspective or another and so is inherently ideological. However, the major contribution that the theory of force-dynamics can make is that it allows us to address the conceptual import of transitivity choices at the interpretation stage of CDA, something which we have suggested is currently under-researched but fundamental to the claims of CDA.

Notes

1. I make no claims to completeness here. There may of course be further force schemas which feature in immigration discourse. Similarly, my examples do not exhaust all of the occurrences of a particular force schema in the corpus from which they have been selected.

2. 'Ideology' is understood throughout as a particular representation of reality or view of the world (Hodge and Kress, 1993: 15).
3. Cognitive Linguistics emerged in the late 1970s in opposition to generative grammar and formal semantics.
4. This last claim, of course, is in line with systemic functional linguistics in which Halliday (1973: 106) states that 'language lends structure to . . . experience and helps determine . . . way[s] of looking at things'.
5. Several alternative typologies of discursive strategies have also been proposed (e.g. Chilton, 2004; Chilton and Schäffner, 1997; Reisigl and Wodak, 2001). Discursive strategies are more or less intentional or institutional plans of practices, including linguistic practices, the adoption of which may have ideological effects (Reisigl and Wodak, 2001).
6. Deictic positioning can, of course, be social, spatial or temporal (see Levinson, 1983).
7. During this period, the European Union expanded twice and two UK General Elections were held. Largely fuelled by the media, the 2005 General Election was heavily focused on the issue of immigration, and extreme right-wing parties like the UK Independence Party and the British National Party gained significant ground.
8. See Croft and Cruse (2004: 45) for a more complete inventory of image schemas.
9. Since immigration is not necessarily construed as a force interaction, all of our examples can be said to instantiate a conceptual metaphor IMMIGRATION AS FORCE INTERACTION in the discourse of immigration. Many other conceptual metaphors constructed through discourse on immigration also contain a force-dynamic element. See, for example, those that construe immigration in terms of WAR or WATER (Charteris-Black, 2006; Dervinytė, 2009; El Refaie, 2001; Hart, 2010; Santa Ana, 2002). We may thus characterize these conceptual metaphors as more specific variants of the general scheme identified as IMMIGRATION AS FORCE INTERACTION, which operates as a 'conceptual key' – a higher-level metaphor that explains how several conceptual metaphors are related (Charteris-Black, 2004: 16).
10. Talmy (2000: 417) treats 'keep' as an honorary auxiliary.
11. These roles should not be confused with the standard participant role categories of Agent and Patient or Trajector and Landmark in Cognitive Grammar.
12. The Antagonist, as in (2), need not be explicitly referred to.
13. See Johnson (1987) for an alternative notation.
14. Note that diagrams such as those in Figure 2 should not be identified as image schemas per se, but are intended only as representations of them (Langacker, 2008: 32). The same schema with the same structural properties and entailments can be represented in alternative ways (cf. Johnson, 1987).
15. Note that laterality is irrelevant in the force-dynamic system (Talmy, 2000: 414) and that in either case the same image schema applies.
16. In this particular example, notice that the dynamic nature of the Ant's oppositional state is marked explicitly by 'is now feeding through', and the onset nature of causation is marked by 'start to'.

References

Cap, P. (2006) *Legitimization in Political Discourse*. Newcastle: Cambridge Scholars Press.
Charteris-Black, J. (2004) *Corpus Approaches to Critical Metaphor Analysis*. Basingstoke: Palgrave Macmillan.
Charteris-Black, J. (2006) 'Britain as a Container: Immigration Metaphors in the 2005 Election Campaign', *Discourse & Society* 17(6): 563–82.
Chilton, P. (2004) *Analysing Political Discourse: Theory and Practice*. London: Routledge.

Chilton, P. and Schäffner, C. (1997) 'Discourse and Politics', in T.A.van Dijk (ed.) *Discourse as Social Interaction*, pp. 206–30. London: SAGE.

Croft, W. and Cruse, D.A. (2004) *Cognitive Linguistics*. Cambridge: Cambridge University Press.

Dervinyté, I. (2009) 'Conceptual Emigration and Immigration Metaphors in the Language of the Press: A Contrastive Analysis', *Studies about Languages* 14: 49–55.

El Refaie, E. (2001) 'Metaphors We Discriminate by: Naturalized Themes in Austrian Newspaper Articles about Asylum Seekers', *Journal of Sociolinguistics* 5(3): 352–71.

Fairclough, N. (1995) *Critical Discourse Analysis: The Critical Study of Language*. London: Longman.

Fauconnier, G. (1994) *Mental Spaces: Aspects of Meaning Construction in Natural Language*, 2nd edn. Cambridge: Cambridge University Press.

Fauconnier, G. (2006) 'Cognitive Linguistics', in *Encyclopaedia of Cognitive Science*. Oxford: Wiley.

Fillmore, C. (1982) 'Frame Semantics', in Linguistics Society of Korea (eds) *Linguistics in the Morning Calm*, pp. 111–37. Seoul: Hanshin Publishing Co.

Fowler, R. (1991) *Language in the News: Discourse and Ideology in the Press*. London: Routledge.

Fowler, R. (1996) 'On Critical Linguistics', in C.R. Caldas-Coulthard and M. Coulthard (eds) *Texts and Practices*, pp. 3–14. London: Routledge.

Fowler, R., Hodge, R., Kress, G. and Trew, T. (1979) *Language and Control*. London: Routledge and Kegan Paul.

Gabrielatos, C. and Baker, P. (2008) 'Fleeing, Sneaking, Flooding: A Corpus Analysis of Discursive Constructions of Refugees and Asylum Seekers in the UK Press 1996–2005', *Journal of English Linguistics* 36(1): 5–38.

Halliday, M.A.K. (1973) *Explorations in the Functions of Language*. London: Edward Arnold.

Hart, C. (2010) *Critical Discourse Analysis and Cognitive Science: New Perspectives on Immigration Discourse*. Basingstoke: Palgrave Macmillan.

Hart, C. (ed.) (in press a) *Critical Discourse Studies in Context and Cognition*. Amsterdam: John Benjamins.

Hart, C. (in press b) 'Moving Beyond Metaphor in the Cognitive Linguistics Approach to CDA: Construal Operations in Immigration Discourse', in C. Hart (ed.) *Critical Discourse Studies in Context and Cognition*. Amsterdam: John Benjamins.

Hart, C. and D. Lukeš (eds) (2007) *Cognitive Linguistics in Critical Discourse Analysis: Application and Theory*. Newcastle: Cambridge Scholars Publishing.

Hodge, R. and Kress, G. (1993) *Language as Ideology*, 2nd edn. London: Routledge.

Johnson, M. (1987) *The Body in the Mind: The Bodily Basis of Meaning, Imagination, and Reason*. Chicago: University of Chicago Press.

Koller, V. (2004) *Metaphor and Gender in Business Media Discourse: A Critical Cognitive Study*. Basingstoke: Palgrave Macmillan.

Kress, G. and Hodge, R. (1979) *Language as Ideology*. London: Routledge and Kegan Paul.

Lakoff, G. and Johnson, M. (1980) *Metaphors we Live by*. Chicago, IL: University of Chicago Press.

Langacker, R.W. (1987) *Foundations of Cognitive Grammar, Vol. I: Theoretical Prerequisites*. Stanford, CA: Stanford University Press.

Langacker, R.W. (1991) *Foundations of Cognitive Grammar, Vol. II: Descriptive Application*. Stanford, CA: Stanford University Press.

Langacker, R. (2008) *Cognitive Grammar: A Basic Introduction*. Oxford: Oxford University Press.

Levinson, S.C. (1983) *Pragmatics*. Cambridge: Cambridge University Press.

Musolff, A. (2004) *Metaphor and Political Discourse: Analogical Reasoning in Debates about Europe.* Basingstoke: Palgrave Macmillan.

O'Halloran, K. (2003) *Critical Discourse Analysis and Language Cognition.* Edinburgh: Edinburgh University Press.

Reisigl, M. and R. Wodak (2001) *Discourse and Discrimination: Rhetorics of Racism and Antisemitism.* London: Routledge.

Santa Ana, O. (2002) *Brown Tide Rising: Metaphors of Latinos in Contemporary American Public Discourse.* Austin, TX: University of Texas Press.

Talmy, L. (1988) 'Force Dynamics in Language and Cognition', *Cognitive Science* 12: 49–100.

Talmy, L. (2000) *Toward a Cognitive Semantics.* Cambridge, MA: MIT Press.

Van Dijk, T.A. (1997) 'Political Discourse and Racism: Describing Others in Western Parliaments', in S.H. Riggins (eds) *The Language and Politics of Exclusion: Others in Discourse,* pp. 31–64. Thousand Oaks, CA: SAGE.

Van Dijk, T.A. (2001) 'Multidisciplinary CDA: A Plea for Diversity', in R. Wodak and M. Meyer (eds) *Methods of Critical Discourse Analysis,* pp. 95–120. London: SAGE.

Van Dijk, T.A. (2002) 'Ideology: Political Discourse and Cognition', in P. Chilton and C. Schäffner (eds) *Politics as Text and Talk: Analytic Approaches to Political Discourse,* pp. 203–38. Amsterdam: John Benjamins.

Widdowson, H.G. (2004) *Text, Context, Pretext: Critical Issues in Discourse Analysis.* Oxford: Blackwell.

Wolf, H.-G. and Polzenhagen, F. (2003) 'Conceptual Metaphor as Ideological Stylistic Means: An Exemplary Analysis', in R. Dirven, R. Frank and M. Putz (eds) *Cognitive Models in Language and Thought: Ideology, Metaphors and Meanings,* pp. 247–76. Berlin: Mouton de Gruyter.

57

Critical Semiotic Analysis and Cultural Political Economy

Bob Jessop

This article seeks to redirect the cultural turn(s) in economic and political investigation by making a case for cultural political economy (CPE; see Jessop & Sum, 2001).[1] This combines concepts and tools from critical semiotic analysis and from critical political economy to produce a distinctive post-disciplinary approach to capitalist social formations. CPE differs from other cultural turns in part through its concern with the key mechanisms that determine the co-evolution of the semiotic and extra-semiotic aspects of political economy. These mechanisms are mediated through the general features of semiosis as well as the particular forms and institutional dynamics of capitalism. Combining these general and particular mediations prompts two lines of investigation. First, given the infinity of possible meaningful communications and (mis)understandings enabled by semiosis, how do extra-semiotic as well as semiotic factors affect the variation, selection, and retention of semiosis and its associated practices in ordering, reproducing and transforming capitalist social formations? And, second, given the contradictions, dilemmas, indeterminacy, and overall improbability of capitalist reproduction, especially during its recurrent crises, what role does semiosis play in construing, constructing, and temporarily stabilizing capitalist social formations? Before proceeding, I should note that analogous approaches could be developed for non-capitalist regimes by combining critical semiotic analysis with concepts suited to their respective economic forms and institutional dynamics.

Source: *Critical Discourse Studies*, 1(2) (2004): 159–174.

In making a case for CPE, I first present some ontological, epistemological, and methodological claims about critical semiotic analysis and critical political economy together with some substantive claims about the role of semiotic practices in constructing as well as construing economic objects and subjects. A second set of arguments concerns the interaction of the semiotic and extra-semiotic in constituting and reproducing agency and structure. This approach is illustrated from the rise of the knowledge-based economy (KBE) as a provisional, partial, and unstable semiotic-material solution to the crisis of Atlantic Fordism. This reveals how semiosis, especially in struggles over accumulation strategies, state projects, and hegemonic visions, contributes to the rise of functioning post-Fordist economies and, in turn, how material preconditions are involved in selecting and consolidating KBE discourses. I conclude with some general remarks on CPE and cultural studies.

On Cultural Political Economy

Three features make CPE distinctive theoretically. First, along with other currents in evolutionary and institutional political economy and in contrast to generic studies on semiosis, CPE opposes transhistorical analyses, insisting that both history and institutions matter in economic and political dynamics. Second, in contrast to other currents in evolutionary and institutional political economy but in common with other variants of cultural materialism, it takes the cultural turn seriously, highlighting the complex relations between meanings and practices. And, third, as opposed to either tradition considered separately, it combines evolutionary and institutional political economy with the cultural turn. It explores these complex relations in terms of three generic evolutionary mechanisms: variation, selection, and retention (Campbell, 1969). This is reflected in its concern with the co-evolution of semiotic and extra-semiotic processes and their conjoint impact in the constitution of capitalist social formations. This general approach can be re-stated in terms of four broad claims.

Ontologically, CPE claims that semiosis contributes to the overall constitution of specific social objects and social subjects and, a fortiori, to their co-constitution and co-evolution in wider ensembles of social relations. Orthodox political economy tends to naturalize or reify its theoretical objects (such as land, machines, the division of labour, money, commodities, the information economy) and to offer impoverished accounts of how subjects and subjectivities are formed and how different modes of calculation emerge, come to be institutionalized, and get modified. In contrast, CPE views technical and economic objects as socially constructed, historically specific, more or less socially (dis)embedded in broader networks of social relations and institutional ensembles, more or less embodied (incorporated and embrained), and in need of continuing social "repair" work for their reproduction. Social construction involves material elements too, of course; but these can be articulated within limits in different ways through the intervention of semiotic practices. Analogous arguments apply to the state and politics (Jessop, 1990, 2002; Mitchell, 1991).

Epistemologically, CPE critiques the categories and methods typical of orthodox political economy and emphasizes the inevitable contextuality and historicity of the latter's claims to knowledge. It rejects any universalistic, positivist account of reality, denies the facticity of the subject-object duality, allows for the co-constitution of subjects and objects, and eschews reductionist approaches to economic analysis. But it also stresses the materiality of social relations and highlights the constraints involved in processes that operate "behind the backs" of the relevant agents. It is especially concerned with the structural properties and dynamics that result from such material interactions. It thereby escapes both the sociological imperialism of pure social constructionism and the voluntarist vacuity of certain lines of discourse analysis, which seem to imply that agents can will anything into existence in and through an appropriately articulated discourse. In short, CPE recognizes both the constitutive role of semiosis and the emergent extra-semiotic features of social relations and their conjoint impact on capacities for action and transformation.

Methodologically, CPE combines concepts and tools from critical semiotic analysis with those from critical political economy. The cultural turn includes approaches oriented to argumentation, narrativity, rhetoric, hermeneutics, identity, reflexivity, historicity, and discourse; here I use semiosis, that is, the intersubjective production of meaning, to cover them all.[2] For they all assume that semiosis is causally efficacious as well as meaningful and that actual events and processes and their emergent effects can not only be interpreted but also explained, at least in part, in terms of semiosis. Thus CPE examines the role of semiosis and semiotic practices not only in the continual (re-) making of social relations but also in the contingent emergence, provisional consolidation, and ongoing realization of their extra-semiotic properties.

Still arguing methodologically, just as there are variants of the cultural turn, political economy also has different currents. My own approach to CPE draws mainly on the Marxist tradition. This examines the specificity of the basic forms, contradictions, crisis-tendencies, and dilemmas of capitalism, their conditions of existence, and their potential impact on other social relations. However, in contrast to orthodox Marxism, which, like orthodox economics, tends to reify and essentialize the different moments of capital accumulation, treating them as objective forces, a Marxist-inspired CPE stresses their contingent and always tendential nature. For, if social phenomena are discursively constituted and never achieve a self-reproducing closure, isolated from other social phenomena, then any natural necessities (emergent properties) entailed in the internal relations of a given object must be tendential. Such properties would only be fully realized if that object were fully constituted and continually reproduced through appropriate discursive and social practices. This is inherently improbable: discursive relations are polysemic and heteroglossic, subjectivities are plural and changeable, and extra-semiotic properties are liable to material disturbances. For example, capitalist relations are always articulated with other production relations and are, at most, relatively dominant; moreover, their operation is always vulnerable to disruption through internal contradictions, the intrusion of relations anchored in other institutional orders and the lifeworld (civil society), and resistance rooted in conflicting interests, competing identities, and rival modes of calculation. The resulting threats to the formal and/or substantive unity of the capital relation mean that any tendencies inherent in capitalism are themselves tendential, that is, depend on the continuing reproduction of the capital relation itself. Combined with critical political economy, critical semiotic analysis offers much in exploring this doubly tendential dynamic (Jessop, 2001).

Substantively, at what orthodox economics misleadingly describes as the macro level, CPE distinguishes the "actually existing economy" as the chaotic sum of all economic activities (broadly defined as concerned with the social appropriation and transformation of nature for the purposes of material provisioning)[3] from the economy (or, better, economies in the plural) as an imaginatively narrated, more or less coherent subset of these activities. The totality of economic activities is so unstructured and complex that it cannot be an object of calculation, management, governance, or guidance. Instead such practices are always oriented to subsets of economic relations (economic systems or subsystems) that have been discursively and, perhaps, organizationally and institutionally fixed as objects of intervention. This involves "economic imaginaries" that rely on semiosis to constitute these subsets. Moreover, if they are to prove more than "arbitrary, rationalistic, and willed" (Gramsci, 1971, pp. 376–377), these imaginaries must have some significant, albeit necessarily partial, correspondence to real material interdependencies in the actually existing economy and/or in relations between economic and extra-economic activities. These subsets are always selectively defined – due both to limited cognitive capacities and to the discursive and material biases of specific epistemes and economic paradigms. They typically exclude elements – usually unintentionally – that are vital to the overall performance of the subset of economic (and extra-economic) relations that have been identified. Such exclusions limit in turn the efficacy of economic forecasting, management, planning, guidance, governance, and so on, because such practices do not (indeed, cannot) take account of excluded elements and their impact. Similar arguments would apply, with appropriate changes, to so-called meso or micro level economic phenomena, such as industrial districts or individual enterprises.

Imagined economies are discursively constituted and materially reproduced on many sites and scales, in different spatio-temporal contexts, and over various spatio-temporal horizons. They extend from one-off transactions through stable economic organizations, networks, and clusters to macro-economic regimes. While massive scope for variation typically exists at an individual transactional level, the medium- to long-term semiotic and material reproduction requirements of meso complexes and macro-economic regimes narrow this scope considerably. The recursive selection of semiotic practices and extra-semiotic processes at these scales tends to reduce inappropriate variation and to secure thereby the requisite variety (constrained heterogeneity rather than simple uniformity) that supports the structural coherence of economic activities. Indeed stable semiotic orders, discursive selectivities, social learning, path-dependencies, power relations, patterned complementarities, and material selectivities all become more significant, the more that material interdependencies and/or issues of spatial and inter-temporal articulation increase within and across diverse functional systems and the lifeworld. Yet this growing set of constraints also reveals the fragility and, indeed, improbability of the smooth reproduction of complex social orders. This highlights the importance of retaining an appropriate repertoire of semiotic and material resources and practices that can be flexibly and reflexively deployed in response to emerging disturbances and crises (Grabher, 1994; Jessop, 2003).

Economic imaginaries at the meso and macro levels develop as economic, political, and intellectual forces seek to (re)define specific subsets of economic activities as subjects, sites, and stakes of competition and/or as objects of regulation and to articulate strategies, projects and visions oriented to these imagined economies. Among the main forces involved in such efforts are political parties, think tanks, bodies such as the OECD and World Bank, organized interests such as business associations and trade unions, and social movements; the mass media are also crucial intermediaries in mobilizing elite and/or popular support behind competing imaginaries.[4] These forces tend to manipulate power and knowledge to secure recognition of the boundaries, geometries, temporalities, typical economic agents, tendencies and counter-tendencies, distinctive overall dynamic, and reproduction requirements of different imagined economies (Daly, 1994; Miller & Rose, 1993). They also seek to develop new structural and organizational forms that will help to institutionalize these boundaries, geometries, and temporalities in an appropriate spatio-temporal fix that can displace and/or defer capital's inherent contradictions and crisis-tendencies. However, by virtue of competing economic imaginaries, competing efforts to institute them materially, and an inevitable incompleteness in the specification of their respective economic and extra-economic preconditions, each imagined economy is only ever partially constituted. There are always interstitial, residual, marginal, irrelevant, recalcitrant and plain contradictory elements that escape any attempt to identify, govern, and stabilize a given economic arrangement or broader economic order (Jessop, 2002; Malpas & Wickham, 1995).

Nonetheless, relatively successful economic imaginaries do have their own, performative, constitutive force in the material world.[5] On the one hand, their operation presupposes a substratum of substantive economic relations and instrumentalities as their elements; on the other, where an imaginary is successfully operationalized and institutionalized, it transforms and naturalizes these elements and instrumentalities into the moments of a specific economy with specific emergent properties. For economic imaginaries identify, privilege, and seek to stabilize some economic activities from the totality of economic relations and transform them into objects of observation, calculation, and governance. Technologies of economic governance, operating sometimes more semiotically, sometimes more materially,[6] constitute their own objects of governance rather than emerging in order to, or operating with the effect that, they govern already pre-constituted objects (Jessop, 1990, 1997). The next section illustrates this with a case study of the KBE.

The Dialectic between Semiotic and Structural Selectivities

CPE is not only concerned with how texts produce meaning and thereby help to generate social structure but also how such production is constrained by emergent, non-semiotic features of social structure as well as by inherently semiotic factors. Although every social practice is semiotic (insofar as practices entail meaning), no social practice is reducible to semiosis. Semiosis is never a purely intra-semiotic matter without external reference and involves more than the play of differences among networks of signs. It cannot be understood without identifying and exploring the extra-semiotic conditions that make semiosis possible and secure its effectivity – this includes both the overall configuration of specific semiotic action contexts and the complexities of the natural and social world in which any and all semiosis occurs. This is the basis of the concept of the economic imaginary outlined above. For not only do economic imaginaries provide a semiotic frame for construing economic events but they also help to construct such events and their economic contexts.

The play of difference among signifiers could not be sustained without extensive embedding of semiosis in material practice, in the constraints and affordances of the material world. Although individual words or phrases do not have a one-to-one relation to the objects to which they refer, the world does still constrain language and ways of thinking. This occurs over time, if not at every point in time. Not all possible discursive construals can be durably constructed materially and attempts to realize them materially may have unintended effects (Sayer, 2000).[7] The relative success or failure of construals depends on how both they and any attempts at construction correspond to the properties of the materials (including social phenomena such as actors and institutions) used to construct social reality. This reinforces my earlier arguments about the dialectic of discursivity and materiality and the importance of both to an adequate account of the reproduction of political economies. It also provides the basis for thinking about semiosis in terms of variation, selection, and retention – since there is far greater scope for random variation in one-off construals than there is in construals that may facilitate enduring constructions. It is to the conditions shaping the selection and retention of construals that we now turn.

Social structuration and, a fortiori, the structuring of capitalist social formations, have three general semiotic aspects. First, semiotic conditions affect the differential reproduction and transformation of social groups, organizations, institutions, and other social phenomena. Second, they also affect the variation, selection and retention of the semiotic features of social phenomena. And third, semiotic innovation and emergence is a source of variation that feeds into social transformation. In short, semiosis can generate variation, have selective effects, and contribute to the differential retention and/ or institutionalization of social phenomena.

Taking for granted the general principles of critical semiotic analysis to focus on broader evolutionary and institutional issues in political economy, we can note that there is constant variation, witting or unwitting, in apparently routine social practices. This poses questions about the regularization of practices in normal conditions and about possible sources of radical transformation, especially in periods of crisis. The latter typically lead to profound cognitive and strategic disorientation of social forces and a corresponding proliferation in discursive interpretations and proposed material solutions. Nonetheless the same basic mechanisms serve to select and consolidate radically new practices and to stabilize routine practices. Simplifying the analysis of evolutionary mechanisms given in Fairclough, Jessop, and Sayer (2003) and extending it to include material as well as semiotic factors, these mechanisms can be said to comprise:

- Selection of particular discourses (the privileging of just some available, including emergent discourses) for interpreting events, legitimizing actions, and (perhaps self-reflexively) representing social phenomena. Semiotic factors operate here by influencing the resonance of discourses in personal, organizational, institutional, and broader meta-narrative terms and by limiting possible combinations of semiosis and semiotic practices in a given semiotic order. Material factors also operate here through conjunctural or institutionalized power relations, path-dependency, and structurally-inscribed selectivities.
- Retention of some resonant discourses (for example, inclusion in an actor's habitus, hexis, and personal identity, enactment in organizational routines, integrated into institutional rules, objectification in the built environment, material and intellectual technologies, and articulation into widely accepted accumulation strategies, state projects, or hegemonic visions). The greater the range of sites (horizontally and vertically)[8] in which resonant discourses are retained, the greater is the potential for effective institutionalization and integration into patterns of structured coherence and durable compromise. The constraining influences of

complex, reciprocal interdependences will also recursively affect the scope for retaining resonant discourses.

- Reinforcement insofar as procedural devices exist that privilege these discourses and their associated practices and also filter out contrary discourses and practices. This can involve both discursive selectivity (for example, genre chains, styles, identities) and material selectivity (for example, the privileging of certain dominant sites of discourse in and through structurally-inscribed strategic selectivities of specific organizational and institutional orders). Such mechanisms recursively strengthen appropriate genres, styles, and strategies and selectively eliminate inappropriate alternatives, and are most powerful where they operate across many sites in a social formation to promote complementary discourses within the wider social ensemble.
- Selective recruitment, inculcation, and retention by relevant social groups, organizations, institutions and so on, of social agents whose predispositions fit maximally with requirements the preceding requirements.

This list emphasizes the role of semiosis and its material supports in securing social reproduction through the selection and retention of mutually supportive discourses. Conversely, the absence or relative weakness of one or more of these semiotic and/or extra-semiotic conditions may undermine previously dominant discourses and/or block the selection and retention of appropriate innovative discourses. This absence or weakness is especially likely in periods of profound disorientation due to rapid social change and/or crises that trigger major semiotic and material innovations in the social world. We should perhaps note here that the semiotic and extra-semiotic space for variation, selection, and retention is contingent, not pre-given. This also holds for the various and varying semiotic and material elements whose selection and retention occurs in this ecological space. In a complex world there are many sites and scales on which such evolutionary processes operate and, for present purposes, what matters is how local sites and scales come to be articulated to form more global (general) sites and scales and how the latter in turn frame, constrain, and enable local possibilities (Wickham, 1987). These interrelations are themselves shaped by the ongoing interaction between semiotic and extra-semiotic processes. To illustrate these arguments, I now introduce the concept of a semiotic order (Fairclough, 2003),[9] define the economic imaginary as such an order, and exemplify this from the KBE case.

A semiotic order is a specific configuration of genres, discourses and styles and, as such, constitutes the semiotic moment of a network of social practices in a given social field, institutional order, or wider social formation.[10] Genres are ways of acting and interacting viewed in their specifically semiotic aspect and, as such, serve to regularize (inter)action. A call-centre script is an example. Discourses represent other social practices (and themselves too) as well as the material world from particular positions in the social world. A case in point would be a particular political discourse, such as the "third way" (New Labour). Styles are ways of being, identities in their specifically semiotic (as opposed to bodily/material) aspect. The new managerial style described by Boltanski and Chiapello (1999) is one instance. Genres, discourses and styles are dialectically related. Thus discourses may become enacted as genres and inculcated as styles and, in addition, get externalized in a range of objective social and/or material facts (for example, second nature, physical infrastructure, new technologies, new institutional orders). The KBE can be read as a distinctive semiotic order that (re-)articulates various genres, discourses, and styles around a novel economic strategy, state project, and hegemonic vision and that affects diverse institutional orders and the lifeworld.

Integrating Critical Semiotic Analysis into Political Economy

I now consider the eventual emergence of the KBE as the hegemonic economic imaginary in response to the interlinked crises of the mass production-mass consumption regimes of Atlantic Fordism, the exportist growth strategies of East Asian national developmental states, and the import-substitution industrializing strategies of Latin American nations. What caused these complex, multi-centric, multi-scalar, and multi-temporal crises is not considered here (Jessop, 2002); instead I focus on the trial-and-error search to identify an appropriate response to these crises. A good starting point is Gramsci's (1971) commentary on an analogous period, the crisis of liberalism, in his notes on "Americanism and Fordism." He indicated that the emergence and consolidation of a new economic regime (mercato determinato) with its own distinctive economic laws or regularities (regolarità) does not occur purely through technological innovation coupled with relevant changes in the labour process, enterprise forms, forms of competition, and other narrowly economic matters. More is required. It also depends critically on institutional innovation intended to reorganize an entire social formation and the exercise of political, intellectual, and moral leadership. One aspect of this is, to use my term, a new economic imaginary. This enables the re-thinking of social, material, and spatio-temporal relations among economic and extra-economic activities, institutions, and systems and their encompassing civil society. And, to be effective, it must, together with associated state projects and hegemonic visions, be capable of translation into a specific set of material, social, and spatio-temporal fixes that jointly underpin a relative structured coherence to support continued accumulation. If this proves impossible, the new project will prove "arbitrary, rationalistic, and willed" rather than "organic" (Gramsci, 1971, pp. 376–377).

This approach implies that crisis is never a purely objective process or moment that automatically produces a particular response or outcome. Instead a crisis emerges when established patterns of dealing with structural contradictions, their crisis-tendencies, and dilemmas no longer work as expected and, indeed, when continued reliance thereon may even aggravate the situation. Crises are most acute when crisis-tendencies and tensions accumulate across several interrelated moments of the structure or system in question, limiting room for manoeuvre in regard to any particular problem. Changes in the balance of forces mobilized behind and across different types of struggle also have a key role in intensifying crisis-tendencies and in weakening and/or resisting established modes of crisis-management (Offe, 1984). This creates a situation of more or less acute crisis, a potential moment of decisive transformation, and an opportunity for decisive intervention. In this sense, a crisis situation is unbalanced: it is objectively overdetermined but subjectively indeterminate (Debray, 1973). And this creates the space for determined strategic interventions to significantly redirect the course of events as well as for attempts to "muddle through" in the (perhaps forlorn) hope that the situation will resolve itself in time. In short, crises are potentially path-shaping moments.

Such path-shaping is mediated semiotically as well as materially. Crises encourage semiotic as well as strategic innovation. They often prompt a remarkable proliferation of alternative visions rooted in old and new semiotic systems and semiotic orders. Many of these will invoke, repeat, or re-articulate established genres, discourses, and styles; others may develop, if only partially, a "poetry for the future" that resonates with new potentialities (Marx, 1852/1996, pp. 32–34). Which of the proliferating alternatives, if any, is eventually retained and consolidated is mediated in part through discursive struggles to define the nature and significance of the crisis and what might follow from it. If the crisis can be interpreted as a crisis in the existing economic order, then minor reforms and a passive revolution will first be attempted to re-regularize that order. If this fails and/or if the crisis is already interpreted initially as a crisis of the existing economic order, a discursive space is opened to explore more radical changes. In both cases conflicts also concern how the costs of crisis-management get distributed and the best policies to escape from the crisis.

In periods of major social restructuring, diverse economic, political, and sociocultural narratives may intersect as they seek to give meaning to current problems by construing them in terms of past failures and future possibilities. Different social forces in the private and public domains propose new visions, projects, programmes, and policies and a struggle for hegemony grows. The plausibility of these narratives and their associated strategies and projects depends on their resonance (and hence capacity to reinterpret and mobilize) with the personal (including shared) narratives of significant classes, strata, social categories, or groups affected by the postwar economic and political order. Moreover, although many plausible narratives are possible, their narrators will not be equally effective in conveying their messages and securing support for the lessons they hope to draw. This will depend on the prevailing "web of interlocution" and its discursive selectivities,[11] the organization and operation of the mass media, the role of intellectuals in public life, and the structural biases and strategically selective operations of various public and private apparatuses of economic, political, and ideological domination.[12] Such concerns take us well beyond a concern for narrativity and/or the constraints rooted in specific organizational or institutional genres, of course, into the many extra-discursive conditions of narrative appeal and of stable semiotic orders. That these institutional and meta-narratives have powerful resonance does not mean that they should be taken at face value. All narratives are selective, appropriate some arguments, and combine them in specific ways. In this sense, then, one must consider what is left unstated or silent, what is repressed or suppressed in official discourse.

Given these general considerations, an effective solution to the search for a meaningful post-Fordist macro-economic order in an increasingly integrated world market would involve an economic imaginary that satisfies two requirements. First, it can inform and shape economic strategies on all scales from the firm to the wider economy, on all territorial scales from the local through regional to the national or supra-national scale, and with regard to the operation and articulation of market forces and their non-market supports. And second, it can inform and shape state projects and hegemonic visions on different scales, providing guidance in the face of political and social uncertainty and providing a means to integrate private, institutional, and wider public narratives about past experiences, present difficulties, and future prospects. The more of these fields a new economic imaginary can address, the more resonant and influential it will be.[13] This explains the power of the KBE as an increasingly dominant and hegemonic discourse that can frame broader struggles over political, intellectual and moral leadership on various scales as well as over more concrete fields of technical and economic reform (see table 1). The basic idea is being articulated on many scales from local to global, in many organizational and institutional sites from firms to states, in many functional systems such as education, science, health, welfare, law, and politics, as well as the economy in its narrow sense, and in the public sphere and the lifeworld. It has been translated into many different visions and strategies (for example, smart machines and expert systems, the creative industries, the increasing centrality of intellectual property, lifelong learning, the information society, and the rise of cybercommunities). And it can be inflected in neo-liberal, neo-corporatist, neostatist, and neo-communitarian ways – often seeming to function like a Rorschach

Table 1: Some representative terms linked to the KBE in different functional systems and the wider society

technology	smart machines – intelligent products – expert systems – new materials – dematerialization – wetware, netware – information and communication technologies – information superhighway – innovation systems
economy	knowledge creation – knowledge management – knowledge-based firm – learning organization – knowledge-intensive business services – infomediaries – embedded knowledge networks – e-commerce – learning economy – reflexive accumulation
capital	knowledge capital – intellectual capital – intellectual property rights – informational capitalism – technocapitalism – digital capitalism – virtual capitalism – biocapitalism
labour	teleworking – intellectual labour – knowledge workers – symbolic analysts – immaterial labour – tacit knowledge – human capital – expert intellectuals – cyborgs
science	knowledge base – innovation – scientific and technical revolution – life sciences – technology foresight – triple helix
education	lifelong learning – learning society – corporate universities – knowledge factories – advanced educational technologies
culture	creative industries – culture industries – cultural commodities – cyberculture – technoculture
law	intellectual property rights – rights to information – immaterial objects – biopiracy
state	virtual state – e-government – science policy – innovation policy – high-technology policy – evidence-based policy
politics	electronic democracy – cyberpolitics – "hactivism"

Source: author's observations.

inkblot to sustain alliances and institutionalized compromises among very disparate interests.

The KBE seems to have become a master economic narrative in many accumulation strategies, state projects and hegemonic visions and, through the 1990s, it gained a key role in guiding and reinforcing activities aiming to consolidate a relatively stable post-Fordist accumulation regime and corresponding mode of regulation. Given the proliferation of discourses during the emerging crisis in/of Atlantic Fordism, different processes were involved in the greater resonance (hence selection) of certain KBE discourses and subsequent institutionalization (or retention) of relatively coherent economic strategies, political projects, and hegemonic visions oriented to, and organized around, the KBE. For there is many a slip between discursive resonance in a given conjuncture and an eventual, relatively enduring institutional materiality.

Nonetheless, with all due caution about the frailty of predictions during a transition from one long wave of capitalist development to another (Perez, 2002), it does seem that the KBE has not only been selected from among the many competing discourses about post-Fordist futures but is now being retained through a complex and heterogeneous network of practices across diverse systems and scales of action. Whether the KBE also offers a scientifically adequate description of today's economy in all its chaotic complexity is another matter. But it does correspond in significant ways to the changes in core technologies, labour processes, enterprise forms, modes of competition, and economic identity politics that had begun to emerge well before the KBE eventually became hegemonic over other accounts of these changes. And it has since gained a crucial role in consolidating them too through its capacity to link different sets of ideal and material interests across a broad range of organizations, institutional orders, functional systems, and the lifeworld and, for this reason, to provide an overall strategic direction to attempts to respond to new threats and opportunities, material disturbances, and a general sense of disorientation in a seemingly ungovernable, runaway world. In short, this is a discursive construal that has good prospects of translation into material reality.

The rise of the KBE as a master narrative is not innocent. While it has material and ideological roots in 1960s debates on post-industrialism, it gained momentum in the 1980s as American capitalists and state managers sought an effective reply to the growing competitiveness of their European and East Asian rivals. Various academic studies, think tank reports, and official inquiries indicated that the US was still competitive in the leading sectors of the KBE. The latter term was an important discursive innovation in its own right, re-classifying goods, services, industries, commodity chains, and forms of competitiveness. This research prompted a concerted campaign to develop the material and ideological basis for a new accumulation strategy based on the deepening and widening of the KBE and the massive extension of intellectual property rights to protect and enlarge the dominance of US capital for the anticipated next long wave. This reflects a neo-liberal policy for productive capital that safeguards US superprofits behind the cloak of free trade in intellectual property and so complements its neo-liberal policy for financial capital. The new strategy was translated into a successful hegemonic campaign (armoured by law and juridical precedents, dissemination of US technical standards and social norms of production and consumption, bilateral trade leverage, diplomatic arm-twisting, and bloody-minded unilateralism) to persuade other states to adopt the KBE agenda. Indeed, the KBE has been warmly embraced as a master narrative and strategy by other leading political forces – ranging from international agencies (notably the OECD and WTO but also the IMF, World Bank, and UNCTAD) through regional economic blocs and intergovernmental arrangements (such as the EU, APEC, ASEAN, Mercosur, NAFTA) and individual national states with different roles in the global division of labour (such as, New Zealand, South Korea, Germany, Colombia) down to a wide range of provinces, metropolitan regions, and small cities.

Like Fordism as a master narrative and strategy before it, the KBE can be inflected to suit different national and regional traditions and different economic interests. It can also be used to guide economic and political strategies at all levels from the labour process through the accumulation regime and its mode of regulation to an all-embracing mode of societalization. Moreover, once accepted as the master narrative with all its nuances and scope for interpretation, it becomes easier for its neo-liberal variant to shape the development of the emerging global KBE through the sheer weight of the US economy as well as through the exercise of economic, political, and intellectual domination.

This said, there is certainly scope for counter-hegemonic versions of the KBE and disputes about how best to promote it. This can be seen in the new international competitiveness benchmarking exercises conducted by the World Economic Forum from 1998 onwards, with the neo-liberal US and neo-corporatist Finland alternating as number one for four years (Porter et al., 2000; World Economic Forum, 2003).[14] Similarly, at its Lisbon summit in 2000, the EU aimed to become the leading KBE in the world whilst protecting the European Social Model and developing modes of meta-governance based on social partnership rather than pure market forces (Telò, 2002). The space available within the KBE discourse for such disputes helps to reproduce the overall discourse within which they are framed.

Concluding Remarks

This article argues for sustained theoretical and empirical engagement between a materially-grounded critical semiotic analysis and an evolutionary and institutional political economy informed by the cultural turn. It is based on my earlier work on state theory and political economy and my critical engagement with Marx's (1996) pre-theoretical discourse analysis[15] and Gramsci's (1971) elaborate philological and materialist studies of hegemony. Others have taken different routes to similar conclusions and have used other labels to describe them. What most distinguishes CPE as presented here from apparently similar approaches are the application of evolutionary theory to semiosis as well as political economy and their resulting mutual transformation.

I conclude with the following remarks. First, insofar as semiosis is studied apart from its extra-semiotic context, resulting accounts of social causation will be incomplete, leading to semiotic reductionism and/or imperialism. And second, insofar as material transformation is studied apart from its semiotic dimensions and mediations, explanations of stability and change risk oscillating between objective necessity and sheer contingency. To avoid these twin problems, CPE aims to steer a path between "soft cultural economics" and "hard orthodox economics." While the former subsumes economic activities under broad generalizations about social and cultural life (especially their inevitably semiotic character), the latter reifies formal, market-rational, calculative activities and analyzes them apart from their discursive significance and broader extra economic context and supports. The former tendency is common in economic sociology or claims about the culturalization of economic life in the new economy (Lash & Urry, 1994); it also occurs in more discourse-theoretical work, such as work on cultural materialism (Milner, 2002; Williams, 1980), the linguistic mediation of economic activities (Gal, 1989), or economic antagonisms (Laclau & Mouffe, 1985). Unfortunately, from my viewpoint, while such currents correctly reject a sharp division between the cultural and material and stress the cultural dimensions of material life, they tend to lose sight of the specificity of different economic forms, contradictions, institutions, contradictions, and so on. The risk here is that one cannot distinguish in material terms between capitalist and non-capitalist economic practices, institutions, and formations – they all become equally discursive and can only be differentiated through their respective semiotic practices, meanings, and contexts and their performative impact. Conversely, hard orthodox economics tends to establish a rigid demarcation between the economic and the cultural, reifying economic objects, naturalizing homo economicus, and proposing rigid economic laws. At its most extreme, this leads to universalizing, transhistorical claims valid for all forms of material provisioning; in other cases, it tends to separate economizing activities from their extra-economic supports, to regard the economy as a self-reproducing, self-expanding system with its own laws, and to provide the theoretical underpinnings for economic reductionism.

In offering a third way, CPE, at least as presented here, emphasizes that capitalism involves a series of specific economic forms (the commodity form, money, wages, prices, property, and so on) associated with generalized commodity production. These forms have their own effects that must be analyzed as such and that therefore shape the selection and retention of competing economic imaginaries. Thus a Marxist CPE would robustly reject the conflation of discourses and material practices and the more general discourse-imperialism that has plagued social theory for two decades. It would also provide a powerful means both to critique and to contextualize recent claims about the culturalization of economic life in the new economy – seeing these claims as elements within a new economic imaginary with a potentially performative impact as well as a belated (mis)recognition of the semiotic dimensions of all economic activities (for sometimes contrasting views, see Du Gay & Pryke, 2002; Ray & Sayer, 1999). And, in addition, as many theorists have noted in various contexts (and orthodox Marxists sometimes forget), the reproduction of the basic forms of the capital relation and their particular instantiation in different social formations cannot be secured purely through the objective logic of the market or a domination that operates "behind the backs" of the producers. For capital's laws of motion are doubly tendential and depend on contingent social practices that extend well beyond what is from time to time construed and/or constructed as economic. CPE provides a corrective to these problems too. In part this comes from its emphasis on the constitutive material role of the extra-economic supports of market forces. But it also emphasizes how different economic imaginaries serve to demarcate economic from extra-economic activities, institutions and orders and, hence, how semiosis is also constitutive in securing the conditions for capital accumulation.

Notes

1. This article derives in part from collaborative work: see Fairclough, Jessop, and Sayer (2003); Jessop and Sum (2000, 2001). It also benefitted from comments by Ryan Conlon, Steven Fuller, Phil Graham, and Jane Mulderrig. The usual disclaimers apply.
2. While semiosis initially refers to the inter-subjective production of meaning, it is also an important element/moment of "the social" more generally. Semiosis involves more than (verbal) language, including, for example, different forms of visual language.
3. Polanyi (1982) distinguishes (a) substantive economic activities involved in material provisioning from (b) formal (profit-oriented, market-mediated) economic activities. The leading economic imaginaries in capitalist societies tend to ignore the full range of substantive economic activities in favour of certain formal economic activities.
4. I am not suggesting here that mass media can be completely disentangled from the broader networks of social relations in which they operate, but I am seeking to highlight the diminished role of an autonomous public sphere in shaping semiosis.
5. Indeed, there is no economic imaginary without materiality (Bayart, 1994).
6. Although all practices are semiotic and material, the relative causal efficacy of these elements will vary.
7. On the pre-linguistic and material bases of logic, see Archer (2000).
8. Horizontal refers here to sites on a similar scale (for example, personal, organizational, institutional, functional systems) and vertical refers to different scales (for example, micro-macro, local-regional-national-supranational-global). The use of both terms must be relative and relational.
9. Semiotic orders are equivalent to "orders of discourse" in Fairclough (1992).
10. This paragraph draws directly and extensively on Fairclough (2003).
11. A web of interlocution comprises meta-narratives that reveal linkages between a wide range of interactions, organizations, and institutions and/or help to make sense of whole epochs (Somers, 1994).
12. On discursive selectivity, see Hay (1996) and Somers (1994); on structural selectivity, see Jessop (1990).
13. My strategic-relational approach is consistent with this claim but also emphasizes that constraints are relative to specific actors, identities, interests, strategies, spatial and temporal horizons, and so on (Jessop, 2002).
14. Neo-statist Singapore "won" second place in 2003, after the US, before Finland.
15. On this, see Fairclough and Graham (2002).

References

Archer, M. S. (2000). *Being human.* Cambridge: Cambridge University Press.

Bayart, J. F. (1994). *L 'invention paradoxale de la mode économique.* In idem (Ed.), *La réinvention du capitalisme* (pp. 9–43). Paris: Éditions Karthala.

Boltanski, L., & Chiapello, E. (1999). *Le nouvel ésprit du capitalisme.* Paris: Gallimard.

Campbell, D. T. (1969). Variation and selective retention in socio-cultural evolution. *General Systems, 14,* 69–86.

Daly, G. (1994). The discursive construction of economic space. *Economy and Society, 20,* 79–102.

Debray, R. (1973). *Prison witings* (R. Sheed, Trans.). London: Allen Lane.

Du Gay, P., & Pryke, R. (Eds.). (2002). *Cultural economy.* London: Sage.

Fairclough, N. (1992). *Discourse and social change.* Cambridge: Polity.

Fairclough, N. (2003). *Analysing discourse: Textual analysis for social research.* London: Routledge.

Fairclough, N., & Graham, P. (2002). Marx and discourse analysis: Genesis of a critical method. *Estudios de Sociolingüística, 3*, 185–229.

Fairclough, N., Jessop, B., & Sayer, A. (2003). Critical realism and semiosis. In J.M. Roberts and J. Joseph (Eds.), *Realism, discourse and deconstruction* (pp. 32–34). London: Routledge.

Gal, S. (1989). Language and political economy. *American Review of Anthropology, 18*, 345–367.

Grabher, G. (1994). *Lob der Verschwendung. Redundanz in der Regionalentwicklung: ein socioökonomisches Plädoyer*. Berlin: Edition Sigma.

Gramsci, A. (1971). *Selections from the prison notebooks* (Q. Hoare & G. Nowell-Smith, Trans.). London: Lawrence & Wishart.

Hay, C. (1996). Narrating crisis: The discursive construction of the 'Winter of Discontent'. *Sociology, 30*, 253–277.

Jessop, B. (1990). *State theory: Putting the capitalist state in its place*. Cambridge: Polity.

Jessop, B. (1997). The governance of complexity and the complexity of governance. In A. Amin and J. Hausner (Eds.), *Beyond markets and hierarchy: interactive governance and social complexity* (pp. 111–147). Cheltenham: Edward Elgar.

Jessop, B. (2001). Capitalism, the regulation approach, and critical realism. In A. Brown, S. Fleetwood, & J.M. Roberts (Eds.), *Critical realism and Marxism* (pp. 88–115). London: Routledge.

Jessop, B. (2002). *The future of the capitalist state*. Cambridge: Polity.

Jessop, B. (2003). Governance and meta-governance: On reflexivity, requisite variety, and requisite irony. In H. Bang (Ed.), *Governance as social and political communication* (pp. 101–116). Manchester: Manchester University Press.

Jessop, B., & Sum, N.-L. (2000). An entrepreneurial city in action. *Urban Studies, 37*, 2290–2315.

Jessop, B., & Sum, N.-L. (2001). Pre-disciplinary and post-disciplinary perspectives in political economy. *New Political Economy, 6*, 89–101.

Laclau, E., & Mouffe, C. (1985). *Hegemony and socialist strategy*. London: Verso.

Lash, S., & Urry, J. (1994). *Economies of signs and space*. London: Sage.

Malpas, J., & Wickham, G. (1995). Governance and failure: On the limits of sociology. *Australian and New Zealand Journal of Sociology, 31*, 37–50.

Marx, K. (1852/1996). The eighteenth brumaire of Louis Bonaparte. In *Marx: Later political writings* (pp. 31–127). Cambridge: Cambridge University Press.

Miller, P., & Rose, N. (1993). Governing economic life. *Economy and Society, 19*, 1–31.

Milner, A. (2002). *Re-imagining cultural studies: The promise of cultural materialism*. London: Routledge.

Mitchell, T. (1991). The limits of the state: Beyond statist approaches and their critics. *American Political Science Review, 85*, 77–96.

Offe, C. (1984). *Contradictions of the welfare state*. London: Hutchinson.

Perez, C. (2002). *Technological revolutions and financial capital*. Chelmsford: Edward Elgar.

Polanyi, K. (1982). The economy as instituted process. In M. Granovetter & R. Swedberg (Eds.), *The sociology of economic life* (pp. 29–51). Boulder: Westview.

Porter, M. E. et al. (2000). *The global competitiveness report 2000*. Oxford: Oxford University Press.

Ray, L., & Sayer, A. (Eds.). (1999). *Culture and economy after the cultural turn*. London: Sage.

Sayer, A. (2000). *Realism and social science*. London: Sage.

Somers, M. R. (1994). The narrative constitution of identity: a relational and network approach. *Theory and Society, 23*, 605–649.

Telò, M. (2002). Governance and government in the European Union: the open method of coordination. In M. J. Rodrigues (Ed.), *The new knowledge economy in Europe* (pp. 242–272). Cheltenham: Edward Elgar.

Wickham, G. (1987). Power and power analysis: beyond Foucault? *Economy and Society*, *12*, 468–498.

Williams, R. (1980). *Problems in materialism and culture*. London: Verso.

World Economic Forum. (2003). *The global competitiveness report 2002–2003*. Oxford: Oxford University Press.

58

On the Problem of Bias in Political Argumentation: An Investigation into Discussions about Political Asylum in Germany and Austria

Manfred Kienpointner and Walther Kindt

1. Introduction

The use of empirical methods taken from linguistic discourse analysis increasingly proves fruitful for the study of argumentation. On the one hand, progress in the development of a theory of everyday argumentation is not possible without a detailed knowledge of the processes and structures of argumentation in natural language; on the other hand such knowledge is indispensable for well-founded analyses of argumentative discourse. Furthermore, the success of empirical research can be demonstrated through the possibility of practical application. The results of empirical studies can be used, for example, to identify problems in everyday instances of political argumentation and to suggest practical solutions. In our paper, we attempt to serve both descriptive and normative interests in the study of argumentation, much in the spirit of Van Eemeren et al. (1993), who study various types of argumentative discourse in less than ideal circumstances in order to enhance both the theory and the practice of argumentation. As empirical data, we have collected a sample of about 80 letters to the editor in German and Austrian journals and magazines of the years 1991–92.

Source: *Journal of Pragmatics*, 27(5) (1997): 555–585.

The central issue of these letters is the problem of political asylum. The sources of all passages quoted below can be found in the Appendix.

A proper discursive treatment of political issues is often hampered by the fact that the respective opponents only use those fragmentary aspects of complex issues which support their case. Therefore, it is difficult to judge the relevance of their arguments for the global issue. In this way, frequently an antagonistic polarization of the debate rather than a consensus on adequate policies is achieved. The problem of bias in political argumentation is discussed in Kindt (1992b), where debates about the Gulf War are used as examples. In this paper, we are going to deal with the problem of bias in some more detail. As we cannot deal with all aspects of political argumentation within the limits of this paper, we would like to present answers to the following three questions:

(1) Which global aspects of the problem are treated and which are left out (= global bias)?

Global bias is to be detected and criticized at the macro-level of the text (sections, chapters), that is, as far as the unbalanced treatment or complete neglect of global dimensions of the problem under discussion is concerned.

(2) Which argument schemes are used to treat more specific aspects of the problem? Are the schemes used in a simplistic and one-sided way (= local bias)?

Local bias is to be analyzed at the micro-level of the text (sentences, paragraphs), that is, as far as the insufficient elaboration of specific arguments within a larger textual unit is concerned.

(3) How can we explain the increasingly aggressive climate of political discussion?

The treatment of our empirical data in Section 2 and 3 is intended to answer the first two of these questions. In Section 4, we shall sum up the descriptive results, give some answers to question (3) and finally try to formulate some recommendations to overcome the shortcomings of the political debate in Austria and Germany.

For our analysis, we have tried to integrate insights from various frameworks. First of all, ancient and modem rhetorical traditions provide attempts at classifying (everyday) arguments as instances of argument schemes. These schemes were called *topoi/loci* by Aristotle (1959, 1960) and Cicero (1951) within the Topical tradition of ancient rhetoric and dialectic, whereas they were termed 'techniques of argumentation' by Perelman and Olbrechts-Tyteca (1971) in their New Rhetoric.

Moreover, we adopt the general strategy of the Pragma-Dialectic approach of Van Eemeren and Grootendorst (1984, 1992, 1994), who want to reconcile descriptive and normative approaches in the study of argumentation (cf. also Kienpointner, 1996). They have developed a code of conduct for rational discussants and study everyday arguments as partial, more or less adequate realizations of these normative rules. Furthermore, they have formulated critical questions for testing the acceptability of instances or argument schemes found in everyday arguments. We also use the many elucidatory studies by Woods and Walton on fallacious arguments (e.g. Walton, 1992; Woods and Walton, 1989), which are based on perspectives of both formal and informal logic (cf. also Blair, 1992). In particular, Walton (1991) provides a useful background for the analysis of bias in political discourse. Walton lists five characteristics of bias in order of importance:

"1. Bias is a lack of appropriate balance or neutrality in argumentation. The problem here is that an arguer supports one side too strongly and/or too often.
2. Bias is a lack of appropriate critical doubt in argumentation. The problem here is a failure of restraint and/or failure to suspect the natural inclination to push for a point of view one supports.
3. Bias is a lack of balance or critical doubt appropriate for a given type of dialogue that a participant is supposed to be engaged in. It is not merely a lack of balance, but a lack of sufficient balance for a particular type of dialogue.
4. Bias is often identified with a particular position supported by an arguer.
5. Bias is often identified with an arguer's having something to gain – a personal interest in the outcome of an argument, e.g. a financial interest." (Walton, 1991: 19)

We add some remarks on the first three characteristics, which are considered the most important by Walton. The first characteristic makes intelligible the intuitive impression that biased arguments lack an impartial treatment of both sides of a question. However, a strong support of one particular point of view need not be inherently fallacious. Therefore, Walton adds the second characteristic, which makes clear that bias is also connected with a specific weakness on the part of the speaker as far as a self-critical distance in relation to his or her own point of view is concerned. The third characteristic adds the important qualification that bias always has to be judged relative to a certain type of argumentative discourse. Of course, it makes no sense to look for impartiality in quarrels (eristic dialogues) or bargains (dialogues of negotiation); and letters to the editor cannot be criticized in the same way as scientific argumentation. In the following, we attempt to critically view the arguments in our sample according to standards which do justice to this particular type of argumentative text. That is, we judge particular arguments relative to standards which are actually followed in many other letters of our sample. Therefore, we criticize weaknesses of argumentation only if they are not found in all letters of our sample.

Bias is not restricted to everyday argumentation. It can also occur in scientific argumentation, especially where problems like political asylum are concerned, where everybody can be expected to have his or her own strong political convictions and commitments. So we have to deal with the problem of how *we* can avoid bias in our treatment of political argumentation. A first step towards the solution of this problem is to be aware of one's own point of view and to make it explicit. In this way, we can try to avoid an unjustified and exaggerated criticism of points of view and arguments which are opposed to our own opinion. Moreover, instead of hiding eventual bias in our analysis behind a pretended 'objective' perspective, we make it possible for the critical reader to judge whether or not we have succeeded in analyzing the texts of our sample as impartially as possible.

So what are our own political commitments? We are opposed to any kind of moderate or radical racism. As far as political refugees are concerned, we support a more liberal policy which does not accept the current severe restrictions for asylum-seekers. The protection of human rights for political refugees takes priority over economic interests.

2. Theoretical Background

2.1. Kinds of Bias

Like most discursive texts, political discourse in its monological form follows the general pattern of a three-part structure: introduction, main part and conclusion. Similar distinctions can be found in modern discourse analysis (cf. Henne and Rehbock, 1982: 186ff., 226ff.) and ancient rhetoric (Aristotle, 1959: 174f.; Cicero, 1951: 2.79ff.). In the case of our letters on political asylum, the main part can very often be further divided according to the following prototypical structure: the status quo of society is described and evaluated as a negative situation which has to be overcome. Next, a more desirable state of society is outlined as a positive goal which should be attained in the future. Then, some possible political measures for reaching this goal are suggested. The conclusion following the main part usually contains an appeal which calls for action according to the policy advocated in the main part.

This structure partially corresponds to an argument scheme called 'pragmatic argument' by Perelman and Olbrechts-Tyteca (1971: 266ff.; cf. below Section 2.3). Given the limited space in letters to the editor, pragmatic arguments quite often appear in a reduced form. The same holds true of other instances of argument schemes appearing in the main part. This should not be criticized as local bias unless an argument clearly deviates from standards of preciseness and plausibility reached in many other letters. In this case, the following criticism is justified: "The suspicion in the case of an arguer who is badly biased is that the accused is not judging the worth of an argument according to the requirements of the argumentation scheme, but always reaching the conclusion, instead, that happens to support the point of view chosen in advance" (Walton, 1991: 3).

Apart from local bias, there is also the danger of global bias. The latter is the result of a neglection of global aspects or dimensions in the controversial issue. In our sample, three global aspects of the problem can be distinguished according to the temporal dimension: the discursive treatment of past, present or future aspects of the problem of political asylum.

Statements oriented towards the past offer causes, reasons and explanations for the negatively evaluated status quo. For instance, one reader writes:

(1) *Die Strömungen von Emigranten und Asylbewerbern sind mittelbare und unmittelbare Folge der früheren europäischen Kolonialpolitik.*

'The flood of emigrants and asylum-seekers is an indirect and direct consequence of the former European colonial policy.'

A discussion orientated towards the *past* should provide prerequisites for answering the following question: what and how much should the persons involved contribute to a solution of the problems of the negatively evalutated status quo? The underlying logical context often remains implicit and can be described as follows: if certain persons are (jointly) responsible for a negative situation, they can be asked to contribute to the solution of the problems involved.

Discussions oriented towards the *present* time are characterized by statements which qualify the status quo in some detail. These qualifications, too, should be justified by suitable arguments. An example of such statements is the following passage:

(2) *Im übrigen zeigt die Zahl der Anerkennungen, daß etwa 98 Prozent der Asylbewerber nicht politisch Verfolgte, sondern Wirtschaftsflüchtlinge sind.*

'Besides, the number of persons accepted as asylum-seekers indicates that about 98% are not political refugees, but economic migrants.'

Argumentation orientated towards the *future* offers statements about the adequacy of measures and tries to justify them with arguments for subsequent policies. In the following example, a reader opposes possible constitutional amendments:

(3) *Jeder weiß, daß wir den Einwanderer-Zustrom bremsen müssen. Dafür müßte das 'Asylverfahrensgesetz' ausreichen. Die Durchsetzung dieses Gesetzes ist wichtiger als eine Zerfledderung des Grundgesetzes mit Einzelheiten.*

'Everyone knows that we have to slow down the influx of immigrants. The asylum laws should suffice for that. The efficient execution of this law is more important than the demolition of the constitution through details.'

Similarly, the textbooks describing and regulating debate tournaments at U.S. academic institutions distinguish global subjects ('stock issues') which have to be dealt with by the competing teams (cf. Freeley, 1986: 55ff.). However, in academic debate it is obligatory to treat *all* subjects in an equally detailed and sophisticated way.

The distinction of the three global dimensions is helpful for the explication of implicit argumentative sequences. It is also useful for the classification of passages as instances of argument schemes which are typical of the respective global subject. We will analyze specific schemes of argumentation in Section 2.3. But first, it is useful to provide a more general classification of the different ways of justifying a statement.

2.2. Procedures of Justification

The efforts made by participants in discussions to justify their own statements or to refute those of their opponents can differ widely (cf. Kindt, 1992a). For the sake of simplicity, we will only discuss procedures of justification.

A statement can be asserted without further justification, if it is trivially evident on the basis of an intersubjectively given perception, or if it is unanimously accepted within a speech community. In example (3) the expression *Jeder weiß* ('everyone knows') is used to allege unanimous acceptance of the statement.

Another type of justification is the argument of authority (cf. Aristotle, 1959: 127f.; Perelman and Olbrechts-Tyteca, 1971: 305ff.). According to this type of justification a statement is valid beyond reasonable doubt if it is confirmed by a qualitatively or quantitatively relevant group of persons with a great deal of competence in the respective area. Writers of letters to the editor can claim a status of authority if they are contemporary witnesses of certain events or have professional knowledge. Here are two examples:

(4) *Ich selber habe die Geschehnisse während der Nazidiktatur im Dritten Reich miterlebt und bin deshalb der Meinung, daß der Grundgesetzartikel auf keinen Fall geändert oder abgeschafft werden darf.*

'I myself was witness to the events that took place during the Nazi dictatorship in the Third Reich; therefore, I believe that the article of the constitution must not be changed or abolished in any way.'

(5) *Wie traurig ist das rapide Zurückweichen der Sozialdemokraten, auf die bisher Verlaß schien, vor den Gegnern des Asylrechts für politisch Verfolgte. Als Richter fühle ich mich zur Kritik daran berufen, besonders soweit es um die Rolle der Gerichte in den neuen 'Ideen' geht.*

'The rapid retreat of the social democrats, who have seemed so reliable thus far, is very regrettable! As a judge, I feel I am the right person to criticize this, especially as far as the role of the courts with reference to the new 'ideas' is concerned.'

Apart from the speaker, other persons or institutions are often appealed to as authorities. In the following example, both individual and institutional authorities are used:

(6) *Der Bonner Korrespondent der Neuen Westfälischen weist in seinem Kommentar dankenswerterweise darauf hin, daß es hierzulande "einen harten Kern von Rechtsradikalen gibt', der keinen besonderen Anlaß 'braucht, um Jagd auf Ausländer zu machen, daß aber auch in den Köpfen anscheinend braver Bürger(innen) fremdenfeindliches Gedankengut schlummert. Diese deprimierende Tatsache wird zwar nach wie vor von den meisten Politikern und auch Journalisten geleugnet, wurde aber bereits vor mehr als zehn Jahren durch die von der damaligen sozial-liberalen Bundesregierung in Auftrag gegebene SINUS-Studie offenbar.*

'In his commentary, the correspondent of the Neue Westfälische newspaper in Bonn laudibly refers to the fact that there is "a hard core of right wing radicals" in this country, who do not need a special excuse for hounding foreigners, but also that xenophobic ideas lie dormant in the heads of seemingly honest citizens as well. This depressing fact is still not acknowledged by the majority of the politicians and journalists, but was already clearly demonstrated more than 10 years ago by a SINUS report commissioned by the then social-liberal federal government.'

Another procedure of justification tries to support a point of view inductively, with the help of suitable examples and illustrations (Aristotle, 1959: 127; 1960: 303; Perelman and Olbrechts-Tyteca, 1971: 350). This procedure is used in the following passage:

(7) *Tatsache aber ist, daß die weitaus meisten Flüchtlinge im ersten Halbjahr 1991 aus Ländern kamen, in denen schwerwiegende Menschenrechtsverletzungen begangen werden oder in denen blutiger Bürgerkrieg herrscht: Jugoslawien, Rumänien, Ostanatolien, Iran, Libanon …*

'It is a fact that in the first half of 1991 the vast majority of refugees came from countries where human rights are severely violated or where bloody civil wars are taking place: Yugoslavia, Romania, East-Anatolia, Iran, Lebanon ….'

Finally, another, particularly important procedure is to justify a point of view by premises and inference rules, because in this way – at least in principle – deductive proof of the controversial point of view can be established. In the following example this technique is used for the refutation of a claim about the xenophobia of Germans. More specifically, the inference rule of contraposition *(modus tollens)* is applied:

(8) *Was heißt eigentlich, die Deutschen haben grundsätzlich einen Ausländerhaß, wie man behauptet? Das Wort 'Ausländerhaß' müßte bei*

diesen Hassern ausgetauscht werden durch das Wort: 'Asylantenhaß'. Diese – meiner Meinung nach gesteuerten – autonomen Jugendlichen gehen doch zu 90 Prozent in die örtlichen 'Ausländerlokale' zum Essen! Warum? Weil sie einen Haß auf 'Ausländer' haben? Das kann nicht sein ...

'What does it mean that Germans have an inherent hatred of foreigners, as is maintained? The expression 'xenophobia', if applied to these people who are full of hate, should be replaced by the expression: 'hate of asylum-seekers'. 90% of these autonomous young people – who are in my opinion manipulated – regularly go to local 'foreigner restaurants'! Why? Because they hate 'foreigners'? That can't be the case ...'

The logical structure of this argument can be reconstructed approximately as follows:

If all Germans were xenophobic, German young people would not go to restaurants of foreigners.
90% of German young people go to restaurants of foreigners.

Therefore: not all Germans are xenophobic.

The last procedure of justification is of vital importance in our analysis in the following sections. The reconstruction of discursive procedures underlying everyday arguments, however, is complicated by the fact that they are usually presented in a highly implicit form. An in-depth analysis and a critical evaluation are only possible if the various underlying logical structures are well known. Therefore, we need detailed typologies of argument schemes underlying everyday arguments like those in our sample.

2.3. Argument Schemes

If the logical structure of argument schemes remains largely implicit in everyday arguments and mutual understanding in discursive dialogues is nevertheless possible, the meaning and use of these schemes must be highly conventionalized and form a stable part of the tacit knowledge of a speech community. Therefore, one of the main aims of empirical discourse studies is to identify the underlying logical structures and ways of realization of these schemes. In the following, we shall present argument schemes frequently found in our sample and illustrate their realization in discourse with some examples. In Section 3, we shall analyze two letters in more detail.

Many of the schemes we are going to examine can already be found in the Aristotelian catalogues of *topoi* (1960 passim, 1959: 119ff.). The way Aristotle presents the *topoi* in his Rhetoric and his Topics varies considerably. Still, it is possible to isolate two main functions: the selective function (hence the name of *topos* as a 'place' where arguments can be found) and the guarantee function. According to the first function, *topoi* are search strategies which enable the speaker to choose relevant arguments from the set of all possible arguments. The latter function allows an equation of Aristotelian *topoi* with inference warrants in the sense of Toulmin (1958): they guarantee the plausibility of the transition from the premises to the conclusion (cf. De Pater, 1965; Green-Pedersen, 1984). In modern typologies, further empirically recognizable argument schemes have been added (e.g. by Perelman and Olbrechts-Tyteca, 1971). Moreover, many authors have tried to develop clear criteria for the demarcation of these schemes and formulated sets of critical questions as to their validity and plausibility (cf. Schellens, 1985; Van Eemeren and Kruiger, 1987; Warnick and Kline, 1992; Kienpointner, 1992a,b; 1993; Kindt, 1992a,b; Garssen, 1994).

We have distinguished three global dimensions in the asylum issue, which are treated more or less extensively in our sample (cf. above, Section 2.1): past, present, and future. Arguments oriented towards the past try to explain the present state of affairs. Therefore, many schemes deal with the causes and reasons of the criticized status quo. Some causal schemes (cf. already Aristotle, 1959: 132ff.) have the following structure:

If event Y would not have happened without event X, X is the cause of Y. Actually, Y would not have occurred without X.

Therefore: X has been the cause of Y.

The following example is an application of this counterfactual way of reasoning, which is used to criticize political lethargy as the cause of the uprise of totalitarian regimes:

(9) *Das, was während des Dritten Reiches an Bösem geschehen ist – die Verfolgung Andersdenkender, Krieg, millionenfache Vernichtung menschlichen Lebens – wäre meines Erachtens nicht eingetreten, wenn bereits 1933 bei vielen der damaligen Zeitzeugen nicht Gleuchgültigkeit, Wegsehen, Weghören, Zurückziehen ins Private vorgeherrscht hätten.*

'The evil things that occurred during the Third Reich – the persecution of opposers of the regime, war. the execution of millions of human beings – in my opinion would never have happened, if many of those who witnessed what was going on already in 1933 had not been so indifferent, had not looked away, had paid attention and not withdrawn into their own private world.'

Another variant of causal schemes uses abductive inferences (cf. Peirce, 1973): if event Y is entailed by X, then X is at least a possible cause of Y. This inference rule is applied in [10]:

(10) *Mit Waffen auch aus deutscher Produktion wird ein Großteil der Flüchtlinge aus ihrer Heimat gebombt – und wir wundern uns dann, wenn sie vor unserer Tür stehen und unseren Schutz erbitten.*

'A majority of the refugees has been bombed out of their native land with weapons partially produced in Germany – and then we are surprised when they turn up at our doorstep and ask for our protection.'

Another kind of causal reasoning tries to refute abductive inferences (cf. Aristotle, 1960: 132f.): the assumption of a causal relationship between X and Y is attacked by the presentation of the 'real' reason of Y, namely Z. In the following example this attack is combined with the charge that the 'real' cause has been concealed:

(11) *Minderheiten werden benutzt, wenn es darum geht, Defizite in unserer Gesellschaft zu verschleiern. Dann heißt es z.B., die Ursache für die große Arbeitslosigkeit, für die steigende Kriminalität oder für die wachsende Unsicherheit auf den Straßen seien die Ausländer.*

'Minorities are used to conceal deplorable states of affairs in our society: for instance, it is claimed that the high rate of unemployment, the rising crime figures, and the growing insecurity in our streets are caused by the foreigners.'

If effects are caused by intentionally acting persons, the following question arises: did these persons freely choose to act (or to refrain from acting) in a particular way or were they forced to? In the first case, they are responsible for any negative consequences and have to justify their acts. Thus a speech act sequence 'reproach-justification' is opened (cf. Kindt, 1992b). In the following passage, the author of the letter emphatically tries to justify a certain group of persons (namely, the children of refugees), arguing that they are not responsible for the negatively evaluated status quo:

(12) *Ich sehe Kinder vor mir, kleine fröhliche Wesen, die sich von anderen Kindern auf dieser Welt kein bißchen unterscheiden. Die sind nicht gefragt worden, ob sie in Deutschland in einem Container oder Asylantenheim wohnen möchten, ob sie ihre Kindheit in beengten Verhältnissen, gehaßt von Menschen, die sie gar nicht kennen, verbringen möchten. Diese Kinder haben nun wirklich nichts mit Arbeitslosigkeit, Wohnungsnot usw. zu tun ...*

'I see children, happy little creatures, who are not at all different from other children in this world. They have not been asked if they would prefer to live in Germany in a container or an asylum-seeker's hostel, if they would like to spend their childhood in cramped conditions, hated by people they do not even know. These children really have nothing to do with unemployment, housing shortage etc. ...'

A contrary position is taken in the following letter, where the asylum-seekers are seen as being responsible for the existing problems:

(13) *Tatsache ist, daß die Mehrheit der zu uns kommenden Menschen nicht aus Gründen politischer Verfolgung, sondern aus rein wirtschaftlichen*

Erwägungen hierher kommt und sich unter Inanspruchnahme unserer sozialen Einrichtungen ein besseres Leben erhofft.

'It is a fact that the majority of the people who come to our country do not arrive because they are politically persecuted, but out of financial reasons, and that they hope for a better life with the help of our social institutions.'

Arguments oriented towards the present time often try to define or classify (elements of) the status quo or to compare it with similar situations and problems. Therefore, argument schemes containing definitions, part–whole or species–genus relationships are used.

Schemes containing definitions (cf. Aristotle, 1959: 126; 1960: 561ff.) often try to define an entity X by a definition Y in a way which makes certain conclusions favoring one's own position possible. In the following passage the author criticizes this strategy:

(14) *Sprache ist verräterisch: Die der späten Achtziger und der jetzt Neunziger ist es auch. Klingt Asylant nicht ein wenig wie Strauchdieb? … So werden aus 'Rabauken' plötzlich 'Ordnungstrupps verunsicherter Bürger' (O-Ton von einem Lokalpolitiker in Hoyerswerda), zusammengehauene Opfer mutieren pauschal zu Sozialhilfebetrügern).*

'Language is very revealing: that of the late eighties, now the nineties, is, too. Doesn't 'asylum-seeker' equate a little bit with 'tramp'? … Thus 'hooligans' become 'vigilante squads consisting of unnerved citizens' (these are the words of a local politician in Hoyerswerda), 'beaten-up victims' universally turn into 'social welfare swindlers'.'

Schemes containing part–whole or species–genus relationships (cf. Aristotle, 1959: 128; 1960: 421ff.; Kienpointner, 1993) are used for inferences of subsumption and classification: properties of parts or species are transferred to the whole or genus and vice versa. For instance, the relative importance of entities can be demonstrated by their inclusion as part X into a whole Y. In the following example, the importance of the number of refugees in Germany is shown to be insignificant, because the refugees form only a very small part of the population of Germany:

(15) *Tatsache ist auch, daß sämtliche bei uns lebenden Flüchtlinge, ob anerkannt oder noch im Verfahren, weit weniger als 1% der Bevölkerung der Bundesrepublik ausmachen.*

'It is also a fact that all refugees living in our country, whether already accepted or still under consideration, represent far less than 1 % of the total population of the Federal Republic.'

Schemes of comparison rely on similarities or differences of entities (cf. Aristotle, 1959: 123; 1960: 371ff.). An important variant of these schemes contains an inference rule which is called 'rule of justice' by Perelman and

Olbrechts-Tyteca (1971: 218ff.). According to this rule, entities X and Y which are identical or similar according to a criterion Z, have to be evaluated and/or treated in the same way. The following example applies this appeal for justice:

(16) *Jeder ausländische Arbeitsnehmer zahlt, genauso wie jeder deutsche, Sozialversicherungen, Steuern und nicht zu vergessen den Solidaritätsbeitrag, der Dank dafür ist Ausländerfeindlichkeit.*

'Exactly like every German worker, every foreign worker has to pay social security contributions, taxes and last but not least the solidarity contribution, all they get for this is xenophobia.'

A strategy counteracting appeals to the rule of justice tries to point out more or less important differences between the compared entities. If entities X and Y, instead of being identical or similar, differ according to a criterion Z, the application of the rule of justice is blocked; see the following example, where the writer tries to demonstrate that Germany is different from other countries as to size and, therefore, is not able to let in many refugees:

(17) *Das verhältnismäßig kleine Deutschland ist eben nicht Kanada oder Australien.*

'Germany, which is relatively small, cannot be compared to Canada or Australia.'

An important variant of the schemes of comparison is the 'a fortiori'-scheme (called *topos* of more/less or 'locus a maiore/a minore' in the ancient tradition, cf. Aristotle, 1959: 124f.; 1960: 407ff.; Cicero, 1951: 2.172; Perelman and Olbrechts-Tyteca, 1971: 343). A general version of the 'a minore'-scheme could be formulated as a norm of action (cf. another version concerning the relative probability of states of affairs in Kienpointner, 1992b: 183):

If even X has property P, and Y's having P is more acceptable than X's having P, then Y should have P.
(Even) X has P.

Therefore: Y should have P.

Within the context of the refugee problem in Austria and Germany, this type of argument can be used to *criticize* a restrictive policy, because even poorer countries accept more refugees; however, it can also be applied to *justify* a restrictive policy, because even richer countries have adopted strategies for reducing the rate of immigration. This is shown by the following two examples:

(18) *Im krisengeschüttelten Ungarn müssen seit den letzten Monaten viermal so viel Flüchtlinge versorgt werden, als unser 'sozialer' Minister Löschnak für ein Jahr zu kontingentieren gedenkt.*

'In crisis-ridden Hungary, for the last few months four times as many refugees have had to be provided for than our 'social' minister Löschnak plans to accept in one year.'

(19) *Selbst die USA, eines der reichsten Länder, haben schon vor Jahren den Zustrom von Einwanderern drastisch reduziert.*

'Even the USA, one of the richest countries in the world, already reduced the influx of immigrants drastically years ago.'

Causal arguments oriented towards the future are quite often instances of the scheme of argumentation which has been called 'pragmatic argument' by Perelman and Olbrechts-Tyteca (1971: 266ff.; cf. also Aristotle, 1959: 129; Toulmin et al., 1984: 369ff.; Freeley, 1986: 181ff.). According to this scheme, the evaluation of an action X depends on the positive or negative consequences Y of X. In its two basic versions, this can be presented as follows:

Action X leads to consequence Y.	Action X leads to consequence Y.
Y is desirable.	Y is undesirable.
There are no other actions Z with even more desirable consequences.	There are no other actions Z with even more negative effects.
X has no or few negative effects.	X has no or few positive effects.
Therefore: X should be done.	Therefore: X should not be done.

Most of the time, actions have both positive and negative consequences. Therefore, all consequences should be considered and weighed up against each other. Action X can only be justified if the positive consequences outweigh the negative ones qualitatively and/or quantitatively. Likewise, X can only be rejected if its negative effects are not outweighed by the positive ones (cf. Kindt, 1992b). As it is often difficult to consider all the direct and indirect consequences of an action and not neglect at least some of them, the danger of local bias in pragmatic arguments is considerably high.

In the following two examples, special emphasis is placed on the qualitatively most important consequences (20) and on possible indirect consequences (21):

(20) *Wenn man zuläßt, daß auch nur eines dieser Rechte auf dem Jahrmarkt deutscher Eitelkeiten verschachert oder gar der Gewalt der Straße geopfert wird, bringt man die Freiheitsrechte insgesamt in Gefahr. ... Die Opferung auch nur eines Grundrechts ließe das Gespenst von Weimar wieder über Deutschlands Straßen und Plätze schleichen.*

'If even one of these rights is permitted to be sold off at the German vanity fair, or sacrificed because of the street terror, the rights of freedom as a whole are endangered. ... Even the sacrifice of only one constitutional right would again let the specter of Weimar creep into the streets and squares of Germany...'

(21) *Wer damit begint, Menschengruppen aus dem gerichtlichen Rechtsschutz herauszunehmen, schafft damit gefährliche Einbruchstellen für die spätere Entrechtung immer weiterer Personenkreise.*

'Whoever starts to remove social groups from the protection of the courts, creates dangerous weak points where ever more persons can be deprived of their rights.'

We have now presented an overview of types of everyday arguments occurring frequently in our sample. Of course, these types are only one step in the justification or refutation of a controversial point of view. They have their place in a sequence of complex argumentation where arguments are related directly or indirectly to the main issue of the discussion. Moreover, their verbalization is accompanied by strategies of foregrounding or backgrounding of relevant information. We will turn to these strategies in the next section.

2.4. Strategic Distribution of Information

Participants in a discussion can touch on themes they do not treat explicitly by giving partial information which requires some reading between the lines (cf. Van Dijk, 1992; 1993: 31f.; Gruber, 1993). For this purpose, they often use the following three strategies: selection of suitable lexical means of expression, backgrounding of incomplete information, foregrounding of incomplete information.

The first strategy consists in the choice of words which provide (e.g. with the help of conversational implicatures in the sense of Grice (1975)) information about a theme not treated explicitly. In the following example, the primary theme is the alleged inconsistency of the asylum policy of the FDP (= the German Liberal Party). Politicians of the FDP are accused of not practising what they preach (cf. Aristoteles, 1959: 132):

(22) *Neben den komfortablen Bungalows aller FDP-Bundestagsabgeordneter sollte man Unterkünfte für Afrikaner, Asiaten und Zigeuner einrichten. Die liberalen Damen und Herren wären dann wohl sehr schnell vom Mitleid für die armen 'politisch Verfolgten' geheilt.*

'Accommodations for Africans, Asians and gypsies should be built next to the comfortable bungalows of all FDP-members of the Bundestag [= the Lower house of the German parliament, M.K./W.K.]. These liberal ladies and gentlemen would quickly be cured of their pity for the poor 'victims of political persecution'.'

The writer of this letter, G. Bittner, explicitly criticizes the behavior of members of the FDP; but by choosing the lexical item *arm* (= poor) and using quotation marks ('victims of ...') he also implies – possibly ironically – that the refugees are not really victims of political persecution and that they are possibly the main cause of the negatively evaluated status quo.

With the help of the second strategy, the writer explicitly introduces the side theme, but refrains from expanding it in the following discourse. Thus, it is backgrounded. In the following letter, political measures suggested by the then German minister of the interior, Schäuble, are criticized:

(23) *Kennt Schäuble die Möglichkeiten des Asylverfahrensgesetzes nicht oder will er nicht darüber sprechen – aus ganz anderen Gründen, die mit der Bewältigung der Asylantenflut gar nichts zu tun habe?*

'Doesn't Schäuble know the asylum laws or doesn't he want to talk about them – for entirely different reasons, which have nothing to do with the influx of asylum seekers?'

The parenthetical comment about personal motivations on the part of the minister are not taken up in the following context. It is only at the end of the letter that the writer provides some further information which implies that Schäuble suggested changes of the constitutional laws in order to annoy the SPD (= the German Social Democratic Party).

The third strategy places explicit information on themes which in the main part are not treated at the beginning or the end of the letter. Thus in a letter which mainly analyzes the present status quo, possible causes are only presented at the end. The prominent position of the last sentence in the published version of the text foregrounds this causal explanation:

(24) *Solange aber junge Leute nicht heiraten können, weil sie keine bezahlbare Wohnung finden, solange alleinerziehende Mütter aus gleichem Grund in Notunterkünfte abgeschoben werden, solange der letzte deutsche Kleinstrentner under der Armutsgrenze lebt, solange hat der Bürger ein Recht auf Angst und Sorgen, denn unsere 'vom Volk gewählten Politiker' sitzen in Bonn und reden, reden und reden!*

'However, as long as young people cannot get married because they can't find an affordable apartment, as long as single mothers are pushed away into temporary accommodation, as long as there is one German retiree living below the poverty line, the citizen has a right to be afraid and worried, because our 'politicians elected by the people' are sitting in Bonn and only keep on talking, talking, talking!)'

On the one hand, these strategies can reduce the danger of bias because they provide implicit or explicit information on side themes not covered in the rest of the letter. On the other hand, they often have the function of transporting positions and judgments without giving explicit arguments which could be attacked and refuted. For instance, in example (24) a reproach is verbalized, but not justified. Thus the readers could more easily be influenced by a potentially biased statement.

3. Detailed Analysis of Two Letters to the Editor

We chose the two letters analyzed in this section in detail according to the following criteria:

(a) They should cover a broad range of themes, that is, they should not be restricted to isolated cases or events.
(b) They should not be too short, which would automatically entail some kind of global bias, that is, the neglect of important global dimensions of the problem under discussion; nor should they be too long, because that would make a detailed analysis impossible within the limits of this paper.
(c) They should be examples of everyday argumentation. Therefore, we chose letters of ordinary people who are not dealing with asylum problems professionally.
(d) They should represent contrary points of view, namely a rather liberal and a rather restrictive position concerning refugee policy.

Following these criteria, we chose the letter *Straffällige müssen abgeschoben werden* ('Criminals have to be deported'), written by Andreas Krämer, Gießen (in *Frankfurter Rundschau,* 16.10.1991; henceforth abbreviated as L1), and the letter *Nur eine kleine Hilfe* ('Only a little help') by Uwe Tünnermann, Lemgo (in *Neue Westfälische,* 24.9.1991; henceforth abbreviated as L2). The full texts and translations are given in the Appendix, Section A2.

In our analysis we will not refrain from giving critical comments on the argumentation of the authors. However, we are not going to criticize them for deviations from high standards of scientific argumentation. Walton (1991: 4ff.) justly remarks that every argument can only be judged as biased relative to a type of argumentative context. Letters to the editors are not intended as scientific inquiries into a problem. Moreover, the writers do not have enough space to treat a problem exhaustively. Besides, quite often the editors of the journal or magazine reserve the right to omit parts of the letter. This is exactly what seems to have happened with two passages of L2. But still, it is justifiable to criticize arguments in letters to the editor if they are globally or locally biased *in comparison to many other letters in the sample, that is, according to standards of argumentation which seem to be followed frequently in this type of argumentative discourse.* Moreover, authors of letters to the editors often explicitly claim that they (are trying to) argue objectively or impartially (cf. our analysis of L1 and L2 below). Especially these passages can be criticized if they do not follow standards of critical discussion like, for example, those established by Van Eemeren and Grootendorst (1984, 1992). If the authors themselves claim a reputable standard of argumentation, they cannot be excused in the same way as the writers of other letters who use their text simply as a means of political polemics or propaganda or want to compensate for strong emotional tensions. Finally, we would like to repeat (cf. Section 1) that we do not claim absolute objectivity in this case and only try to analyze the letters as impartially as possible.

In the following, we first present the argumentative macrostructure (cf. Van Dijk and Kintsch, 1983: 15) of L1 and L2. This reconstruction of the basic propositions conveyed by the texts will be used as a starting point for critical comments on possible global bias.

According to the macrostructure depicted in Fig. 1, L1 can be characterized as a text which mainly gives reasons for the deplored status quo and suggests measures for improving the situation. Krämer almost completely refrains from analyzing the present situation. Differently from many other letters in the sample, Krämer does not try to define crucial concepts nor to classify or compare the status quo (using relationships of species–genus or part–whole or similarities and differences). Especially problems of justice, which are treated in many letters of comparable length, are almost entirely neglected. Therefore, L1's almost exclusive orientation towards the past and the future can be criticized as a global bias. However, L1 is a reaction to an earlier article *Rechtsextremismus weit verbreitet* (Attitudes of the extreme right are widespread) in *Frankfurter Rundschau* (26.9.1991). The analysis of the status quo in this earlier article seems to be included implicitly. In our detailed analysis of L1, we will have to consider whether the abstention from an explicit treatment of the present situation is dysfunctional also for the claims concerning possible reasons and measures.

The macrostructure of L2 can be reconstructed as in Fig. 2. As can clearly be seen, Tünnermann treats all global dimensions of the problem. However, the focus of his treatment is clearly directed towards the present and the past situation. Measures suggested for the future are not compared with the possible alternatives or evaluated as to negative consequences. The negative consequences expected by Krämer are apparently not a central issue for Tünnermann. Therefore, also L2 can be criticized as globally biased: it is too strongly orientated towards an analysis of past reasons for the status quo and questions of justice in the present situation.

In our detailed analysis of L1, we shall mainly be dealing with three problems:

(1) How are the schemes of argumentation verbalized?
(2) Which strategies of foregrounding or backgrounding are used?
(3) Which local forms of bias and/or other forms of uncorrect or fallacious argumentation can be detected?

3.1. Analysis of L1

3.1.1. Verbal Strategies

Strategies of verbalization are used to make one's own arguments as strong as possible. They can be used to reject possible objections to one's own

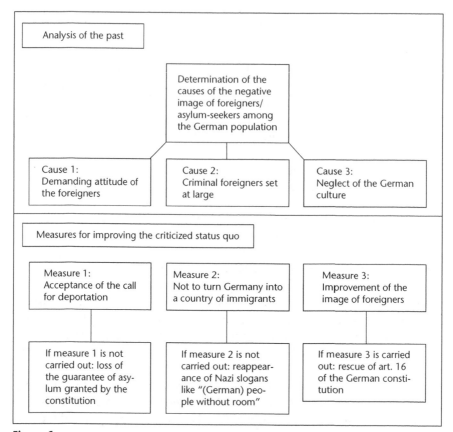

Figure 1

arguments (defensive strategies) or to produce the impression that one's own arguments are (almost) evident proof (offensive strategies).

An example of a defensive strategy is the opening sentence of Krämer's letter: *So entsetzlich die Vorkommnisse … sind* ('However terrible the events… are'); this is an instance of the strategy called 'concessio' (concession) in ancient rhetoric (cf. Quintilian, 1970: 500; Van Dijk, 1993: 93ff.). This rhetorical strategy consists in conceding a weak argument in order not to have to defend it in detail. Then the speaker goes on to argue in favor of a stronger point of view. Krämer concedes that the violent attacks on asylum-seekers' hostels are dreadful in order to prevent the impression that he would play down these events. The latter could not be justified in a democratic society.

Similarly, with the formulation *So ist es keinesfalls 'rechtsextrem'* ('It is, therefore, in no way an 'attitude of the extreme right')' in the third paragraph he wants to prevent his urgent recommendation of the deportation of refugees from being evaluated negatively as a right wing extremist's point of view. Preventive strategies are called 'praemunitio' (preventive defense) in

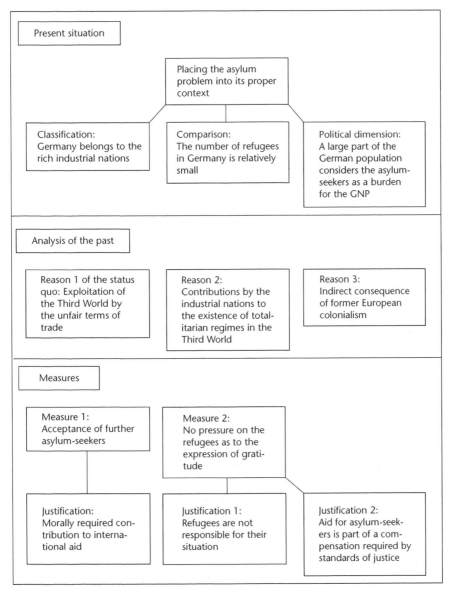

Figure 2

ancient rhetoric (cf. Quintilian 1970: 485). This technique is also used in the immediately following defense of this measure: *Dies sollte … nicht so einfach … abgetan werden* ('This should not simply be dismissed'). At the same time, Krämer's continuous attempts at dissociating himself from positions of the extreme right are used as strategic means of positive self-presentation (cf. Van Dijk, 1992; 1993: 76ff.).

Offensive strategies try to present one's own arguments as maximally relevant and/or conclusive. To reach this aim, Krämer presents the global focus of his argumentation, namely, the negative image of the asylum-seekers, as maximally pertinent to the asylum discussion. According to his formulation in the first paragraph, it is inevitable to think about the low degree of acceptance of the refugees (*... so kommen wir nicht umhin, darüber nachzudenken ...* 'we cannot avoid considering ...'). In the second paragraph, he considers the demanding attitude of the foreigners as one reason for their negative image. This argument is presented as trivially true: *So ist doch letztlich unbestritten ...* ('After all, it cannot be denied ...'). However, this formulation is mildly mitigated by the particles *doch letztlich* ('after all').

Another offensive strategy consists in presenting the own point of view as relevant for all or the vast majority. This strategy is realized by the use of the 'inclusive we': for example; Krämer uses *wir* in this at the end of the third paragraph: *Wir riskieren ... zu verlieren* ('We risk losing ...').

3.1.2. Distribution of Information

As we have seen above, part of the information conveyed by the text is quite often backgrounded. The backgrounded information can trigger inferences which the reader is supposed to make. However, a more explicit presentation of the inferences could be detrimental to the position of the author. Thus, backgrounding information serves a double purpose.

In the second paragraph of L1, Krämer, using a parenthesis (*– aus dessen Sicht –* 'according to his view'), restricts the claim about the demanding attitude of the foreigners to Mr. Average (*Otto Normalverbraucher,* literally: 'Otto Average Consumer'). However, by simply using the name and a parenthesis, Krämer backgrounds this restriction. It is only a secondary theme, the importance of which is thereby reduced. Compare other possible formulations like 'Of course, the demanding attitude exists only in the mind or Mr. Average', which would express the restriction with much more informative weight. In this way, Krämer can admit that his argument is not tenable for all Germans without having to withdraw it completely.

In the third paragraph, the use of the expression *Zauberwort* ('magic word') creates an implicature which connects the right of asylum with the influx of (criminal) desperate people: magic words like 'asylum' create an impression of a paradise in Germany, which attracts innumerable people without hope. Again, Krämer could not have claimed this implicature explicitly without weakening his own arguments: after the violent attacks on refugees it has become difficult to claim that Germany is a magic kingdom for asylum-seekers.

The last sentence of L1 calls for active participation by the foreigners in Kramer's program in creating a better image for the refugees (*Hierzu bedarf es aber auch der Mitwirkung der Ausländer*). Krämer leaves possible ways of participation implicit. In this way, it is easier for the readers of L1 to share Krämer's point of view because an explicit mentioning of possible measures could include kinds of policies not acceptable for many of them.

3.1.3. Schemes of Argumentation

The quality of the arguments in a text can be evaluated in two steps: firstly, they can be criticized as locally biased arguments because they are *incomplete* instances of an argument scheme. This is the case when relevant premisses are left out, for example important causes or consequences.

Secondly, they can be criticized as *incorrect* applications of an argument scheme because they create misunderstandings due to the use of ambiguous expressions or contain hasty generalizations or falsely present temporal succession as causal relationships or are connected with unjustified personal attacks (cf. Van Eemeren and Grootendorst, 1992).

We will begin with an evaluation of the completeness of the argumentation. At the beginning of L1, Krämer uses causal arguments. These can be criticized as incomplete because Krämer does not discuss or at least mention further possible causes for the negative image of foreigners, for example:

(a)   insufficient strategies by the politicians,
(b)   deeply rooted prejudices against foreigners,
(c)   persuasion by emotionalizing propaganda directed against foreigners,
(d)   insufficient information about the situation in the developing countries and the individual and collective fate of asylum-seekers before their arrival in Germany.

Without consideration of these causes, which are treated explicitly in many other letters in our sample, Krämer's analysis necessarily remains incomplete. He could at least have stated that there are further possible causes for the negative image. Thus, the omission of further causes cannot be simply ascribed to the lack of space within a particular text type like letters to the editor. Furthermore, the local bias resulting from the neglect of other possible causes of the status quo also reduces the plausibility of the measures suggested by Krämer later on.

Of course, Krämer's concentration on measures to improve the image of foreigners could be justified if he did not want to suggest an overall solution of the problem. However, the opening sentence in the last paragraph of his letter creates the impression that the improvement of the image would be the *main* step towards a solution (*Das Ziel zur Rettung des Artikels 16 GG muß sein, wieder eine breite Akzeptanz in der Bevölkerung zu schaffen.* 'In order to save article 16 of the constitution [= which grants the right of asylum, M.K./ W.K.], one needs to recreate broad foreigner acceptance by the population').

Moreover, even if Krämer only wanted to provide a partial solution to the problem, he could have strengthened the relevance of his suggestions by comparing the number of foreigners with the total population of Germany or by giving data concerning the number of criminal foreigners in proportion to criminal German citizens.

Finally, further measures, which are treated repeatedly in other letters, are simply missing in Krämer's discussion of possible policies:

(a) a better explanation of the asylum laws by the politicians;
(b) job opportunities or even obligatory work for asylum-seekers,
(c) reduction of the welfare contributions for the refugees to the necessary minimum.

As far as the correctness of the arguments in L1 are concerned, we have to distinguish three aspects:

(a) The sincerity of Krämer's personal statements cannot be judged by looking at the text alone. Moreover, often it is not easy to tell how we have to interpret statements which are not explicitly marked as subjective. Therefore, in these cases a judgment of correctness is not possible.
(b) Most statements in L1 are formulated as if they were accepted by all or most members of the German speech community. Again, it would be very difficult to judge the correctness of these assumptions. It would be particularly difficult to decide whether the alleged facts really are the (only) causes of the negative image of foreigners.
(c) Therefore, within the limits of a textual analysis, a more feasible way of analysis is the critical assessment of the correctness of the inferences drawn by Krämer. The truth and the sincerity of the statements used as premises are accepted provisionally.

This does not mean that the facts presupposed by Krämer are uncontroversial. In the first paragraph of L1, he asks why *in der nahezu gesamten deutschen Bevölkerung die Akzeptanz gegenüber Ausländern/Asylbewerbern ... gering ist*. This presupposes that *almost all* Germans have a negative view of foreigners. However, the title of the article in the *Frankfurter Rundschau* which Krämer quotes only says that right wing extremism is widespread (*Rechtsextremismus verbreitet*). Krämer's presupposition could be criticized as an instance of the fallacy of hasty generalization. However, this generalization is necessary for his further arguments. Only if the vast majority of the population really has a negative attitude towards foreigners, can Krämer's conclusions be justified: he considers the improvement of the negative image as the main problem to be solved.

The correctness of Krämer's inferences suffers particularly from the fact that he does not sufficiently distinguish between foreigners in general and asylum-seekers. In the passage quoted above he treats foreigners and asylum-seekers as *one* group (*Ausländer/Asylbewerber*). In the second paragraph he talks about foreigners (*Ausländer*), but seems to have asylum-seekers and economic migrants in mind. In the third paragraph he mentions foreign drug dealers, gamblers, thieves and gangs (*ausländische Drogendealer, Hütchenspieler, Diebes- und Unterweltbanden*), which cannot be equated with political refugees in the sense of §16 of the constitution, which grants asylum. But this is exactly what Krämer does when he falsely claims that many of the respective criminals are attracted to Germany by the magic word 'asylum' (*das Zauberwort 'Asyl'*). Therefore, even if this statement is true about the criminals referred to, it cannot be used to infer the conclusion concerning the deportation of criminal asylum-seekers. Due to the ambiguity of crucial terms used by Krämer, the logical relationship between his premises and his conclusion remains unclear and his inference is, therefore, not correct.

Krämer's sloppy use of *Ausländer* could be justified because he talks about the political views and emotions of the German citizens, who do not carefully distinguish different senses of the word either. This is the way in which the negative image of specific groups of criminal foreigners is transferred to the refugees. However, any discussion about possible political measures to improve the situation should avoid confusing clearly different groups. Writers of other letters in our sample, differently from L1, do attempt to distinguish 'foreigners' in general from 'refugees', 'asylum-seekers' and 'economic migrants'.

Twice, Krämer uses instances of the pragmatic argument (cf. Section 2.3.) to justify political measures through the negative consequences which will follow if the measures are not realized.

In the third paragraph, he justifies his call for deportation with undesirable consequences for the negatively evaluated status quo. His inference, which proceeds in three steps, can be reconstructed as follows (for the sake of brevity, we only provide the warrants, that is, the inference rules justifying the step from the premisses to the conclusions):

(1) If the deportation of criminal foreigners is not undertaken, the negative image of asylum-seekers will remain unchanged. This inference rule remains implicit, but has been justified by Krämer in the preceding context. Therefore, the rule, which is necessary for the correctness of the inference, can be supplemented. However, as we have shown above, this inference rests on a premise ('Criminal foreigners cause the negative image of asylum-seekers') which confuses different groups of foreigners.

(2) If the negative image of the refugees remains unchanged, §16 can no longer be carried out. This step is explicitly stated by Krämer (cf. *Jedes Recht kann nur solange durchgesetzt werden, wie es … trifft*).

(3) If §16 can no longer be carried out, it runs the risk of being abolished. Again, this inference rule remains implicit. But Kramer can correctly

suppose that his readers know the rule, given the many recent requests for the abolition of §16 from the constitution.

All in all, Krämer's argumentation seems to be a correct application of the pragmatic argument scheme. However, as we have seen, some premisses of the inference are problematic due to an ambiguity of crucial terms. Moreover, the presupposed causal relationship between the foreigners' negative image and the abolition of §16 remains doubtful because some further possible causes are not considered.

Krämer uses a second instance for the pragmatic argument in the fourth paragraph. This time, he argues by pointing out negative consequences if certain political measures are taken: If Germany is made an immigration country through certain legal measures, right wing theories of *Volk ohne Raum* (= Hitler's claim: 'Germans do not have enough space to live') can be expected to be revived.

Krämer also seems to imply that further negative consequences would go hand in hand with these extremist theories. However, he himself does not seem to consider this argument to be sufficient because he adds an argument of comparison: Germany is considerably smaller than traditional immigration countries. But again, his use of the pragmatic argument seems to be basically correct. Still, he can be criticized for not discussing possible advantages of a more liberal immigration policy, which could outweigh negative effects, like the creation of dubious theories by small groups of the extreme right. To a certain extent, this incompleteness makes Krämer's argument biased. Moreover, his way of warning about the danger of right wing reactions can be accused of being a kind of concealed racist strategy: this way, restrictive measures can be justified at any time as the lesser of two evils (cf. Van Dijk, 1993: 99ff.).

To sum up, we conclude that our detailed analysis of L1 has shown a number of weaknesses. The plausibility of Krämer's arguments is reduced by two main factors: the incompleteness of some of its arguments make L1 locally biased, the correctness of the inferences in L1 is partially endangered by the ambiguity of crucial terms.

3.2. Analysis of L2

In our treatment of L2, we shall deal with our three basic questions simultaneously. We recall that the questions are: (1) the verbalization of arguments, (2) the informational strategies, (3) the plausibility of the arguments. Tünnermann's letter has apparently been shortened by the editors of the *Neue Westfälische* in three places. However, this seems to be relevant for our discussion of possible local bias only in one instance, namely, at the end of the letter.

In the first two paragraphs of L2, Tünnermann uses a technique called 'dissociation of concepts' by Perelman and Olbrechts-Tyteca (1971: 411ff.).

In its most general form, it consists in refuting a position by pointing out that it relies on 'appearance' rather than 'reality' (ibid.: 415).

In the first paragraph, Tünnermann contrasts the position based on stereotypes of the mass and mass media ('appearance') with expert knowledge about the status quo ('reality') mentioned in the second paragraph. He points out his reserve against such stereotyped attitudes by using quotation marks and the subjunctive (*als stünde Deutschland in der 'Asylantenfrage' vor einem Überlebensproblem.* 'The impression that Germany is facing problems of survival because of the 'asylum-seekers' question')'. Moreover, the use of the lexical item *Überlebensproblem* (problem of survival) can be analyzed as a backgrounded criticism. That is, Tünnermann implicitly criticizes exaggerated claims in the asylum discussion: quite often, causal 'arguments of direction' (Perelman and Olbrechts-Tyteca, 1971: 281ff.) are used to support the view that a liberal asylum-policy ultimately leads to a catastrophe. His use of the form *Bundesbürger(innen)* (male and female citizens of the Federal Republic) makes clear that Tünnermann is also opposed to sexist norms of usage. At the same time, he indirectly introduces himself as someone who knows more than the average citizen.

In the second paragraph, Tünnermann tries to prove that the facts refute the stereotype of an apparently disastrous status quo. To do this, he uses two arguments; First, he classifies Germany as a rich industrial nation. Possible counter-arguments against this instance of a species–genus argument scheme are preventively blocked by the qualifications *trotz ihrer immensen finanziellen Verpflichtungen* ('despite its immense financial commitments') and *nach wie vor* ('notwithstanding the economic changes in Germany'). Tünnermann's argumentation can be criticized because it does not provide comparisons with the relative wealth and financial problems of other 'rich industrial nations'. Moreover, it falsely pretends that 'rich industrial nation' is a precise, clear-cut category. Therefore, it is not compelling to conclude that a rich industrial nation cannot have problems of survival.

Secondly, Tünnermann presents statistical evidence which puts the absolute number of refugees in Germany into perspective: 1% of all refugees in the world does not seem to be much. Moreover, he quotes Amnesty International as a reliable source of the data, thereby using an argument from authority (cf. above Section 2.2). The following argument is an instance of the a fortiori-scheme (cf. above 2.3): if even developing countries have to cope with many more asylum-seekers, Germany should not worry about 1% of them. Both arguments suffer from incompleteness because Tünnermann does not present data concerning other industrial nations and does not mention the huge problems caused by the influx of refugees into neighboring Third World countries.

The lack of a precise demarcation of crucial concepts and the incompleteness of Tünnermann's argumentation in the second paragraph justifies a criticism of local bias. Tünnermann cannot simply be excused by a lack of space; for instance, in many other letters of comparable length the financial situation of Germany is dealt with explicitly and compared with that of other industrial nations.

In the third paragraph of L2, Tünnermann treats a further central aspect of the asylum discussion: even if there is no doubt as to the survival of Germany, he has to deal with the fact that many German citizens cannot understand why they have to bear the costs incurred by the refugees. The strong emotions involved are only hinted at by the lexical items *wurmt* and *fleißig*: many Germans are annoyed because part of their money, which they have worked hard for, in used for the refugees. However, Tünnermann does not deal explicitly with the emotional problems of these groups of the German population, he rather tries to refute their assumed cost–benefit reasoning, which can be reconstructed as follows:

If we pay for the refugees without getting anything in return, this situation is not acceptable.
We pay for the refugees without getting anything in return.

Therefore: This situation is not acceptable.

Tünnermann criticizes this way of reasoning with the following general type of objection: relevant premises have been left out; hence, the argument is incomplete, which means that it is locally biased (cf. Kindt, 1992a: 114).

Tünnermann offers three factual claims to show that his criticism is justified. All claims try to demonstrate that Germany shares some responsibility for the economic and historical facts which have led to the asylum-problems. Like Krämer, he uses the 'inclusive we' to make the emotional impact of his charge stronger. The same function is fulfilled by the negatively connotated nouns *Ausbeutung/Produktionsdiktate/Kolonialpolitik* (exploitation, constraints of production, colonialism). Tünnermann mitigates his accusation by claiming only co-responsibility for Germany. Still, a more balanced view should have considered the considerable involvement of local rulers and politicians in the exploitation of people in Third World countries.

In the last paragraph, Tünnermann draws conclusions which are wholly based on variants of the rule of justice (cf. above, Section 2.3.):

(a) every nation has to contribute an adequate amount towards international aid,
(b) the countries who have more should help those countries who have less,
(c) the Germans, at least partially, have to compensate for their profits due to the unfair terms of trade with their financial aid.

Tünnermann has provided some background for these arguments in the preceding paragraphs: he has argued that Germany's contribution to international aid is not unreasonably high (second paragraph) and that there are economic and historical reasons which compel Germany to compensate its (earlier) profits made in the Third World. Therefore, his application of the rule of justifice is basically correct.

Arguments based on the rule of justice have to show the equivalence of the compared things, persons, situations etc., however. Given the fact that many refugees come from the former Eastern Bloc, the rule of justice does not apply here, at least not in the same way as in the case of refugees coming from the Third World. Moreover, again using the 'inclusive we', Tünnermann does not even try to distinguish between different degrees of responsibility of subgroups of the German population (e.g. owners of big enterprises in contrast to the mass of the population). These differences should have resulted in a less apodictic use of this argument scheme.

Finally, it can be criticized that Tünnermann justifies possible measures for improving the status quo only by using moral arguments. That is, he does not consider the possible consequences of the suggested measures nor does he mention the possibility of removing possible causes of the deplored status quo. In general, the arguments offered by Tünnermann suffer from the fact that he does not try to combine his remarkable ethical standards with an analysis of advantages and disadvantages of possible measures and their alternatives.

To sum up, we can conclude the following: though we are more sympathetic to the position defended by Tünnermann, L2, like L1, contains several flaws and weaknesses of argumentation. While Krämer's L1 is strongly centered round the feelings of the German people and pragmatic arguments about consequences of possible measures, Tünnermann's L2 deals mainly with Germany's moral obligations and arguments based on the rule of justice. Both letters often lack appropriate balance. They are undoubtedly biased to a certain degree. While it may have been impossible for them to deal with every aspect with sufficient sophistication, Krämer and Tünnermann could at least have mitigated their claims a little.

4. Conclusion

We have tried to present a framework for the analysis of argumentation which combines theoretical and empirical approaches. We have studied the problem of bias in political argumentation on the basis of a sample of letters to the editor. Of course, the limited space makes it difficult for the writers of these letters not to produce locally or globally biased arguments. However, the analysis of other types of political discourse clearly shows that bias is a general problem in political discussions (cf. Kienpointner, 1992a: 250ff.; Kindt, 1992b; Walton, 1991 on bias in oral and written discourse in newspaper articles, TV-discussions, election campaigns etc.). In the following, we will list a few possible explanations for the fact that bias is so frequent in political argumentation:

(a)   it is cognitively simple and emotionally more pleasant to recognize only those aspects of a problem which are important to oneself and support one's own point of view. In this way, cognitive dissonance and unpleasant feelings of shame and guilt are avoided or at least reduced.
(b)   Prevailing styles of education and communication in our culture enhance antagonistic rather than cooperative procedures in the solution of conflicts. The resulting competitive styles of argumentation are prone to produce biased arguments.
(c)   Many social and political problems are so complex that an adequate treatment is almost impossible on the basis of everyday argumentation.

An approach like ours, which is directed at descriptive and normative goals, should provide strategies and recommendations for overcoming the problems posed by the factors listed above. What, then, are viable solutions for improving the quality of political argumentation?

First of all, it has to be stated that it is neither possible nor necessary that political argumentation in its everyday form has to treat every aspect of the respective problems in a detailed way; some degree of global bias is inevitable, given the various limits of time and space. This inevitable bias has to be compensated for by appropriate political structures which grant pluralism and free expression of political opinions. In democratic societies, the writing of discursive texts, for example editorials or letters to the editor, can be seen as a cumulative process where only the collection of all texts written from widely diverging perspectives can be seen as a sufficiently balanced treatment of complex political problems: it results in a compensation of individual bias. Therefore, individual writers like those in our sample may choose certain dimensions of the problem and neglect others. But they should become aware of the fact that they contribute only partial solutions to the problem. Moreover, they should avoid drawing hasty conclusions without qualification. If Krämer and Tünnermann had followed this recommendation, they would have stated that their concentration on pragmatic (L1) or justice-oriented (L2) arguments, respectively, was only a contribution towards a partial solution of the complex asylum problem.

Secondly, bias in political argumentation could be mitigated if people were willing to avoid the use of crucial political terms with strong positive or negative connotations. Usually, these terms are used because they favor one's own position: if somebody is an 'economic migrant' rather than a 'political refugee', he or she does not deserve asylum; if somebody is a 'fascist' rather than a 'conservative', his or her political arguments need not be taken seriously in a democratic society. Therefore, in political debates 'semantic fights' are quite often carried out by participants who want to push through their own rules of usage. Many political discussions could become more fruitful if the participants were willing to use impartial terms wherever available.

Thirdly, the improvement of the standards of political argumentation requires institutional changes in our system of education. If people are to become ready to produce balanced arguments and to behave cooperatively in discussion, this ability has to be formed at school and in other pedagogical institutions. It should be trained much more than it is the case nowadays, for example in the educational system of Austria and Germany. Similar claims hold true for many other countries. It is strange to see the following discrepancy: on the one hand, modem societies have become completely dependent on successful communication; on the other hand, differently from the Ancient World and the Middle Ages, wide-ranging and efficient training of the techniques of argumentation are widely neglected in the educational institutions (perhaps with one major exception: the debate tradition in England, the U.S.A., the Netherlands and some other countries). Important political issues like the asylum problem often lead to tedious and frustrating decision procedures. This makes clear that deliberate attempts to improve the practice of argumentation are necessary.

A change in educational policy is also suggested by the alarming increase of nationalism and right wing radicalism in Europe. The brutal attacks on asylum seekers, foreigners, and gypsies in Austria and Germany call for adequate measures by the opinion leaders and politicans. Amongst other measures, the educational policies have to be adjusted to oppose racist tendencies of all kinds (cf. Wodak et al., 1990; Van Dijk, 1993). Parts of the argumentative competence which should be taught (more) are: knowledge about the strength and weaknesses of specific schemes of argumentation, the balanced application of these schemes, strategies of verbalization, the ability of critical thinking (cf. Paul, 1987), particularly the critical analysis of prejudiced thought and its inhuman consequences.

Appendix

A. 1. Sources of passages of letters to the editor quoted in Section 2

(1) Frankfurter Rundschau, 18.10.91; A. Belfellah.
(2) Neue Westfälische, 7.11.91; P. Nipko.
(3) Frankfurter Rundschau, 26.10.91; H. Wagner.
(4) Neue Westfälische, 1./2.11.91; F. Martens.
(5) Frankfurter Rundschau, 10.10.91; K. Beer.
(6) Neue Westfälische, 14.11.91; U. Tünnermann.
(7) Frankfurter Rundschau, 9.10.91; A. Müller.
(8) Neue Westfälische, 19.10.91; G. Arronge.
(9) Haller Kreisblatt, 16.10.91; K.-H. Galling.
(10) Frankfurter Rundschau, 9.10.91; A. Müller.

(11) Neue Westfälische, 19.10.91; L. Brade.
(12) Neue Westfälische, 19.10.91; W. Brockmeyer.
(13) Neue Westfälische, 19.10.91; K.-M. Hartrampf.
(14) Neue Westfälische, 17.10.91; C. Willmann.
(15) Frankfurter Rundschau, q. 10.91; A. Müller.
(16) Neue Westfälische, 19.10.91; R. Bruzesse.
(17) Frankfurter Rundschau, 16.10.91; A. Krämer (= L1).
(18) Profil, 9.12.91; S. Szalachy.
(19) Neue Westfälische, 19.10.91; K.-H. Hartrampf.
(20) Frankfurter Rundschau, 29.10.91; H. Oberst.
(21) Frankfurter Rundschau, 10.10.91; H. Beer.
(22) Spiegel, 19.8.91; G. Bittner.
(23) Frankfurter Rundschau, 26.10.91; H. Wagner.
(24) Neue Westfälische, 19.10.91; Ch. Beyer.

A.2. Full texts and translations of the two letters analyzed in Section 3

L1: Andreas Krämer, Gießen: *Straffällige müssen abgeschoben werden.* **In: Frankfurter Rundschau, 16.10.91:**

So entsetzlich die Vorkommnisse vor dem Ausländerheim in Hoyerswerda sind, so kommen wir nicht umhin, darüber nachzudenken, warum in der nahezu gesamten deutschen Bevölkerung, die Akzeptanz gegenüber Ausländern/Asylbewerbern so gering ist ('Rechtsextremismus verbreitet', FR vom 26.9.).

So ist doch letztlich unbestritten, daß nicht wenig Ausläder mit einer unheimlichen Anspruchsmentalität nach Deutschland kommen und Dinge verlangen, für die Otto Normalverbraucher hart arbeiten muß und die – aus dessen Sicht – über die Rettung des an Leib und Leben bedrohten hinausgehen.

Es ist ferner für die Masse der Bevölkerung einfach unverständlich, warum etwa ausländische Drogendealer, Hütchenspieler, Diebes- und Unterweltbanden nach deren Festnahme umgehend wieder auf freien Fuß gesetzt werden, anstatt sie abzuschieben. Hier liegt wahrlich der Verdacht nahe, daß vieles davon auf das Zauberwort 'Asyl' zurückzuführen ist. So ist es keinesfalls 'rechtsextrem' wenn man fordert, daß Asylbewohner ihr Recht verwirkt haben, wenn sie es dahingehen (sic! M.K./W.K.) mißbrauchen, daß sie in dem Land, das sie aufnimmt und von dessen Steuergroschen ihr Aufenthalt bezahlt wird, straffällig werden. Dies sollte m.E. nicht so einfach als Stammtischgerede abgetan werden. Jedes Recht kann nur solange durchgesetzt werden, wie es auf die Akzeptanz der Bevölkerung trifft. Wir riskieren andernfalls das kostbare Asylversprechen des GG gänzlich zu verlieren.

So stößt etwa die multikulturelle Gesellschaft auf wenig Gegenliebe, wenn man sich des Eindrucks nicht erwehren kann. daß die eigene Kultur als letztes kommt. In diesem Zusammenhang sei auch davor gewarnt, Deutschland formell zu einem Einwanderungsland zu machen. Es graut einem schon heute vor den dann zu erwartenden 'Volk ohne Raum'-Theorien. Das verhältnismäßig kleine Deutschland ist eben nicht Kanada oder Australien.

Das Ziel zur Rettung des Artikels 16 GG muß sein, wieder eine breite Akzeptanz in der Bevölkerung zu schaffen. Hierzu bedarf es aber auch der Mitwirkung der Ausländer.

'However terrible the events in front of the asylum-seekers' hostel in Hoyerswerda are; we cannot avoid thinking about the reasons for the low opinion of foreigners/asylum-seekers among almost the entire German population ('Widespread right-wing extremism', FR, 26.9.).

After all, it cannot be denied that a large number of foreigners come to Germany with an unbelievably demanding attitude, asking for things which Mr. Average Consumer has to work hard for and which – in his opinion – go above and beyond rescuing life and limb.

What is more the vast majority of the population cannot understand why foreign drug dealers, gamblers, thieves and gangs are set free immediately after having been arrested instead of being deported. The definite suspicion arises that a lot of this is due to the magic word 'asylum'. It is, therefore, in no way an 'attitude of the extreme right' if one demands that asylum-seekers lose their rights if they abuse the laws of a country which welcomes them and pays for their upkeep with its taxes. In my opinion this should not simply be dismissed as ale-house politics. A law only can be enforced as long as it is accepted by the population. Otherwise we risk losing completely the precious promise of asylum granted by our constitution.

Thus a multi-cultural society will not find a great deal of support if one cannot avoid the impression that one's own culture is of less importance. In this context I would like to warn against formally turning Germany into an immigration country. I already now shudder at the thought of the 'A people without enough room' theories which will then be heard. The relatively small Germany cannot be compared to Canada or Australia.

In order to save article 16 of the constitution, one needs to create broad foreigner acceptance by the population. However, this will only be possible with the help of the foreigners.'

L2: Uwe Tünnermann, Lemgo: *Nur eine kleine Hilfe*. In: Neue Westfälische, 24.9.91:

Die Bundesbürger(innen) haben in diesem Sommer wieder einmal den Eindruck, als stünde Deutschland in der 'Asylantenfrage' vor einem Überlebensproblem. Es vergeht kaum ein Tag, an dem nicht in den Zeitungen ein Artikel ... zum Thema Asylbewerber erscheint. ...

Die Bundesrepublik Deutschland ist trotz ihrer immensen finanziellen Verpflichtungen nach wie vor ein reicher Industriestaat. Sie hat nach Angaben von Amnesty International noch nicht einmal ein Prozent der Weltflüchtlingsmenge bei sich aufgenommen; die meisten Asylsuchenden der 'Dritten Welt' fliehen immer noch in angrenzende Entwicklungsländer.

Dennoch wurmt es hierzulande viele, daß diese Menschen aus aller Welt von unserem fleißig erwirtschafteten Bruttosozialprodukt leben. Dabei sollen wir nicht verdrängen, daß wir als Industrienation teilhaben an der Ausbeutung der Rohstoffe und Arbeitskräfte der 'Dritten Welt', deren Länder wir durch Schutzzölle, Niedrigpreise, Produktionsdiktate und Kreditbedingungen hindern, sich zu entwicklen (sic! M.K./W.K.). Wir tragen auch über unsere unsere atlantischen Bündnisverpflichtungen mit dazu bei, daß in Asien, Afrika und Lateinamerika undemokratische Regime aus militärpolitischen Gründen an der Macht bleiben. Wir sind auch als Europäer historisch mit hineinverflochten in die Spätfolgen der früheren abendländischen Kolonialpolitik.

Wenn wir Asylsuchende bei uns aufnehmen, leisten wir als Staat eigentlich nur unseren schuldigen Beitrag zur gemeinsamen internationalen Hilfe gegen das Weltflüchtlingselend. Wir sollten deshalb die Asylbewerber nicht ständig unter einen Dankbarkeitsdruck setzen, denn der einzelne Flüchtling kann nichts dafür, daß er im Schatten geboren ist, während wir im Licht leben. Über die Flüchtlingshilfe geben wir den unterentwickelten Ländern eigentlich nur einen kleinen Teil dessen zurück, was wir ihnen weltwirtschaftlich weggenommen haben und militärpolitisch heute noch wegnehmen. ...

'This summer, the citizens of the: Federal Republic are once again under the impression that Germany is facing problems of survival because of the 'asylum-seekers' question. Almost every day articles concerning the issue of the 'asylum-seekers' appear in the newspapers. ...

Despite its immense financial commitments, the Federal Republic is still a rich industrial nation. According to figures published by Amnesty International, it has not even taken up 1% of all refugees in the world; most asylum-seekers in the Third World still flee into neighboring developing countries.

Nevertheless many people living here are annoyed by the fact that these people from all over the world are living on our gross national product created by our hard work. However, as an industrial nation, we should not forget that we are participating in the exploitation of raw materials and manpower in the Third World, whose development is blocked by our protective trade duties, dumping prices, production constraints and credit terms. Moreover, through our NATO commitments we are contributing to the fact that undemocratic regimes can remain in power in Asia, Africa, and Latin America for reasons of military policy. Furthermore, as Europeans we are historically involved in the indirect consequences of the former European colonial Policy.

If we take in asylum-seekers, our country is only providing the contribution which it owes to joint international aid which tries to fight the misery suffered by the world's refugees. Therefore, we should not constantly force the refugees to be grateful because the individual refugee is not responsible for having been born in the darkness while we live in the light. By means of financial aid for the refugees we are only giving back to the underdeveloped countries a small part of what we have taken away from them through the global economy and are still taking away from them through military policy ....'

References

Apothéloz, Denis, Pierre-Yves Brandt, and Gustavo Quiroz, 1993: The function of negation in argumentation. Journal of Pragmatics 19: 23–38.

Aristotle, 1959. Rhetoric. Ed. by W.D. Ross. Oxford: Oxford University Press.

Aristotle, 1960. Posterior analytics. Ed. and transl. by H. Tredennick. Topica. Ed. and transl. by E.S. Forster. London: Heinemann.

Blair, J. Anthony, 1992. Premissary relevance. Argumentation 6: 203–217.

Cicero, 1951. De oratore. Ed. by A.S. Wilkins. Oxford: Oxford University Press.

Freeley, Austin J., 1986. Argumentation and debate. Belmont: Wadsworth.

Garssen, Bart, 1994. Recognizing argumentation schemes. In: F.H. Van Eemeren and R. Grootendorst, eds., Studies in pragma-dialectics, 105–111. Amsterdam: Sic Sat.

Green-Pedersen, Niels J., 1984. The tradition of the topics in the Middle Ages. München: Philosophia.

Grice, H. Paul, 1975. The logic of conversation. In: P. Cole and J.L. Morgan, eds., Syntax and semantics, 41–58. New York: Academic Press.

Gruber, Helmut. 1993: Political language and textual vagueness. Pragmatics 3: 1–28.

Kienpointner, Manfred, 1992a. Alltagslogik. Stuttgart: Frommann-Holzboog.

Kienpointner, Manfred, 1992b. How to classify arguments. In: F.H. Van Eemeren, R. Grootendorst, J.A. Blair and Ch.A. Willard, eds., Argumentation illuminated, 178–188. Amsterdam: Sic Sat.

Kienpointner, Manfred, 1993. The empirical relevance of Perelman's New Rhetoric. Argumentation 7: 419–437.

Kienpointner, Manffed, 1996. Vernünftig argumentieren. Reinbek: Rowohlt.

Kindt, Walther, 1988. Zur Logik von Alltagsargumentationen. Fachberichte Informatik der EWH Koblenz 3: 1–48.

Kindt, Walther, 1992a. Organisationsformen des Argumentierens in natürlicher Sprache. In: H. Paschen and L. Wigger, eds., Pädagogisches Argumentieren, 95–120. Weinheim: Deutscher Studienverlag.

Kindt, Walther, 1992b. Argumentation und Konfliktaustragung in Äußerungen über den Golfkrieg. Zeitschrift für Sprachwissenschaft 11: 189–215.

Pater, W.A. de, 1965. Les topiques d'Aristote et la dialectique platonicienne. Fribourg: Ed. Saint Paul.

Paul, Richard W., 1987. Critical thinking in the strong sense and the role of argumentation in everyday life. In: F.H. Van Eemeren, R. Grootendorst, J.A. Blair and Ch.A. Willard, eds., Argumentation: Across the lines of disciplines, 379–382. Dordrecht: Foris.

Peirce, Charles S., 1973. Lectures on pragmatism/Vorlesungen über Pragmatismus. Ed. and transl. by E. Walther. Hamburg: Meiner.

Perelman, Chaim and Lucie Olbrechts-Tyteca, 1971. The New Rhetoric. A treatise on argumentation. Notre Dame, IN: University of Notre Dame Press.

Quintilianus, 1970. Institutio oratoria. Ed. by M. Winterbottom. 2 vols. Oxford. Oxford University Press.

Schellens, Peter J., 1985. Redelijke argumenten. Utrecht: ICG Printing-Dordrecht.

Toulmin, Stephen, 1958. The uses of argument. Cambridge: Cambridge University Press.

Toulmin, Stephen, Richard Rieke and Allan Janik, 1984. An introduction to reasoning. New York: Macmillan.

Van Dijk, Teun A., 1992. Racism and argumentation: Race riot rhetoric tabloid editorials. In: F.H. Van Eemeren, R. Grootendorst, J.A. Blair ind Ch.A. Willard, eds., Argumentation illuminated, 243–259. Amsterdam: Sic Sat.

Van Dijk, Teun A., 1993. Elite discourse and racism. Newbury Park, CA: Sage.

Van Dijk, Teun A. and Walter Kintsch, 1983. Strategies of discourse comprehension. New York: Academic Press.

Van Eemeren, Frans H. and Rob Grootendorst, 1984. Speech acts in argumentative discussions. Dordrecht: Foris.

Van Eemeren, Frans H. and Rob Grootendorst, 1992. Argumentation, communication and fallacies. Hillsdale, NJ: Erlbaum.

Van Eemeren, Hans H. and Rob Grootendorst, eds., 1994. Studies in pragma-dialectics. Amsterdam: Sic Sat.

Van Eemeren, Frans H. and Tjark Kruiger, 1987. Identifying argumentation schemes. In: F.H. Van Eemeren, R. Grootendorst, J.A. Blair and Ch.A. Willard, eds., Argumentation. Perspectives and approaches, 70–81.

Van Eemeren, Frans H., Rob Grootendorst, Sally Jackson and Scott Jacobs, 1993. Reconstructing argumentative discourse. Tuscaloosa, AL: University of Alabama Press.

Walton, Douglas, 1991. Bias, critical doubt, and fallacies. Argumentation and Advocacy 28: 1–22.

Walton, Douglas, 1992. The place of emotion in argument. University Park, PA: Pennsylvania State University Press.

Warnick, Barbara, and Susan L. Kline, 1992. The New Rhetoric's argument schemes: A rhetorical view of practical reasoning. Argumentation and Advocacy 29: 1–15.

Woods, John and Douglas Walton, 1989. Fallacies: Selected papers 1972–1987. Berlin: Foris/De Gruyter.

Wodak, Ruth et al., 1990. 'Wir sind alle unschuldige Täter'. Diskurshistorische Studien zum Nachkriegsantisemitismus. Frankfurt a. M.: Suhrkamp.

59

Discourses and Concepts: Interfaces and Synergies between *Begriffsgeschichte* and the Discourse-Historical Approach in CDA

Michał Krzyżanowski

1. Introduction

Developed since the early 1990s by Ruth Wodak and her collaborators – initially at the University of Vienna and later also at Lancaster University in the UK – the Discourse-Historical Approach (hereinafter DHA) remains one of the most open and interdisciplinary traditions in Critical Discourse Analysis. The claim that, just like the majority of CDA, the DHA "is by its nature interdisciplinary, combining diverse disciplinary perspectives in its analysis" (Wodak, 1996: 17) has been one of the standard premises of the approach. As the most recent credo of the tradition also suggests, its interdisciplinarity "involves theory, methods, methodology, research practice and practical application" (Reisigl and Wodak, 2009: 94; cf. also Wodak, 2001). The interdisciplinary devotion of the linguistically-rooted DHA has been particularly visible in a multitude of theoretical and analytical approaches which have been applied by the trend to its research of diverse research objects in different contexts (cf. Krzyżanowski, 2010; for an overview). The diverse theoretical and analytical approaches applied by the DHA over the years have originated in a range of social sciences and cognate areas, including,

Source: Rudolf de Cillia, Helmut Gruber, Michael Krzyżanowski and Florian Menz (eds), *Diskurs Politik-Identität/Discourse-Politics-Identity* (Tübingen: Stauffenburg Verlag, 2010), pp. 125–135.

inter alia, social theory, (political) sociology, political science, legal studies, social anthropology, organisational research and, last but not least, history.

It is the discipline of history which has recently immensely contributed to the DHA research. Initially, history was providing DHA studies with necessary (and always desired) in-depth contextual information in its widely-known diachronic explorations (e.g. Wodak et al., 1990 and 1994 and 1999). However, in the last decade, we have also seen that many analytical and conceptual tools which developed within history – or more specifically a branch of social history known as *conceptual history* or *historical semantics* – have been used widely in the DHA explorations. A particularly prominent role has been played here by the German tradition of history of concepts – or *Begriffsgeschichte* (hereinafter BG) – which was widely present in the DHA studies of the last decade.

The aim of this (short) chapter is to provide a synthesis of multiple interfaces between, on the one hand, the German *Begriffsgeschichte*, and, on the other hand, the Discourse-Historical Approach. As most of the readers of this volume are familiar with foundations, aims and key concepts in DHA which has been elaborated widely in recent years (cf. Wodak, 2001 and 2008; Reisigl and Wodak, 2001 and 2009), the chapter will start from a brief sketch of foundations of BG and its key theoretical and analytical foundations, particularly those relevant to DHA work. Then, the contribution will outline interfaces between BG and DHA by pointing to the several levels at which BG ideas have been incorporated in DHA works as well as by referring to some joint BG-DHA research foci.

2. Key Concepts and Terms in the German Begriffsgeschichte

Initiated in the 1950s and 1960s by the German historian Reinhart Koselleck (1923–2006), 'history of concepts' or *Begriffsgeschichte* (cf., inter alia, Brunner et. al, 1972, Koselleck, 2002) remains one of the most progressive currents in social history. It is also one of the most interdisciplinary oriented approaches within the historical science and the one which, following broader trends in the social sciences, initiated 'linguistic turn within the discipline of social history' (Ifversen, 1997, in Åkerstrøm-Andersen, 2003: 33). Unlike other historical semantic approaches represented by, inter alia, the so-called Cambridge School (Q. Skinner, J. Pocock, et. al.; cf. Richter, 2003) and traditionally placed within the broader trend of history of ideas (cf. also Åkerstrøm-Andersen, 2003), German *Begriffsgeschichte* (BG) must be viewed as linguistically-oriented social history. For this reason, while strongly influenced by the history of social and political thought, representatives of BG have increasingly turned to linguistically-inspired or discourse-based and discourse-oriented analyses (cf. Ifversen, 2003). So far – contrary to the rather strictly-Anglo-Saxon Cambridge School – BG has become most popular in the German-speaking area in which it originated (in the works of Koselleck himself or his collaborators, such as Conze or Brunner and many others) as well as in various Scandinavian countries where scholars such as Bo Stråth, Jan Ifversen or Kari Palonen have become the most prominent in popularising BG. The only exception in the Anglo-Saxon Academia, generally rather reluctant towards BG (cf. Munslow, 2007), is the work of Melvin Richter who undertook several successful attempts to popularise BG in the English-speaking countries where he also contributed to many debates between BG and the history of ideas (cf. e.g. Richter, 1987, 1995 and 2003; Lehmann and Richter, 1996).

The basic interest of BG is in both synchronic and diachronic analysis of *key social and political concepts.* BG views concepts as "central to the constitution of society, including the constitution of action as well as agents of action" (Åkerstrøm-Andersen, 2003: 34). The becoming or constitution of society takes place in a form of "a semantic battle about the political and the social; a battle about definition, defence and occupation of conceptually composed positions" (ibid.). Accordingly, concepts are viewed by Koselleck (1982a) as basic elements of all social fields of action, whereas the former and the latter remain in a state of dialectical relation. Koselleck sees concepts in a very close relation to their lexical representation, yet clearly argues that whereas "each concept is associated with a word (…) not every word is a social and political concept" (Koselleck, 1982a: 418). Thus, only selected lexical items may become key concepts which "possess a substantial claim of generality and always have many meanings" (ibid.). Richter (2003: 94) outlines the following groups of concepts which are traditionally in the focus of BG:

> "(1) concepts long in use, such as 'democracy', the meaning of which can still be understood by the speaker of the language today; (2) concepts such as 'civil society', the earlier meanings of which have been so effaced that they can now be understood only after scholarly reconstruction of their prior meanings; (3) neologisms such as 'caesarism', 'fascism' or 'Marxism', coined in the course of revolutionary changes they helped to shape or interpret".

Analysing development and recurrence of such social and political concepts, BG distinguishes between three types of concepts: (a) the so-called basic or key social and political concepts (*Grundbegriffe*), (b) their neighbouring or sister-concepts (*Nebenbegriffe)* and (c) their adversary or counter-concepts (*Gegenbegriffe*). *Grundbegriffe*, it seems, are at the core of BG's interests as such concepts which possess a mobilising force and which, as such, always appear in critical moments of history known as periods of crisis and transformation (in line with Koselleck's earlier claims on the fundamental importance of critique and crisis, or *Kritik und Krise,* in the development of socio-political reality; cf. Koselleck, 1959). It is for this reason that the BG's search for *Grundbegriffe* has inter alia focussed on France (1680–1820) or

German-speaking Europe (1750–1850) in the very pregnant period of enlightenment and early modernity.

Whereas, in a diachronic perspective, only recurrence of the *Grundbegriffe* can be considered, the synchronically-oriented analyses in BG focus on the larger semantic webs defined as *semantic fields*. The latter are formed in the process of positioning *Grundbegriffe* vis-à-vis their *Nebenbegriffe* and their *Gegenbegriffe*. The general question in the diachronic analyses remains concerned about the *singularity or generality* of particular concepts – that is, plainly speaking – the likelihood of their uniqueness for particular contexts or their ability to become universal concepts (cf. Koselleck, 1985; Åkerstrøm-Andersen, 2003). On the other hand, the synchronic analyses operate on a number of dimensions which can help to not only discover concepts and relationships between the concepts, but to also view how the thus constructed semantic fields contribute to the constitution of society and social fields of action. Accordingly, BG's analyses and interpretations are guided by the following key categories (also known as 'pre-linguistic distinctions' or 'couples of opposition', cf. Åkerstrøm-Andersen, 2003: 43):

(a) *Before and After*, which, expressed in Koselleck's famous distinction between the 'scope of experience' (*Erfahrungsraum*) and 'horizon of expectations' (*Erwartung–shorizont*) (cf. Koselleck, 1979 and 1985; Schinkel, 2005), allow to view the (historical) formation of space-time relationship in "continuously changing patterns and relations" (Åkerstrøm-Andersen, 2003: 44) born out of "tension between expectation and experience"(ibid.);
(b) *Inside and Outside*, which allow distinguishing between inside and outside of every society as in case of the concepts of 'enemy/friend' etc. (cf. Åkerstrøm-Andersen, 2003: 45) and which are also reproduced in categories of 'us' and 'them';
(c) *Up and Down*, which allow for the ordering of concepts along the lines of intra-societal divisions and which define "political self-organisation" (cf. Åkerstrøm-Andersen, 2003: 45) as well as "distribution of relationships and dependency" (ibid.) as in, e.g., the master/slave relationship.

Though present also in diachronic investigations, the listed categories are the foundation of BG's synchronic investigation of how concepts as well as their counter- or sister-concepts form semantic relations and how, thus, semantic fields are constructed and effectively displaced.

3. Interfaces and Synergies between Begriffsgeschichte and the Discourse-Historical Approach

Though there have been different (mainly theoretically-oriented) studies which pointed to the plausibility of merger between *Begriffsgeschichte* and diverse discourse-theoretical and discourse-analytical approaches (cf. Ifversen,

2003; Åkerstrøm-Andersen, 2003; Foxlee, 2009a and 2009b), the DHA definitely remains one research tradition which has created many links with BG. Those links, or interfaces, can be considered at several levels including theoretical and conceptual foundations, analytical and interpretative links as well as common research foci.

3.1. (Some) Theoretical and Conceptual Interfaces between DHA and BG

Though 'discourse' as a term does not function as predominantly in BG as in some other trends of conceptual history (cf. Foxlee, 2009a), BG and DHA clearly share many ideas of which the central one is that *language (and discourse) constitute social and political reality.* It is for this reason that both BG and DHA emphasise the role of combination of synchronic and diachronic dimensions of analysis in order to discover how different forms of linguistic realisation ('texts' in DHA, 'words' or 'lexical items' in BG) re-appear in different contexts thus becoming symptomatic for the re-emergence of deeper social and political meanings and perspectives ('discourses' in DHA, 'concepts' in BG). Whereas different aspects of discourse are highlighted in DHA (cf. Wodak, 2008; Reisigl and Wodak, 2009), it views discourses as predominantly historical as well as inherently dependent on the contexts of their social production and reception. Accordingly, as Wodak (1996: 19) suggests:

> "Discourse is historical: Discourse is not produced and cannot be understood without taking the context into consideration. (...). Discourses are always connected to other discourses which were produced earlier, as well as to those which are produced synchronically or subsequently".

It is precisely the DHA's strong *reliance on contexts* which constitutes another link to the BG. Unlike sometimes suggested by opponents of BG, the latter is not only interested in diverse types of concepts as such (or in their surface-level lexical representations only) but draws heavily on the in-depth knowledge and analysis of social and political contexts in which those concepts emerge (and effectively, as postulated by BG, which the concepts quasi-outlive by becoming elements of standard social and political vocabulary). It is here that another crucial synergy appears between DHA and BG. Just like BG, DHA ascribes a unique role to context and postulates its broad definition ranging from text-internal structures up until the broad socio-political and indeed historical context. In DHA the context is explored at four levels which include (Wodak, 2001: 67):

> (a) "the immediate, language or text internal co-text"; (b) "the intertextual and interdiscursive relationship between utterances, texts, genres and discourses"; (c) "the extra-linguistic social/sociological variables and

institutional frames of a specific 'context of situation'" (…) and; (d) "the broader socio-political and historical contexts, which the discursive practices are embedded in and related to".

It is important that, whereas both BG and DHA emphasise the necessary connection between language and discourse and the broader (incl. historical) context, the multi-level approach to context in DHA points to the necessity of approaching relationship between discourse and context in a gradual and systematic way (somewhat missing in BG), thus also allowing for the necessary 'micro-macro mediation' between text, discourse and society (cf. Wodak, 2006).

Finally, the salient DHA concept of *recontextualisation* (cf. Wodak, 2000 and 2001) also yields itself here by grasping processes where certain meanings or arguments outlive the contexts in which they were produced (in BG) by being taken out of their original contexts and put into new ones (in DHA). The idea of recontextualisation draws on the post-Bakhtinian concept of *intertextuality* (cf. also de Beaugrande and Dressler, 1981) as well as the key DHA idea of *interdiscursivity* (cf. Wodak, 2001). Just like many other key concepts and terms in DHA, recontextualisation is understood in a systematic and gradual way which consists of three levels (cf. Wodak 2000 and 2001; for further details): *contextualisation* (when a discursive element is put into a certain context), *decontextualisation* (when a discursive element is taken out of its original context) and, finally, *recontextualisation* (when a discursive element is being put into a new context). Recontextualisation points to the way in which DHA approaches the historical and diachronic nature of discourse. By analysing how certain discursive elements (most notably arguments or *topoi)* can be re-accommodated across spatial and temporal dimensions (in different contexts, and at different points in history). Whereas BG is quite similarly interested in a parallel process of re-accommodation of concepts along the spatio-temporal lines, it rarely seems to look systematically at how those processes take place, and how concepts become attached to, or detached from, their contexts. Thus, the gradual and phased description of such processes offered by the analytical concept of recontextualisation would certainly be of value in BG's conceptual-historical analyses.

3.2. Interfaces between DHA and BG at the Interpretative and Analytical Level

The key elements of the BG's conceptual apparatus which have been present in DHA works is the idea of existence of *'scope of experience' (Erfahrungsraum)* and *'horizon of expectations' (Erwartungshorizont,* cf. Koselleck, 1979 and above). The idea has been used widely in many of the recent DHA studies. Starting from the work by Wodak et. al. (1999) – which initiated a very lively DHA trend of explorations on social and political identities in different national and supranational contexts (cf. inter alia, Wodak, 2009; Wodak and Weiss, 2004; Weiss, 2002a; Krzyżanowski and Oberhuber, 2007; Krzyżanowski, 2010) – the experience/expectations categories have become crucial in the process of highlighting discursive construction of identifications within different fields of social action. Those categories allowed, inter alia, highlighting the importance of spatio-temporal distinctions in the formation of identities in and through discourse. The categories also helped to discover analytically how diverse the subjects' (individual and collective) identifications are formed by means of referring to individual and common past and future in discourse.

A more analytical, rather than interpretative of BG concepts used widely in DHA analyses is that of *semantic fields* (cf. above). The latter is investigated by DHA – quite similarly to BG – with the aim of discovering the variety of arguments and themes (or other discursive elements) which are used in relation to different widely-debated social and political concepts or other highly-connotative and necessarily polysemous lexemes incl. proper names. Whereas, similarly to BG (cf. above), DHA looks at diverse semantic fields in a mainly synchronic way, it remains devoted to diachronic comparisons of similarities and differences within and between those fields over time.

From DHA studies, my own work (cf. Krzyżanowski, 2002) provides a conceptually-oriented analysis of ideological connotations that exist in media discourse between widely-recogonised political figures (e.g. 'Haider' vs. 'Hitler', etc.). The study analysed Polish press discourse about the 'Austrian Crisis 2000' i.e. a spectacular electoral gain of Jörg Haider's rightwing populist Austrian Freedom Party, its subsequent joining of Austrian government and the ensuing sanctions of the EU-14 against the Austrian government. The work also included analysis of semantic fields which were formed in the process of forming relation between the two key concepts – one historical and one contemporary – and their semantically- and connotatively-defined *Nebenbegriffe* and *Gegenbegriffe*. The analysis aimed to show how, despite their real-world spatio-temporal differences, the semantic field of the two name-concepts – defined in the 2002 study as 'symbolic elements of discourse' – became to a large extent convergent, mainly due to the fact of Haider's own actions and his frequent and overtly positive recalling of Nazi times and of the Austrian NS past. Performed mainly at the thematic level of DHA exploration (of *discourse topics*, cf. e.g. van Dijk, 1988), the analysis also helped showing how the semantic field of 'Haider' (cf. Figure 1) was constructed from content-based relations of the past- and present-oriented elements of discourse.

Conducted in a context of a wider research programme 'DYLAN' looking at multilingualism in post-enlargement European Union[1], a very recent DHA study (cf. Krzyżanowski and Wodak, 2010) proposed a somewhat different application of the notion *of semantic fields*. The latter – applied to the diachronic analysis of the meaning of 'multilingualism' and related concepts

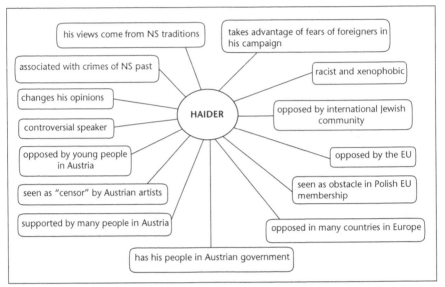

Source: Krzyżanowski, 2002: 151.

Figure 1: Semantic Field of Connotations related to Symbolic Element 'Haider' in Polish Press Discourse about the 'Austrian Crisis 2000'

in EU language policy documents – have been followed in a way close to the understanding of semantic fields within BG. The study did not look as much on the, e.g., content-related elements of discourse (themes or discourse topics), as on the other concepts – mainly in the meaning of *Nebenbegriffe* (cf. above) – related to the central idea of 'multilingualism' as well as, at a further stage of exploration, at the diversity of arguments used in discourse to support those notions. The analysis was performed in order to trace the changing meaning of 'multilingualism' in EU language policy over time as well as to emphasise the impact of broader and equally evolving EU-political agenda on that particular policy field. As it has been established, the meaning of the concept of 'multilingualism' in EU language policy changed significantly over the analysed period and reached the most complex stage of development in mid-2000s (cf. Figure 2). At this stage, the concept of 'multilingualism' was related to three major *Nebenbegriffe* (multilingual economy, multilingual society and multilingualism in European Commission's relations with citizens) which all broke down into further concepts (as well as related arguments). Interestingly, the analysis helped discovering how the 'old' topics of EU policy (e.g. its interest in economic aspects of European integration, or its traditionally problematic concept of 'social Europe') all became integral parts of the semantic field of 'multilingualism' along with the more contemporary concepts (democratic aspects of 'communicating EU' to its citizens) salient to the EU agenda at that time, i.e. so far at the heyday of EU language policy.

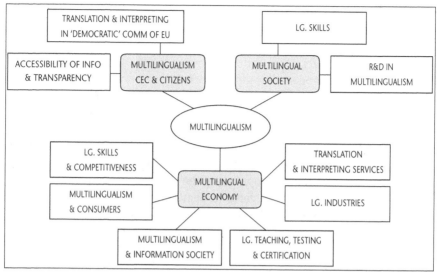

Source: Krzyżanowski and Wodak, 2010.

Figure 2: Semantic Field of Multilingualism in EU language policy documents in 2005

3.3 Common Research Foci in BG and DHA

Finally, the obvious connections between BG and DHA have taken place at the *focal level* with both research traditions sharing interest in the same or very similar research foci. Of the latter, the most important remains the very polysemous concept of 'Europe' (cf. also Koselleck, 1982b) together with its sister- and counter-concepts.

In BG, scholars such as Stråth (2000, 2002, 2005 and 2008), Malmborg and Stråth (2002) or Ifversen (2002) emphasised different conceptualisations of *Europe, European civilisation* or *European identity* in diverse contexts. Of these, it is exactly the idea of European identity (cf. also above) which eventually drew DHA researchers into Europe-related research. DHA works by, inter alia, Weiss (2002a and 2002b), Wodak (2003 and 2009), Wodak and Weiss (2004) or Krzyżanowski (2003, 2008 and 2010) and Busch and Krzyżanowski (2007) concentrated on discourses of European identity while ascribing key importance to the ways in which 'Europe' (as a social and political concept) was defined in different contexts. More recently, a DHA study by Krzyżanowski and Oberhuber (2007; published in a BG-related book series on 'Multiple Europes' edited by Stråth) has – while explicitly referring to key premises of BG – looked at how concepts of 'Europe' and 'European Union' were discursively constructed as convergent and divergent in intra- and extra-institutional, national and supranational discourses of the so-called EU-constitutional debate. The main finding of those analyses was that, while using a similar set of structures of arguments for/against Europe/EU, many of the key figures of the EU constitutional debate and of its most prominent event i.e. the 2002–03 European Convention saw those concepts very differently and in an almost individually-specific manner (cf. also Krzyżanowski, 2010; for related analyses).

Whereas the earlier focal synergies between BG and DHA resulted in many parallel studies on similar topics (such as those on 'Europe', cf. above), some of the recent work has been undertaken in a close collaboration of the two approaches. For example, in a recent cross-national research project EMEDIATE[2], several BG scholars (incl. Stråth and Schulz-Forberg) and DHA researchers (incl. Wodak and Krzyżanowski), as well as other scholars from within media studies and political science, worked jointly on the process of historical and diachronic development of the European Public Sphere. Here, BG and DHA researchers investigated in-depth (while using an interpretative apparatus inspired by BG, and a mainly DHA-based methodological framework) how media discourses on key periods of crisis of the post-war European history contributed to the change in social and political conceptualisation of 'Europe' (as well as of its *Nebenbegriffe* of 'European values' or 'European identity', cf. Krzyżanowski, 2009; Triandafyllidou, Wodak and Krzyżanowski, 2009). Among the main findings of that collaborative BG-DHA study was a conclusion that the concept of 'Europe' never comes to the foreground on media reporting on (European and other) crises in the post-War period (quite differently to, e.g., the ways of reporting of events related to the EU in 1990s and 2000s). Accordingly, media had very limited impact on any far-reaching (re-) conceptualisation of Europe in the post-War period, with Europe's key *Nebenbegriffe* (European values, European identity) also making place for other, strictly-national considerations and concepts (cf. ibid.; for further details). Equally, the research proved that the role of Koselleck's idea of *Kritik and Krise* (cf. above) is limited in the media which, though actively involved in its construction, quasi stand aside of the socio-political reality cyclically reconstructed by transformation and crisis.

4. (Very Short) Conclusions

The provided synthesis has aimed to enumerate the key areas in which many synergies have already been worked out between the followers of the German *Begriffsgeschichte* and of the *Discourse-Historical Approach in CDA*. Severely constrained by the limitations of space, the presented synthesis has surely been selective. Written by a DHA researcher, the provided outline has also been one-sided and has looked at the BG-DHA interfaces mostly from the perspective of DHA and of applications therein of several BG conceptual and interpretative tools. However, the chapter has also, though in a limited fashion, pointed to DHA concepts and analytical tools which could be applied more widely within BG (e.g. at the very analytical or interpretative level, cf. above). The main closing postulate of this contribution is that a constructive dialogue between the BG and DHA – initiated by Ruth Wodak and her followers (incl. the author of this chapter) – must be furthered and deepened to the benefit of both approaches and their inherently interdisciplinary character.

Notes

1. DYLAN (Language Dynamics and Management of Diversity) is an Integrated Project carried out under the EU Sixth Framework Programme between 2006 and 2011 (www.dylan-project.org).
2. EMEDIATE 'Media and Ethics of European Public Sphere – From the Treaty of Rome to the War on Terror' was an EU-FP6 research project carried between 2004 and 2007 at eight European Universities (http://www.cui.cu/RSCAS/Research/EMEDIATE/Index.shtml).

References

Åkerstrøm-Andersen, N. (2003). *Discursive Analytical Strategies. Understanding Foucault, Koselleck, Laclau, Luhmann*. Bristol: The Policy Press.

Brunner, O./ Conze, W./ Koselleck, R. (1972). *Geschichtliche Grundbegiffe: Historisches Lexikon zur politisch-sozialen Sprache in Deutschland*. (Vol. 1). Stuttgart: Klett-Cotta.

Busch, B./ Krzyżanowski, M. (2007). Outside/Inside the EU: Enlargement, Migration Policies and the Search for Europe's Identity. In: J. Anderson and W. Armstrong (eds). *Geopolitics of European Union Enlargement: The Fortress Empire*. London: Routledge, 107–124.

de Beaugrande, R./ Dressler, W. U. (1981). *Introduction to Text Linguistics*. London: Longman.

Foxlee, N. (2009a). *Concepts, Texts and Discourses: Contextualist Approaches to Intellectual-Historical Discourse Analysis*. Presentation to the Language, Ideology and Power Research Group (LIP), LAEL, Lancaster University, January 19th, 2009.

Foxlee, N. (2009b). *Initiating a Dialogue: Critical Discourse Analysis, Corpus Linguistics and the History of Concepts*. Paper delivered at 'New Directions in the History of Concepts' 10th annual conference of the History of Political and Social Concepts Group, London and Oxford, 17–19 September 2009.

Ifversen, J. (1997). Og magt, demokrati og diskurs. *Begrebshistoriske Studier No 2*. Århus: University of Århus.

Ifversen, J. (2002). The Meaning of European Civilization – A Historical-Conceptual Approach. *European Societies*, 4(1), 1–26.

Ifversen, J. (2003). Text, Discourse, Concept: Approaches to Textual Analysis. *Kontur*, No. 7, 60–69.

Koselleck, R. (1959). *Kritik und Krise. Eine Studie zur Pathogenese der Bürgerlichen Welt*. Freiburg: Alber.

Koselleck, R. (1979). *Vergangene Zukunft. Zur Semantik geschichtlicher Zeiten*. Frankfurt am Main: Suhrkamp.

Koselleck, R. (1982a). Begriffsgeschichte and Social History. *Economy and Society*, 11(4), 409–427.

Koselleck, R. (1982b). *Europa im Zeitalter der europäischen Revolutionen*. Frankfurt am Main: Suhrkamp.

Koselleck, R. (1985). *Futures Past. On the Semantics of Historical Time*. Boston, MA: MIT Press.

Koselleck, R. (2002). *The Practice of Conceptual History. Timing History, Spacing Concepts*. Palo Alto, CA: Stanford University Press.

Krzyżanowski, M. (2002). Haider: The New Symbolic Element in the Ongoing Discourse of the Past. In: Wodak, R./ Pelinka, A. (eds). *The Haider Phenomenon in Austria*. New Brunswick, N.J.: Transaction Publishers, 121–157.

Krzyżanowski, M. (2003). My European feelings are not only based on the fact that I live in Europe: On the new mechanisms in European and national identification patterns emerging under the influence of EU Enlargement. *Journal of Language and Politics* 2(1), 175–204.

Krzyżanowski, M. (2008). On the Europeanisation of Identity Constructions in Polish Political Discourse after 1989. In: Galasińska, A./ Krzyżanowski, M. (eds). *Discourse and Transformation in Central and Eastern Europe*. Basingstoke: Palgrave Macmillan, 95–113

Krzyżanowski, M. (2009). Europe in Crisis: Discourses on Crisis-Events in the European Press 1956–2006. In: *Journalism Studies,* 10(1), 18–35.

Krzyżanowski, M. (2010). *The Discursive Construction of European Identities*. Frankfurt a.M.: Peter Lang.

Krzyżanowski, M./ Oberhuber, F. (2007). *(Un)Doing Europe. Discourses and Practices of Negotiating the EU Constitution*. Brussels: P.I.E.-Peter Lang.

Krzyżanowski, M./ Triandafyllidou, A./ Wodak, R. (2009). Conclusions: Europe, Media, Crisis and the European Public Sphere. In: Triandafyllidou, A./ Wodak, R./ Krzyżanowski, M. (eds). (2009), 261–268.

Krzyżanowski, M./ Wodak, R. (2010). Hegemonic Multilingualism in/of the EU Institutions: An Inside-Outside Perspective on the European Language Policies and Practices. In: Böhringer, H./ Hülmbauer, C./ Vetter, E. (eds). *Mehrsprachigkeit in europäischer Perspektive*. Frankfurt/Main: Peter Lang, in press.

Lehmann, H./ Richter, M. (eds) (1996). *The Meaning of Historical Terms and Concepts: New Studies in Begriffsgeschichte*. Washington, D.C.: German Historical Institute.

Malmborg, M. af/ Stråth, B. (eds) (2002). *The Meaning of Europe*. Oxford: Berg.

Munslow, A. (2007). Book Review: Futures Past: On the Semantics of Historical Time. *Theory, Culture and Society* 24(1), 156–160.

Reisigl, M./ Wodak, R. (2001). *Discourse and Discrimination: Rhetoric of Racism and Anti-Semitism*. London: Routledge.

Reisigl, M./ Wodak, R. (2009). The Discourse-Historical Approach (DHA). In: Wodak, R./ Meyer, M. (eds) *Methods of Critical Discourse Analysis* (2nd Edition). London: Sage, 87–121.

Richter, M. (1987). Begriffsgeschichte and the History of Ideas. *Journal of the History of Ideas,* 48(2), 247–263.

Richter, M. (1995). *The History of Political and Social Concepts: A Critical Introduction*. New York: Oxford University Press.

Richter, M. (2003). Towards a Lexicon of European Political and Legal Concepts. A Comparison between Begriffsgeschichte and the Cambridge School. *CRISPP*, 6(2), 91–120.

Schinkel, A. (2005). Imagination as a Category of History. An Essay Concerning Koselleck's Concepts of *Erfahrungsraum* and *Erwartungshorizont*. *History and Theory* 44/2005, 42–54.

Stråth, B. (ed.) (2000). *Europe and the Other and Europe as the Other*. Brussels: P.I.E. – Peter Lang.

Stråth, B. (2002). A European Identity: To the Historical Limits of a Concept. *European Journal of Social Theory*, 5(4), 387–401.

Stråth, B. (2005). Future of Europe. *Journal of Language and Politics,* 5(3), 427–448.

Stråth, B. (2008). Belonging and European Identity. In: Delanty, G./ Jones P.R./ R. Wodak. (eds). *Identity, Belonging and Migration*. Liverpool: Liverpool University Press, 21–38.

Triandafyllidou, A./ Wodak, R./ Krzyżanowski, M. (eds) (2009). *European Public Sphere and the Media: Europe in Crisis*. Basingstoke: Palgrave Macmillan.

van Dijk, T. A. (1988). *News as Discourse.* Hillsdale, NJ: Lawrence Erlbaum Associates.

Weiss, G. (2002a). Searching for Europe: The Problem of Legitimisation and Representation in Recent Political Speeches on Europe. *Journal of Language and Politics,* 1(1), 59–83.

Weiss, G. (2002b). A.E.I.O.U. – Austria Europae Imago, Onus, Unio? In: Mamborg, M. af/ Stråth, B. (eds)(2002), 263–285.

Wodak, R. (1996). *Disorders of Discourse.* London: Longman.

Wodak, R. (2000). Recontextualisation and Transformation of Meanings: A Critical Discourse Analysis of Decision-Making in EU Meetings about Employment Policies. In: Sarangi, S./ Coulthard, M. (eds). *Discourse and Social Life.* London: Longman, 185–207.

Wodak, R. (2001). The Discourse-Historical Approach. In: Wodak, R./ Meyer, M. (eds). *Methods of Critical Discourse Analysis.* London: Sage, 63–94.

Wodak, R. (2003). Multiple Identities: The Roles of Female Parliamentarians in the EU Parliament. In: Holmes, J./ Meyerhoff, M. (eds). *The Handbook of Language and Gender.* London: Blackwell, 671–699.

Wodak, R. (2006). Mediation between Discourse and Society: Assessing Cognitive Approaches in CDA. *Discourse Studies* 8(1), 179–190.

Wodak, R. (2008). Discourse Studies – Important Concepts and Terms. In: Wodak, R./ Krzyżanowski, M. (eds) (2008), 1–29.

Wodak, R. (2009). *The Discourse of Politics in Action. Politics as Usual.* Basingstoke: Palgrave Macmillan.

Wodak, R./ de Cillia, R./ Gruber, H./ Mitten, R./ Nowak, P./ Pelikan, J. (1990). *"Wir sind alle unschuldige Täter!" Diskurshistorische Studien zum Nachkriegsantisemitismus* Frankfurt/Main: Suhrkamp.

Wodak, R./ Menz, F./ Mitten, R./ Stern, F. (1994). *Sprachen der Vergangenheiten.* Frankfurt/ Main: Suhrkamp.

Wodak, R./ de Cilia, R./ Reisigl M./ Liebhart, K. (1999). *The Discursive Construction of National Identity.* Edinburgh: Edinburgh University Press.

Wodak, R./ Weiss, G. (2004). Visions, Ideologies and Utopias in the Discursive Construction of European Identities: Organising, Representing and Legitimising Europe. In: Pütz, M./ van Dijk, T. A./ Neff-van Aertselaer, J-A (eds). *Communicating Ideologies: Language, Discourse and Social Practice.* Frankfurt am Main: Peter Lang, 225–252.

Wodak, R./ Krzyżanowski, M. (eds) (2008). *Qualitative Discourse Analysis in the Social Sciences.* Basingstoke: Palgrave Macmillan.

60

Discursive Technologies and the Social Organization of Meaning

Jay L. Lemke

1. Introduction

The concept of meaning, like that of cognition itself, is increasingly being conceptualized today as the outcome of a process of interaction between the organism and its environment. Meanings are made by the interaction of brains and bodies with texts, artifacts, ecologies and persons, according to the social conventions of cultures, in particular situations and settings. The semantic systems of language and the typical forms of narratives and other genres of text and discourse are widely recognized today as essential cultural resources mobilized by individuals to do the work of institutions, relationship- and identity-building, and cultural innovation. Because language is made to do the work of organizing society, social technologies of organization get written into the forms of language and inscribed in the bodies and meaning-making habits of people. The thesis I would like to propose, somewhat tentatively, in this article is that contemporary changes in the organization of society, such as globalization, are associated with significant shifts in the dominance of particular discursive technologies.

The dominant discursive technology of late modernism has been the standardized text or discourse genre, epitomized perhaps in the bureaucratic 'forms' we fill in again and again in our lives, and which function to organize society, and us, on larger scales. I want to explore the relationship

Source: *Folia Linguistica*, XXXVII(1–2) (2001): 79–96.

between this discourse technology and the social technology of organization that it serves. This relationship is highlighted when we begin to consider the ways in which such post-modern discourse technologies as hypertext afford us the possibility of creating new kinds of syntagmatic meanings by linking across the re-contextualized elements of traditional genres and forms. The meaningful traversal of a hypertext database is but one instance, I will argue, of a more general re-organization of the possibilities for post-modern identities, societies, and meanings. These *traversals* of many kinds suggest the emergence of new principles of social organization and control.

Critical discourse analysis is primarily concerned with understanding how we use language to maintain, resist, and change the social, cultural, economic, and political organization of society. I want to suggest that it can also be used to identify emergent new discourse technologies and modes of social organization and control, and that we need to study not just how language sustains the *status quo* in society, but how it is implicated in the profound changes now taking place in the global re-organization of society (cf. Gee, Hull, & Lankshear 1997; Fairclough 2000; Language in the New Capitalism website). This project is profoundly relevant to the study of cognition, i.e. to understanding how people make situated local meaning, because it tells us something essential about how and why the meanings we make here and now are connected to those made by others with whom we form, if not necessarily a community, at least a network of mutual interdependence. Because we cannot survive alone, we do not think thoughts that are entirely our own.

An even more direct connection to issues of cognition arises from our understanding that we frame our identities through the narrative and other discourse genres of our community. If we still tell our lives as narratives, we may nonetheless be coming today to experience them more as hypertexts. We are learning to make meaning on multiple scales of human experiencing, and as we come do so more and more outside the limitations of standardized cultural genres, new kinds of lives, new kinds of communities, and new forms of personal humanity become possible.

In the sections that follow, I will first try to sketch a theoretical framework for understanding the role of texts and other semiotic-material artifacts in organizing the coherence of social-ecological systems across time and space. I will then outline briefly what I see as the connection between text genres as a technology of social organization and the characteristic principles of social control in late modern society. Finally, I will try to characterize some newly emergent forms of textuality as representative of a new technology of meaning-making practices that I call 'traversals' and then address the critical questions of the new modes of social control they may portend and the new human possibilities they may afford.

2. From Complex Material Systems to the Role of Texts

Complex systems theory is an attempt to characterize the common and distinctive features of dynamical systems in which large numbers of elements interact to produce determinate but unforeseeable new phenomena (Bar-Yam 1997). Human organisms, ecosystems, and human communities such as cities are all examples of complex dynamical systems of this sort. Living systems in general are complex dynamical systems, and they are characterized by a hierachical organization across multiple levels (Salthe 1985, 1993) each with its characteristic time scales (for characterizing the rates of processes) and spatial-extensional scales (for typical sizes, masses, and energies).

In many such systems and across many such levels of organization, two general principles appear to hold (Lemke 2000a):

> (1) Adiabatic separation – processes which occur at radically different rates (50–100 times faster or slower) tend not to readily exchange energy with one another, and so not to exchange information efficiently, across distinct levels of system organization

> (2) Informational alternation – as we move from level to level, information from lower levels is re-organized by intermediate levels for higher levels in such a way that differences of degree at the level below matter as differences of kind at the level above, and vice versa

More specifically, in most complex material and biological systems, intermediate levels of organization emerge from the potentialities of a lower level under the organizing constraints of a pre-existing higher level. When these new intermediate levels emerge, they have the effect of filtering only some sorts of information through to the higher level, while buffering that higher level against other information (noise) from below. Only directly adjacent levels significantly influence one another.

In this model timescales (or rates) are a more general parameter for identifying a level of organization than are distances, sizes, masses, or energies. As Latour (1987) has noted in a critique of social systems models, the topology of social systems is more like that of an extended network than like that of a set of nested spheres of increasing size. For simpler biological and other material systems, scaling by time and by size produces the same definitions of levels, but even in these realms there are exceptions (Lemke 2000a, 2000b) and it is time that is the more reliable and general differentiator among levels because of the physical basis of the principle of adiabatic separation. One can describe social networks as consisting of interpenetrating and interlocking subnetworks, which are still relatively insulated from one another by their typical timescales for action or completion of some process. Conversations, for example, occur too quickly to be directly affected by the much slower processes of language change; those longer-term processes are normally mediated and buffered by many intermediate levels of social organization (communities, institutions, extended social networks) from the linguistic innovations in any particular conversation.

As Latour (1987) also notes, the networks that make society possible do not consist solely of humans. Human communities, whether villages or cities, are also ecosystems or components of ecosystems. We depend as much on soils, bacteria, plants, animals, and our own tools, buildings, and artifacts of all kinds as we do on one another, not just for our survival, but also for the functioning of our institutions and cultures. The systems we belong to and depend on are ecological-social systems or networks of humans and non-humans. You cannot understand a technological civilization apart from its artifacts and ecosystem. You cannot account for the flows of matter and energy in the ecosystem itself without taking into account cultural values and discourses that mediate how we build and design, what plants we sow or root out, which species we cultivate or exterminate, and how we distribute resources geographically and socially. There are only ecosocial systems or networks, not separate purely social systems and purely 'natural' ones.

3. Texts, Heterochrony, and Mediation by Semiotic Artifacts

The role of meaning and values, of semiotic practices, in ecosocial systems (which could equally be called ecological-social-semiotic systems or actant-networks) creates some interesting paradoxes. How is it possible for human communities, in partnership with tools and raw materials, to coordinate the building of a cathedral over a centuries-long timescale? How can centuries-old traditions and rituals be maintained in the actions of people and artifacts that take place on the timescale of minutes or hours or even days? Such things do not normally happen across such disparate timescales of organization in non-social, non-semiotic complex systems. If our own ecosocial feats of cross-temporal coordination seem unsurprising to us, it is because we are not looking at them from the perspective of more general kinds of complex dynamical systems where there are few violations of adiabatic separation across widely disparate timescales. Climate change and local weather tend to be highly buffered from one another; the long-term ecological succession in a large area of forest is not influenced by the cutting of one tree, and vice versa.

Heterochrony (which has several meanings in biology) is a convenient name for phenomena in which processes on non-adjacent, and more generally on many radically different timescales (taking place at radically different typical rates) strongly interact with one another to determine the phenomenon of interest (Lemke 2000c). In the case of human culture and history, M.Serres (1995) has referred to such phenomena in terms of the metaphor of 'folded time' in which events remote in time from one another may be culturally more relevant to a present event than other events nearer in time. There are two kinds of violation of simple notions of causality in complex dynamical systems: first, the complexity of coupling among processes on a single scale-level means that causal chains become circular, with the result that system-level, aggregate phenomena cannot be said to be 'caused' by any particular constituent or process (*contra* reductionism); and, second, across scale-levels, heterochrony permits the "folding" of time, so that nearness in time is no longer any guarantee of the greater causal relevance of an event.

It is not particularly unique to my own formulation to identify a critical role for written texts in producing coherence across time and space in human social systems (cf. Olson 1994 and many references therein). What is more specific to this model is to generalize the case of written texts to all material objects that persist over timescales long compared to the local and ephemeral events in which the objects are produced, circulated, and used on particular occasions, provided only that these objects carry information which is crucial in accounting for relationships between events distant in time. In a more detailed account, we would consider in detail the role of cross-scale semiotic processes, which imply that higher levels of social organization are required to determine the meaning of these objects for particular events (Lemke 2000a). Briefly, the cultural codes by which the objects are interpreted as meaningful are themselves phenomena of a higher level of organization and change on a much slower timescale than that of any interpretative particular event or meaning-sensitive use of the object.

In a more Latourian actant-network model, Star, & Griesemer (1989) have identified the same role for what they call 'boundary objects' highlighting the fact that such objects knit together different subnetworks by functioning in different ways in each, but preserving their own material integrity as they circulate from one to another. Thus information value is readily seen to lie not in the form of the artifact itself, but only in its relations to the practices of interpreting and using such objects in the different communities or subnetworks.

Finally, we should recognize that it is not just 'texts' in the ordinary sense of written language, or even texts in the extended sense that includes various forms of visual-graphical representation as well as language (e.g. Lemke 1998a), but tools and built environments, modifications of the natural environment, and even the malleable human body itself, which can function as semiotic 'artifacts'. A special case of great interest is that identified by Bourdieu (1990) as 'bodily habitus', the sense in which culture and life experience are written into the body, not just in gait and physique, but in the subtler dispositions of our likes and dislikes, our habits of spontaneous reaction to cultural situations (sports, work, sexual play), and so forth.

Both Bourdieu and Foucault (1979, 1980) have documented the sense in which various social and cultural 'disciplines of the body' make us material products of our culture, who in turn carry that culture forward by how we act and react. Foucault in particular has seen such processes as technologies of social control.

My hope is that we can learn to read this analogy between disciplined bodies or bodily habitus and 'texts' backwards and ask more generally in what different ways, historically and contemporaneously, 'texts' and other semiotic artifacts index different modes of social control.

4. Beyond Standardized Genres and Modernist Social Control

The meanings we make are a product not only of our immediate needs but also of the modes of social organization in which we participate. We fill out forms, give job-talks, write essays, and make small-talk because we participate in larger- and smaller-scale social institutions from the nation-state to the family and the business office. Within these settings we deploy the resources appropriate to various more- and less-prescribed written and spoken genres as our immediate needs and longer-term ambitions dictate. What is true of the meanings made specifically with language is true more generally of the meanings made with every form of human action: each act participates in local constructions of meaning on shorter timescales at the same time that it also participates in the systematic networks of interdependent activities that sustain institutions and societies over much larger distances and longer times.

The high modern world is characterized by standardization: different people in widely separated times and places recreate similar forms and documents, acts and practices. As I have argued elsewhere (Lemke 2000a, c), it is the material embodiment of meaning in physical texts, documents, tools, artifacts, architecture, designed land- and city-scapes, and in our own human bodies that enables us to coordinate activities over long periods of time and so over global societies and virtual communities of millions of people and billions of artifacts. There is standardization of infrastructure and classification schemes (Star & Bowker 1999), standardization of instruments and measures, standardization of textual genres both written and spoken, and standardization of the routine activities of daily life and specialist practice. The making of texts and tools, the using of texts and tools, the enactment with our own bodies of familiar rituals and routines does not just get some job done in the here and now. It also repeats key features familiar to others, which they in turn can make sense of and make use of, often for very different purposes in other times and places. In this basic way activities remote in time and space come to be articulated, coordinated, and ultimately inter-dependent.

Not surprisingly many of us rebel against this standardization. We magnify the significance of small variations, we seek novel meanings and creative practices. We also worry that over-standardization makes our social system too rigid, too little able to respond to the waves of change that pass through it, many of its own unplanned making. We live in practical terms only by conforming to standardization; we depend on the predictable practices and products of others in every aspect of our lives. We are caught in the web. Within the prescriptions of our modern genres of text and action, our standard templates for artifacts and institutions, we do find latitude. We can deploy the constituents of these genres in different ways that are still meaningful and still useful, and we sometimes deploy them tactically against the strategic interests of institutions we find oppressive (de Certeau 1984). More importantly perhaps, we can mix and combine genre templates and their components in novel ways with results unpredictable even to ourselves. Insofar as genres and standardized forms represent institutional idealizations, we do in fact never produce perfect instances of them, but always instead some sort of hybrid bricolage that is, we hope, functional enough to get by on, perhaps personal enough to be proud of, sometimes odd enough to be interesting in its own right.

Standardization is our solution to the problem of ecosocial scale. In many ways it is Nature's solution also. Large ecosystems are not simply made from the diversity of species, but from the endlessly repeated webs of relationships among different members of the same species (plural), identical enough for ecological purposes. Nature hedges her bets with many layers of redundant diversity: there are many phenotypically and genotypically different individuals of each species, each ready to play its role in the great webs in a slightly different, but often enough functionally equivalent manner. There are many species that occupy homologous niches, not quite but almost equally good as substitute food-source, competitor, predator, decomposer, or transporter. There are many fractally self-similar ecological patches on many spatial scales, each ready to function as the seed for regeneration of the larger ecosystem after its periodic and predictable local traumas. In species with wide ranges, individual organisms can in principle pick up their lives and survive even if artificially transported far from their native habitat. This is perhaps less true of the most highly social species, who may have individual attachments to particular mates and troops or hives and broods. Human cultural standardization extends our range as individuals and as members of social subgroups, not yet as widely as our species range (linguistic and cultural barriers are still serious obstacles), but much more widely than in earlier eras of the human past.

Social control under modernism, as Foucault has often described it (e.g. Foucault 1979, 1980), consists essentially of technologies of standardization: artifactually mediated means of comparing people and events to idealized standardized forms and rewarding closer matches and sanctioning divergences outside some narrow range of tolerance. Society prescribes for us ideal patterns of conformity; some we internalize, some we resist, but they all take this same form. This is a historically specific mode of social control. Although no doubt something like it has existed through all of human history, it only became the dominant mode of social control in modern times. It is part and parcel of the technology of social organization for large-scale, modern mass societies. In smaller-scale societies it is usually sufficient to assemble *ad hoc* applications of precedent and abstract values for each particular instance. There is no special need to enforce widespread conformity to codified norms; it is sufficient to adjust individual instances within local social tolerances (cf. tribal dispute resolution, witch-doctoring, mandarin courts, *qadi* justice).

Standardization is here to stay, but it is not the last word in human organizational technologies or social forms. The logical endpoint of this strategy is global uniformity on such a scale as to diminish the diversity of the human 'meme-pool' to dangerously low levels. There must be countervailing tendencies at work. Those which operate solely within the tolerances of standardized genres and templates, the limited creativity of 'normal science' and 'normal life' while wondrously diverse under the microscope of micro-analysis, cannot account for the emergence of radically new ecosocial and cultural-natural phenomena. What *can* account for them, in the view of complex systems theory, is the unpredictability of strong-coupling: multiple feedback loops and nonlinear reinforcement of small effects toward the larger scale by the collective and cooperative phenomena of whole systems (Kauffman 1993; Lemke 2000a, b; Bar-Yam 1997). Most simply it is new networks, new couplings, connections, and interdependencies that can surprise us.

What do new networks look like in their embryonic forms, before we can say whether they, too, will in their turn become standardized? Do they *need* to become standardized in order to play a significant role in ecosocial systems? in culture, identity, and behavior? or as grounds of meaningful activity?

I wish to propose here a new class of theoretical object, which I am calling *traversals*. Traversals are temporal-experiential linkings, sequences, and catenations of meaningful elements that deliberately or accidentally, but radically, cross genre boundaries. A traversal is a traversal *across* standardized genres, themes, types, practices, or activities that nevertheless creates at least an ephemeral or idiotypical meaning for its human participants, and represents at least a temporarily functional connection or relationship among all its constituent processes and their (human or nonhuman) participants (i.e. *actants*).

I believe that traversals are becoming a particularly significant ecosocial and natural-cultural phenomenon in this period of world history, the late 20th and the 21st century, in the same sense in which genres and standardization became particularly significant in the high modern era of the 19th and early 20th centuries. As there have come to be in the high modern period more genres, more standardized types, and so stronger and more rigid boundaries and principles of classifications to define and separate them, so there have also come to be more more resources for hybridization, for creative and stylistic combination and catenation of these types as elements separated from their usual contexts.

But why now? For this we have to look still further outward to the level of social organization achieved for the first time only at the beginning of the high modern era, when genres and standardization became particularly important because they were absolutely necessary to the coordination and coherence of ecosocial systems of unprecedented scale, not just geographically, but in terms of numbers of people and numbers and types of artifacts. It is the dependence of our lives on organization at this mega-scale which has raised the dangers of over-standardization at the same time that it provides us with abundant boundaries to be transgressed and types and constituents to be combined, concatenated, and serialized.

But still, why now? We must finally, I think, look still further outwards, because we are today once again at the threshhold of a still larger scale of ecosocial organization: global and planetary. Global, species-wide standardization really would threaten our biological survival. Whatever coutervailing possibilities are available to us, they are now likely to start being seriously explored. It is a general principle of complex systems theory that as new higher levels of organization emerge, they provide new criteria for fault-tolerance at lower levels, freeing up what was formerly constrained, so that now many different possibilities are equally functional so long as they sustain the new higher level's needs (cf. Lemke 2000a).

I believe that it is becoming safer to break the rules that were formerly necessary to the survival-by-standardization of nation-states and national cultures because the global economy and its emerging meta-culture provides a stabilizing outer-envelope within which transgressions need not be disastrous for individuals or social networks. Traversals are, I believe, the characteristic form that is becoming salient and significant in the transition to globalization; the form that will truly characterize the successor to modernism.

5. What Are Traversals?

Definitions belong to the end-days of theory-building; they are never truly starting points. I gave a notional definition of traversal above; do not regard it as definitive or generative, but only as a way in to the intellectual construction and examination of a putative phenomenon.

Examples are more helpful at this early stage of theory construction. Traversals include such phenomena as:

hypertexts, experienced in time as jumping from one element in one modern genre or type to another that may be quite disparate, e.g. narrative to poem to diagram to table to dialogue to video to quantitative graph, etc. (Landow 1997; Lemke, in press) and also linking across topics and themes that may have no typical cultural collocations;

    websurfing, which generalizes the simple hypertext across radically different content categories, linguistic registers, and domains of human activity, but with some logical connective relations at each juncture or link, and with a sense, like that for hypertext, of a coherent meaning-experience along a whole experiential trajectory;

    channel-surfing, the immediate predecessor of web-surfing, in which the viewer jumps at various rates among the widely different television programs and genres (adventure to cooking to news to talkshow, etc.), again creating a unique and in some sense coherent meaning-making experience, in which the viewer is a more active creator of the trajectory than s/he could be in relation to any single program;

    mall-cruising, an architectural experience, or 'reading' of assembled space, in which, whether as shopper or social visitor, over a relatively short span of time, individuals move from food-court to clothes-mart to movie theatre to furnished public space, again assembling the trajectory of a coherent visit-to-the-mall.

To these we can add such less radically heterogeneous precursors as: video montages, disco sound and record 'mixes', the distinctive mixed-period style of some postmodern architecture, and even that hybrid reality of all texts that leads to the famous dictum of Derrida that you cannot *not* mix genres. Let me analyze this dictum as a way of making salient the role of *scale* in defining and characterizing traversals.

    Of course you *can* produce a pure, idealized genre (boring and predictable as that is likely to be), but only if it is short, brief, or simply repetitive within prescribed limits of variation. Every standardized bureaucratic document-form is such a pure genre. So are simple genres like the sonnet, sonata, or haiku, extending perhaps to the folktale, to ritual speech genres, the simple mathematical proof, the patent application, perhaps the typical scientific research article. We can produce pure instances of ideal genres of indefinite length by recursion, as with dictionaries, encyclopedias, or linked folktales as in the 1001 Arabian Nights. But once we try to produce really long single texts, or really long-term sequences of action, the inherent messiness of life intrudes. There are always 'circumstances beyond our control', lapses of memory, errors of production, interruptions, intrusions, our own perverse need to diverge, and digress. There are improvisations, irrefusable opportunities to improve, create, individualize. There is the simple impossibility of prescribing in sufficient detail all the elements of a text or activity that is semantically heterogeneous (i.e. does not keep repeating the same meaning patterns over and over) or functionally developmental (i.e. having got to some point in the sequence of action, new possibilities emerge just because of what we have done so far, possibilities that could not have been foreseen before we did it; cf. Lemke 1991). There is simply no functional point in trying to pre-specify the total course of a lengthy activity or the total shape of a lengthy text. Lengthy activities must allow for unforeseeable opportunities and contingencies, for emergent goals. Long texts are written to make meanings that do not serve only standardized functions (Lemke, forthcoming).

The novel is not a genre; even the most predictable 'genre novel' is not actually written to a formula, or if it is, it does not serve for us all the important functions of a novel. No book which develops a related cluster of themes for its entire length of hundreds of printed pages can be said to be an instance of a predictable, formulaic genre. An ode or an elegy may be highly standardized, but an epic is not. The *interest* of a long text lies partly in its unpredictability, whether narrative (the novel, the drama) or informational (the essay, the treatise). Standardized scientific textbooks are perhaps the longest texts to realize pure genres in both form and content; they represent an epitome of modernism, texts so similar in form and content that they are more like translations of one another than like original works.

What is important, however, for the theory of traversals, is that we make new kinds of meanings across very long texts which are qualitatively different from those we make with short texts. If every possible meaning could be made in a single clause, we would have no need of complex sentences. If moderate length sentences afforded the entire meaning potential of language, we would have no occasion to create longer texts. It is a very important and largely unanswered question in the theory of text semantics just what kinds of meanings we can and do create with longer-scales texts that we cannot make with shorter texts? (Lemke, in forthcoming). Traversals are also conceptualized as meaning-makings, and what characterizes a traversal is precisely that some kind of coherent meaning is made in the unpredictable sequencing of unlike types over 'text-scales' that are longer than the scales of the standardized elements which are strung together along the traversal.

Hypertext and its extension to hypermedia afford the most text-like instances of traversals. The user's trajectory or pathway through a hypertext environment (a set of texts or other media objects, with specific links among them) may afford the possibility of moving from text page to video playback to map display, and from poetry to expository argument to narrative, in many possible sequences, some planned by the creators of the hypertext and many not (Lemke 1998b). Of course hypertext also affords, like print, the simultaneous display of different genres of text and other media, and we know that the reading experience of print is also one in which our eye and attention move at different rates along various visual and logical pathways to attend to these elements sequentially (including alternately, back and forth). Hypertext simply extends this affordance but also make it possible for reader-users to create much more original and unpredictable traversals through the resources of the hypertext environment. What is most important about hypertext traversals, and traversals in general, are the kinds of meanings that we make, coherently and cumulatively, along the traversal, on its longest scales.

Organized hypertexts often have relatively thematically constrained textual and other media resources. But the WorldWideWeb is itself the largest scale hypertext known, or probably today imaginable. Following its links across only a few webpages can readily shift the thematic domain quite radically and unpredictably, and many of us have often found ourselves enjoying 'surfing the web' in this way. A complete surfing 'session' may have for us, retrospectively or even in real time as it is occurring, a sense of meaningfulness, of idiosyncratic coherence. Taken as a whole, or perhaps retrospectively and more selectively assembled from various of its constituent experiences/pages, we can feel that we have 'done something' or 'got somewhere' or just had a good exploratory tour. This experience is I think akin to 'channel-surfing' and the cumulative experience of a unique juxtaposition (really serialization) of moments from programs and commercials of widely different genres (weather, beer, comedy, action, feminine deodorant, news). Sometimes the results are hilarious, sometimes depressing; sometimes we linger, sometimes we keep moving along, but this is 'an activity' – it is 'viewing' or 'surfing' and not simply a meaningless instrumental interlude *en route* to real television viewing. It is a mode of television use or experiencing, and one that has a lot of popularity, especially among younger people for whom the organized content of television is often boring or irrelevant.

This notion of traversal began to emerge in a conversation I had with Jerome Bruner in 1998 about his useful view that our identities are constructed along narrative principles, and often constructed and reconstructed in the actual telling of stories about ourselves in daily life, in family groups, etc. (Bruner 1990; see also Gergen 1991, Wortham 2001). There is a critical tradition in the theory of autobiography (e.g. Freeman 1993), as also for the evaluation of testimony in trial law (e.g. Jackson 1995), which points out that we organize the stories of our lives, what we have done and what we have witnessed, according to the standardized genres of culturally valued narratives. We want to make our lives sound heroic or tragic, or at least interesting, as stories. We tell stories of events in ways that seem to make sense because they fit familiar patterns in which sensible motives seem to lie behind actions and events. So on this view, while constructed identities very likely are narrative effects, there must be a pre-narrative mode in which we actually experience our lives as meaningful as they happen, rather than only retrospectively. My proposal to Bruner was that 'we tell our lives as narratives, but we experience them as hypertexts'.

So it is not just the more specialized forms of traversal experience in channel- and web-surfing that I have in mind, but the way in which we experience the meaningfulness of a day in our lives as having some whole-ness or coherence to it, as being some sort of unique 'text' – retrospectively seen and told as a narrative, perhaps, but originally experienced meaning-fully as a traversal or hypertext. I believe that we are now passing historically from the era of simply making sense of our lives as they happen, at various timescales, to a more deliberate and artificial, historically specific, cultural *practice* of creating days of our lives as works of art, or at least as works of craft. It may not of course be the whole day, though I rather suspect that the day is a culturally salient scale for traversal meaning. The work of 'making the day interesting' may well be partly responsive to or in reaction against those parts of it that were boring or unpleasant, or began and promised to be so. Leisure days are the most obvious instances of this, but I think that increasingly some people, perhaps again younger people, are looking at all of their days in this way. Not necessarily to make a good tellable story of the day, though we also do that, but at least to make a day that has a certain sat-isfaction to it, taken as a whole.

6. Traversal Repertoires: Emergent Modes of Social Control

How do traversals matter to the larger ecosocial system? What difference does it make if this person or that makes some sense of a traversal across a disparate and unusual collection of genre fragments and otherwise standard-ized activities or events? More specifically, how do traversals have conse-quences on much longer timescales?

Let us go back again to the case of genres and standardized activities. These too take place, instance by instance, on relatively short timescales, times of the order of hours or days in most cases. How does it happen that their *forms* recur in different times and places, so that the typical lifetime of influence of the form is decades or centuries? As I have argued elsewhere, this heterochrony or linkage across radically different timescales is always mediated by the tem-poral persistence of material artifacts, including the human body itself (Lemke 2000c). In brief, material texts and other semiotic artifacts persist and circulate in society over timescales much longer than the characteristic time-scale on which they are written or read and used in shorter-term activities. The conventions for making meaning with these artifacts (i.e. meanings above and beyond, yet made by reference to, their strictly physical and biological affordances) are themselves also preserved and circulated through such arti-facts. Ecosocial systems, at least insofar as human culture matters in them, are made both more complex and more tightly coupled at larger scales by these practices/processes, these material technologies of ecosocial organization.

A particular traversal may of course be the precursor to a future standardized genre. It may be repeated, exactly or with some tolerable variation, by the same person, or by other persons, on occasions nearer or more remote in time and place. It may become regularized by word of mouth, by written accounts, by arrangements of artifacts and land- or city-scapes that make it more likely for a similar traversal to be made again. The traversal must leave some enduring trace, in an account or record of itself (symbolic signs), or by its effects on the world (indexical signs). Its near-replicas, of course, are also (iconic) signs renewing its meaning and possibility for us.

But all this is distinctly a matter of timescale, and timescales are matters of degree, however much discrete, order-of-magnitude differences of timescale are the basis of system organization. A single traversal persists on its own timescale; its memory may persist longer in an individual. There may be indexical traces of its having occurred that persist in the environment; it may be visible to others; accounts of it may circulate. This does not mean that it will ever be replicated or imitated. But in addition to standardized genres and institutionalized repertoires of activities, ecosocial systems are characterized on shorter timescales by *repertoires of possibility*. Sometimes called 'the thinkable' or 'the imaginable' in contrast with the presumptively not-imaginable, with doings that have no meanings and which therefore cannot be imagined through their meanings, and so can only be encountered by circumstance or accident. There are things we can fall into that we could not have imagined. Most times these happenings are not, for us, events at all, just confusions, lacking even so much meaningfulness as identifiability as discrete or segmentable occasions or events. But sometimes we encounter an event, a happening in the world, even one in which we find ourselves an unintentional participant, that has meaning during or after the experience even though it had no place in our system of possibles and thinkables before. The repertoire of possibles is thereby expanded for us. Sometimes its structural organization is even overturned or modified, though probably more often such events are added as singulars, still not part of any generative systemic potential.

Traversals can enlarge the repertoire of possibles. This is, after all, part of the motivation I gave at the beginning for their species-survival value. And in particular what they can do is to create local and ephemeral possibilities of meaningful connection or catenation among otherwise radically distinguished and separated genres and domains of activity. And not just one to another, but whole *sets* of genres, domains, topics, themes, and categories of persons, experiences, actions, or activities that are united by the thread of even a single traversal that passes through all of them.

Local and ephemeral (on some timescale), traversal repertoires can potentially become regularized, standardized, repeated, and disseminated over larger scales and for longer times. Or they may not. A traversal repertoire may portend a new category-in-the-making or a new activity-genre-in-the-making, or it may not. History is contingent, at many scales. There may be a place or function for the new activity in some larger-scale structure, or not. The smaller-scale enabling events needed to promote institutionalization may occur, or they may not.

But this way of thinking about the sequelae of traversals is still modernist, still privileges the way of standardization, as if all that mattered in human life or the dynamics of an ecosocial system were its relatively fixed invariant forms. This importance, I believe, attaches to invariants because they mediate modernist social control. Is there an emerging mode of social control analogously associated with traversals and traversal repertoires? If so, then it may well become the dominant mode in a future where global meta-culture operates above, beyond, and to some extent outside of traditional modernist norms of conformity and standardization. I would no more expect norm-conformity to disappear in such a future than I would expect standardization to do so, but just as the emergence of higher levels of organization in the global economy permit relaxing the rigidity of many standardized practices such as standardized career paths or loyalty to national cultural ideals, so the corresponding global meta-culture will depend less on strict predictability of longer-term traversals (such as biographical-scale ones) and more on these traversals sharing some less restrictive features.

Here, finally, is my guess and my quandary about what seems to me to be the mode of social control that will grow in importance as traversals are added on top of activity genres and conformity to genre norms, which will in turn grow less important, at least on the longer timescales now to be dominated by traversals instead. My guess is that traversals will be characterized by something like a *style*. Something more like a holistic aesthetic judgment rather than, as with genre-like norms, by objective conformity to codified criteria that specify analytical components. We judge genre-conformity by looking at the separate parts and their criterial features; if all the parts are present, if each has the canonical features, if they are all ordered in the normative manner, the text or activity passes muster. There is no special sense of the whole; no emergent quality of the whole that is taken to be more than the sum of its parts. Genre-conformity is an eminently linear and summative strategy, a true product of the machine age. Traversal judgments, on the other hand, are eminently holistic, or at least they operate 'in the large', with the meaningfulness and quality of the longer-scale portions of the traversal more important than the smaller-scale ones. Traversals are emergent all the way down. They are characteristic of the age of complex (including biological and ecosocial) systems theory.

Late modernist technologies of mass social organization require a historically unprecedented degree of social control and widespread standardization and conformity. As they expand, modernist societies find that each effort to enforce standardization runs afoul of the messiness of complex systems, their inherent unpredictability arising from multiple cross-couplings and interlocking, circular causal loops. Each effort to enforce conformity in such a system requires that more and more aspects of life must in turn also be controlled. A global-scale society built on modernist principles will be extremely precarious, teetering permanently at the edge of collapse, requiring the most minute control of every aspect of human life and ecological processes to maintain itself. We will, I think, never actually reach this stage. Rather we will shift uneasily between the last gasps of modernism, its periodic crises of regional or global collapse (economic and ecological) arising from over-control, and an emerging counter-system predicated on relaxing control over people and ecosystems, reducing expectations, accepting disasters as inevitable rather than further increasing control in futile efforts to prevent them that only lead to other greater disasters. We will have to finally let go of the modernist Faustian fantasy of total control over the world and our own lives, and embrace instead a value system which privileges the whole over the part, the complete ecosocial system over humanity alone, and the quality of a day or a life over the standardization of a word or an action.

In all these scenarios, the new ways we learn to use language to make new, emergently possible kinds of meanings in traversals across widely different scales (of time, text, or experience), will play a key role. It is the work of critical discourse analysis and applied linguistics to tell us *how*.

References

Bar-Yam, Y. 1997. Dynamics of Complex Systems. Cambridge MA: Perseus Publishing.

Bourdieu, P. 1990. The Logic of Practice. Stanford CA: Stanford University Press.

Bruner, J. 1990. Acts of Meaning. Cambridge, MA: Harvard University Press.

De Certeau, M. 1984. The Practice of Everyday Life. Berkeley: University of California Press.

Fairclough, N. 2000. Language in the New Capitalism. http://www.uoc.es/humfil/nlc/CA-15egd.doc.

Foucault, M. 1979. Discipline and Punish. New York: Random House.

Foucault, M. 1980. The History of Sexuality. Volume 1. New York: Random House.

Freeman, M. 1993. Rewriting the Self: History, Memory, Narrative. New York: Routledge.

Gee, J.P., Hull, G. & Lankshear, C. 1997. The New Work Order: Behind the Language of the New Capitalism. New York: Westview.

Gergen, K. 1991. The Saturated Self. New York: Basic Books.

Jackson, B.S. 1995. Making Sense in Law: Linguistic, Psychological and Semiotic Perspectives. Liverpool: Deborah Charles Publications.

Kauffman, S. 1993. The Origins of Order. New York: Oxford University Press.

Landow, G. 1997. Hypertext 2.0. Baltimore: Johns Hopkins University Press.

Lankshear, C. 1997. "Language and the New Capitalism." The International Journal of Inclusive Education. 1(4): 309–321. Online at: http://www.geocities.com/Athens/Academy/1160/langnewcap.html

Language in the New Capitalism (Website): http://www.uoc.es/humfil/nlc/LNC-ENG/lnc-eng.html

Latour, B. 1987. Science in Action. Cambridge, MA: Harvard University Press.

Lemke, J.L. 1991. "Text Production and Dynamic Text Semantics." In E. Ventola, (Ed.) Functional and Systemic Linguistics: Approaches and Uses. Berlin: Mouton/deGruyter (Trends in Linguistics: Studies and Monographs 55). 23–38.

Lemke, J.L. 1998a. "Multiplying Meaning: Visual and Verbal Semiotics in Scientific Text." In: J.R. Martin & R. Veel, Eds., Reading Science. London: Routledge. 87–113.

Lemke, J.L. 1998b. "Hypertext Semantics." Paper presented at the International Congress of Systemic-Functional Linguistics, Cardiff, 1998. Online at: http://academic.brooklyn.cuny.edu/education/jlemke/webs/hypertext/tsld001.htm

Lemke, J.L. 2000a. "Opening Up Closure: Semiotics Across Scales." In: J. Chandler and G. van de Vijver, (Eds.) Closure: Emergent Organizations and their Dynamics (Volume 901: Annals of the NYAS). New York: New York Academy of Science Press. 100–111.

Lemke, J.L. 2000b. "Material Sign Processes and Ecosocial Organization." In: P.B. Andersen, C. Emmeche, and N.O. Finnemann-Nielsen, Eds. Downward Causation: Self-organization in Biology, Psychology, and Society. Aarhus University Press (Denmark). 181–213.

Lemke, J.L. 2000c. "Across the Scales of Time: Artifacts, Activities, and Meanings in Ecosocial Systems." Mind, Culture, and Activity 7(4): 273–290.

Lemke, J.L. In press. "Multimedia Genres for Science Education and Scientific Literacy." In: M. Schleppegrell & M.C. Colombi, (Eds.) Developing Advanced Literacy in First and Second Languages. Mahwah, NJ: Erlbaum.

Lemke, J.L. Forthcoming. The Role of Texts in the Technologies of Social Organization. To appear in R.Wodak & Weiss, Eds., Theory and Interdisciplinarity in Critical Discourse Analysis. London: Macmillan/Palgrave.

Olson, D.R. 1994. The World on Paper. New York: Cambridge University Press.

Salthe, S.N. 1985. Evolving Hierarchical Systems. New York: Columbia University Press.

Salthe, S.N. 1993. Development and Evolution. Cambridge: MIT Press.

Serres, M. 1995. Conversations on Science, Culture, and Time. (R. Lapidus, Trans.) Ann Arbor, MI: University of Michigan Press.

Star, S.L. & Bowker, G. 1999. Sorting Things Out: Classification and its Consequences. Cambridge, MA: MIT Press.

Star, S.L. & Griesemer, J.R. 1989. "Institutional Ecology, 'Translations' and Boundary Objects: Amateurs and professionals in Berkeley's Museum of Vertebrate Zoology, 1907–39." Social Studies of Science 19: 387–420.

Wortham, S. 2001. Narratives in Action. New York: Teachers College Press.

61

On Combining Pragma-Dialectics with Critical Discourse Analysis

Constanza Ihnen and John E. Richardson

Introduction

Recently, an academic 'front' has been opened between Critical Discourse Analysis (CDA) and more 'orthodox' argumentation scholarship. Specifically, in a keynote conference address, Žagar (2009) argued that the work of some Critical Discourse Analysts not only misuses but misunderstands certain key concepts of classical rhetorical theory – in particular *topoi* – and permanently blots its analytic copy book through a fundamental disconnect between the analytic and political goals of CDA. From a different, though not wholly unrelated argumentative tack, Ietcu-Fairclough (2010, p. 2) argued that the Discourse Historical Approach to CDA applies the notion of *topos* "in ways which do not seem to correspond" to the way it is defined in classical rhetoric. Instead, her own critical analysis of public and political discourse (cf. Fairclough & Ieţcu-Fairclough, forthcoming) favors "an approach that draws on the highly technical and rigorous analytical apparatus of argumentation theory in order to engage in argument reconstruction and analysis" (Ietcu-Fairclough, 2010, p. 3). However, she is quite clear that she now feels "the pragma-dialectical model is not sufficient" for such a task, since "Public debate and deliberation do not easily fit the CD [critical discussion] model" (Ibid.). In more detail, she argues that while critical discussion "ends ideally in consensus, politics is not a realm where consensus is always

Source: Eveline T. Feteris, Bart Garssen and Francisca Snoeck Henkemans (eds), *Keeping in Touch With Pragma-Dialectics: In Honor of Frans H. van Eemeren* (Amsterdam: John Benjamins, 2011), pp. 231–244.

possible or desirable". Ignoring the fact that the resolution of a difference of opinion is not the same as achieving consensus, Ietcu-Fairclough (2010) argues this is not always possible because there are "differences of opinion that have to be left in peace and have to coexist peacefully *without agreement*, without attempting to reduce one view to another"; similarly, resolution is not always desirable because "practical reasoning in the political public sphere occurs against a background of value pluralism, as well as a plurality of goals, and there are typically good arguments on both sides of a debate" (Ibid.). Finally, Forchtner and Tominc (forthcoming) argue against the use of pragma-dialectics in the Discourse Historic Approach to CDA since, to do so, entails an incommensurable "epistemological conflict" between the Critical Theory (Habermas) of the Discourse Historic Approach and Critical Rationalism of Pragma-Dialectical theory.

In sum, there is a growing body of work that asserts a basic incompatibility between CDA and pragma-dialectics. In contrast, we consider this putative divide between CDA on the one hand and argumentation – and in particular, pragma-dialectical theory – on the other to be both mistaken and undesirable. Indeed, in this contribution we argue that pragma-dialectics can play a significant role in a CDA research agenda. We develop our argument in two steps. First, we outline the similarities and differences between these approaches. Since the readership can be expected to be more or less familiar with the pragma-dialectical theory but not necessarily with CDA, we start with a brief introduction to the latter. Following this, we specify the benefits of combining the two perspectives.

1. Two Approaches to (Argumentative) Discourse

The principal theoretical and analytic foci of Critical Discourse Analysis (CDA) remain the relationships between text and context. Like most other approaches to discourse analysis, CDA is interested in examining "what and how language communicates when it is used purposefully in particular instances and contexts" (Cameron, 2001, p. 13). We assume that language is a social practice that, like all practices, is dialectically related to the contexts of its use. In other words, "speaking and writing always represent, produce and reproduce attitudes, beliefs, opinions and ideologies" (Heer & Wodak, 2008, p. 10) and, in so doing, language use contributes to the production and *re*production of social realities.

Despite its name, CDA is not a singular method of analysis. Rather, it is a perspective on critical scholarship, aimed at analyzing the ways that individuals and social groups *use* language. Critical discourse analysts focus "on social problems, and especially the role of discourse in the production and reproduction of power abuse or domination" (van Dijk, 2001, p. 96). Hence, "CDA sees itself as politically involved research with an emancipatory requirement: it seeks to have an effect on social practice and social relationships"

(Titscher *et al*, 2000, p. 147), particularly relationships of disempowerment, dominance, prejudice and/or discrimination.

Given the variance of approaches to CDA – or, more broadly still, of Critical Discourse *Studies* – inevitably, any account of what CDA *is* will be partial. Here, we discuss Ruth Wodak's Discourse Historical Approach to discourse analysis (see Reisigl and Wodak 2001, 2009; Richardson & Wodak, 2009a, 2009b; Wodak, 2009), since this is currently the only significant approach that, from inception, has built argumentation formally into its analytic framework.[1] The Discourse Historical Approach (DHA) aims to integrate and triangulate knowledge about historical sources and the background of the social and political fields within which discursive events are embedded. Such an aim is based on the principle that a text only creates sense when its manifest and latent meanings (implicature, presupposition, allusion and so on) are read in context. Thus, context, contextualization and *recontextualisation* need to be taken seriously in analysis – aspects of textual sensemaking that are often signaled and accomplished through intertextual relations. No text is ever isolated in space and time as many studies illustrate; thus, intertextuality is inherently part and parcel of meaning making in context (see, van Dijk, 2008a).

The Discourse Historical Approach (DHA) uses four 'levels of context' as heuristics to locate discursive practices, strategies and texts in a specific socio-political context. First, the immediate, language or text internal co-text, which take into account issues such as textual coherence, cohesion, and "the local interactive processes of negotiation" (Reisigl & Wodak, 2001, p. 41), such as turn-taking, question/answer and so on. Further, following Billig *et al* (1988), we argue that texts are multi-vocal – they present more than one view, or are based on "ideological dilemmas", tensions and inconsistencies which should be drawn out in analysis. Second, there are the intertextual and interdiscursive relationships between utterances, texts, genres and discourses. This level of context takes into account the history and intertextual references of terms and concepts used, or the ways that a concept is mentioned, discussed or argued about, in different texts and in different genres. For example: in what ways has immigration been discussed historically? Does this differ between genres or between argumentative activity types? These intertextual and interdiscursive relationships can, and should, be examined in terms of both continuities and discontinuities with the current period.

Third, there are the social/sociological variables and institutional frames of a specific 'context of situation'. Accordingly, if the object of analysis is a party election leaflet, this would need to be contextualized *as* a party election leaflet – that is, a text produced at a particular time, by a particular organization according to a particular set of discursive criteria. Fourth, we take into account the broader socio-political and historical contexts within which the discursive practices are embedded. This fourth level of context is 'history' as it is conventionally understood – the broad stories of the complex interactions of people, organizations, institutions and ideas. Such a consideration is based on the principle that discourse is "situated in, shaped by and constructive of circumstances that are more than and different to language" (Anthonissen, 2003, p. 297). Therefore, these social, political and historical contexts need to be brought back into analysis. These four layers enable researchers to better situate and analyze the meanings of discourse and how they relate to context.

In addition, the DHA seeks to identify the effect of particular discursive strategies which may serve to represent an individual or a group either positively or negatively (see Reisigl & Wodak, 2009). Specifically, the DHA offers five types of discursive strategies which underpin the inclusion/exclusion of self/other, and the constructions of identities. 'Strategy' in this sense generally refers to a (more or less accurate and more or less intentional) plan of practices, including discursive practices, adopted to achieve a particular social, political, psychological or linguistic goal. First, there are referential, or nomination, strategies, by which social actors are named and, in so doing, discursively represented and positioned as, for example, part of in-groups and/or out-groups. This can be achieved through a number of more or less explicit membership categorization devices, from open nomination through to metaphor, metonymy and synecdoche. Second, social actors as individuals, group members or groups as a whole, are linguistically characterized through predications. These predicational strategies may, for example, be realized as evaluative attributions of negative and positive traits in the linguistic form of implicit or explicit predicates and so aim at labeling social actors, processes, things (etc.), in a more or less positive or negative manner.

Third, there are argumentation strategies and here Reisigl and Wodak (2001) place particular emphasis on topoi, through which positive and negative attributions are often justified. Typically, topoi in prejudicial or discriminatory discourse are employed to justify the exclusion of migrants through quasi-rational arguments such as 'they are a burden for the society', 'they cost too much', 'their culture is too different', and so forth (see Krżyzanowski & Wodak, 2008; Reisigl & Wodak, 2001; Wodak & van Dijk, 2000). Analyzing a text/discourse's argumentation strategies also requires analysts to examine the argumentative potential of visual elements (Richardson, 2008). Indeed, given both legal constraints and salient social taboos against overtly stated racist argumentation in party politics, prejudicial arguments are usually not spelt out explicitly, and can rely on certain pictorial elements in advancing a coherent standpoint (Richardson & Wodak, 2009a). Fourth, one may focus on strategies of perspectivation, framing or discourse representation. Through framing, speakers express their involvement in discourse, and position their point of view in the reporting, description, narration or quotation of relevant events or utterances. Fifth, there are strategies of intensification and mitigation, both of which help to qualify and modify the epistemic status of a proposition by intensifying or mitigating the illocutionary force of utterances.

These strategies can be an important aspect of the presentation inasmuch as they operate upon it by either sharpening it or toning it down.

The DHA to critical discourse analysis thus contextualizes text and talk in relation to other discourses, social and institutional reference points, as well as socio-political and historical contexts and events.

Pragma-dialectics shares with CDA an interest in describing (argumentative) discourse and in carrying out these descriptions from a pragmatic point of view. The pragmatic principle, for instance, that the meaning of a (fragment of) discourse is linked to the context of its use is not only basic to CDA but also to pragma-dialectics. Not surprisingly then, a pragma-dialectical analysis also falls back on empirical warrants that go beyond the discourse itself. Typical sources used to analyze argumentative discourse in pragma-dialectics are insights concerning conventional structures and strategies of discourse and ethnographic evidence relating to the specific context of activity type – or genre – in which a discourse is embedded. Likewise, the broader socio-political and historical context of the discourse plays a significant role in the analysis of implicit and indirect speech acts such as unexpressed premises (van Eemeren, Grootendorst, Jackson & Jacobs, 1993; van Eemeren, 2010).

Connected to this pragmatic orientation to discourse is the shared assumption that language is a goal-oriented activity, taking place amid a set of contextual constraints, and that speakers want their utterances not only to be understood but also accepted. This common view of discourse may explain another broad area of agreement between the two perspectives: their interest in studying the strategic dimension of (argumentative) discourse. In pragma-dialectics, the speaker's quest for effectiveness is studied from the point of view of 'strategic maneuvering' and in the Discourse Historic Approach under the more general concept of the 'discursive strategy'.

Interestingly, it is not only in the description of (argumentative) discourse that these perspectives on discourse meet. Pragma-dialectics and CDA also converge in their interest to carry out some sort of 'evaluation' or 'critique' of discourse. In pragma-dialectics, argumentative discourse is evaluated from the point of view of the ideal model of a critical discussion, which specifies the stages and rules instrumental to the rational resolution of a difference of opinion. An argumentative move that violates any of these rules is negatively evaluated as 'unreasonable' or 'fallacious', because it obstructs the rational resolution of the dispute. In CDA, analyst are interested not just in describing how social reality is represented in the discourse but also in labeling and characterizing certain representations as being 'unacceptable' or 'unreasonable', because they play a role in (re)creating relations of inequality and disempowerment. Such a characterization, of what is communicated in discourse, is clearly also evaluative in nature.[2] Approaches to CDA that draw on argumentation theory also employ ideal models of communicative interaction in the critical analysis of discourse. Indeed, analysts working from the Discourse Historical Approach have used pragma-dialectics, including the model of a critical discussion, as part of their critical analysis of linguistic strategies of argumentation (Reisigl & Wodak, 2001). However, discourse evaluation, from a CDA perspective, usually means more than assessing dialectical reasonableness.[3]

In line with van Dijk's (2008b, p. 823) suggestion that CDA should address "the lack of theory about the norms and principals of its own critical activity", recently, certain scholars within CDA have become a little more engaged with the task of providing an explicit, and more coherent, theoretical justification for the normative judgments at the heart of critique.[4] Such work remains in its developing stages, meaning that more effort will be required before normative critique can be rescued from its current ghettoized location in political and moral philosophy (Sayer, 2006). However, we can identify two promising theoretical approaches: adapting and applying Habermas' notion of deliberative discourse (cf. Forchtner, forthcoming; Forchtner & Tominc, forthcoming); and Sayer's anti-reductionist, objectivist, stance on social suffering.

There are, of course, also some striking differences between pragma-dialectics and CDA. The first and, perhaps, most obvious contrast relates to the type of discourse activity each is concerned with. CDA is not specifically and primarily interested in argumentation. A CDA perspective can be applied to any type of discourse, and to any element of a discourse, no matter whether its function is argumentative, informative or explanatory. Pragma-dialectics, in contrast, deals exclusively with argumentative discourse and, hence, with moves that have an argumentative function.

There is, moreover, a fundamental difference as regards their *methods* of analysis. On the one hand, CDA does not have a singular methodology, but draws on insights and applies categories from a variety of sources. Linguistics is one of them, of course, but also political theory, political philosophy, sociology, and history. Indeed Sayer (2006, p. 463) argues that "CDA can never be a self-contained activity", and necessarily needs to draw on "specific scholarly knowledge regarding the issues addressed in the discourse in question" (see also Wodak, 2001). On the other hand, pragma-dialectics has a method of analysis of its own. This method consists in carrying out a 'normative reconstruction' of discourse. The point of such a reconstruction is to recover from a sequence of pragmatically organized speech acts a set of *argumentatively relevant moves* to which the standards and categories of the ideal model for a critical discussion apply and represent them in an analytic overview (van Eemeren *et al*, 1993). The overview specifies the type of dispute, the propositions that make up the substance of the standpoints and arguments, the starting points of the discussion, the type of argument schemes used in each single argument, and the way in which those arguments relate to one another.[5]

Different also is the focus of analysis. What is relevant to CDA might not be relevant to pragma-dialectics, and vice versa, and different perspectives on relevance are likely to result in different descriptions of one and the same discourse. CDA typically describes texts from the point of view of a specific social problem (e.g. discrimination against Muslims) and concentrates on the discursive manifestation of power abuse and axes of domination in relation to that problem (e.g. the representation of the Muslim veil in news media).[6] A pragma-dialectical analysis focuses, in contrast, on argumentatively relevant moves, that is, moves that can play a (positive or negative) role in a critical discussion. These argumentative moves can relate to any subject matter.

There is also a subtle difference concerning the relation between the analysis of discourse, on the one hand, and the evaluation or critique, on the other, in each of these approaches. In pragma-dialectics, analysis and evaluation are worked out independently and the outcome of each of these processes is presented separately. In CDA, in contrast, the results of the analysis –an examination of discourse processes in their widest sense – and the critique of the discourse are often presented simultaneously.

The strategic dimension of discourse is analyzed differently as well. As mentioned earlier, central to the pragma-dialectical approach is the concept of strategic maneuvering. The notion is premised on the pragma-dialectical assumption that "engaging in argumentative discourse always means being at the same time out for critical reasonableness and artful effectiveness" (van Eemeren & Houtlosser, 2009, p. 4). Strategic maneuvering aims to influence the result of a particular dialectical stage to one's own advantage, through choosing from the topical potential available at this stage, by adapting argumentative moves to those most agreeable to an audience and through the purposive choice of presentational devices including, but not exclusively, the various figures and tropes of classical (rhetorical and dialectic) argumentation theory. However, the *specific* choices that arguers make in their strategic maneuvering can nevertheless be treated as non-obligatory structures, meaning we should regard their inclusion pragmatically, showing how and in what respects the use of particular maneuvers can be explained by the particular opportunities afforded by a certain dialectical stage (see also Perelman & Olbrechts-Tyteca, 1969, p. 168). This characterization of strategic maneuvering already points to some important contrasts with CDA: CDA is not solely concerned with argumentative strategies, and even when the strategy under study is argumentative, the analyst does not necessarily explain those strategies by reference to the dialectical framework of a critical discussion.[7]

Finally, there are also significant differences concerning the evaluation of the discourse. Pragma-dialectics aims at identifying fallacious argumentative moves – moves that obstruct the rational resolution of a difference of opinion. To this end the analyst checks whether the moves comply with the rules of a critical discussion. In CDA, the main concern is to link linguistic analysis with social analysis, examining the relations between text and context in general and specifically between discourse (language in use) and social, political and economic disempowerment.

2. Prospects for a Dialogue between Pragma-Dialectics and CDA

Before specifying in which ways CDA might benefit from a pragma-dialectical approach, it is important to set out clearly the limits of a pragma-dialectical contribution. Pragma-dialectics, being a theory of argumentation, can be relevant to a critical discourse analysis only as regards the argumentative dimension of the discourse under study. Thus, a discourse may comprise statements, presuppositions, and implicatures, for instance, which are extremely interesting from a CDA perspective but that would not be taken up by a pragma-dialectical reconstruction because they are not argumentatively (i.e. dialectically) relevant.

Having said this, we think pragma-dialectics can contribute to a critical analysis of argumentative discourse in at least three respects.[8] First of all, pragma-dialectics offers a theoretical apparatus to establish what is communicated in argumentative discourse. The attribution of a large number of implicit elements in argumentative discourse – propositional commitments, functional relations, structural organization and overall coherence of argumentative discourse – can only be properly justified by reference to some set of expectations regarding the way argumentation should proceed. This is precisely what pragma-dialectics provides. Argument schemes provide a theoretical grounding to reconstruct implicit premises and standpoints, and to identify the type of justificatory relation between arguments and standpoints (Atkin & Richardson, 2007). Likewise, the different types of argumentation structures distinguished in pragma-dialectics – subordinative, coordinative and multiple – supply a theoretically motivated tool to describe the relation between the arguments used in the justification of one and the same standpoint. In short, we consider that the pragma-dialectical methods of analysis can provide a theoretical and systematic grounding to the interpretive-descriptive claims of CDA. And this, in turn, can prevent charges against CDA of interpretive bias – that is, of forcing an ideologically motivated reading upon a text.[9] This contribution at the level of analysis should not be underestimated, since any appropriate social critique of discourse presupposes an adequate description.

Secondly, we would like to point at the potential of strategic maneuvering for enriching the strategic analysis of DHA. This applies not only to the analysis of DHA's 'argumentation strategies' (*topoi*) but also to the study of strategies pertaining to argumentative moves that go beyond the speech act of argumentation such as framing a difference of opinion in an advantageous way at the confrontation stage or presenting starting points at the opening stage as if they were matters of "fact".

Moreover, we believe that CDA can benefit from the pragma-dialectical methods for evaluating argumentative discourse. In our view, a social critique of discourse should not consist simply in a juxtaposition of the ideas conveyed in a discourse and the points of view expressed by the critical discourse analyst on social reality. Rather, the critique should involve a justification – a justification that takes due account of the arguments advanced in the discourse under analysis. We think that the pragma-dialectical instruments for evaluation – critical discussion rules and critical questions in particular – can play an important role in such justificatory process.

3. Towards an Integrated Approach to Argumentation Analysis

Concretely, we propose to conceive of critique as a process in which the critical discourse analyst assesses the soundness of argumentative moves from a critical discussion perspective. To do justice to the emancipatory interests of CDA, however, the evaluation of the author's argumentation should go beyond the question of whether this stands up to the criticism actually advanced by the real opponent or the criticism projected by arguers themselves. The evaluative process should allow the analyst to put forward criticisms that have not been taken into account by the real or projected parties to the dispute. In other words, we think that the critical discourse analyst should be allowed to engage as if another party to the dispute, who assumes (at least) the role of antagonist to the viewpoints expressed by the author.[10] In doing so, the analyst will necessarily rely, explicitly or implicitly, on some normative political model or ideas.

In this way, critical discourse analysts can systematically justify their critique that a certain discourse is biased (in the sense of being based on ignorance or a partial understanding of social reality) or ideologically objectionable (since it contributes to suffering or hinders interpersonal flourishing, cf. Sayer, 2006), by arguing against the acceptability of the premises, or the relevance and sufficiency of the arguments adduced. In addition, the standards for a critical discussion could help in the identification of prejudice and relations of dominance at discursive levels that go beyond the process of advancing arguments. For instance, a pragma-dialectical evaluation might bring to view interactional drawbacks such as restricting the other party's freedom of action at the confrontation stage (violation of rule 1). If the opponent is a member of some disempowered social group this fallacy could point to the (re)creation of social inequality in discourse. Also, treating a mixed dispute in terms of a non-mixed difference of opinion (violation of rule 2) could be a way of neglecting the existence of other, contradictory and non-dominant discourses in the public sphere.

We believe that our proposal does justice to the principles lying at the basis of each of these approaches: dialectical reasonableness, on the one hand, and a political commitment to those who suffer the most, on the other. Dialectical reasonableness is preserved so long as we require the analyst to show that the viewpoints expressed in the discourse are unacceptable *because* they do not stand to a critical test. At the same time, the socio-political drive of CDA is upheld by allowing the analyst to take an active role in the (implicit or explicit) discussion presupposed by the discourse under consideration. In exercising this right, the analyst can bring to the discussion criticisms of the argumentation that are not taken up by the author and dominant discourses in the public domain.[11]

Notes

1. This is not to suggest that other approaches to CDA are not interested in analysing argumentative discourse. In an early programmatic article, van Dijk (1993) states that 'critical discourse analysts want to know what structures, strategies or other properties of text, talk, verbal interaction or communicative events play a role' in relations of social dominance, later listing 'topics, local meanings, style and rhetoric' as candidate examples of such structures, strategies or other properties of text and talk. Similarly Fairclough (1996: 286) argues that analysis of a particular discursive event requires an 'orientation to how it reworks the social resource of the existing order of discourse; but it also includes the concerns of stylistic, pragmatic and rhetorical analysis'. Fairclough (2003) draws briefly on Toulmin's work in discussing 'dialogical' and 'monological' arguments, though has moved away from argumentation towards a more fluid notion of construal in his recent Dialectical-Relational Approach (2009). As a rule, the methods of discourse analysis used in CDA cannot be prescribed in advance, since their selection depends mainly on specific research questions. That said, the DHA is the only approach that explicitly, and consistently, cites argumentation as a key discourse strategy, hence our focus on this approach in this chapter.
2. This is, by the way, key to the distinction between 'critical discourse analysis' on the one hand, and 'discourse analysis', on the other. The latter is solely concerned with the description and interpretation of discourse.
3. Though, as we detail below, CDA can nonetheless integrate pragma-dialectical analysis into a wider socio-political critique.
4. Cf. the day conference *Critique: An interdisciplinary conference on 'being critical'* held at Loughborough University, 26th June 2009
5. To be sure, there is a partial overlap between pragma-dialectics and CDA as regards the use of (socio)linguistic sources in the analysis. Still, there is a crucial difference in that the model for a critical discussion specifies what to look for in the discourse and provides a framework to systematically interpret, place and organize relevant empirical data.
6. That said, a further point is worth stressing: CDA does not – or at least, should not – render every negative representation of someone pertaining to a disempowered social group as, in and of itself, illegitimate (i.e., racist, sexist, anti-Muslim, etc.). A critical discourse analysis must distinguish between legitimate criticism of (people who happen to be), for instance, Muslims and illegitimate (in other words, prejudiced or racist) attacks. For an elaboration of this view, see Richardson (2006).
7. Though see Richardson (2001) and Ieţcu-Fairclough (2008), who incorporate a strategic maneuvering approach in their analyses.
8. Due to space limitations we will only examine ways that pragma-dialectics can contribute to CDA. However, CDA can also contribute to pragma-dialectics, for example by uncovering modes, or 'species', of argumentative practice where strategies of unequal

power relationships are enacted. In relation to the DHA in particular, the four 'levels of context' used to locate practices, strategies and texts in a specific contexts could be very useful in refining analysis of argument activity types.

9. Schegloff (1997), for instance, considers CDA descriptions problematic because he regards the analyst's interpretation as one based on ideological commitment rather than an analytic perspective.

10. A critical discourse analyst can – and probably will – assume also the role of protagonist of the opposite standpoint. In addition, s/he may assume at the level of a subdispute the standpoint that the argumentation is insufficient and advance objections to the protagonist's argumentation to justify his/her criticism.

11. On the face of it, it might seem that the critical discourse analysts' vested interest in discovering an author's argumentative missteps jeopardizes the principle of dialectical reasonableness. We think, however, that this is too hasty a conclusion. It is true that analysts will have an interest in 'winning' the dispute, but not less than any antagonist to a difference of opinion. In line with the notion of strategic maneuvering, we believe that the analysts' rhetorical goals may, but need not, be in conflict with their dialectical aims.

References

Anthonissen, C. (2003). Interaction between visual and verbal communication: changing patterns in the printed media. In G. Weiss & R. Wodak (Eds.), *Critical Discourse Analysis: Theory and Interdisciplinarity* (pp. 297–311). Houndmills: Palgrave.

Atkin, A. & Richardson, J.E. (2007). Arguing about Muslims: (Un)Reasonable argumentation in letters to the editor. *Text and Talk*, *27*(1): 1–25.

Billig M., Condor, S., Edwards, D., Gane, M., Middleton, D. & Radley, A.R. (1988). *Ideological Dilemmas*. London: Sage Publications.

Cameron, D. (2001). *Working With Spoken Discourse*. London: Sage.

Dijk, T. A. van (2001). Multidisciplinary CDA: a plea for diversity. In R. Wodak & M. Meyer (Eds.), *Methods of Critical Discourse Analysis* (pp. 95–120). London: Sage.

Dijk, T. A. van (2008a). *Discourse and Context. A Sociocognitive Approach*. Cambridge: Cambridge University Press.

Dijk, T. A. van (2008b). Critical Discourse Analysis and nominalization. *Discourse & Society*, *19*(6), 821–828.

Eemeren, F.H. van (2010). *Strategic Maneuvering in Argumentative Discourse: Extending the Pragma-Dialectical Theory of Argumentation*. Amsterdam/Philadelphia: John Benjamins.

Eemeren, F.H. van, Grootendorst, R., Jackson, S., & Jacobs, S. (1993). *Reconstructing Argumentative Discourse*. Tuscaloosa/London: The University of Alabama Press.

Eemeren, F.H. van & Houtlosser, P. (2009). Strategic maneuvering: Examining argumentation in context. In F.H. van Eemeren (Ed.), *Examining Argumentation in Context: Fifteen studies on strategic maneuvering* (pp. 1–24). Amsterdam: John Benjamins.

Fairclough, N. (1996). Rhetoric and Critical Discourse Analysis: A Reply to Titus Ensink and Christoph Sauer. *Current Issues in Language & Society 3*(3): 286–289.

Fairclough, N. (2003). *Analysing Discourse: Textual Analysis for Social Research*. London: Routledge.

Fairclough, N. (2009). A dialectical-relational approach to critical discourse analysis in social research, in R. Wodak & M. Meyer (Eds.), *Methods of Critical Discourse Analysis* (Second edition) (pp. 162–186). London: Sage

Fairclough, N. and Ieţcu-Fairclough I. (forthcoming). Argumentation Theory in CDA: Analyzing Practical Reasoning in Political Discourse. In R. de Cillia, H. Gruber, M. Krzyzanowski & F. Menz (Eds.), *Discourse-Politics-Identity*. Vienna: Stauffenburg Verlag.

Forchtner, B. (forthcoming). Critique, the discourse-historical approach, and the Frankfurt School.

Forchtner, B. & Tominc, A. (forthcoming). Critique in the Discourse-Historical Approach: Between Habermas' Critical Theory and Popper's Critical Rationalism.

Freeley, A. J. (1996). *Argumentation and debate: Critical thinking for reasoned decision making* (9th ed.). Belmont, CA: Wadsworth.

Heer, H. & Wodak, R. (2008). Introduction: Collective Memory, National Narratives and the Politics of the Past. In H. Heer, W. Manoschek, A. Pollak & R. Wodak (Eds.), *The Discursive Construction of History: Remembering the Wehrmacht's War of Annihilation* (pp. 1–13). Basingstoke: Palgrave.

Hultzén, L. S. (1966). Status in deliberative analysis. In D.C. Bryant (Ed.), *The rhetorical idiom: Essays in rhetoric, oratory, language and drama.* New York: Russell and Russell.

Iețcu-Fairclough, I. (2008). Legitimation and strategic maneuvering in the political field. *Argumentation, 22*: 399–417.

Iețcu-Fairclough, I. (2010). Argumentation and CDA, presentation at *Language, Ideology, Politics Workshop*, Lancaster University 27 January 2010.

Krżyzanowski, M. & Wodak, R. (2008). *The Politics of Exclusion. Debating Migration in Austria.* New Brunswick, NJ: Transaction Publishers.

Lemke, J. (1995). *Textual Politics: Discourse and social dynamics.* London: Taylor & Francis.

Reisigl, M. & Wodak, R. (2001). *Discourse and Discrimination. Rhetorics of Racism and Antisemitism.* London: Routledge.

Reisigl, M. & Wodak, R. (2009). The Discourse-Historical Approach. In R. Wodak & Meyer. M. (Eds.), *Methods of Critical Discourse Analysis* (2nd edition) (pp. 87–121). London: Sage.

Richardson, J. E. (2001) 'Now is the time to put an end to all this': Argumentative discourse theory and letters to the editor. *Discourse and Society, 12*(2): 143–168.

Richardson, J. E. (2006). On delineating 'reasonable' and 'unreasonable' criticisms of Muslims. *Fifth Estate Online*, August 2006.

Richardson, J. E. (2008). 'Our England': discourses of 'race' and class in party election leaflets. *Social Semiotics, 18*(3), 321–336.

Richardson, J. E. & R. Wodak (2009a). The impact of visual racism: Visual arguments in political leaflets of Austrian and British far-right parties. *Controversia 6*(2): 45–77.

Richardson, J. E. & Wodak, R. (2009b). Recontextualising fascist ideologies of the past: right-wing discourses on employment and nativism in Austria and the United Kingdom. *Critical Discourse Studies, 6*(4): 251–267.

Sayer, A. (2006) Language and significance – or the importance of import: Implications for critical discourse analysis. *Journal of Language and Politics, 5*(3): 449–471.

Schegloff, E. A. (1997). Whose Text? Whose Context? *Discourse & Society, 8*(2): 165–187.

Shaw, W.C. (1922). *The art of debate.* Boston: Allyn & Bacon.

Titscher, S., Meyer, M., Wodak, R., & Vetter, E. (2000). *Methods of Text and Discourse Analysis.* London: Sage.

Van Dijk, T. A. (1993). Principles of Critical Discourse Analysis. *Discourse and Society, 4*(2): 249–283.

Wodak, R. (2001). What CDA is about. In R. Wodak & M. Meyer (Eds.), *Methods of Critical Discourse Analysis* (pp. 1–13). London: Sage.

Wodak, R. (2009). *The Discourse of Politics in Action: Politics as Usual.* Basingstoke: Palgrave.

Wodak, R. & Dijk, T. A. van (Eds.) (2000). *Racism at the Top.* Klagenfurt: Drava.

Žagar, I. Z. (2009). The Use of Topoi in Critical Discourse Analysis (CDA), Keynote Lecture, *2nd International Conference on Political Linguistics*, University of Łódź, Poland, 17–19 September 2009.

62

The Impact of Visual Racism: Visual Arguments in Political Leaflets of Austrian and British Far-right Parties

John E. Richardson and Ruth Wodak

Introduction

In this paper, we apply the Discourse Historical Approach to Critical Discourse Analysis (DHA; see Wodak 2001, 2004, 2008b) combined with argumentation theory and visual grammar (Kress & Van Leeuwen 1996, 2001) to visual texts. Specifically we examine election posters and brochures to investigate the explicit and indirect persuasive rhetorical and argumentative devices employed to construct fear of foreigners, migrants, and asylum seekers, and to convince voters of their potential danger. Our texts are drawn from recent election materials produced by Austrian and British right-wing parties with an explicit xenophobic agenda. Our analysis seeks to detect similarities and differences in these new-old 'law and order' campaigns. We claim that the methodology, which we first present, is adequate to deconstruct the implied racist visual meanings.

In the second section of the paper, we introduce the Austrian and British examples and locate them in their respective national and ideological contexts. Finally, we compare the British and Austrian rhetoric and relate the results to the different socio-political developments and traditions of the two EU member states.

Source: *Controversia: An International Journal of Debate and Democratic Renewal,* 6(2) (2009): 45–77.

Due to space restrictions, we focus mainly on the visual argumentative texture of the examples and necessarily have to neglect many other salient features of right-wing populist and fascist rhetoric.[1]

Methodology: Discourse Historical Analysis (DHA)

According to Reisigl and Wodak (2001:1), racism/discrimination/exclusion manifests itself discursively: 'racist opinions and beliefs are produced and reproduced by means of discourse… through discourse, discriminatory exclusionary practices are prepared, promulgated and legitimized'. Hence, the strategic use of many linguistic indictors to construct in- and out-groups is fundamental to political (and discriminatory) discourses in all kinds of settings. It is important to focus on the latent meanings produced through pragmatic devices (e.g. implicatures, hidden causalities, presuppositions, insinuations and certain syntactic embeddings), as frequently manifest in the rhetoric of rightwing-populist European politicians, such as Jörg Haider, Jean Marie Le Pen or Silvio Berlusconi (see Wodak and Pelinka 2002; Rydgren 2005). To be able to analyse our examples, it is important to introduce some analytic concepts of DHA:

Systematic qualitative analysis in DHA takes four layers of context into account:

- the *intertextual and interdiscursive relationships* between utterances, texts, genres and discourses,
- the extra-linguistic social/sociological variables,
- the *history and archaeology of texts and organizations*,
- and institutional frames of the specific *context of a situation*.

In this way, we are able to explore how discourses, genres, and texts change due to socio-political contexts.

"Discourse" in DHA is defined as being

- related to a macro-topic (and to the argumentation about validity claims such as truth and normative validity which involves social actors who have different points of view).
- a cluster of context-dependent semiotic practices that are situated within specific fields of social action;
- socially constituted as well as socially constitutive;
- integrating various differing positions and voices.

Furthermore, we distinguish between "*discourse*" and "*text*": Discourse implies patterns and commonalities of knowledge and structures, whereas a *text* is a specific and unique realization of a discourse. Texts belong to "*genres*". Thus, a discourse on exclusion could manifest itself in a potentially huge range of genres and texts, for example in a TV debate on domestic politics, in a political manifesto on immigration restrictions, in a speech by an expert on migration matters, and so forth (Wodak 2008a). A text only creates sense when its manifest and latent meanings (*inter alia*, implicature, presupposition, allusion) are read in connection with knowledge of the world.

In accordance with Bakhtin's (1981; 1986) seminal work, we take "*intertextuality*" to refer to the linkage of all texts to other texts, both in the past and in the present. Indeed, no text is ever isolated in space and time as many studies illustrate; thus, intertextuality is inherently part and parcel of meaning making in context (see, Van Dijk, 2008). Bakhtin's term 'hereoglossia' captures this point adequately: every text manifests and integrates many voices – the voice of the author as well as (possibly contradictory) voices of 'others' who are talked or written about (Lemke, 1995). Intertextual links can be established in different ways: through continued reference to a topic or to its main actors; through reference to the same events as the other texts; or through the reappearance of a text's main arguments in another text. The latter process is also labeled "*recontextualization*". By taking an argument out of context and restating it in a new context, we first observe the process of de-contextualization, and then, when the respective element is implemented in a new context, of recontextualization. The element then acquires a new meaning, because, as Wittgenstein (1967) demonstrated, meanings are formed in use. Hence, arguments from parliamentary debates on immigration, from political speeches or in the mass media, are recontextualized in a genre-adequate way in the texts we analyse below through the use of salient visual and verbal features and elements.

The construction of in-and out-groups necessarily implies the use of *strategies of positive self-presentation and the negative presentation of others*. We are especially interested in five types of discursive strategies, all involved in positive self- and negative other-presentation, which underpin the justification/legitimization of inclusion/exclusion and of the constructions of identities. '*Strategy*' generally refers to a (more or less accurate and more or less intentional) plan of practices, including discursive practices, adopted to achieve a particular social, political, psychological or linguistic goal.[2]

First, there are *referential*, or *nomination*, *strategies*, by which social actors are constructed and represented, for example, through the creation of in-groups and out-groups. This is done through a number of categorization devices, including metaphors, metonymies and *synecdoches*, in the form of a part standing for the whole (*pars pro toto*) or a whole standing for the part (*totum pro parte*).

Second, social actors as individuals, group members or groups as a whole, are linguistically characterized through predications. *Predicational strategies* may, for example, be realized as evaluative attributions of negative and positive traits in the linguistic form of implicit or explicit predicates. These strategies aim at labelling social actors in a more or less positive or negative manner. They cannot be neatly separated from the nomination strategies.

Third, there are *argumentation strategies* and a fund of *topoi* through which positive and negative attributions are justified. For example, it can be suggested that the social and political inclusion or exclusion of persons or policies is legitimate. We say more about such *topoi* below.

Fourth, one may focus on the *perspectivation, framing* or *discourse representation*. Through framing speakers express their involvement in discourse, and position their point of view in the reporting, description, narration or quotation of relevant events or utterances.

Fifth, there are *intensifying strategies* on the one hand and *mitigation strategies* on the other. Both of these help to qualify and modify the epistemic status of a proposition by intensifying or mitigating the illocutionary force of utterances. These strategies can be an important aspect of the presentation inasmuch as they operate upon it by either sharpening it or toning it down.

Positive self and negative other-presentation requires justification and legitimation strategies, as elements of 'persuasive rhetoric'. Reisigl and Wodak (2001) define "*topoi*" as parts of argumentation which belong to the obligatory, either explicit or inferable premises. *Topoi* are the content-related warrants or 'conclusion rules' which connect the argument or arguments with the conclusion or the central claim. As such they justify the transition from the argument or arguments to the conclusion. Less formally, *topoi* can be described as reservoirs of generalised key ideas from which specific statements or arguments can be generated (Ivie, 1980, cited in Richardson, 2004: 230). As such, *topoi* are central to the analysis of seemingly convincing fallacious arguments which are widely adopted in prejudiced and discriminatory discourses (Kienpointner 1996: 562).

In Table 1, we list the most common *topoi* which are used when writing or talking about 'others', specifically about migrants. These *topoi* have been investigated in a number of studies on election campaigns (Pelinka and Wodak 2002), on parliamentary debates (Wodak and van Dijk 2000), on policy papers (Reisigl and Wodak 2001), on 'voices of migrants' (Delanty, Jones, Wodak 2008; Krżyzanowski and Wodak forthcoming), and on media reporting (Baker et al 2008). Most of them are used to justify the exclusion of migrants through quasi-rational arguments ('they are a burden for the society', 'they are dangerous, a threat', 'they cost too much', 'their culture is too different', and so forth). In this way, migrants are constructed as

Table 1: List of Prevailing Topoi in Immigration Discourse

1- Usefulness, advantage	9- Economy
2- Uselessness, disadvantage	10- Reality
3-Definition	11- Numbers
4-Danger and threat	12- Law and right
5-Humanitarianism	13- History
6- Justice	14- Culture
7- Responsibility	15- Abuse
8- Burdening	

scapegoats; they are blamed for unemployment or for causing general discontent (with politics, with the European Union, etc.), for abusing social welfare systems or they are more generally perceived as a threat for 'our' culture. On the other hand, some *topoi* are used in anti-discriminatory discourses, such as appeals to human rights or to justice.

Similarly there is a more or less fixed set of metaphors employed in exclusionary discourse (Reisigl and Wodak 2001), such as the likening of migration to a natural disaster, of immigration/immigrants as avalanches or floods, and of illegal immigration as 'dragging or hauling masses'.

Furthermore, Reisigl and Wodak (2001) draw on Van Eemeren and Grootendorst (1994) and Kienpointner (1996) when providing the list of general common fallacies. Frequently employed fallacies include, first, *argumentum ad baculum*, i.e. 'threatening with the stick', thus trying to intimidate instead of using plausible arguments. Second, *argumentum ad hominem*, which can be defined as a verbal attack on the antagonist's personality and character (of her or his credibility, integrity, honesty, expertise, competence and so on) instead of discussing the content of an argument. Finally, the *argumentum ad populum* or *pathetic fallacy* which consists of appealing to prejudiced emotions, opinions and convictions of a specific social group or to the *vox populi* instead of employing rational arguments. These fallacies frequently prevail in rightwing populist rhetoric (see Rydgren 2005).

Visual Rhetoric

As Willard (1979) argued, for too long the study of argument was unfortunately "coloured by the assumption that the claims and the reasons [of argumentation] must be linguistically serialised" (1979: 212). Adopting such a logocentric position when examining multi-modal discourse genres, such as political leaflets, will only ever provide an inadequate account of how their standpoints are advanced and/or derailed. In response, academic work on rhetoric and persuasion has recently taken a visual turn, expanding empirical and analytic foci from linguistic discourse (whether spoken or written) to include pictorial and visual artefacts in many disciplines and fields, from text linguistics and discourse analysis to literary criticism and rhetoric (Kostelnik & Hassett 2003; Hart & Daughton, 3rd revised edition, 2006; van Leeuwen & Jaworski 2002; Olsen et al, 2008b). This growth in visual rhetoric was driven by an "emerging recognition that such symbols provide access to a range of human experience not always available through the study of [linguistic] discourse" (Foss, 2004: 301). However, such preoccupations are hardly a new thing. Indeed, Gronbeck (2008: xxii) shows evidence, from a variety of Greek and Roman sources on rhetoric, for "knowing and believing grounded in seeing and the visualised." Yet, as he goes on to state, "scholars of communication have only begun to scratch the surface of the political and social implications" of the visual (Ibid.). The increasing attentiveness to the *analysis* of visual rhetoric has resulted in studies examining visual discourse as varied as fine art (Helmers, 2004; Willard, et al 2007), cartoons (Edwards & Winkler, 2008; Groarke, 2007) film (Alcolea-Banegas, 2007; Blakesley, 2004), advertising (Burridge, 2008, Ripley, 2007) political leaflets (Cairns, forthcoming; Richardson, 2008) and other visual artefacts.

However, there is still a great deal of debate regarding the possibility of visual rhetoric, and specifically whether it is possible for images to offer *arguments*. After all, we may agree that visual and multi-modal media – whether a photograph, a television documentary, a war memorial or a human body – can, and do, communicate meanings. We may equally agree that "visuality" plays a powerful role in "shaping our public symbolic actions" (Olsen et al, 2008a: 1). But can we say that they advance standpoints and supply supporting arguments? Some readers may think it unnecessary to recount such debates, given the recent publication of several visual rhetoric anthologies (Handa, 2004; Hill & Helmers, 2004; Olsen et al, 2008b; Prelli, 206). However, such an account is useful to outline the position of our own work. As Blair (2004: 46) discusses, those who argue against the possibility of arguments being visual tend to base this claim on two reasons. The first "is that the visual is inescapably ambiguous or vague. The other is related to the fact that arguments must have prepositional content", or, more specifically, that images cannot assert and so cannot advance a standpoint. First, we would agree that the meanings of the visual are frequently ambiguous. However, ambiguity and vagueness are also a feature of verbal argumentation, which, when serious enough to breach the pragma-dialectical language use rule (which states 'Parties may not use any formulations that are insufficiently clear or confusingly ambiguous'), can indeed be an obstacle for resolution. Hence, vagueness, on its own should not be viewed as a reason against the possibility of arguments being visual. Quite the contrary: we believe vagueness to be an inherent feature of political communication and also for advertising, particularly in images or metaphors (see Charteris-Black 2006 for a detailed discussion). As Wodak & de Cillia (2007: 335) also argue, commemorative speeches and accompanying iconic symbolism which are needed for the discursive construction of national identities, are also inherently vague to allow for a maximum of identification by as many people as possible (see also Billig 1995).

It is equally true that arguments advanced visually "are implicit and indirect in the sense that they are not explicit verbal statements of the sort that we typically take to be the paradigm instances of argumentative speech acts" (Groake, 2002: 144). However, in this way too, visual argumentation is comparable to its verbal counterpart, given that "in practice, the explicit performance of a speech act is the exception rather than the rule" (van Eemeren & Grootendorst, 1992: 44). As with verbal arguments, if we are to assess visual argument properly, we need to make an accurate extraction of the premises left implicit – that is, we should aim to offer a 'maximally argumentative inter- pretation' of the ways in which a standpoint is advanced, supported or defended visually. Indeed, we suggest that several interpretations could be offered due to the inherent ambiguity of visual arguments, where contextual information becomes decisive in opting for one or another reading. This is why we endorse the DHA as a specifically context-sensitive discourse-analytic approach as will be illustrated below. Such a linguistic reconstruction cannot fully replace the original, given the evocative power of visual communication (Hill & Helmers, 2004), but rather is comparable to the translation of one language into another. It is only with a comprehensible and charitable recon- struction of the implicitly advanced argumentation that we can properly iden- tify the argument scheme and implicatures employed, and hence the type of connection between premises and the standpoint (van Eemeren & Grootendorst, 1992; van Eemeren, Grootendorst & Snoeck Henkemans 2002).

On this basis, in this article we maintain that it is possible to argue visu- ally, since it is possible for images to advance and defend standpoints. More specifically, "visual arguments constitute the species of visual persuasion in which the visual elements overlie, accentuate, render vivid and immediate, and otherwise elevate in forcefulness a reason or set of reasons for modifying a belief, an attitude or one's conduct" (Blair, 2004: 50). Hence, if it is possi- ble to reconstruct from an image, a reason for accepting or believing some proposition or for modifying a belief or action – that is, if the meaning of an image can be reconstructed as advancing or defending a standpoint – it should be regarded as a visual argument. We should also emphasise at this point that we are aware of the fact that visual texts which are used as adver- tisements or for political election campaigns also strongly address emotions and cause affective responses (as does pathos-oriented rhetoric in general). Such rhetoric and argumentation frequently relies on fallacies which try to evoke positive or negative responses by applying simplistic 'we-discourses' or seductive metaphors as unifying elements. Hence, we are dealing with pat- terns of argumentation which are very complex and integrate cognitive and emotional, rational and irrational (fallacious) elements. Moreover, 'unrea- sonable' argumentation strategies can also form an intentional and inherent part of rightwing populist rhetoric, frequently relying on pragmatic devices such as irony and sarcasm. We will point to such uses below.[3]

Only systematic reception studies would allow investigating the many and predictably systematically differing ways of understanding such images and slogans. Lutz and Wodak (1987), Wodak et al. (1999 [2009]) and Kovàcs and Wodak (2003), for example, were able to illustrate in large stud- ies about media reception in various contexts that focus group participants offered different readings of the same text due to social class, previous experience, ethnic origin, and political affliation. Unfortunately, no empirical study about the leaflets under investigation exists to date. However, opinion polls and election results are referred to whenever appropriate which, however, do not allow establishing any causal links between visual argumentation and political party preference (see also Krzyżanowski, 2008, for the use of focus groups in reception studies and the newly coined term 'dog-whistle' politics by Poynting and Noble, 2003).

Inclusion and Exclusion – The Examples

Austria: The Freiheitliche Partei Osterreichs (FPÖ) and the Bundnis Zukunft Osterreich (BZÖ)

After the Second World War, in 1949, "liberals" with a strong German National orientation and no classical liberal tradition (see Bailer-Galanda and Neugebauer 1993: 326), who felt unable to support the SPÖ or the ÖVP, founded the VDU ("*Verband der Unabhängigen*"). This party became an electoral home for many former Austrian Nazis. The FPÖ, founded in 1956, was the successor party to the VDU, retaining an explicit attachment to a 'German cultural community' (for further political and historical information about the FPÖ as successor party to the former NSDAP, see Scharsach 2000, Scharsach and Kuch 2000, DöW 1993, Bailer-Galanda and Neugebauer 1997). In its more than 50-year-old history, the FPÖ has, therefore, never been a 'liberal' party in the European sense, although there were always tensions between more liberal and more conservative members of the party. For instance, in 1986, Haider was elected as leader of the party and unseated Norbert Steger, a liberal leader.

Since 1986, the FPÖ has gained many votes, peaking with 26.9% of all the votes cast in Austrian elections of October 1999 (1,244,087 voters). By 1993, the FPÖ's party policy and politics were conspicuously anti-foreigner, anti-European Union and widely populist, close to Le Pen's *FN* in France (Reisigl & Wodak 2000; Wodak & Iedema 2004; Wodak & Pelinka 2002). From the summer of 1995, the FPÖ almost completely ceased to stress the closeness between the Austrian and the German cultural community because opinion polls demonstrated that the majority of Austrian citizens no longer accepted such a self-definition. In the autumn of 1997, the FPÖ presented a new party programme, which, in its strategically employed 'calculated ambivalence' (see Reisigl & Wodak 2002), emphasizes Christian values.

From February 4th, 2000, the FPÖ constituted part of the Austrian government, having formed a coalition with the conservative ÖVP. This development caused a major upheaval internationally and nationally, and led to the so-called 'sanctions against the Austrian government' by the 14 other member states of the European Union (see Pelinka & Rosenberger 2001). In September 2000, the EU found an exit strategy and the sanctions were lifted due to a report of "Three Wise Men" (see Möhring ed. 2001). Nevertheless, the report stated that the FPÖ should be regarded as a "right wing extremist populist party, a right wing populist party with radical elements".

Figure 1: BZÖ, Graz Kampagne Aufsteller ('We are cleansing Graz' say Peter Westenthaler and Gerald Grosz; they are cleansing Graz of 'political corruption, asylum abuse, beggars, and foreign criminality')

In May 2005, a section of the FPÖ splintered off to form a new party, the *Bündnis Zukunft Österreich (BZÖ)*. Haider, a chief architect of the creation of the BZÖ, remained regional governor in Carinthia, but Peter Westenthaler took over the leadership of the party. Heinz-Christian Strache, a kind of 'modern clone' of Haider, took over the more far right, traditional and less populist FPÖ *(Freiheitliche Partei Österreichs)*. The FPÖ still thrives on explicit xenophobia, pan-Germanic sentiments, anti-Semitism, and Islamophobia in contrast to the BZÖ, which has continued its more populist programme with xenophobic and anti-Semitic subtexts (Turner–Graham 2007; Wodak 2007). However, the BZÖ continuously lost votes, as the governmental role does not seem to fit rightwing populist parties – their strength seems to lie in their oppositional role, not in taking over governmental responsibilities (Krżyzanowski and Wodak 2008). In the elections of October 1ˢᵗ 2006, the left Social-democratic Party (SPÖ) gained the majority in Austria after having been in opposition for six years. The BZÖ proportion of the vote was reduced to barely 5%, securing only 7 seats in parliament; the FPÖ attracted around 11% of the vote and is also represented in parliament.

In sum, for a considerable period of time, the FPÖ has, more than any other Austrian party, persuasively set a "xenophobic" anti-foreigner tone in

Austrian domestic policies. For more than a decade, the FPÖ has almost always profited electorally from the populist business of sowing uncertainty and irrational xenophobic and anti-Semitic anxieties, which – as already mentioned above – have been harboured or willingly adopted, for different reasons, by a considerable proportion of voters. This mantle has now been adopted by the younger and more populist BZÖ, as we demonstrate below.[4]

In December 2007 and January 2008, both traditional and less known exclusionary discourses suddenly (re)appeared in the public sphere. This was triggered by three primary factors: the expansion of the Schengen area (border controls between Austria, Slovakia, the Czech Republic, Hungary, and Slovenia were abolished on December 21st, 2007); the possible accession of Turkey; and new and very strict immigration laws in Austria and in other EU member states. New xenophobic slogans from the FPÖ, such as '*Lieber Schweinskotelett statt Minarett*' ('Rather pork cutlets than minarets'), "decorated" the streets of Vienna. In the city of Graz, during its city council elections in early 2008, a great deal of exclusionary racist rhetoric was posted by the BZÖ, which focused on the term '*säubern*' (to clean/cleanse). This functions as an obvious allusion to Nazi propaganda and anti-Semitic ideology proposing 'cleansing cities of Jews' – a euphemism for ethnic cleansing and genocide ('*Säuberung von Juden; Judenrein*'). The images below, taken from leaflets and postcards distributed by the BZÖ, illustrate this exclusionary rhetoric and the many negative ethnic, religious, and national stereotypes which were (re)produced during this campaign, i.e. stereotypes of the 'Poles as thieves' and the 'drug-dealing African':

These three Austrian posters condense many features of racist and discriminatory rhetoric. Most importantly, the allusion to Nazi rhetoric is apparent both in the choice of words, and in the use of visual metaphors, insinuations, and symbols ('cleansing the streets with brooms'). This also applies to the stereotypes of 'drug dealing black asylum seekers', and 'Polish thieves' (as nominations), which are common in Austria. In this way, by applying several visual and verbal *topoi*, the BZÖ attempts to construct itself as the "law and order" party that can save Austrians, and the citizens of Graz specifically, from 'immediate and huge threats'.

The posters employ many nominative and predicative strategies whereby the 'others' are named and certain generic characteristics are attributed to them. Both the men in Figures 2 and 3 are referred to by using the same combination of referential and predicative strategies:

Wojciech K, Serienautoknacker   [Wojciech K, serial car thief]

Amir Z, Asylwerber und Drogendealer [Amir Z, asylum seeker and drug dealer]

The first component in each construction – providing their given name but only the initial of their family name – paradoxically acts to anonymise

Figure 2: BZÖ, Graz 'Postkarte Autoknacker' (Wojciech K., serial car thief, states: 'Do not vote for the BZÖ because I would like to continue with my business dealings')

Figure 3: BZÖ, Graz 'Postkarte Drogendealer' (Amir Z, asylum seeker and drug dealer, states: 'Please do not vote for the BZÖ because I would like to continue with my business dealings')

the two men – they are constructed as generic types. This strategy works in conjunction with the ways that both their faces are concealed, either by a balaclava in Figure 2 or the black censor's rectangle in Figure 3. Following their (foreign sounding) given names, the second component of the nominalization attributes negative generic characteristics to the men. The predicative strategy in each case is an intensified criminalisation. This, Wojciech K is not *just* a car thief, but is a serial, or *career*, car thief. In the case of Amir Z, this intensification is achieved through an additional negative actional anthroponym (Reisigl & Wodak, 2001): thus, he is not *just* a drug dealer, but is also an asylum seeker – that is, someone who, in the eyes of the BZÖ, is already 'burdening Our society' (*topos* of burden) and so should not be 'taking advantage of Our generosity' (*topos* of abuse).

The BZÖ leaders are also labelled and characterized, albeit contrasted in positive ways. They are not generic, but individuals, with full given and family names, colourful, handsome, and fore-grounded, whereas the 'others' are back-grounded through the dark – 'dirty' – colours used. In this way, even the colours are employed as part of the argument: cleaning the streets of dirt which is – conventionally – brown and black, not white and orange. The two men are also smiling while 'cleaning the street'. This ironic (or sarcastic) connotation can be viewed as integrating intentionally unreasonable argumentation strategies and part of 'calculated ambivalence'; in this way, they are addressing viewers in multiple ways and also signal that they knowingly employ the embedded allusion to Nazi rhetoric.

Moreover, all posters utilize layout and fonts in black and white and explicit paradoxical statements which serve as *presuppositions* to contrasting latent meanings: the real and right norms and values are implied through the subtext – the opposite meanings. These persuasive strategies (*implicature by contrast*) all belong to the political sub-field of advertising; hence we are dealing with a case of hybridity, *mixing the genres* of advertising and political communication (Fairclough 2003).

If we continue briefly with a *multi-modal analysis*, we have to point to colours and contrast between dark and light which are salient features (see Kress and van Leeuwen 1996): dark for the 'others', the bad people who steal and deal drugs; light, white and orange for the 'good guys' who 'will cleanse' the city of threatening inhabitants. In this way, the images combine *metaphorical, metonymic, and pragmatic devices* in intricate ways. The latter devices are employed as *argumentation and intensification strategies*. The *topoi* range from 'abuse, criminality' to 'law and right' 'threat for our culture', and 'justice'.

Due to the fact that we are discussing images where the depiction of the 'others' employs biological characteristics, like skin colour, certain hairstyles, dark eyes, etc., we necessarily conclude that racist meanings are intentionally (re)produced as persuasive devices. At this point, we should explore the context of the election campaign in much greater detail, the history of the two parties involved, as well as the broader historical context in Austria, where similar slogans and meanings were employed by Nazi rhetoric before and during WWII. The *topos* of 'cleansing' streets/stores/towns of 'others' (Jews, Slavs, Roma, etc.) stems from such fascist rhetoric and has now been redeployed and recontextualized to apply to Poles and migrants from Africa, among others, for this context.

The concept of 'Säuberung' (cleansing; using precisely this wording in German) is readily notable in historical Nazi sources or reading old dictionaries.[5] Looking in in Nazi brochures, propaganda, Nazi editions of dictionaries, and even in Hitler's *Mein Kampf* (270, 359) the concept is frequently related to, or collocated with, 'Judenrein' as well as 'Rassenrein' (clean of Jews, pure race, respectively, again precisely this wording in German). There, the purity of blood depends on 'cleansing Germany and the German race from Jewish influence and destruction' (*Zersetzung*). The 'cleansing' should, so Nazi ideology argues, lead to *Entjudung* (De-Judaification) (see Schmitz-Berning 2007: 189). Accordingly, Jews should, first, be removed from all professions and business; second, all alleged and so-called 'Jewish influence' should be destroyed; third, all Jewish possessions and properties should be taken over by force ('*Arisierung*'); and fourth, in the well-known so-called 'final solution' (*Endlösung*), Säuberung referred euphemistically to the policy of murder, deportation, and mass extermination (gassing). (See also *Duden*, 10th edition, 1929; 11th edition 1934, 12th edition 1941). In the 13th edition of *Der Duden* from 1947, these concepts were deleted – which provides even more evidence for the fact that everybody knew that these terms were part of Nazi jargon!

It should also be noted that 'cleansing the streets' in this leaflet does not only refer to the way the Nazis used the term '*Säuberung*'. It also implicitly indexes the material consequences of this policy, in the form of the Jews who had to kneel on their knees and wash the streets, often with their tooth brushes, while the SA and SS and many bystanders jeered and laughed. Thus, this image is doubly meaningful. On the one hand, the rather clear insinuation to Nazi jargon and cleansing. On the other hand there is the subtext, related to the 'washing and cleaning of Austrian streets by Jews'. Now 'the Aryans' are doing this themselves, though smiling cheerfully, standing, and with brooms.

We do not claim that everybody who views the above-depicted poster will be able to make these associations and be able to deconstruct the visual and textual insinuation (see above). However, many viewers certainly will be able to guess the latent meanings and the intended subtext as these terms are strongly and explicitly taboo in public and official discourses. Schoolbooks, films, and documentaries all contain pictures of Nazi times with such slogans – for example of Jewish shops where these words were painted on the windows, and or of Jews forced to wash the streets. Thus, one can assume a wide collectively shared knowledge of these historically connotated words in the Austrian context which politicians refer to intentionally – although they would, of course, always deny such intentions (see Wodak and Reisigl, 2002).

The argumentative chain that is implied runs as follows:

1) The BZÖ cleans the streets and keeps our city clean – they stand for 'law and order'
2) Wojciech, a Polish foreigner, steals cars as his daily business
3) If you vote for BZÖ, Wojciech will not be able to continue stealing

4) Hence, Wojciech (and all other criminals) oppose the BZÖ
5) Voting for the BZÖ will establish 'clean – orange-streets' once more;
6) BZÖ stands for law and order

Moreover, explicit actions are depicted. The BZÖ actually 'cleans' the streets which implies that they 'clean out' the – generically depicted – criminals and drug dealers. They do not have to promise or appeal for action in indirect or coded ways; they are, if one follows the very explicit metaphorical argument, already acting! Here, the broken, distressed font of the 'undesirable elements' being cleansed from the streets of Graz acts as an intertextual link between the Campaign Leaflet and the Postcards. For each of the four problems that the BZÖ will brush away, there is a more detailed postcard providing an exemplar or illustration. Thus, if we were in any doubts about Wojciech's nationality ('he sounds foreign, but he could be Austrian...'), the campaign leaflet provides "*Ausländer kriminalität*" as a transformed generalisation of his activities. Similarly, the transformed generalisation relating to "Amir Z" explicitly reiterates the interpretative gloss that draws on the *topos of abuse*, implicit in the postcard. These intertextual links, signalled visually through the use of the distressed font, function to project the exemplars, detailed in the postcards, into the principal Campaign Leaflet (*argumentum ad exemplum*): the visual rhetoric leads us to visualise 'undesirables' like Amir Z and Wojciech K being swept away by the cleansing broom of the BZÖ.

Debates about immigration and nationhood are also crucially linked to *assumptions about place,* thus to *deixis*. 'Our' culture belongs 'here' within the bounded homeland, whilst the culture of 'foreigners' belongs 'elsewhere' (*topos of culture*). The theme of place is particularly threatening to groups who are seen to have no 'natural' homeland, such as the Roma or other diasporic communities today, or the Jews in the first half of the twentieth century. Religion as a central condition for inclusion/exclusion, frequently triggered by indexical markers such as the 'headscarf' worn by Muslim women, has recently become dominant in some EU countries.

The United Kingdom: The British National Party

The British National Party (BNP) is currently Britain's largest far-right political party. The BNP was founded in 1982, through the merger of a faction of the neo-Nazi *British Movement* and John Tyndall's openly anti-Semitic *New National Front* (itself a splinter from the, at that time, larger *National Front*). Nick Griffin joined the BNP from the *International Third Position* in 1995. Soon after joining the party, in July 1998, he was charged with race hatred offences in connection with a magazine that he edited called *The Rune*. Issue 12 of the magazine (published in 1996) was judged to contain both anti-Semitic libel and Holocaust denial material, and Griffin was convicted and received a nine-month prison sentence, suspended for two years. Recently, the leadership of the BNP have argued that this anti-Semitism is a thing of the past, and are focusing instead on the putative threat posed by what they call the 'Islamification' of Britain. The extent to which anti-Semitism remains at the ideological core of the party is a matter of debate. There is evidence, for example, that the decline of anti-Semitic rhetoric in party literature is attributable to simple political opportunism rather than a genuine change of party ideology. Thus, in an article published in the magazine *Patriot,* soon after his trial (that is, before he deposed Tyndall as chairman), Griffin outlined to BNP activists his plans for the "modernisation" of the party. He wrote:

As long as our own cadres understand the full implications of our struggle, then there is no need for us to do anything to give the public cause for concern [...] we must at all times present them with an image of moderate reasonableness. [...] Of course, we must teach the truth to the hardcore, for, like you, I do not intend this movement to lose its way. But when it comes to influencing the public, forget about racial differences, genetics, Zionism, historical revisionism [i.e. Holocaust denial] and so on – all ordinary people want to know is what we can do for them that the other parties can't or won't. (cited in Brown, 2007)

A racist anti-immigrant policy, based on nativist principles, remains unquestionably at the heart of the Party however. As the Party's Constitution states, they remain "committed to stemming and reversing the tide of non-white immigration and to restoring, by legal changes, negotiation and consent the overwhelmingly white makeup of the British population that existed in Britain prior to 1948."

In the 2005 General Election, the BNP polled 193,000 votes for the 119 candidates it fielded, significantly higher than the 47,000 amassed in 2001. Across the United Kingdom as a whole, they attracted 4.3 per cent of the vote, obtaining more than 5 per cent of the vote in 33 of the seats they contested and more than 10 per cent in three constituencies. The highest of these was the Barking constituency, its main target seat, where the party polled 16.9 per cent, its highest share of the vote anywhere in the country (John et al, 2006).

On May 1st 2008, local government elections took place in England and Wales, along with elections for the Greater London Authority and London Mayor. The BNP stood over 600 candidates across 74 wards in England and Wales – enough that they qualified for a party political broadcast. The BNP also entered 10 candidates for the GLA London-wide candidate list, one constituency candidate (for the London constituency of City and East) as well as Richard Barnbrook as their Mayoral Candidate. The London Assembly is made up of 25 members, and is a unique case in British politics, being decided by a partial system of proportional representation: 14 members of the Authority are elected via a 'first past the post' system to represent constituencies; these are supplemented by 11 London-wide members elected

Figure 4: The BNP 'Londoner' campaign leaflet

through PR. Political parties need 5% of the vote to get one of these 11 seats, 8% for two and 11% for three.

Their results were below what had been widely predicted and were judged a disappointment by the party (Lowles, 2008). Across the country, the party added 10 local councillors, significantly lower than the 40 they were reported as aiming for (Ibid.). Barnbrook came fifth in the Mayoral Elections, placing behind the three major Parties as well as the Green Party, with only 2.84 per cent of the first choice votes (69,710 votes).[6] This was down marginally on the percentage of first choice votes that the BNP candidate Julian Leppert received in the 2004 London Mayoral election.[7] In City and East, Robert Bailey came fourth with 9.82 per cent (18,020 votes) for the BNP, in a constituency that also saw sizable returns for the UK Independence Party (3,078 votes; 1.68%), the English Democrats (2,048 1.12%) and the National Front (2,350, 1.28%). However, the party attracted 5.33% of the vote for the London-wide candidate list (130,714), marginally more than the 4.8% share of the vote they achieved in 2004, and sufficient to elect Richard Barnbrook as a member of the GLA.

A BNP leaflet, headed The LONDONER was a prominent feature of the party's London campaign. During every weekend in the run up to Election Day, party activists leafleted a variety of London's boroughs, including the predominantly Jewish communities in the North of the city (Taylor, 2008). On their first 'National Weekend of Action' alone, the party apparently delivered over 100,000 leaflets across the capital (BNP, 2008). Laid out in the style of a newspaper – complete with a clear san-serif masthead – the remainder of front page is arranged under the headline "The Changing Face of London":

Here, the expression 'Changing Face' is used both metaphorically, to refer to the ways that the character, persona or disposition of London has (apparently) changed, as well as literally, referring to actual faces of London's inhabitants who metonymically represent the city. With this in mind, a productive initial analytic strategy may be to examine the ideational content of the images used on this front page.

The upper of two images shows white families – the vast majority of whom are women and children – out socialising on a terraced street; food and drink are clearly included on stalls in the foreground of the image and flag bunting between the housing. From this, and the fashions worn by the women and children, we can conclude that the photo was taken on the day of a significant social event during the late 1940s or early 1950s. A candidate example could be the Queen's Coronation in 1952, but given the almost total lack of men, we presume the event depicted is the 'Victory in Europe' Day Celebrations. It is therefore rather ironic that the BNP chose this image, given that a large proportion of the men 'missing' from the image would have still been stationed in Europe after fighting fascism (a war that the BNP maintains was unnecessary). Overall, the sense is of a happy occasion – a street Party – enjoyed by friendly, welcoming women. This is achieved in no small part due to the emphasis placed on a woman at the extreme left of the image, photographed with a large, open and welcoming smile. The arrow on the left – headed "From this…" – points the attention of the viewer directly at her, providing a welcoming entry point into the image.

The photograph has an open aspect, a light palette (which connotes an aged photograph as well as imbuing it with a clean, bright aesthetic) and is composed in such a way that the people only take up the lower half of the frame. The majority of remainder of the image is open sky, giving it the sense of space and liberty, into which is interspersed the Union Flags on the bunting. The combination of fun, friendliness and the place of the Nation (metonymically represented by the flag) in everyday life is highly conducive to the BNP constructing an idealised past for working class Londoners (this is a terraced street, not one filled with Georgian mansion houses). In addition, the event pictured is atypical. Street parties of this nature were rare, even during this period of time, and restricted to major Royal Weddings, Coronations and other events of high social significance. Opting to use such an image to represent the conviviality and social inclusiveness of London in the past is therefore misrepresentative and, potentially, counter-productive to the success of the BNP's argument.

The women in the image below are far less welcoming. It's immediately apparently that they're Muslim; wearing the *niqab* means that you can't see their faces, only their eyes, which look out at the viewer in an expressionless way. Repeating the structure of the image above, the viewer's attention is directed by the use of the arrow on the left, this time pointing to a woman putting up two fingers – a gesture directed towards the photographer and hence transferred to the viewer. This is an interesting, and ironically rather English, gesture, usually taken as a sign of defiance or abuse – in effect meaning 'fuck off'. The palette of the lower image is much darker than the one above, predominantly the result of the black *niqabs* and dark clothing worn by each of the three women. Here, again in contrast with the image above, the composition is dominated by the three women, who practically fill both the height and width of the frame. The poor print quality and pixelation of the image suggests that it was enlarged from a much smaller image to create this looming presence of the women dominating the frame.

It is interesting that the BNP chose to use two pictures of women in this leaflet. This is an unusual approach for the party, and marks a shift compared to the pictorial content of their leaflets produced over the past two years, which tended to emphasise the threat of the *male* Other. In the case of this LONDONER leaflet, the more archetypally prejudicial image of 'the (male) Muslim horde', taken at a London protest against the publication of 'the Danish cartoons', is relegated to the back page (see Richardson, 2008, for an examination of the BNP's use of this image). On the front page, the party have set up a figure of contrast between the *women qua women* of London's past and women presented as more typical of London's present. The white women of the past are friendly and welcoming, pictured smiling with children and food, in an image that acts to domesticate them: they appear happy to be home, providing food for family and friends. This symbolic domestication is particularly significant historically, since this image would have been taken immediately after a period of intense involvement in the public sphere and with 'war effort' employment in particular. The selection of this image, therefore, at the very least represents a "modern traditional" patriarchal view, in which women may well be 'allowed' to work, but "remain primarily responsible for the family and the home" (Amesburger & Halbmayr, 2002, cited in Mudde, 2007: 93). In the lower image, the leaflet portrays a group of expressionless, but nevertheless *un*friendly Muslim women of the present. In contrast with the white women above, who were pictured with children of a variety of ages, a pram pushed by the woman in the middle, has been specifically cropped from the original image. This cut – which removed around a quarter of the original image – severed the woman from the domestic role *she* was performing when the photograph was taken. Along with the removal of social context from the image, this drastic edit further reduces the woman's range of discernible social and personal roles – she is reduced to being only *a Muslim woman*, not a mother, sister, aunt, etc. The extent of the cut also required the BNP to stretch the image in order to fit the width of the page. As a result of this enlargement, the shape of the women has been distorted – they look more squat and dumpy than they are in the original.[8]

In fact, while tracing the origin of this lower photo, we were able to find out that the photograph wasn't taken in London at all, but rather in the Sparkhill area of Birmingham (UK) on 31 January 2007. The night before, eight Muslim men were arrested in Sparkhill, and neighbouring areas, as part of what Police and Security sources described as an alleged plot to kidnap and behead a British soldier; a further man was arrested the following day.[9] The Muslim Maktabah bookshop was also raided along with four further commercial premises. The social disruption this brought, along with the way that the news media widely described the region of the city as being a hotbed of radicalization, led some Muslims in the local community to feel angry at the way that they were being portrayed. The image has since been used in further news reports regarding the alleged self-imposed segregation of Muslims in the UK, as well as on the cover of the 2007 paperback edition of Melanie Philips' book *Londonistan*. This book appears to be the first instance where the image was used in direct reference to Muslims in London.

The layout of image and inference on this front page supports the ideal/ real layout proposed in the multi-modal approach – the BNP's ideal picture of London positioned at the top of the composition, whilst their idea of the City's terrible reality underneath. The layout also implicitly indexes and plays on an inversion of the 'before and after' personal transformations used in adverts for cosmetics and other beauty products. This page layout, and rhetorical position, is also used in a leaflet distributed in Stoke-on-Trent.

The repeated use of "this" is a particularly effective rhetorical device on the front page, and the principal element that allows a rhetorical cross-fertilisation between visual and verbal components of the argument. The first use ("CONSIDER THIS,") forms part of a directive to cue up the argument presented on the front page – "this" functions as a cataphoric pronoun, referring the reader 'forward' to the argument that the BNP wishes the viewer to consider. The second "this" is a far more complex pronoun, simultaneously referring to the image above, of the white street scene, as well as the qualities that London used to possess, listed in the sentences that follow. The pronoun is linked to the upper photograph through the semantic consonance between "the way London used to be", "From this…", as a starting point of a change of state used on the intrusive arrow, and the global topic of Change, introduced in the headline. The photo and the description of London-past that it is meant to represent, should be viewed and understood together: the street scene, depicting a universally white and predominantly female group of people, should be taken to denote a city "At ease with itself, friendly, happy and secure". Thus:

[this picture above depicts] the way London used to be

[London used to be] At ease with itself, friendly, happy and secure.

This indexical slippage, between image and description, allows the BNP to offer one account of the event taking place in the image. Specifically, how the "community values" of the past are something to be desired and which the BNP aims to encourage or reintroduce. However, the use of the second image, in opposition to the street party photographed, enables the BNP to project issues of race and religion onto this putative loss of "community values". The choice to depict Muslim women in *niqab*, the selection of this particular point in time (of someone making an abusive gesture) and the production decision to frame them in enlarged close up, thereby denying them a sense of place and context, makes it difficult to construct any interpretation of the image other than one that emphasises their Muslimness. In turn, this foregrounding of the women's Muslimness acts to emphasise the white, non-Muslimness of the women and children in the upper image. Hence, from this contrast, we can construe that London has changed:

"From this [white] to this [Muslim]"
and it is this change that has apparently brought with it the loss of a variety of positive social characteristics:
"From this [friendly] to this [abusive]"
"From this [happy] to this [unexpressive]"
"From this [secure] to this [insecure]"
"From [a sense of community values] to [anti-social]"

The leaflet doesn't go as far as to explicitly state that the presence of Muslims living in London resulted in the loss of these positive social characteristics, but then it doesn't have to. The standpoint is derived from the complex interplay of visual and verbal dimensions: that London has changed "From [Image 1] to [Image 2]"; and that London used to be at ease with itself [etc.]

The final use of "this" in the central verbal component of the front page – "If you would like London to be like this again..." – retains the complex way that this pronoun is used on the front page. Here, "this" refers anaphorically to the list of positive social and civic qualities listed immediately beforehand, as well as the image from London's past. Hence, to the uncritical eye, the leaflet could be proposing a return to the positive social values listed – a list that invokes certain bedrock values of contemporary liberal, social democratic political thought, that most people would have difficulty opposing.

However, in concert with the images, the racialised assumptions of the proposition cannot be overlooked. Like the Austrian leaflets we examined above, this is an argument for the racial purification of a City. From this, it is possible to reconstruct a standpoint and its arguments.

1. London used to be white
2. When it was white, London was at ease with itself, friendly, happy and secure.
3. The BNP wants London to be at ease with itself, friendly, happy and secure.
4. Being at ease, friendly, happy and secure means being white
5. Therefore, the BNP will make London white again

Like with any reconstruction, ours involves the transformation of certain argumentative elements and the interpretation, clarification and substitution of others (principally, in this case, the visual elements). During our reconstruction, we considered using 'non-Muslim' rather than 'white' (thus: '(1) London used to be non-Muslim; (2) When it was non-Muslim...' etc.), given the way that the BNP are clearly making the 'Muslim-ness' of the women in the lower image the problematic aspect of their identity. By this alternative reconstruction, the BNP would be arguing to remove (only) Muslims from London and hence 'make London free of Muslims again'. However, the agenda of the BNP is significantly wider than this. As their Party constitution, quoted in an earlier section, shows, they do not limit their discrimination to Britain's Muslim populations. They argue – and, with the advent of a BNP Councillor on the Greater London Authority will be *agitating for* – the wide-spread repatriation of Britain's non-White populations. Our reconstruction therefore takes into account this wider agenda, and reads the use of the Muslim women to metonymically stand in for Britain's non-white, that is, minority ethnic, communities in general.

Comparative Discussion

At this stage we can perhaps offer a comparative examination of the leaflets of these two political parties, and their relations to their respective national and ideological contexts of production and consumption.

Prejudicial Topoi

As should already be clear, there are significant parallels and overlaps between the prejudicial *topoi* employed in the leaflets of both parties. In each, minority communities are positioned as objects the 'We' must deal with – explicitly as a form of polluting dirt in the case of the BZÖ, or as a vaguely delineated, but nevertheless socially disruptive (Muslim) community in the case of the BNP. The reader of each leaflet is placed in a position of power relative to these negatively described social groups and asked to grant each party the mandate to act on a shared sense of revulsion and deal with the problem communities in 'responsible ways'; i.e. both parties appeal to be trusted to change the current situation and transform it into a 'clean' community again. The BZO requests the reader grant them their vote so they can 'cleanse' Graz, whilst the BNP requires 'your support' to return London to the 'friendly, happy and secure' state of the pre-1950s through removing (that is, if their Constitution is anything to go by, the repatriation) of British Muslims. Thus, both leaflets are based on what one may term a *global*, or organising *topos of disadvantage*: that 'having these kind of people here, in Our city, is harmful and disadvantageous and, as such, they should be removed'. Connected to the macro *topos of disadvantage* is a second macro-*topos*: the *topos of threat* ('they bring insecurity and unhappiness').

In turn, these two macro-*topoi* are constituted by a series of supporting *topoi*, which draw variously on, the *topos* of law and justice ('they are drug dealers and criminals'), the *topos* of history ('things were better here before they arrived'), the *topos* of culture ('they don't have Our sense of community values'; 'they are different'; 'they beg outrageously'; 'they do not want to integrate'), and the *topos* of abuse ('they abuse our asylum system'; 'they abuse our tolerance'). Singly, these *topoi* offer prejudicial, indeed racist, accounts of minority communities, as 'things which bring social problems and danger'. Collectively, each of these constitutive *topoi* contributes to a higher order rhetorical aim of the analysed leaflets: for the purification of the national space.

Visual Argumentation

Given the focus of this article, it is pertinent to assess the role of the visual relative to linguistic aspects of the argument advanced. Specifically, we can ask to what extent do the visual, and particularly the pictorial, elements of the leaflets stand as independent arguments supporting the standpoints of each political party? The literature on argument structures is useful here, suggesting three types of argumentation:

- first, *subordinate argumentation*, in which "one of the reasons [or arguments] supports the other" forming a serial chain of reasons (Snoeck Henkemans, 2001: 101);
- second, *coordinate argumentation*, in which "each of the reasons given is directly related to the standpoint and the reasons work together as a unit" (Ibid.);
- and, third, *multiple argumentation*, in which "each reason separately supports the standpoint" (Ibid.).

Here, we suggest that these leaflets represent visual examples of co-ordinatively compound argumentation, given that the pictorial (and other visual devices) and linguistic elements "together constitute a defense [of their respective parties' standpoints] only in combination with one another" (van Eemeren & Grootendorst, 2004: 121). However, this does not mean that the visual elements of each leaflet perform an identical rhetorical function. In the case of the BZÖ, the *linguistic* aspect of the argumentation is explicit in the way that it advances the party's standpoint and proposed action to implement the standpoint– that the BZÖ stands for law and order and hence voting for the BZÖ will establish 'clean streets' once more. The verb *'säubern'* is a material verb (in Halliday's classification). The history of the term *Säuberung*, and the Nazis specific use of it, remain implicit and function pragmatically as insinuation. The image therefore in general functions as an enactment, or demonstration (in the non-logical sense) of the proposed policy. This takes the form of a statement (or slogan), visual specification (what is being cleansed), and finally, explicit metonymic visual enactment. We say metonymic in the sense that two brooms and the two party leaders stand for the whole party and many brooms cleansing the whole city.

The linguistic element of the BNP leaflet, on the other hand, is more equivocal in what exactly it is arguing for (and, conversely, the problem that it is arguing against). In the absence of explicit elaboration, the two images fill in the referential blanks created through the repeated use of the indexical but vague and ambiguous 'this'. Thus:

This [Image 1] is how London used to be.
This [Image 2] is what London has changed into
The BNP intends to make London more like *this* [Image 1]…
…by cleansing the city of *this* [Image 2]

In this way, the images perform a double function: they, first, convey in a vivid and evocative way a putative change in the 'face of London', and they do this without explicitly raising the issues of race or religious difference in the text; they actually rely mostly on the difference in clothing and their presupposed religious significance. In fact, their implicit indexing of religion removes the need for the linguistic element of the leaflet to use these terms, thereby fulfilling their second function: they inject a degree of deniability to the argumentation – that is, the BNP could, conceivably (though rather implausibly) claim 'they weren't being racist'. Indeed, the linguistic element of the BNP leaflet carefully avoids the kind of explicit referential and predicative strategies used by the BZÖ. The 'good people' – that is, the people who the BNP is willing to represent and to whom they are hoping to appeal – are described using a proximate spatialisation "local people". According to their self-description, the BNP are "the party that puts local people first" rather than the party that wishes to purge a city of asylum seekers (negative actional anthroponym) and *Ausländer* (negative de-spatialised anthroponym), and only the inferential content of the two images exposes the chauvinistic implications of this partiality.

National Contexts

The equivocal and indirect nature of the standpoint advanced in the BNP leaflet is no doubt due, in no small part, to the restrictions laid out in race relations legislation to avoid inciting racial and religious hatred. The BNP are, of course, aware of the precise nature of these restrictions having had first hand experience of defending themselves against criminal charges. In addition to being found guilty of race hatred offences in July 1998 (discussed above), in April 2005, Nick Griffin was charged with four offences of using words or behaviour intended or likely to stir up racial hatred. During their trial in February 2006 (and subsequent re-trial in November 2006), both Griffin and his co-accused, Mark Collett, were found not guilty of all charges, given that their hatred had been directed at Muslims and Islam – described by Griffin as a "wicked and vicious faith" – and not against persons on racial grounds. Since the Racial and Religious Hatred Act 2007 came into force at the start of October 2007, this loophole, which essentially allowed incitement to hatred against Muslims so long as they were defined by reference to their religious belief, has been closed.

However, the restrictions on visual communications in this legislation are vague. For example, Section 29B(1) of the Act states that a person is guilty of an offence if s/he uses "threatening *words* or *behaviour*, or displays any written material which is threatening" (emphases added) in order to stir up religious hatred. Similarly Section 29C(1) refers only to publishing or distributing "*written* material", and the only references to visual images are made in relation to broadcast, time-based programming (cf. Sections 29E-G). Given this lack of attention to visual communication in the Act, it is interesting that the BNP relied so centrally on visual elements, that rely so much on decoding and interpretation, to support their standpoint.

The context dependency on Austrian texts is equally salient, corresponding to the de-tabooization of xenophobia since 1989 and more specifically 1993. The recontexualization of anti-Semitic slogans, and recycling them for xenophobic purposes, originates about this period. So, suddenly, from 1989, we have anti-Semitism and xenophobia enacted in parallel and also merged ways. Old images have since been used to vilify new out groups as well as for the old out-group. Moreover, due to the six years rightwing government of ÖVP and BZÖ (FPÖ) from 2000 – 2006, and the BZÖs role in the government, a kind of normalization and accommodation to discriminatory linguistic practices has taken place in the Austrian public sphere. Since then, even explicit xenophobic and anti-Semitic utterances rarely cause any scandals (Pollak and Wodak 2001). Sanctions usually only occur if the international media (interestingly metonymically labelled as *Das Ausland* and frequently insinuating a World Jewish Conspiracy of the US media; see Mitten 1992; Wodak 2003, 2007) start writing about such incidents. The level of taboo has fallen significantly. One absolute taboo, however, still persists: Holocaust Denial, which is punishable with sentences up to 10 years. Otherwise, the so-called *Verbotsgesetz* (Prohibition Law) which punishes all Nazi activities (in whatever form) defines these as 'gross trivialization of Nazi ideology' (*'gröbliche Verharmlosung'*) which frequently – due to the coded character of racist discourse in Postwar Austria – needs linguistic expertise to decode systematically (Pelinka and Wodak, 2002).

Final Remarks

In this article we have used the Discourse Historical Approach (DHA) to Critical Discourse Analysis to analyse the implicit and explicit argumentative structures and manoeuvres used in two election campaign leaflets. DHA maintains that the analysis of complex rhetorical discourse requires precise examination of differing layers of text and context and the theoretical and methodological contributions of cognate disciplines. The BZÖ and BNP are both political parties with a long and well-established record of xenophobic, racist and anti-Semitic rhetoric. In keeping with this record, we showed that the campaigns of both parties were based on two organising prejudicial mac-ro-*topoi* – the *topos* of disadvantage and the *topos* of threat. These *topoi*, in combination, support the rhetorical standpoints of the analysed leaflets: for the purification, racial and religious, of the national space.

However, given both legal constraints and salient social taboos against overtly stated racist argumentation in party politics, such arguments were not spelt out explicitly in the leaflets, but rather relied, in varying degrees, on their pictorial elements in advancing a coherent standpoint. We suggest that, given that the pictorial and linguistic elements only constitute a defence in combination with each other, the leaflets represent visual examples of co-ordinatively compound argumentation. It is only when a thorough examination of the linguistic content – including their insinuations, allusions and presupposition and their significance to specific national and historic contexts – is offered in concert with a close reading of the pictorial and visual content of the leaflets, that the chauvinistic, racist and anti-Semitic implications of the visual standpoints can be fully appreciated.

Notes

1. See, for example, Krżyzanowski & Wodak 2008; Pelinka & Wodak 2002; Reisigl 2002, 2008; Reisigl & Wodak 2000, 2001, 2003; Richardson 2004, 2008; Rydgren 2005; van Dijk 1984, 1993; Wodak 2003, 2008b; Wodak & Iedema 2004; Wodak & Pelinka

2002; Wodak & Reisigl 2002; Wodak & van Dijk 2000; for more extensive analyses of the 'politics of exclusion' and 'othering' in right-wing populist rhetoric.

2. All these strategies are illustrated by numerous categories and examples in Reisigl and Wodak (2001: 31–90). It would be impossible to present all these linguistic devices in this paper, owing to space restrictions.

3. We are grateful to Michael Billig who pointed us in this direction when viewing our data and commenting on our paper.

4. In this paper, we focus mainly on xenophobic exclusionary meanings; however, the BZÖ attacks the Jewish community, specifically its president Dr. Ariel Muzikant, from time to time with different agenda and functions: 2001, in the regional election campaign in Vienna, Jörg Haider tried to raise his chances by opposing restitution claims for Jewish victims of the Shoah (this restitution should compensate the so-called 'Aryanisation' of Jewish belongings, etc.). However, these agenda were opposed vehemently by the SPÖ and Haider lost many votes (see Pelinka and Wodak 2002, Wodak 2007). April 2008, the BZÖ started a new anti-Semitic campaign; this time solidarity with Palestinians is functionalised for sentiments against Austrian Jewish citizens. They are labelled as uncivilised and juxtaposed to the civilised Western (Christian) world.

5. For example: *Meyers Lexikon*, 8th edition, Leipzig 1936–1942; *Duden*, 12th edition, Mannheim 1941, 13th edition, Mannheim 1947) or consulting specialist diction-aries of NS jargon (Leon Poliakov, Josef Wulf, *Das dritte Reich und die Juden*, Frankfurt: Athenaeum: 146–149, 179; Cornelia Schmitz-Berning 2007, *Vokabular des Nationalsozialismus*, 2nd edition, Berlin: De Gruyter: 333–334; 511–519.

6. Barnbrook also received 5.23%, or 128,609 of the second choice votes.

7. In 2004 Julian Leppert (BNP) received 3.04% of the first choice votes, 0.20% higher than Barnbrook;

8. The original image, entitled 'Many British Asians don't feel British', taken by a Press Association photographer, is available to view here: http://prints.paphotos.com/pictures_679845/Many-British-Asians-dont-feel-British.html (accessed 19 May 2008).

9. Of the nine men arrested, two were released a week later with no charge; another of the nine was released in the month that followed. Of the remaining five men, only one – Parviz Khan – was charged, and found guilty, of charges relating to kidnapping; the remainder were convicted for offenses related to supplying materials to foreign fighters for terrorist purposes or for not informing the Police of Mr Khan's activities (http://news.bbc.co.uk/1/hi/uk/7246646.stm).

References

Alcolea-Banegas, J. (2007) Visual Arguments in Film, in F. H. van Eemeren, J. A. Blair, C. A. Willard & B. Garssen (eds) *Proceedings of the Sixth Conference of ISSA*, pp.35–42. Amsterdam: Sic Sat.

Bailer-Galanda, B. & Neugebauer, W. (1997) *Haider und die Freiheitlichen in Österreich*. Vienna: Braumuller

Bakhtin, M. (1981) *The Dialogical Imagination*. Austin: University of Texas Press.

——. (1986) The Problem of Speech Genres, in *Speech Genres and Other Late Essays*, pp.60–102. Austin: University of Texas Press.

Billig, M. (1995) *Banal Nationalism* London: Sage.

Blair, J. A. (2004) The Rhetoric of Visual Arguments, in C, A. Hill & M. Helmers (eds) *Defining Visual Rhetorics*, pp.41–62. Mahwah, NJ: Lawrence Erlbaum Publishers.

Blakesley, D. (2004) Defining Film Rhetoric: The Case of Hitchcock's *Vertigo*, in C, A. Hill & M. Helmers (eds) *Defining Visual Rhetorics*, pp.111–134. Mahwah, NJ: Lawrence Erlbaum Publishers.

BNP (2008) 100,000 Leaflets: 250 Activists: The BNP's Biggest Ever Push in London! *BNP Online*, www.bnp.org.uk/2008/01/21/100000-leaflets-250-activists-the-bnp%e2%80%99s-biggest-ever-push-in-london/ (accessed 6 May 2008).

Brown, G. (2007) Why the BNP is still fascist, What Next? No.31, http://www.whatnext-journal.co.uk/Pages/Latest/Current.html (accessed 6 May 2008).

Burridge, J. (2008, forthcoming) The Dilemma of Frugality and Consumption in British Women's Magazines 1940–1955, *Social Semiotics* 18(3).

Cairns, J. (forthcoming) Politics? Fear not! The rise of The Average Superhero in the visual rhetoric of Bill Davis' 1971 election pamphlet, in G. Allen and D.J. Robinson (eds) *Communicating Canada's past: Approaches to the history of print and broadcast media*, Chap. 7. Toronto: University of Toronto Press.

Charteris-Black, J. (2006) *Politicians and Rhetoric. The Persuasive Power of Metaphor.* Basingstoke: Palgrave.

Delanty, G., Jones, P. & Wodak, R. (Eds.) (2008) *Identity, Migration, and Belonging* Liverpool: University of Liverpool Press.

Dokumentationsarchiv des osterreichischen Widerstandes (1993) *Handbuch des Rechtsextremismus in Osterreich.* Wien: DOW.

Edwards, J. L. & Winkler, C. K. (2008) Representative form and the Visual Ideograph: The Iwo Jima Image in Editorial Cartoons, in L. C. Olsen, C. A. Finnegan, D. S. Hope (eds.) *Visual Rhetoric: A Reader in Communication and American Culture*, pp.119–138. Thousand Oaks: Sage.

Fairclough, N. (1995) *Media Discourse.* London: Arnold

——. (2003) *Analyzing Discourse* London: Routledge.

Foss, S. K. (2004) Framing the Study of Visual Rhetoric: Toward a Transformation of Rhetorical Theory, in C, A. Hill & M. Helmers (eds) *Defining Visual Rhetorics*, pp.303–314. Mahwah, NJ: Lawrence Erlbaum Publishers.

Groake, L. (2002) Towards a Pragma-Dialectics of Visual Argument, in F. H. van Eemeren (ed) *Advances in Pragma-Dialectics*, pp.137–152. Amsterdam: Sic Sat.

——. (2007) Four theses on Toulmin and visual argument, in F. H. van Eemeren, J. A. Blair, C. A. Willard & B. Garssen (eds) *Proceedings of the Sixth Conference of ISSA*, pp.535–540. Amsterdam: Sic Sat.

Gronbeck, B. E. (2008) Visual Rhetorical Studies: Traces through Time and Space, in L. C. Olsen, C. A. Finnegan, & D. S. Hope (eds.) *Visual Rhetoric: A Reader in Communication and American Culture*, pp.xxi–xxvi. Thousand Oaks: Sage.

Handa, G. (2004) (ed.) *Visual Rhetoric in a Digital World: A Critical Sourcebook.* New York: Bedford-St Martin's.

Heer, H., Manoschek, W., Pollak, A. & Wodak, R. (Eds.) *The Discursive Construction of History. Remembering the Wehrmacht's War of Annihilation.* Basingstoke: Palgrave/Macmillan.

Helmers, M. (2004) Framing the Fine Arts Through Rhetoric, in C, A. Hill & M. Helmers (eds) *Defining Visual Rhetorics*, pp.63–86. Mahwah, NJ: Lawrence Erlbaum Publishers.

Hill, C. A. & Helmers, M. (2004) Introduction, in C, A. Hill & M. Helmers (eds) *Defining Visual Rhetorics*, pp.1–24. Mahwah, NJ: Lawrence Erlbaum Publishers.

H. Margetts, D. Rowland & P. Weir (2006) *The BNP: the roots of its appeal.* London: Joseph Rowntree Charitable Trust.

Kienpointner, M. (1992) *Alltagslogik.* Stuttgart: Fromann & Holzboog.

Kovàcs, A. & Wodak, R. (Eds.) (2003) *Nato, Neutrality and National Identity. The Austrian and Hungarian Case.* Vienna: Böhlau.

Kress, G. & Van Leeuwen, T. (1996) *Reading Images.* London: Routledge (2nd edition 2001).

Krżyzanowski, M. (2008) 'Analysing Focus Group Discussions', in R. Wodak & M. Krżyzanowski (Eds.). *Qualitative Discourse Analysis in the Social Sciences* 162–181. Basingstoke: Palgrave.

Krżyzanowski, M. & Wodak, R. (2008) 'Migration und Rassismus in Österreich', in B. Gomes, A. Hofbauer, W. Schicho & A. Sonderegger (Eds.). *Rassismus. Beiträge zu einem vielgesichtigen Phänomen*, 257–279. Wien: Mandelbaum.
——. (2008) *The Politics of Exclusion. Debating Migration in Austria*. New Brunswick, NJ: Transaction Publishers.
Lemke, J. (1995) *Textual Politics: Discourse and social dynamics*. London: Taylor & Francis.
Lowles, N. (2008) Waking up to a different London, *Searchlight Online*, http://www.hope nothate.org.uk/2008_HOPE_not_hate_campaign_blog (accessed 6 May 2008).
Lutz, B. & Wodak, R. (1987) *Information für Informierte*. Vienna: Akademie der Wissenschaften.
Mitten, R. (1992) *The Politics of Antisemitic Prejudice. The Waldheim Phenomenon in Austria*. Boulder, Co: Westview Press.
Möhring, R. (Ed.) (2001) *Österreich allein zuhause*. Politik, Medien und Justiz nach der politischen Wende. Frankfurt/Main: IKO-Verlag.
Mudde, C. (2007) *Populist Radical Right Parties in Europe*. Cambridge: Cambridge University Press.
Olsen, L. C, Finnegan, C. A, & Hope, D. S. (2008a) Visual Rhetoric in Communication: Continuing Questions and Contemporary Issues, in L. C. Olsen, C. A. Finnegan, D. S. Hope (eds.) *Visual Rhetoric: A Reader in Communication and American Culture*, pp.1–14. Thousand Oaks: Sage.
——. (2008b) (eds.) *Visual Rhetoric: A Reader in Communication and American Culture*. Thousand Oaks: Sage.
Pelinka, A. & Wodak, R. (Eds.) (2002) *"Dreck am Stecken"* Vienna: Czernin Verlag
Pelinka, A. & Rosenberger, S. (2001) *Österreichische Politik. Grundlagen, Strukturen, Trends*. Vienna: Universitätsverlag.
Poynting, S. & Noble, G. (2003) 'Dog-whistle Journalism and Muslim Australians since 2001' *Media International Australia: Culture and Politics*, 109: 41–49.
Prelli, L. J. (2006) (ed.) *Rhetorics of Display*. Columbia: University of South Carolina Press.
Reisigl, M. (2002) 'Dem Volk aufs Maul schauen, nach dem Mund reden und angst und bange machen' – Von populistischen Anrufungen, Anbiederungen und Agitationsweisen in der Sprache österreichischer PolitikerInnen, in Eismann, W. (ed.) *Rechtspopulismus in Europa. Österreichische Krankheit oder europäische Normalität?* pp.149–198. Vienna: Czernin.
——. (2008) Analysing Political Rhetoric, in R. Wodak & M. Krżyzanowski. (Eds), 96–120.
Reisigl, M. & Wodak, R. (2001) *Discourse and Discrimination. Rhetorics of Racism and Antisemitism*. London: Routledge.
——. (2002) Nationalpopulistische Rhetorik – Einige diskursanalytische und argumentations-theoretische Überlegungen zur österreichischen Debatte über den "nationalen Schulterschluss, in A. Demirovic & M. Bojadzijev: *Konjunkturen des Rassismus*, pp.90–111. Münster: Verlag Westfälisches Dampfboot.
——. (Eds.) (2000) *The Semiotics of Racism. Approaches in Critical Discourse Analysis*. Vienna: Passagen Verlag.
——. (forthcoming). The Discourse-Historical Approach, in R. Wodak & M. Meyer (Eds.) (2009) *Methods of CDA*. London: Sage (in press).
Richardson, J. E. (2004) *(Mis)Representing Islam: the racism and rhetoric of British Broadsheet newspapers*. Amsterdam: John Benjamins.
——. (2008) 'Our England': discourses of 'race' and class in party election leaflets, *Social Semiotics* 18(3): 321–333.
Ripley, M. L. (2007) The ad as argument, in F. H. van Eemeren, J. A. Blair, C. A. Willard & B. Garssen (eds) *Proceedings of the Sixth Conference of ISSA*, pp.1173–1180. Amsterdam: Sic Sat.

Rydgren, J. (Ed.) (2005) *Movements of Exclusion.* New York: Nova.

Scharsach, H.-H. (2000) *Haider. Österreich und die Rechte Versuchung.* Hamburg: Rororo.

Scharsach, H.-H. & Kuch, K. (2001) *Haider – Schatten uber Europa.* Berlin: Kiepenheuer & Witsch.

Snoeck-Henkemans, A. F. (2001) Argumentation Structures, in F.H. van Eemeren (ed) *Crucial Concepts in Argumentation Theory,* pp.101–134. Amsterdam: Amsterdam University Press.

Swales, J. (1990) *Genre Analysis.* Cambridge: CUP.

Taylor, M. (2008) BNP seeks to bury antisemitism and gain Jewish votes in Islamophobic campaign, *Guardian,* www.guardian.co.uk/politics/2008/apr/10/thefarright.race (accessed 6 May 2008).

Turner-Graham, E. (2007) *'Austria First': H.C.Strache, Austrian identity and the current politics of Austria's Freedom Party.* Unpubl. Ms.

Van Dijk, T. (1984) *Prejudice in Discourse.* Amsterdam: Benjamins.

——. (1993) *Discourse and Elite Racism.* London: Sage.

——. (2008) *Discourse and Context – a Sociocognitive Approach.* Cambridge: CUP.

Van Eemeren, F. H & Grootendorst, R. (1992). *Argumentation, Communication and Fallacies: A Pragma-Dialectical Perspective.* Hillsdale, NJ: Lawrence Erlbaum.

——. (2004) *A Systematic Theory of Argumentation.* Cambridge: Cambridge University Press.

Van Eemeren, F. H, Grootendorst, R. & Snoeck Henkemans, F. (2002) *Argumentation: Analysis, Evaluation, Presentation.* Mahwah, NJ: Lawrence Erlbaum.

Van Leeuwen, T. & Jaworski, (2002) The discourses of war photography: Photojournalistic representations of the Palestinian-Israeli war, *Journal of Language and Politics,* 1(2): 255–275.

Van Leeuwen, T. & Wodak, R. (1999) Legitimizing Immigration Control: A discourse-historical analysis. *Discourse Studies* 1(1): 83–118.

Willard, C. A. (1979) Arguing as epistemic II: A constructivist/interactionist view of reasons and reasoning. *Journal of the American Forensic Association,* 15, 211–219.

Willard, C. A., Hart, J. & Willihnganz, S (2007) Using the Goodman/Schwed model to analyze artistic arguments, in F. H. van Eemeren, J. A. Blair, C. A. Willard & B. Garssen (eds) *Proceedings of the Sixth Conference of ISSA,* pp.1491–1494. Amsterdam: Sic Sat.

Wittgenstein, L. (1967) *Philosophische Untersuchungen.* Frankfurt: Suhrkamp.

Wodak, R. (2001) The discourse-historical approach, in R. Wodak & M. Meyer (eds) *Methods of Critical Discourse Analysis,* pp. 63–95. London: Sage.

——. (2003) Populist discourses. The rhetoric of exclusion in written genres, *Document Design. Journal of Research and Problem Solving in Organizational Communication* 4(2): 133–148.

——. (2004) Critical discourse analysis, in C. Seale, G. Gobo, J. F. Gubrium & D. Silverman (Eds.) *Qualitative Research Practice,* 197–213. London: Sage.

——. (2007) Pragmatics and Critical Discourse Analysis. A cross-disciplinary inquiry' *Pragmatics and Cognition,* 15(1): 203–227.

——. (2008a) 'Us' and 'Them': Inclusion/Exclusion – Discrimination via Discourse, in G. Delanty, P. Jones & R. Wodak (Eds) *Migration, Identity, and Belonging,* pp. 54–78. Liverpool: Liverpool Univ. Press.

——. (2008b) Introduction: Important terms and concepts. In Wodak, R., Krżyzanowski, M. (Eds.) (2008) pp.1–41.

Wodak, R. & De Cillia, R. (2007) Commemorating the past: the discursive construction of offcial narratives about the 'Rebirth of the Second Austrian Republic'. *Discourse & Communication,* Vol 1(3), 337–363.

Wodak, R. & Iedema, R. (2004) Constructing Boundaries without being seen: the case of Jorg Haider, Politician, *Revista Canaria de Estudios Ingleses* 49, 157–178.

Wodak, R., De Cillia, R., Reisigl, M., Liebhard, K. (1999 [2009]) *The Discursive Construction of National Identity.* Edinburgh: EUP.

Wodak, R. & Krżyzanowski, M. (Eds.) (2008) *Qualitative Discourse Analysis in the Social.* Basingstoke: Palgrave.

Wodak, R. & Meyer, M. (Eds.) (2009) *Methods of Critical Discourse Analysis.* London: Sage (2nd revised edition, 1st edition 2001).

Wodak, R. & Pelinka, A. (Eds.) (2002) *The Haider Phenomenon.* New Brunswick, USA: Transaction Press.

Wodak, R. & Reisigl, M. (2002) „... WENN EINER ARIEL HEISST ... " Ein linguistisches Gutachten zur politischen Funktionalisierung antisemitischer Ressentiments in Österreich, in: A. Pelinka & R. Wodak (Eds.) *"Dreck am Stecken",* pp. 134–172. Vienna: Czernin Verlag.

Wodak, R. & Van Dijk, T. (Eds.) (2000) *Racism at the Top.* Klagenfurt: Drava.

63

Language and Significance – or the Importance of Import: Implications for Critical Discourse Analysis

Andrew Sayer

Introduction

When people talk about what things mean to them, they are usually *not* providing a definition of terms, but alluding to how things affect their well-being, to what matters to them. For example, an unemployed person talking about the meaning of unemployment already knows what the *term* 'unemployed' means; they are likely to be referring to things like how prolonged unemployment has led to lack of money, loss of social contact and status, demoralisation, shame, depression, and increased vulnerability to illness. While they are partly providing a fuller, richer description of unemployment and its effects, they are also doing much more than this, for they are simultaneously evaluating it and explaining what seems significant about it, that is, why it has import. Similarly, when asked what our friends mean to us, what we say will have something to do with how and why we value them, what it is about them that we value. So this kind of meaning concerns what is of significance or of value in terms of some notion – usually vague – of well-being, not necessarily of ourselves, but of anything we care about.

One of the main things that texts do is assess the significance or value of their objects. Newspaper articles on the latest government budget say 'what the budget means for you' by explaining what will make a significant difference to us, pointing out changes that may impinge on our well-being in

Source: *Journal of Language and Politics*, 5(3) (2006): 449–471.

some way. Such cases might be glossed as 'evaluative' uses of language, or as expressive of the author's feelings. But the evaluations and feelings are *about* something, including the well-being or ill-being of actors, and perhaps the flourishing or decline of particular practices and institutions, and they are explained in terms of the attributes of the things being valued. While they also tell us something about the valuer, they are justified by claims about the nature of their objects, and thus simultaneously involve the informative function of language.

In this paper I wish to argue that this kind of meaning eludes the standard ways of categorising the functions of language. Not only that, it eludes classification as *either* fact *or* value, reason *or* emotion, positive *or* normative, for in important cases, these distinctions break down. Given the dominance of such dualisms over ways of thinking in contemporary social science, the very things which are most important to us, which have significance or import, are liable to be reduced to the status of matters of subjective judgement lying beyond the scope of reason, and perhaps accordingly ignored by social science as *in*significant, producing an alienated and alienating social science. Thus, well-being itself may be viewed sceptically as no more than a matter of subjective opinion having nothing to do with any objective condition. On this account, for example, whether one takes a patriarchal or feminist view of what enables women to flourish is just a matter of personal taste. This undermines critique, including critiques of discourse, for they then appear to be no more than arbitrary, 'subjective' views. The point of valuation and critique is often to assess whether some situation involves flourishing or suffering, or well-being or ill-being. When we evaluate discourses critically, part of what we are doing is assessing what they say about import or significance. Thus, a feminist critique of patriarchal discourse might argue that its claims about what is good for women are false, and argue instead that women are currently oppressed.

If we are to remedy these problems we have to deconstruct the dualisms that prevent understanding of significance or import, and confront the nature of well-being. In particular, it is essential to challenge the common view that values are beyond the scope of rational deliberation. I shall begin by showing how common classifications of the functions of language fail to capture the very things that matter to us most. I relate this failure to the estrangement of positive and normative thought and the rise of related problematic dualisms in social science over the last 250 years. I then comment on the implications of this for the nature of critique with special reference to discourse analysis and in particular, CDA, and conclude.

Significance and Conceptions of Language

It is standard to think of meaning in terms of relations among signifiers, signifieds and referents, as elements of a communications system. Within this approach one can show how meaning is constituted through the play of difference among systems of terms, though as the postmodernists overlook, not wholly independently of reference, including practical reference, in which actors materially interact with the world and get feedback from it. One can think of whole discourses in this way. But there is something missing here, or at least something implicit and unacknowledged, for this conception of discourse and meaning in society can be propounded and applied without any recognition of the signif*icance* of things for people in terms of their well-being, and what they care about or value (Graham 2003).

Significance eludes standard classifications of the functions of language, for example, as comprising informative, performative, expressive, evocative and evaluative functions. Although it is common to note that more than one of these functions can be evident simultaneously in a specific speech act, accounts of significance involve a combination of functions which many find particularly difficult to acknowledge, for they seem to combine the incommensurable. Talk of what something means to us in terms of significance or import is not merely expressive or evaluative, for it refers to or informs us about particular objects such as ways of living. When we say, for example, that hooding prisoners causes suffering, it seems difficult to classify this as either factual or evaluative but also difficult to categorise it as both. The latter option seems awkward because we are accustomed to assuming that we can and should distinguish sharply between statements of fact, which are either true or false, and 'value-judgements' which supposedly can be neither true nor false; indeed, according to positivism, it *makes no sense* at all to think of value judgements as true or false. Yet we may want to insist that the practice in question really or truly does cause or involve suffering, and that in making this claim observers are not merely describing their subjective state of being upset ('emoting') or telling others how to feel, but describing a real state of affairs. Of course such a claim, like any other, is fallible, but it purports to be about some state of affairs which exists, and those who make it are likely to justify their judgement by elaborating on the kind of suffering caused and what it is about people that makes them susceptible to it. (Statues, by contrast, do not suffer when hooded.) In other words, while it is common to classify such statements as 'value-judgements', they might be argued to be similar to factual judgements.

Some may view this as an attempt to deduce 'ought' from 'is', a procedure which many regard as illegitimate. I shall come to the is-ought problem presently but for now we should note that many 'is' (factual) statements are already likely to be 'valuey', that is about things we can hardly avoid valuing in some way (Collier 1994). This is convergent with Volosinov's argument regarding the evaluative orientation of utterances as inseparable from their referential function (Volosinov 1973: 105).[1] We are evaluative beings and we can no more stop evaluating the world than we can stop breathing. Our vulnerability, our neediness, our capacity for flourishing and suffering, our psychological dependence on others and our need of their approval and cooperation – all of these make us evaluative beings, assessing the implications of changes in the environment and in others' behaviour towards us in terms of their likely effect on our well-being and that of others or other causes we care about. We simply could not survive, let alone flourish, if we did not continually evaluate our circumstances. At the same time, the valuations say something about the world; they make or imply claims about what it is that promotes or threatens flourishing or suffering. This, as we shall see, has major implications for the nature of critiques of discourses, for while categorisation of such matters simply as 'value-judgements' seems to relativise and subjectivise them, and put them beyond the scope of reason and science, viewing them as involving matters of fact makes their critique continuous with the usual objectives of social science.

At one level, we always do expect texts to impute and interpret significance, though often the form of the discourse is not overtly evaluative, indeed it may be disguised (see Fairclough 2003: 96–98, 110–115, 177ff; Graham 2003). On occasions where we cannot identify what a discourse is saying in terms of significance, we ask questions like 'so what?', 'what's your point?' In some cases these may be merely calls for clarification, but often they are requests to be told what matters, what is significant or good or bad that we weren't already aware of. Often the purpose of a discourse is to argue that something is more or less significant than we had imagined, or significant in a different way. But we fail to grasp what is involved here if we reduce significance to mere expressions of subjective opinion (the 'boo-hooray theory of value'), for that is to confuse the source of statements with what they are about. I wish to argue that they are fallible judgements of independently existing states.

Underlying Problematic Dualisms

In order to pursue this question further we need to address the underlying dualisms that have come to structure social scientific thought about such matters, in particular fact/value, reason/emotion, positive/normative and objective/subjective. Note that I am not criticising them simply because they are dualisms, which seems to me extraordinarily dogmatic (how can one know whether a dualism is problematic until one has investigated what it's about and how it's used?). Nor am I claiming that they have no use whatsoever. Rather, I am claiming that while there are circumstances in which they may be useful, there are others where they obstruct understanding. As we shall see, the cases that do not fit are not mere curiosities but turn out, ironically, to involve precisely the things that are most important for our welfare.

These oppositions have emerged and hardened over the last 250 years. During this period there has been a gradual estrangement of positive and normative thought so that where once they were often blended seamlessly, normative thought has now been largely expelled from social science, and ghettoised in political and moral philosophy. Contemporary social scientists are taught to bracket out normative thought and prioritise positive matters of what exists and how things work. What is generally overlooked is that this attempted expulsion of values from science was accompanied by an expulsion of reason (or science) from values, so that values and valuation now tend to be thought of as 'subjective' – at least as having nothing to do with understanding and explanation, and at worst as a contaminant threatening the objectivity of science. Of course, this has not made social science value-free, but it has successfully marginalized normative thought as a worthwhile activity in its own right. More recently, in a new twist, postmodernists tend to suspect normativity as authoritarian and repressive of difference, and therefore to be avoided.[2]

An important consequence of this major shift has been that social science has become ill-equipped to understand lay normativity. As lay actors, the most important questions we face tend to be normative ones, as we continually evaluate how we and people and things we care about are faring. They range from what to say next in a conversation to momentous decisions such as what to do about a troubled relationship, whether to migrate, or whether to make a political protest. Normative judgements are an unavoidable part of everyday life. Many social scientists are not only unpractised in normative reasoning but do not see this as a problem precisely because they regard it as 'merely subjective' and a threat to objectivity. This leads to a particularly damaging variant of the scholastic fallacy identified by Bourdieu (2000). Here it is not just the tendency of academics to project their special contemplative, cognitive relation to the world onto those they study, but the tendency to project a *de-normativized* relation to the world onto actors for whom normative questions are likely to be the most important.[3] Thus, what they care about is either marginalized, as if it were mere noise, or else treated as mere contingent facts about actors (opinions, 'affect'), rather than something that reveals much about themselves and their condition and whether they are flourishing or not. Thus, the import of the situation for the actor is likely to be regarded by the social scientist as of little import.

Alternatively, we may recognise the normative character of everyday discourse and life, but be wary of assessing its evaluative judgements because they are considered to be matters of opinion or value rather than fact and reason, and as beyond the scope of social science. I shall argue that, ironically, this handicaps our positive understanding of the world, not only in paying insufficient attention to the fact of lay normativity itself, but in ignoring what it tells us about people's circumstances. Thus, I have argued elsewhere that people's normative responses to class inequalities, involving for example, envy, resentment and guilt and shame, tell us a great deal about the nature of class relations (Sayer 2005).

Let us take the positive/normative distinction itself first. A positive judgement is 'world-guided', involving an attempt to adjust our ideas to correspond to the way the world is. A normative judgement is 'world-guiding', implying that the world should change to correspond to our ideas. It would seem that the difference could hardly be clearer. But matters of value and significance involve both simultaneously. If we reflect on adjectives like 'oppressive', 'abusive', 'cruel', 'kind', or 'generous' we can see that they are both descriptive and evaluative, and one cannot separate the two components from one another (Taylor 1967; see also Haines 1998). Thus, when we decide to accept a description of some practice, say, as 'oppressive' or 'racist', we simultaneously accept the implicit valuation.

In effect, the distinction splits us in two. We are needy beings, characterised by lack and desire, and we are capable of flourishing or suffering.[4] In noting a need, such as the need of a homeless person for a home, I am *simultaneously* positively registering a need or lack that exists (world-guided judgement) and normatively, implying that there is something wrong that ought to be changed (world-guiding judgement).[5] It would not be a need if the world were such that it could never fail to be fully met. Similarly, when we say something like 'unemployment tends to cause suffering', we are not merely 'emoting' or expressing ourselves, or offering a subjective opinion, but making a claim (fallible, like any other, of course) about what objectively happens. Nor are we simply providing a purely positive description, for in identifying suffering we can hardly avoid the normative implication that the situation is bad and in need of remedying. If we think about the 'flourishing' or 'suffering' of humans or other species, then although these are vague terms, covering wide ranges of conditions, they seem to be both positive descriptions and normative evaluations. Some claims about the elements of well-being, like being free from disease and physical violence, might seem straightforward, while others, such as the need to participate in political decisions affecting one's own community,[6] might seem more contestable, but this situation is not unlike that of straightforwardly positive sciences such as geology, where some claims seem to be well-established and uncontroversial and others are very uncertain. We do not imagine that the presence of the latter renders the whole enterprise of geology 'mere subjective opinion', but thanks to the pervasive influence of the dualisms, and the estrangement of positive and normative thought, many find it hard to regard questions of well-being in the same way, tending to relegate them all to the de-rationalised realm of 'values'.

We may feel we should try to find more neutral or less value-laden words to describe such matters, but if we do, one of two things will happen: either we will mislead by euphemising, so that we allow others to fail to understand that flourishing or suffering is involved (in which case the description will be deficient positively as well as normatively), or the new words will come to take on a similar evaluative load as the old ones. This implies that the positive and normative content of such descriptions are not necessarily inversely related. Consider the following famous example, comparing two statements about the Holocaust: 'thousands died in the Nazi concentration camps' and 'thousands were systematically exterminated in the Nazi concentration camps'.[7] The second is both more value-laden and more factually accurate than the first: the prisoners did not just die naturally, nor were they killed randomly and individually, but according to planned mass executions. Therefore, refraining from using evaluative terms may weaken rather than strengthen the descriptive adequacy or truth status of our accounts.

This tells us something about the relationship between beliefs that are subjective in the sense of value-laden and their objectivity in the sense of their truth status: value-ladenness and truth are not necessarily inversely related, hence neutrality is not the same thing as objectivity in this sense. This means that it is a mistake to regard values as a contaminant threatening the objectivity (i.e. truth, practical adequacy) of social science, which we must root out or at least minimise. For example, using terms like 'arrogant', 'condescending', 'vain', 'oppressive', or 'humiliating' in describing social behaviour need not be a problem. We may sometimes use them mistakenly, but then we can also be mistaken in our choice of non-evaluative descriptions.

This is not to claim that all positive statements about the world are simultaneously normative – which would be implausible; for example, 'the trees are over there' is in most contexts unlikely to have any normative implications or message. But it is interesting that it is not just any concepts which seem to be simultaneously positive and normative, but ones which concern the very things which matter most to us – needs, well-being, etc. So the dogma that statements must be *either* positive or normative, either informative or evaluative, but not both, has the effect of making it difficult to acknowledge precisely the things which are most important to us.

Some readers may want to argue that I am guilty of the 'naturalist fallacy', in which one imagines that 'ought' can be logically deduced from 'is'. Whether or not this is a fallacy – and it is still debated in philosophy – it is a red herring. Logic concerns the relationships between statements, but I am not referring to the relationship between statements but among objects or processes of the world, such as the relationship between our bodies (or rather 'mindbodies') and food or its absence, or violence, or respect or disrespect. A starving person has no need of a logical warrant for trying to find food. The attribution of the naturalistic fallacy to such cases is itself an example of the linguistic fallacy that such matters are governed by relationships internal to language.[8]

It is common for social scientists, especially those who regard themselves as *critical* social scientists, to accept that value-freedom is impossible, and to argue that factual statements cannot be separated from value judgements. However, many of those same social scientists regard values and evaluations as beyond the scope of reason, as merely subjective. They may happily describe their own judgements, like any other, as 'subjective', making us wonder why we should take them seriously, or say that their values are 'political' rather than scientific, as if this were no reasons for pursuing one political agenda rather than another. Again, far from challenging fact/value and cognate dualisms they merely change sides from the objective and value-neutral to the subjective and openly value-laden. Alternatively, they may opt for a relativistic point of view, claiming that evaluative judgements are purely internal to particular world views, such that it is impossible to arbitrate between them by reference to anything other than those same world views.[9] Far from being generously liberal, this is a conservative view that legitimizes any politics, including oppressive ones, and indeed both Hitler and Mussolini embraced relativism because it gave them free rein to assert their power.[10]

An important cognate dualism, and one that relates to well-being, is that of reason and emotion, in which emotion is positioned as irrational. There is now growing support in philosophy for the idea of 'emotional reason', according to which emotions are evaluative judgements of things believed to affect our well-being or that of others or things we care about (Archer 2000; Helm 2001; Nussbaum 2001). They are "... highly discriminating evaluative responses, very closely connected to beliefs about what is valuable and what is not" (Nussbaum 1993: 239). Thus, emotions such as compassion, anger, pride, embarrassment, guilt, shame and humiliation are all *about* various events or circumstances. They do not arise purely unprompted from within, but have referents.[11] They are not merely expressive but evaluative and informative. Although the differences between emotions are fuzzy, they differ according to the situation and the specific kind of harm or benefit involved and have their own normative structures, so that for example, the circumstances in which we feel embarrassed differ from those in which we feel ashamed (see Williams 1993).

Emotional judgements are fallible – we may be falsely proud, or mistakenly angry – but then so too is unemotional reason. Reasoning and rationality are not to be confused with infallibility. But in any case, the very fallibility of emotions implies that there is something independent of them – the events or states being evaluated – about which one can be mistaken. However, it would be difficult to explain how we have survived if our emotions were *always* radically mistaken (for example, consider fear). Failing to see how the expressive response is coupled to this reference to things believed to bear upon well-being has the effect of de-rationalizing values. The use of the term 'affect' by academics to refer to emotions also tends to de-rationalise (and belittle) them, so that they seem no more than an a-rational or irrational accompaniment to the serious business of life, rather than a form of commentary on often serious events, real or imagined. It is perhaps significant that when we speak of 'affect*ations*', or 'affect*ing*' a certain manner, we mean precisely to draw attention to their simulated – or rather dissimulated and false – character.

A further source of confusion is the dualism of objective/subjective. This is more complex, for the problem lies not so much in the opposition itself as in the differences which each term conceals within it. Here we need to distinguish these, not 'overcome the opposition', which generally means absorbing everything into subjectivism or discourse in idealist fashion. Each term has at least three different and contingently-related senses, yet users often slide among them unknowingly. 'Subjective' may mean firstly 'value-laden', secondly, 'pertaining to subjects', or thirdly, 'probably untrue'. Equivalently, 'objective' may mean 'value-free', 'pertaining to objects' or 'true' (Sayer 2000, Collier 2003).

Values and judgements are clearly subjective in the second sense since they are held and made by knowing subjects. But values and judgements are also *about* something – either something independent of the subject or, as in internal conversations, about the subject's own thoughts and feelings, which can be treated as objects of reflection. Imagine we have two identical objects, say two copies of the same issue of this journal; it would make no sense to say that one of them was good, while the other was not. How could they be if they were exactly the same? There must be something different about them such that we think they should be valued differently.[12] The simple philosophical point here is that valuation cannot be purely subjective in the second sense, but has also to relate to the properties of its objects. So valuation has both subjective and objective aspects (in the second pair of senses), in fact it involves a relation between the two. When we say here that valuation has an 'objective' aspect we do not mean that it involves claims which we can confidently know to be true in some absolute sense, but that it is objective in the sense of pertaining to objects and their properties. Our statements about just what the nature of particular objects is, what their properties are, are fallible, that is, capable of being mistaken. However, again, for it to be possible for statements to be fallible, there must be something independent of them, something which is not merely their 'construction', about which they can be mistaken; in other words, something objective in the sense of existing independently of their observation by a subject.[13] Thus, objective in the sense of pertaining to objects does not entail that our statements about their nature are objective in the sense of 'true': on the contrary, the fallibility of knowledge and truth claims derives from the very independence of objects from what we think about them. If the objective world in the sense of the world of objects were to be collapsed into our subjective states of mind, so that there was nothing outside knowledge or discourse, then these would be infallible, for there would be nothing external to them about which they could be mistaken. Consequently, far from implying privileged access to the truth, the insistence on the objective or object-related dimension of valuation renders fallibility comprehensible (Sayer 2000; Collier 2003).

How do well-being or flourishing and their opposites relate to this disaggregated view of objectivity and subjectivity? There may be occasions in which we can think ourselves into a more or a less contented state, though even here, wishful thinking has its limits and we may be able to register whether we have succeeded or failed in doing this, sometimes deciding that we are deluding ourselves about our circumstances. While we are relatively malleable beings, we cannot be made into just anything, and we are not indifferent to how we are shaped. If we argue that flourishing and suffering are not mere products of wishful thinking but objective states, it is vital not to confuse this with a claim to objectivity in the third sense of knowing exactly what these states are, what their characteristics are. Rather, it is to suggest that flourishing and suffering are forms of being that are largely independent of an observer's recognition of them, and hence states that we may struggle to identify and achieve. This is implied, for example, in the claim that women were oppressed even before feminist discourses identified them as being oppressed, just as the earth was round even before it was identified as such, and did not suddenly change from flat to round when people changed their minds about it. When people find that what they had expected would produce well-being does not do so – when, for example, women found that a life of subordination to men did not enable them to flourish – they are registering the fact that well-being is not just a self-fulfilling or merely discursively-constituted state but something that has to be pursued and developed. A further example: capitalist culture encourages us to believe that greater riches will make us happier, yet a large volume of empirical research on this suggests that beyond a basic level increased wealth does not have this effect (Lane 1991). This again implies that this aspect of well-being has objective qualities which some discourses may fail to identify (Eagleton 2003).

Of course, there are many kinds of flourishing and cultures provide both their own forms of flourishing and their own conceptions of the good life. However, some of these conceptions may be blatantly ideological, typically representing domination as fairness and the lives of the dominated as free and full. Not just any practice or situation can be passed off as flourishing. Starvation, sensory deprivation and abuse and contempt produce palpable forms of suffering whatever the available discourses may claim. This is again because people are not products of collective wishful thinking but have capacities for flourishing and suffering which may or may not be identified or acknowledged adequately by prevailing discourses.

This kind of naturalistic claim has become controversial, as various forms of anti-naturalism (often under the banners of anti-essentialism and social constructionism) have become popular in recent social science. They are bolstered by a normative concern, for they appear to liberate those whose oppression has been legitimized by being represented as naturally-grounded, for example in the case of racism by the kind of spurious naturalism that claims racial differences in ability. However, if we respond to this spurious naturalism by denying that people have any particular natural properties as human beings, as organic bodies, and assume instead that these properties are no more than cultural or discursive constructions, then we lose all critical purchase on any oppressive exercise of power, particularly through torture, mutilation or abuse (Soper 1995a:138). To accept this point is not to deny that some forms of flourishing are more completely cultural.[14] Their assessment is a good deal more complex than that of physical well-being. Cultures provide discourses, forms of life or practices through which people make sense of themselves and their worlds, and they provide conceptions of the good life, indeed whole systems of valuation of things, people and practices. Actors generally become committed to certain relationships and practices not only in the sense that they feel they ought to pursue them, but in the sense that they become so deeply embodied and 'embrained' that they would find it difficult *not* to pursue them. To prevent someone participating in such practices would in itself inflict psychological pain or bereavement – as well as threaten a form of social life. For example, preventing the religious from practising their religion would cause suffering, and psychological and cultural loss. Cultural goods are emergent from (i.e. dependent on but irreducible to) our social and biological nature. Our relationship to and investment in those goods affects whether we flourish or suffer, and it would be unethical to ignore this; we are not, therefore, recommending a reductive naturalism, but an approach which is responsive to cultural emergence (Archer 1996). At the same time, as there are culturally-specific forms of life, there are also cross-cultural or universal psychological characteristics, in particular a capacity for fellow-feeling, a need for the support and approval of others, and moral sentiments such as shame, pride and guilt. It is these universal characteristics which make us susceptible to particular cultural forms of influence (Collier 2003).

It is possible, however, that certain cultural conceptions of well-being may be illusive, and sometime progress may depend on replacing those favoured ways of life. It is also possible for evaluations to be adaptive, that is, for people to want to regard their lot as good even if it is not, particularly where they feel unable to change their situation, so as to avoid a life of regret. If we are serious about the fallibility of judgements of value, then we cannot regard them as authoritative or as an inviolable feature of people's identities. To take a form of thinking seriously is to engage critically with its arguments; to refuse to do so is patronising and demeaning. Some may feel uncomfortable about the implicit notion of 'false consciousness' in such a view, but we presuppose such a possibility every time we argue with someone – including arguing against the possibility of false consciousness itself – and when we accept that knowledge is fallible. Cultures are also internally complex and invariably internally inconsistent, so that their members can formulate critiques within them by playing off ideas against others, for example, by showing how democratic or egalitarian ideals professed in some parts of society are not upheld in others. Often, local forms of flourishing exist within and depend on wider systems of oppression. The fallibility of cultural assumptions can be registered from within: no Archimedean critical standpoints are needed. Thus, it is possible to come to see that wealth does not guarantee happiness, that subservience to men does not enable women to flourish, and so on.

The plurality of possible forms of flourishing (and suffering) is likely to go beyond those currently and historically experienced. In developing new ways of living, people can acquire new cultural emergent powers, and discover new ways of flourishing – and suffering (Archer 2000). Thus ethics (both descriptive and prescriptive) must allow a creative dimension, albeit not creation out of nothing, as if it meant denying any kind of natural limits and enablements, as seems to be implied in some of Foucault's work (Foucault 2000), but creation through the use and development of existing materials. There therefore need be no conflict between an ethics of authenticity and an ethics of creativity.[15] We learn as best we can what is objectively possible and what objectively expands human flourishing through social experimentation. That such social experiments, such as those of Talibanism, state socialism or global neoliberalism can go horribly wrong, is precisely in keeping, rather than in contradiction, with the idea that what constitutes human flourishing is an objective matter in the strong sense, that is, partly independent of 'social construction'.

The kind of position developed here, which relates matters of significance, and especially ethics, to flourishing, is opposed to Habermas's idea that moral values are ultimately legitimized by reference to religion or philosophies, such as utilitarianism (see van Leeuwen 2003). While religion is certainly influential in this respect, Habermas surely inverts the relationship between philosophies and practice and involves a scholastic fallacy. Thus, people did not need utilitarian philosophy to legitimize appeals to usefulness; philosophers are largely involved in reflecting on and evaluating such lay normativity, but the latter operates mainly at the level of actors' 'feel for the game' rather than formal ethical reasoning.

These are just some of the complexities of arguments about well-being, but I would argue that it is better to confront them rather than dismiss it as 'subjective', or purely relative to cultures, for these just undermine critique, or replace it with a directionless scepticism.

Implications for *Critical* Discourse Analysis

These arguments about the simultaneously evaluative and informative character of judgments of value and significance not only help us understand the nature of discourse, but also have major implications for our understanding of *critique*.

They bear on the controversy of whether discourse analysis can be both critical *and* scientific (e.g. see Graham 2003; Rajagopalan 2004; Reisigl and Wodak 2001; Wodak 2001).

CDA might be said to be critical in a number of ways. At a minimum it produces analyses of discourse which differ from, and hence are critical of, lay understanding of discourse. One respect in which it might do this is by showing the influence of discourse in structuring practices and influencing or shaping subjects rather than in merely externally representing them.[16] We can also endorse Horkheimer's point that the fundamental premise of criticism is that things did not have to be the way they currently are. CDA demonstrates this point in highlighting the constructed and contingent nature of discourses. However, this is far from sufficient, for a fascist could exploit it as easily as could a progressive.[17] There is no point in critique if it doesn't contribute or at least point towards the reduction of illusion and improvements in well-being.

The Foucauldian concept of 'regimes of truth' and the associated rejection of the concept of ideology is of little help here,[18] for in relativising truth it merely undermines its own standpoint, or that of any critique (Foucault 1977). Post-structuralism tends to invite scepticism or universal doubt, rather than criticism, although scepticism may be intellectually invigorating in making us examine our assumptions. A post-structuralist discourse analysis might therefore be called '*Sceptical*' rather than '*Critical* Discourse Analysis'.[19] And if we further adopt the kind of scepticism which also relativises objects, such as bodies, by imagining them to be no more than the voluntaristic constructions of discourses, then as Soper argued, an important kind of critique becomes impossible.

Discourse ethics, à la Habermas, is more constructive; but although interesting and useful from a normative point of view, it doesn't explain why actors should prefer any way of life to any other by relating this to their vulnerabilities and capabilities, indeed how or why flourishing should be distinguishable from suffering. It also fails to connect to their moral sentiments – which are largely products not of learned academic discourses but of their social being, their experiences of flourishing and suffering, their fellow-feeling and their need for others' approval in the context of the informal moral education provided by everyday interaction.[20] These are the kinds of criteria which actors appeal to in normative argument, whether the speech situation is ideal or not.

In so far as discourses have an informative function, CDA can show in what respects they are untruthful, insincere or inappropriate, as Habermas argued. This implies that CDA can never be a self-contained activity, for it must always engage with and assess the specific scholarly knowledge regarding the issues addressed in the discourse in question (Wodak 2001). Thus, a CDA of political discourses on immigration has to be cognisant of research and data on this topic in order to assess whether they are truthful, etc. In addition, on the basis of our discussion of valuation and significance we can suggest that critique can go further and analyse and assess how discourses identify or impute significance, value and well- or ill-being by making assumptions or claims which are simultaneously positive and normative. Thus, regarding the expression 'collateral damage', CDA might argue that it is a dangerous euphemism because it conceals the import of what it refers to – it is both positively and normatively misleading.

Concepts of ideology and hegemony have obvious attractions in critical social science, and especially in CDA. However, the popularity of these concepts in these fields has tended to decline in the last two decades, not only as a result of the decline of Marxism but as part of a wider turn away from explicit normative theory and critique, ironically especially in recent self-styled 'critical theory'. 'Ideology' is distinguished from other knowledge claims insofar as it is not merely false in some respect but contributes "to the production, reproduction or transformation of relations of domination" (Fairclough 1992: 87). Four things should be noted about this. It exemplifies Marxism's ambivalence towards normative ethics in that while it clearly regards domination as bad, the reasons for this are left implicit. Secondly, while domination is an important source of suffering it is not the only one, and discourses may contribute to other sources. For example, for children or the sick, lack of care is a cause of suffering, and some discourses may be problematic because they contribute to the devaluation of care. Thirdly, to say why these things are bad we need some conception of well-being and ill-being. Indications of such conceptions are a common feature of lay and political discourses (what it is to be a good father, for example). Fourthly, some problematic concepts may simply be mistakes; they are not necessarily the product of domination in blocking recognition of what well-being is.[21] As we have seen, the identification of just what constitutes (an improvement in) well-being may in some cases be very difficult.

Similarly, the concept of hegemony is no more specific about what is problematic (or good) about the phenomena it identifies, that is, why the leadership and domination of popular ways of thinking is bad, other than through their association with the dominant classes and their interests. Like the concept of ideology, its use depends not on an explicit critique of the ideas in question (though this may be added) but on an assumption that the reader will in any case share the same (usually negative) view of them. The same often applies to 'symbolic violence' and 'misrecognition' in the work of Bourdieu (e.g. Bourdieu 1984).

According to the audience, radical social scientists can normally use a few terms which deal directly with matters of ill-being – such as 'domination', 'oppression', or 'racism' – without being challenged, because it can be assumed that the audience will agree on them. But if they go beyond these terms and dwell upon evaluations, they are likely to be accused of importing their values into the analysis, as if these could only be a contaminant, distorting otherwise objective analysis.[22] Alternatively they may be asked 'where their critique hails from', which again implies that the evaluation is problematic because it is 'subjective' and arbitrary, or deriving from an Archimedean point, or imposing some kind of repressive universalism. Tactically, then, radicals may find that it is best not to reveal too much of their critical standpoints, for the more they do so, the more likely they are to be dismissed as subjective or as implying an authoritarian foisting of views on others.

Again, it has to be acknowledged that the evaluation of well-being is extremely difficult, and even where *feelings* about what is bad are widely shared and uncontentious, it may be very difficult to *articulate* exactly what the problem is. However, unless we try, we risk misidentifying the problem and hence impeding attempts to remedy it. For example, many young people today feel that class inequalities are bad, but some of them tend to think of them as primarily products of misrecognition and prejudice, rather than unequal economic distribution, thus producing the illusion that if only people of different classes could get rid of their prejudices about one another, they would become equal and the problems would disappear (Sayer 2005).

When Habermas criticized Foucault's work as 'crypto-normative' he was attacking a more heavily disguised form of criticism, one that merely insinuates that some object is problematic without giving any indication why, so that the reader is left unsure of what the problem is. This crypto-normativity has become common and the associated normative disorientation it produces is even valued in post-structuralism, as if there were some virtue in this.[23] But this is not the only problem, for given the fusing of positive and normative in matters of needs and well-being, crypto-normative approaches are also *crypto-positive*, since they sacrifice descriptive richness through their refusal of valuation. In avoiding comment on whether something causes suffering or flourishing we miss important positive information. Thus in response to vaguely dystopic accounts of ubiquitous power and subjectification we may feel unsure whether to ask 'is everything bad?' or 'so what?'.

Against these de-normativising tendencies, I am arguing that there is a need for a more explicit kind of critique which articulates its standpoints and that of the texts it analyses in terms of arguments about flourishing and suffering. Far from being authoritarian in intent and effect, it would adopt the risky, deliberative-democratic strategy of airing such arguments so that others can criticise them, instead of assuming agreement on them or hiding them for fear of allowing values to 'intrude' into social science.

Finally, my argument also implies a different attitude towards values in texts from that implied by the prevailing dualisms that I have criticised. In some cases, CDA is concerned with making explicit evaluations that are only implicit in texts, and with indicating in what respects those implicit valuations are misleading or otherwise suspect. Thus, for example, Graham (2001) demonstrates how managerial discourses on topics such as the 'knowledge economy' use language that appears purely 'factual' and blurs the distinction between the actual and the possible in a way that makes certain future possibilities seem both inevitable and desirable, when they are arguably neither. But the problem with such discourses is not that they imply particular valuations, for discourses about how our lives are changing and likely to change in future could hardly do otherwise, indeed they would be uninteresting if they didn't. Nor is the problem necessarily that the valuations are not made more explicit by separating them out from the descriptions, for descriptions of matters impinging on our well-being are unavoidably evaluative and the two aspects are only separable at the price of obscuring the relation between the evaluations and what they are about, hence making them seem beyond the scope of reason. Rather, the problem with such discourses is that *both* the descriptions and the implicit valuations are suspect. For instance, the implicit valuations of the term 'collateral damage' are dubious because the descriptions of their objects are seriously deficient. Take the statement 'CDA helps us understand the many different functions of language and how discourse relates to other aspects of the social world, revealing many processes that would be difficult to notice otherwise'. Here I am using factual language but it would be perverse to deny that it implied a positive valuation. If I were to follow it up with a more explicit evaluation, such as 'CDA is good', that would not add anything; indeed, it might detract from the point, since such assertions are or may be divorced from the descriptions of their referents and hence may seem arbitrary. This is why, as Fairclough (2005) notes, the more concrete and specific the evaluative terms we use – for example, 'generous and witty', rather than 'nice' or 'good' – the more appropriate they seem, because it is clearer what they are about, indeed the normative and the positive have not been separated.

Conclusion

There would be no point in criticism if nothing mattered, if nothing had any significance – that is any implications for whether people flourished or suffered. But I suspect that like other critical social sciences, CDA is inhibited by the tendency to regard values as merely subjective – both in the sense of 'probably not correct' and 'pertaining only to the subject' – and not also related to the nature of the object being evaluated and to capacities for flourishing and suffering.

What can be done about this? First, we can recognise that the point of much discourse is to identify or attribute significance in some way, not merely to describe and explain the world but to imply what we should care about, what involves flourishing and suffering, what is lacking and needed, and assess the implications of events for these things. To make a *critical* analysis requires us to make an assessment of these matters and where this is at variance with the discourse under analysis, to decide which is better. For example, a crucial aspect of 'framing' in political discourse (Lakoff 2004) is the way in which it highlights or occludes flourishing or suffering, and in which it encourages us to narrow or broaden our moral imaginations, and positions us as self-centred or other-regarding, parochial or cosmopolitan, and so on.[24] Secondly, we need to start taking normative discourse, both lay and academic, more seriously, since it is both part of the object of study and a rival account to any we may come up with. Thirdly, we need to attempt to clarify and assess the nature and bases of particular critiques we make. To do this we need to avoid the epistemic fallacy of converting questions of being – for example, suffering – into matters of beliefs and knowledge about them, while acknowledging that the latter can only be developed through available discourses. To treat the things that most trouble us as 'merely subjective', is to confuse values with what they are about. In effect, it is strange to call responses to, say, cruelty, a product of our values, for they are products of our valuations of something that causes suffering (MacIntyre 1971). We need also to avoid the positive scholastic fallacy of de-normativising social life: it is extraordinary how little interest contemporary social science shows in explaining why people value things as they do, why they think some things are good and some bad, without resorting to a sociological reductionism which renders them as no more than products of their social position and interests, or of social or cultural norms. This creates theory-practice contradictions: in the seminar room many today will argue that normative matters such as those of ethics are subjective, relative to culture, purely conventional or culturally-constituted. However, outside the seminar room, when someone mistreats them they generally do not say things like 'in my subjective view that was wrong', or 'in my culture that's wrong' or 'don't you know that's culturally-constituted as bad?' Rather than resort to such pathetically weak arguments, they say things like 'look at the damage you have done', which implies objective harm. In the face of such glaring theory-practice conditions we should take normativity more seriously, and deconstruct the dualisms that have prevented us from doing so.

Notes

1. My own claim about the overlap of the evaluative and the informative is less sweeping. Some judgements are merely 'characterising judgements' rather than 'appraising judgements', as Nagel put it, though in my view the former are always needed to defend the latter (Nagel 1961). Volosinov's treatment of the relation between subject and object in valuation is also unclear.
2. Of course, this is itself a normative judgement.
3. Bourdieu himself failed to avoid this variant of the fallacy, because of his reluctance to take actors' accounts as anything more than functions of their position and habitus. On the one hand, this means that otherwise serious academics can be breezily anti-intellectual about normative reasoning, scoffing at the interminable arguments of moral and political philosophy; on the other, it allows them to loftily ignore lay normativity.
4. Anti-humanists should note that I am not claiming that humans are unique in these respects.

5. Such inferences are of course fallible and involve an implicit ceteris paribus clause, but the same goes for more straightforwardly positive claims about how the world works. There are also difficult issues here regarding the difference between needs and wants, but they do not affect the argument presented here.

6. Amartya Sen's and Martha Nussbaum's research on 'capabilities' attempts to identify these elements of flourishing and suffering (Sen 1999; Nussbaum 2000).

7. For a fuller discussion, see Taylor 1967.

8. Of course, people *can* order the material world according to discursive structures, but they can only do this successfully to the extent that they do so in ways which accord with the objective properties of the materials which they mobilize and attempt to manipulate.

9. Lemke's discussion of 'value preferences' comes close to this subjectivism and relativism (Lemke 1995).

10. "There is no such thing as truth. Science is a social phenomenon and like every other social phenomenon is limited by the benefit or injury it confers on the community". Hitler, cited in G.Daniel *The Idea of Pre-History*, London, C.A.Watts and Co. 1962, p.118) "Everything I have said and done in these last years is relativism by intuition ... From the fact that all ideologies are of equal value, that all ideologies are mere fictions, the modern relativist infers that everybody has the right to create for himself his own ideology and to attempt to enforce it with all the energy of which he is capable." Mussolini, cited in Veach, 1962.

11. The referents may be past events, which may in some cases be vividly remembered or in others almost forgotten. The possibility of emotions responding to such events and not purely to present ones is the most likely reason why we tend to think of them as irrational.

12. Of course whether the differences warrant these different judgements might be disputed, but the comparative judgement cannot even get off the ground if it is not related to any identifiable differences.

13. Many of the objects we judge are social constructions, which obviously owe their existence to the subjects that produced them. But production or construction is different from mere observation or construal. The U.S. neoconservatives are a social construction, but they are not *my* social construction, just something I externally construe, and they have proved indifferent to my critical construals of them. My construals may be more or less 'objective' in the sense of true, but they are fallible because the neoconservatives are whatever they are regardless of how I think about them. They are objective in the sense of existing independently of others' observations at any moment. In using the metaphor of construction it is vital to distinguish participants (constructors) from spectators (construers) and acknowledge that constructions succeed or fail according to how they use the properties of the materials – physical and ideational – involved in the construction process.

14. Cultural variation is itself dependent on natural capacities for enculturation. Not just anything can be culturally shaped (as opposed to merely externally culturally construed); only certain species which have the particular properties which make them susceptible to cultural variation.

15. It is not only absurd to call, as Foucault does, for an ethic of creativity that is not based on truth about desire, life, nature or body (Foucault 2000: 262), as if these would prevent creativity and new discoveries; it is also dangerous to call for an ethics which disregards the affordances and limits of human social being.

16. I do not use the stronger language of 'constitution' or 'construction' because of their tendency to imply that anything can be constructed on the basis of collective wishful thinking, come what may, in other words the tendency to lapse into a voluntarism or in the Foucauldian case 'subjectivism without a subject'.

17. Defenders of the status quo as 'the best of all possible worlds' are clearly *not* denying that things could be different.
18. Pace Rajagopalan (2003).
19. Where the nihilistic implications of this skeptical orientation to normative as well as positive matters are realised as a problem, it sometimes prompts not a rejection of universal skepticism but a move towards various kinds of romanticism, in which appeals are made to 'conscience' (e.g. Bauman 1993).
20. Here I am alluding to a view of lay morality which owes much to Adam Smith's analysis of moral sentiments (Smith 1759; Sayer 2005).
21. This has been a fatal weakness of Marxism – the optimistic belief that all problems derived from domination and repression such that their removal would automatically augur in a better social order.
22. Again, this accusation confuses different senses of 'objective' – as value-free, as true, and as pertaining to objects.
23. This complements a rather adolescent tendency to value transgression in itself, regardless of what is being transgressed.
24. While Lakoff's approach is helpful, unless it is supported by normative arguments about well-being, it need not necessarily be progressive.

References

Archer, Margaret S. 1996. 2nd ed. *Culture and Agency*. Cambridge: Cambridge University Press.

Archer, Margaret S. 2000. *Being Human*. Cambridge: Cambridge University Press.

Bauman, Zygmunt. 1993. *Postmodern Ethics*. Oxford: Blackwell.

Bourdieu, Pierre. 1984. *Distinction: A Social Critique of the Judgement of Taste*. London: Routledge.

Bourdieu, Pierre. 2000. *Pascalian Meditations*. Cambridge: Polity.

Collier, Andrew. 2003. *In Defence of Objectivity*. London: Routledge.

Eagleton, Terry. 2003. *After Theory*. London: Penguin.

Fairclough, Norman. 1992. *Discourse and Social Change*. Cambridge: Polity.

Fairclough, Norman. 2003. *Analysing Discourse: Textual Analysis for Social Research*. London: Routledge.

Fairclough, Norman. 2005 Analyzing values in texts: The contribution of Critical Discourse Analysis to researching moral economies. Draft paper.

Foucault, Michel. 1977. *Discipline and Punish*. Harmondsworth: Penguin.

Foucault, Michel. 2000. *Michel Foucault: Ethics*. ed. Paul Rabinow. London: Penguin.

Graham, Philip. 2001. Space: Irrealis objects in technology policy and their role in a new political economy. *Discourse and Society* 12(6), 761–788.

Graham, Philip. 2003. Critical discourse analysis and evaluative meaning: interdisciplinarity as a critical turn. In: G. Weiss and R. Wodak. (eds). *Critical Discourse Analysis: Theory and Interdisciplinarity*. Basingstoke: Palgrave, 108–129.

Haines, Simon. 1998. Deepening the self. In: Jane Adamson, Richard Freadman and David Parker (eds). *Renegotiating Ethics in Literature, Philosophy and Theory*. Cambridge: Cambridge University Press, 21–38.

Helm, Bennett W. 2001. *Emotional Reason: Deliberation, Motivation and the Nature of Value*. Cambridge: Cambridge University Press.

Lakoff, George. 2004. *Don't Think of an Elephant! Know Your Values and Frame the Debate*. White River Junction, VT: Chelsea Green Publishing Co.

Lane, Robert E. 1991. *The Market Experience*. Cambridge: Cambridge University Press.

Lemke, Jay. 1995. *Textual Politics*. London: Taylor and Francis.

MacIntyre, Alasdair. 1971 *Against the Self-Images of the Age*. London: Duckworth.

Nagel, Ernest. 1961. *The Structure of Science*. London: Routledge and Kegan Paul.

Nussbaum, Martha. C. 1993. Charles Taylor: explanation and practical reason. In: Amartya Sen and Martha C. Nussbaum (eds). *The Quality of Life*. Oxford: Clarendon Press, 232–241.

Nussbaum, Martha C. 2000. *Women and Human Development: The Capabilities Approach*. Cambridge: Cambridge University Press.

Nussbaum, Martha C. 2001. *Upheavals of Thought: The Intelligence of Emotions*. Cambridge: Cambridge University Press.

Rajagopalan, Kanavilil. 2004. On being critical. *Critical Discourse Studies* 1(2), 261–266.

Reisigl, Martin and Wodak, Ruth. 2001. *Discourse and Discrimination*. London: Routledge.

Sayer, Andrew. 2000. *Realism and Social Science*. London: Routledge.

Sayer, Andrew. 2005. *The Moral Significance of Class*. Cambridge: Cambridge University Press.

Sen, Amartya. 1999. *Development as Freedom*. Oxford: Oxford University Press.

Smith, Adam. 1984[1759]. *The Theory of Moral Sentiments*. Indianapolis: Liberty Fund.

Taylor, Charles. 1967. Neutrality and political science. In: Alan Ryan (ed.). 1973. *The Philosophy of Social Explanation*. Oxford: Oxford University Press, 139–170.

Soper, Kate. 1995. *What is Nature?* Oxford: Blackwell.

van Leeuwen, Theo. 2000. The construction of purpose in discourse. In: Srikant Sarangi and Michael Coulthard (eds). *Discourse and Social Life*. London: Longman, 66–81.

Volosinov, Valentin N. 1973. *Marxism and the Philosophy of Language*. Cambridge, MA: Harvard University Press.

Williams, Bernard. 1993. *Shame and Necessity*. Berkeley, CA: University of California.

Wodak, Ruth. 2001. The discourse-historical approach. In: Ruth Wodak and Michael Meyer (eds). *Methods of Critical Discourse Analysis*. London: Sage, 63–94.

64

Future of Europe

Bo Stråth

I will begin this article on the future of Europe by a few words about what was before Europe, namely the nation-states, and then discuss *past* futures of Europe. How was Europe's future imagined in the *past*? At the end I will connect the sequence of past futures into our present European future.

The nineteenth and most of the twentieth century were dominated by the perspective of the nation-state. The perspective of most nation-state histories was teleological with a linear process towards national unity where the regions were seen as remnants of tradition, social inequalities were played down, and national unity was emphasised. This process was reinforced through the experiences of two world wars. National mobilisation for war promoted social integration and feelings of community. The response to the Great Depression was the emergence of the modern welfare state. The idea of the modern welfare state culminated during some two or three decades after World War II. This culmination built on a centenary development beginning with the debate on the social issue from the 1830s. The debate addressed the question of political responsibility and political action against what was identified as a social problem beyond the capacity of the individuals to solve. The problem was referred to as a systemic one. The debate accelerated from the 1870s with attempts to unify and reconcile the discourses on nation and class struggle. This was obvious in Germany where the *Verein für Sozialpolitik* founded in 1873 tried to approach both the national and the social questions (Wagner 1990; Zimmermann 1996 and 2000; Didry, Wagner and Zimmermann (eds) 1999).

Source: *Journal of Language and Politics*, 5(3) (2006): 427–448.

The invention of the concept of unemployed in the 1880s was a milestone in this process. At that time, unemployment was still a theoretical concept: unemployment (as opposed to poverty caused by 'want of work' to use the terminology of the English Poor Laws) was first recognised in Britain in the late 1880s. The concept was a social construct. It reflected a prescriptive approach closely aligned to a desire to improve industrial performance in the face of increasing competition for foreign markets. From the very beginning, the concept was an element of a utopian economic theorisation of society that clearly demarcated the unemployed from the poor and pauperism. It was a new concept for a new form of society: not yet the fully employed society, but at least the potentially prosperous society (Topalov 1994: 13–35; Stråth 2000a).

The future in this master narrative, with various national versions, was at the beginning teleologically imagined as stronger and bigger. After 1945 the imagination of a linear progressive march was rather understood in terms of richer and more liberal in demarcation to Eastern Europe in the framework of the Cold War.

The point I want to make here is that the social issue was at the core of the nation building. The question today is what role it plays in the building of Europe. The European unification movement has often been seen in terms of parallelism to the nation building: integration of smaller units into larger. There is a bias in this reference to history. Integration in the historical examples is seen in terms of market integration from which somehow social integration more or less automatically emerged. The European integration is with the same bias analogically seen as a market integration, which will unify Europe also socially. The analogy between Europe and the European nineteenth century nation state building is biased because it neglects how closely the national (rather than the market) and the social questions were from the 1870s onwards when the effects of industrial capitalism became palpable during the long economic depression and provoked protests and responses by the ruling classes. National socialism competed with class struggle socialism in the search for remedy, and protectionism became the instrument to correct market forces. The mix that these processes contained exploded in 1914. After a brief European armistice, it exploded once more in the 1930s.

We do not learn from history and history does not repeat itself. It is nevertheless important to be attentive to recurring structural elements. One crucial element of such attention is to get history right and to resist simplistic analogies irrespective whether they are based on ideological bias or historical ignorance. Integration does not come from just market freedom. Karl Polanyi convincingly demonstrated that market integration often leads to social disintegration (Polanyi 2001 [1944]). This is a historical experience to pay attention to in the ongoing construction of Europe.

The teleological national modernisation narrative culminated in the early 1970s. In the framework of the economic crisis, and the doubts that future could be managed according to schedule, the image of national communities of destiny based on welfare eroded in the wake of the collapse of labour markets and of economic performance, yes, indeed, of the whole international order. Regional networks emerged as alternative sites of profitability and economic expansion. The nation became perceived as more fragmented, multiple and contingent than it had been so far. The network metaphor invaded social sciences not caring about the question of power and social hierarchies. Instead of power, large scale and centralised hierarchy the network connoted small scale, nearness and decentralised structures of local autonomy. Societies were seen in horizonal and smooth transnational terms. A mutually reinforcing academic debate in Western Europe as well as the United States of America propagated the narrative with great conviction (Sabel 1989; Sabel and Zeitlin 1997). The image of state power as a counterweight to capitalist power evaporated in the idea of self-regulating networks, which even were equipped with democratic capacities. The networks guaranteed both liberty and solidarity as opposed to eroding state sclerosis structures. This was the beginning of the globalization narrative, which from the 1990s replaced the old national modernisation narrative and infused new hopes in future. The success of this new teleology was confirmed through the collapse of the Soviet Empire. In some versions, the history had even come to an end. Karl Marx' socialist utopia got a liberal version where history stopped one step earlier (Fukuyama 1992).

The concept of a European identity was launched in 1973, at the European Community summit in Copenhagen. This concept was advanced and elaborated in a context marked by an experienced *lack* of identity and the erosion of interpretative frameworks and orientation. If there had been a sense of identity, there would have been no need to invent the concept as a means by which to induce a new community in the European Community. Exactly what is meant by the concept of a European identity is unclear (Niethammer 2000). The European identity discourse can be seen as an alternative to the network and globalisation narrative. As an alternative it represented both overlappings and differences. The backdrop of both narratives was quite clearly the collapse of the Bretton Woods order. The collapse of the old order provoked the search for new meaning and new interpretation. The network and the identity discourses were mobilising instruments for orientation and political action.

In retrospect, it is striking how, at the same time as 'identity' was being launched, attempts within the European project to intensify the process of 'integration', the watchword of the 1950s and 1960s, were running into difficulty. European integration connoted milk lakes and butter, egg and meat mountains in the wake of the EEC agricultural subsidy politics, and stagnating industries. In political terms, Charles De Gaulle rhetorically emphasised the limits of the European integration already in the 1960s with his argumentation for *l'Europe des patries*. In brief, integration was by the beginning of the 1970s no mobilising concept any more. In a situation in which both labour markets and the capacity of national economies for political government was diminishing, identity was launched by the European Council as a key concept in order to infuse new confidence in the project of unification. From our perspective today, it seems clear that identity replaced integration as the buzzword for the European unification project at a time when the project was experiencing severe strains (Stråth 2000b). The concept emerged in a situation in which the very legitimacy of the European integration project was at stake (below).

Integration as a Political-Academic Concept for the Design of Future

If the concept of 'identity' is vague, then the term 'integration' is no less so. The concept of integration originally meant 'to make whole', or 'to form an entirety or entity'. Elements are brought together to become 'integral' parts of a larger whole. This meaning establishes 'integration'as an antonym for 'dissolution'. In the social sciences, integration refers to processes of unification of separate units, processes in which societies are established and maintained, or in which they merge to form larger entities.

After the early use of the concept in classical sociology, 'integration' re-emerged after the Second World War as a key social science concept in the federalist, functionalist and neo-functionalist discourses on Europe. It was used to describe not only the transformation of Western European societies after World War II, but also in the wake of the Cold War. By 1945, nationalism and national arrogance were discredited as political instruments and interpretative frameworks, yet, ironically and paradoxically, this was at precisely the same moment that the nation-state emerged as more consolidated than ever, following the mass participation involved in the mobilisation for war. The contradiction between transnational free-trade theories and national welfare strategies for promoting mass production and mass consumption was concealed behind the concept of integration. This merger of transnational ideas and national performance was particularly distinct in Western Europe. Alan Milward (1994) talked about the European integration as a rescue of the nation-states rather than transgressing them.

Integration became a buzzword with a high political charge. The phenomenon that the concept claimed to describe was twofold: first, the institutionalisation of intragovernmental co-operation, in which the point of departure was the nation-state, reinforced through welfare strategies, and secondly, the simultaneous condensation of transnational networks of communications and organised interests in Western Europe. A corresponding process of political, economic, and communicative condensation occurred in Soviet-dominated Eastern Europe, although this was through the use of Soviet military power and physical repression rather than through the concept of integration. It is clear that there was a connection between the two processes and the mutually reinforcing debates on them. The West saw itself in the mirror of the East and vice versa.

The idea of European integration was a child of World War II and the Cold War. As a matter of fact, the concept was a compromise in a situation where the USA, as opposed to the situation today, wanted an ever tighter degree of European unification, a United States of Europe in analogy to the United States of America. Integration became a key concept not only in the social sciences but also in politics. As such, its value was in its vagueness and ambiguity and its openness to interpretations. It produced both a political contestation over the precise content of the concept and, at the same time, political concord that integration was a good thing. In 1949, when the US administration realised the magnitude of European resistance to the economic and political unification of Western Europe implicit in the Marshall Plan and in the American ideas of a United States of Europe, the concept of integration became the palliative to avoid a deadlock situation in the relationship between the US and Western Europe. While the Marshall administration (ECA) continued to talk about 'European unification' and supranational institutions, the State Department preferred 'integration', because it provided more room to manoeuvre, with respect both to the European nations and Congress. To continue to require European 'unification' would have provoked resistance from several European governments because of its connotations of surrendering national sovereignty (af Malmborg 1994. Cf Stråth 2000c). From a political language making use of an old concept in the social sciences, 'integration' was re-induced in the scientific theorising around a specific political process. The concept of integration was thus launched with the intention of introducing meaning that went beyond that which was contained in the concept of co-operation. The emerging phenomenon that 'integration' claimed to describe was, in Western Europe, understood to be the construction of a new entity that represented something more than the sum of its participating elements. While 'co-operation' described a static structure of interaction between separate elements, 'integration', which had the goal of holistic unification, had more processual and transformative connotations.

The term 'integration' was soon embedded in a symbolic context. Integration became a concept charged with signification and value. From the earliest moments, the connotations of 'integration' moved in one specific direction. In its European context, 'integration' became a functionalist concept, heavily dependent upon theory in mainstream American sociology. Integration began to imply a smooth, linear evolutionary development towards ever higher or more condensed levels of co-existence. Thus, European integration became an illustration of functionalist and teleological theorising about society.

Born as a concept of high politics, integration became an analytical instrument in the social sciences. From the academic debate the term fed back on politics. The term also became politically attractive, since it promised to prevent war and promote peace through the intensification of communication and trade, of economic and political networks throughout industrial societies. The social sciences operated as a form of feedback, legitimising the policy-making. In their optimistic scenario, political scientists and Europe's political élite argued that the merging and interweaving of Europe into this new functional system of elements, which had previously been oppositional and competitive, would dramatically decrease the risks of warfare and increase the prospects of welfare in Europe. This was how the concept was generally understood in both the social sciences and politics. The welfare was thought to emerge through free trade and market performance.

In the debate, which took place at both intellectual and political levels, over the construction of this (Western) European image, and on how to describe the envisaged new functional system, historical prototypes were mobilised. The question was whether the emerging entity was best described in terms of a 'confederation' or a 'federation', in terms of interstate or suprastate co-operation (for this debate, see Schmitter 1996). In the social sciences, this was a debate with clear political undertones, while, in the political debate, the concept had pretensions of scientific legitimisation. The target of the debate, and the object for the concept of integration, was the European Community. While integration was a concept with generalised ambitions, its test bed was Western Europe as a project for peace and social welfare. The ramework for the experiment was the Cold War and the demarcation of the Soviet sphere. In this framework, the liberal market order was seen as the guarantee of peaceful co-operation and increasing welfare, not in a neoliberal sense, but in the context of ideas of politically managed economies. The opposing image in the emerging Western world-view was the Soviet Union and its Eastern European satellites.

The confidence in this interpretative framework eroded heavily in the 1970s, as has been mentioned. It was in this framework of lost legitimacy that the concept of European identity was launched in 1973. European identity was put on the agenda at the moment that political economy, in its form that had been established since the 1950s, was becoming exposed to severe strains.

The Idea of a European Identity

The concept of 'European identity' was diffused in the 1970s in the framework of attempts to establish a European tripartite order of corporatist bargaining between the governments, the employers and the employees. This European order was outlined to replace the collapsing national corporatist frameworks. The identity concept emerged in a situation in which Europe was experiencing a profound crisis in national economic government.

The idea of a European identity was more precisely designed at the Copenhagen EC summit in December, 1973 (Passerini 1998 and 2000). The idea of identity was based on the principle of the unity of the Nine – this was just after the first enlargement – on their responsibility towards the rest of the World, and on the dynamic nature of the European construction. The meaning of 'responsibility towards the rest of the World' was expressed in a hierarchical way. First, it meant responsibility towards the other nations of Europe with whom friendly relations and co-operation already existed. Secondly, it meant responsibility towards the countries of the Mediterranean, Africa and the Middle East. Thirdly, it referred to relations with the USA, based on the restricted foundations of equality and the spirit of friendship. Next in the hierarchy was the narrow co-operation and constructive dialogue with Japan and Canada. Then came *détente* towards the Soviet Union and the countries of Eastern Europe. At the bottom of the list came China, Latin America, and, finally, a reference was made to the importance of the struggle against underdevelopment in general. The fact that the USA was mentioned after the Middle East must be understood in the framework of the prevailing oil price shock.

This mode of argument for a European identity demonstrates the danger contained in the concept. Beyond this emergence of a rhetoric of European identity, seemingly of a rather innocent kind, history shows in more general terms how risky the ideological charge built into the identity concept can be, and how entrenched the processes of exclusion and inclusion which it involves can become. At the end of the road, the 'Europe as an identity' project took on essential proportions. The extreme of identity in essential terms was identity politics on the Balkans and a new European genocide.

The liberal end of history scenario eroded rapidly at about the same time, at the mid–1990s. The European people that had been conjured up in the identity discourse never appeared. Instead, the reappearance of nationalism was obvious. Instead of a European people unified in a supranational EU managed by a strong Commission, as the Maastricht Treaty and the shift of name from the European Economic Community to the European Union indicated, the European political practice as it developed meant a migration of power from the centralised level of the Commission to the member state governments assembled in the Council. The regulative framework based on compelling directives, with the pretension of a supranational law *sui generic*, is gradually being transformed into intergovernmental agreements in the so-called open method of coordination process. Instead of a tighter political union as a higher level of integration, in comparison to the economic free trade unification, the trend is towards a looser kind of intergovernmental cooperation and coordination. This trend is obvious since some ten years. The European summits in Luxembourg 1997 and Lisbon 2000 outlined this transformation from the image of a Europe beyond the nations to a Europe of the nations. High politics in Europe had to recognise that the nation had returned on the European scene and to find political responses to this fact.

Against the backdrop of this development, the concept of a European identity does not serve a purpose any more. The image of a European people as it was designed in the framework of the Cold War seems to be more distant than ever. Or, put in other and more provocative words, the guidance provided by the Cold War does not exist any more. It seems as if the new buzzword launched to fulfil the function of unification was 'constitution'. The identity concept has become irrelevant. The loss of orientation, confidence and political legitimacy was around 2000, ten years after the cease of the Cold War, as massive as in the 1970s. The infusion of new confidence among Europe's citizens required a new language. In this framework, 'constitution' should be seen as an attempt to introduce a new *Zauberwort*.

The collapse of the 'identity' image was demonstrated in an as striking as embarrassing way in Nice 2000. When the European leaders met in Nice in December, 2000 it could have been in a kind of euphoria under proud proclamations of a project on march. A time schedule was set for the biggest EU enlargement ever, marking the definite end of the Cold War and the whole post-war period, the start of a new era. The agenda of the unification of Europe in quite a new sense, the whole of Europe, was proclaimed.

However, this potential moment of a euphoria collapsed in a general chaos when the *grande geste*, the opening towards the East, was translated into institutional questions about how many votes each Member State should have and what kind of majority a decision required. Member State representatives accused each other of narrow interest politics. Media described how the leaders of Europe tried to see and dark the cards of one another like in a big European poker game. The distance to the populations was emphasised by the police barricades against violent demonstrators in what best can be described in terms of a paramilitary street battle of the kind which has become the more or less 'normal' framework of political summits.

The mood certainly shifted at the occasion of the introduction of the euro one year later on 1 January, 2002. The day was a remarkable manifestation of European unification. The Euro was celebrated as the symbol of a new Europe, more unified than ever since the Roman Empire. Political leaders getting their first banknotes from cash machines among ordinary people in the streets dissolved hierarchies between elites and masses. Europe was really unified horizontally as well as vertically. The euphoria was a europhoria, and it was exactly as a symbol for unity that the new currency was celebrated. The media and the elites did not talk very much about the strictly economic side of the event, but about the symbol for unity.

One conclusion of the two events is how fast the moods change and how transient and inconsistent Europe is, far from frequent imaginations of Europe as a fixed and rigidly institutionalised category, be it a market or a polity. In the seeming stability is instability. Solutions to one problem are pregnant with new challenges and new problems. In one version, Europe can be seen as a project towards ever deeper and more refined, and at the same time ever larger stages of integration, 'functional incrementation'. In another version, Europe has for half a century been a project from crisis to crisis. The media cover of the two events demonstrate how fast the moods shift and what an important role the media – as much as the events themselves – play in this shift. It is like an acceleration of time itself (Stråth and Triandafyllidou forthcoming).

The Umbrella over the Fiasco in Nice: The Constitution for a New European Future

'Constitution' emerged as an umbrella over the fiasco in Nice. It would solve the problems that the Nice summit failed to do. The constitution would provide institutional arrangements to prevent overstretching and break down of the European project when it was extended from 15 to 25 and more members.

Normally, constitution refers to a moment of condensed political foundation in which a new entity of transgressing dimensions emerges. The cases in point are the constitutions in the wake of the French and the American Revolutions. Constitution in this sense connotes a distinct, not to say charismatic, text. Constitution creates a political community that abolishes previous unifications.

It is difficult to see anything of these dimensions in the proposal for a European constitution, which was put on the table in 2004. In crucial respects, the act remains an intergovernmental agreement. In referendums, it is evaluated by the European peoples (in plural) nation per nation, not a European people as the constitutive entity. On the symbolic level Giscard d'Estaing as the main responsible for the draft could possibly be conceivable as one of the founding fathers in Paris or Philadelphia, but as a representative of a European will in the twenty-first century his aristocratic manners and arrogant style radiated neither charisma nor democratic values. Hopes and expectations were invested in the Constitution as a concept to conjure up a 'community', and as such it can be seen as a new link in the chain of integration and identity. However, as opposed to the two precursors the hopes evaporated very soon after the referendums in France and the Netherlands in the spring of 2005 and were after the summit in Brussels in June rather turned into a horror scenario like after Nice five years earlier.

The process towards a European constitution intended to speed up the emergence of a European political community through the creation of thicker relations between citizens. It was a process based on the ambition to reshape identities and memories where the integration and identity concepts did not work anymore. This ambition was confronting the limits set by an intergovernmental order.

The Mythical Foundation of Europe

The conclusion is that we should be sceptical *vis-à-vis* the mythical underpinning of the institutional dimension of European society. This mythical underpinning goes deeper than the concepts of integration, identity, and constitution. It tells stories about Europe formed by a specific Christian or Antique heritage emphasising values of Enlightenment, tolerance and benevolence, ignoring the dark sides of European history. Those dark sides are rather condensed to a German history without a more general European responsibility. This myth construction has been obvious in the debates about the drafting of a European constitution. The considerations about the invocation of a specific Christian heritage, ignoring the role of the Jewish and Islamic religions in the creation of a perceived European culture, is a case in point (see for a discussion of the role of Christian values in the work on the constitution Schlesinger and Foret forthcoming).

The risk in such mythical projections of an imagined cultural heritage with essential proportions *à la longue durée* is to become myopic towards the powerful and apparently banal myths that we live by. History becomes nostalgia. In the case of the European Union, at least two political myths are at work (Botticci 2004: 259). One is the political myth of Europe as the land of freedom and welfare. The clearest sign of the working of this myth is the number of immigrants that are prepared to die at Europe's borders. The question is whether after the recent enlargement new borders are about to emerge within the EU between new and old member states. The second myth is derived from the banal history of the European construction itself, first born as an institution which aimed to solve the historical conflict between Germany and France over coal and steel, then developed into the European common market through integration, and later into the European Union through identity. This is the myth of Europe as a teleological progress.

According to the official historiography, today's EU is built on the Schuman Plan. One important dimension of the European Coal and Steel Community, which continued in the EEC and the EU, is that political power and authority is more centralised than the possibility of claiming political responsibility. This is an obvious difference in comparison to national parliamentary democracies. There is a discrepancy between the European Union as an economic project and as a political and social project.

Interestingly enough, this discrepancy can be attributed to the experiences of Fascism and Communism at the time of the foundation of the European Coal and Steel Community in 1951. Out of bitter experiences, the Christian Democrats in Europe after 1945 had learnt how the rule of the people could be abused. Democracy had brought Fascism and Nazism to power. At the time of the Berlin Blockade and the Korean War, the Moscow-controlled Communist Parties in France and Italy had the support of some 25–30 per cent of the electorate. Through the institutional construction of the European Coal and Steel Community, Robert Schuman, Konrad Adenauer and Alcide de Gasperi thought that they would create an order where the executive power was safeguarded from attacks from populism and unreliable voters, as well as made more robust than the League of Nations had been. They were keen to avoid a new Weimar scenario. The framework was the Cold War and Communism was the big threat.

Their primary aim was never to create a democratic organisation but to establish a system of protection that would make their nation-states safe for democracy. The language to describe the new institutional setting is a case in point, with the High Authority, which later became the Commission, as the body of centralised power. There is no better source of this interpretation than the European Coal and Steel Community Treaty itself, signed in Paris in May, 1951 in the middle of the Korean War

The official historiography of the European project of unification, with 1945 or 1950 as the starting point, is too simplistic and too propagandistic. It is a historiography in which the men of 1950 saw the light and where the Good stood up against the Evil, an Evil located both in space and time, in the East and in History, as Communism and Nazism/Fascism. The political task has, ever since, been to convince the citizens of the superiority of the model that was shaped.

The Democratic Deficit

The problems are obvious when this teleology is confronted with claims for democracy, and when claims are raised to transfer democratic power from the Member States to the Union level. Such a transfer would mean a clash with the ideas of the founding moment of the European post–1945 project, ideas which received intentional expression in the High Authority. The difficulty for the European Parliament to define its role is obvious. In its self-understanding, the Parliament is the expression of the will of a European people that does not, however, exist. The enactment of a people's will in democratic societies emerges not in terms of consensus, as is so often erroneously argued, but through contention, debate and compromise. Political conflict has historically since the French Revolution been measured along a right-left scale. The social issue is thereby a key dimension. This right-left dimension is the core axis that has been institutionalised in national parliamentary democracies. In the European Parliament, however, it is much less developed. The issue of the debate is much more a contention with the Commission and the Council about the power distribution within the institutional government triangle of the EU. The institutional setting from the early 1950s is, in this respect, still in operation. National sovereignty was not transferred to the European Parliament but to the High Authority/the Commission. It is in this light that the talk about the democratic deficit at European Union level should be seen. The ongoing migration of power from the Commission to the member states brings in a certain sense politics closer to the citizens, but is in no way a solution to the problem of a democratic deficit at the European level. The open method of coordination and the government negotiations are as opaque and as shrouded in mystery as a Vatican conclave.

In 1992 with the Maastricht Treaty an economic and a political union was designed. German Minister of Foreign Affairs Joschka Fischer in 2000 in a speech at the Humboldt University of Berlin outlined the contours of a federal Europe. Already in 1997 the EU Council had decided on a strategy of simultaneous deepening and broadening of EU. The Maastricht process towards a political union was supplemented with the decision on enlargement. The illusion prevailed that it would be possible to maintain both targets without any deeper analysis of to what extent they were compatible. In this vein Fischer's plea for a federal Europe should be seen (Fischer 2000. Cf Baublöck, Mokre and Weiss 2003). Fifty years earlier almost to the day of Fischer's speech, Robert Schuman presented, according to Fischer, his vision of a 'European Federation' for the preservation of peace. This heralded 'a completely new era' in the history of Europe. European integration was the response to centuries of a precarious balance of powers on this continent which again and again resulted in terrible hegemonic wars culminating in the two World Wars between 1914 and 1945. The core of the concept of Europe after 1945 was and still is a rejection of the European balance-of-power principle and the hegemonic ambitions of individual states that had emerged following the Peace of Westphalia in 1648, a rejection which took the form of closer meshing of vital interests and the transfer of nation-state sovereign rights to supranational European institutions.

At the time of Fischer's speech, the migration of power from the Commission to the Council was fully visible as the transformation of the *acquis communautaire* to the open method of coordination as the motor of decisionmaking. This was a development towards the EU of the Member States, De Gaulle's *l'Europe des patries*. It is difficult to imagine that the German Foreign Minister was not fully aware of this development. If so, his speech must be seen as a warning and a last heroic attempt to revert this development. "Fifty years on, Europe, the process of European integration, is probably the biggest political challenge facing the states and peoples involved, because its success or failure, indeed even just the stagnation of this process of integration, will be of crucial importance to the future of each and every one of us, but especially to the future of the young generation", Fischer said. This process of European integration had by the time of his speech been called into question by many people; it was viewed as a bureaucratic affair run by a faceless, soulless Eurocracy in Brussels – at best boring, at worst dangerous.

Fischer did not expressly address the operative challenges facing European policy over the next few months, not the ongoing intergovernmental conference, the EU's enlargement to the east or all those other important issues calling for rapid solution, but rather the possible strategic prospects for European integration far beyond the coming decade.

Fischer's appeal for a federal Europe in an attempt to avoid overstretching of EU in the framework of the envisaged enlargement soon abated. In the convent on a European constitution his vision had no place. In parallel to the conjuration of a European political union, although hardly federal, the political practice of the governments spoke another language, which emphasised the inter-state character of EU. The power concentration to the representatives of the member state governments, who try to negotiate and hammer out ad hoc responses to emerging problems, is a much more fragile construction than what was envisaged in the Maastricht Treaty. The development of the Growth and Stability Pact is a case in point. The fragility did not directly decrease with the enlargement. Fischer tried in vain to draw the attention to this fragility. The contradictions between the fiasco at the European summits in Nice 2000 on a revision of the institutional rules in the light of the enlargement, or in Brussels in 2005 about the financial distribution, and between these two events the solemn proclamation of a Constitution in Rome 2003 are clear evidences of the fragility. The contradictions take on schizophrenic proportions.

Instead of the transformation of the earlier confederation into a federation with a full European parliamentarisation, which would be the logic consequence of the idea of a political union, the idea of a constitution could be seen as an attempt to hide the failure through a flight forward. As I have already argued, despite the language, the concept has not much similarity with the historical use of the term.

Europe has until today remained an elite project with an emphasis on the economic integration of Europe. The power migration from the Commission to the Council only means that the Commission is made responsible for politics that it cannot control. The Commission, and with the Commission the whole EU, is seen as being governed by technocratic and bureaucratic principles exclusively guided by the demands of economic efficiency. The political and social consequences of the politics for economic efficiency are ignored according to the reproaches against the Commission. The reproaches are not unjustified, but the problem is less the Commission than the member states, which do not allow for the construction of a social Europe. The hands of the Commission are back-tied. We are in a certain sense in a situation that Karl Marx described as the *verselbständigte Macht der Exekutivegewalt*, the autonomisation of the power of the executive authority, when he in

18 Brumaire analysed the Bonaparte regime of Napoleon III. However, only in a certain sense, since the Commission can only partly be blamed for the development. The power of the Commission is challenged by the governments. They have, in *closed* meetings, called *open* method of coordination, developed a habit of decision-making of historical range in a pre-democratic almost absolutistic manner without real public debate. The notorious democratic deficit of the EU is about to erode the political legitimacy of Europe (Scott Wright 2004; Wodak and Wright 2005; Muntigl, Weiss and Wodak 2000).

The erosion of the political legitimacy must be related to the fact that EU remains an economic integration. The protests against the constitution in France and the critique of the new capitalism in Germany are hints of the risks in ignoring the social dimension. We might be in a Polanyian situation where the dis-embedding of the market forces provokes social protests and the subsequent political re-embedding of the economy through a correcting regulation to integrate the protests. This would be a rather optimistic scenario where the political response to the protests comes in time. The strong and convincing argument that Karl Polanyi made in 1944 in his outline of a long-term scenario of the development of industrial capitalism in *The Great Transformation* was that economic integration tended to lead to social disintegration. The social protest was the mechanism that called for political intervention to correct the ravages of the market. The economic forces became politically embedded through new rules of the game and social peace was restored. However, the economic forces tended to transgress their new embedding, to 'disembed' themselves again, and so the process continued.

There is an emerging debate that there is a connection between the way in which the euro was constructed with prize stability as utmost goal and the low performance of the European economy. However, there are more marks of questions than answers around the functioning of the EMU. Nobody can convincingly explain why the growth in some of the EMU economies, as for instance Ireland and Finland, while the stagnation is evident in Italy and Germany (EMU after Five Years 2004; European Central Bank 2005). The debate seems to look for answers to the overall weak performance of the euro economies, increasingly referred to in terms of 'crisis', in two opposing directions. The one set of arguments envisage a kind of clearing centre in Brussels with the task to adjust differences in growth. Parallel and synchronous finance and tax politics would enforce economic convergence. The other line of argument requires more flexibility on the labour markets in order to adjust the differences in economic performance.

The first line of argumentation seems to confirm the 18 Brumaire scenario. The erosion of the Growth and Stability Pact speaks against this kind of arguments. The precondition for successful politics in this direction, i.e. to avoid the autonomisation, and at the same time the erosion of the executive power, is probably a much tighter binding of the financial politics through the involvement of the member state governments and parliaments and the European Parliament, which would mean a federal development. The second line of argumentation comes close to seeing competition about social standards as the solution. Competition about social standards is also, and more adequately, called social dumping.

Another scenario, in the extension of the second one, is much worse but nevertheless fully conceivable. Polanyi analysed how the protest of the masses in the 1930s broke down the gold standard. We should be aware that the euro is much more similar to the gold standard than to the US Dollar in terms of institutional structure and monetary power. The erosion of the GSP referred to above is a clear hint of how fragile the euro is. The rigid monetary regulation of the euro by the ECB, with no inflation as primary goal, has certain similarities with the administration of the gold standard.

The enlargement without a tighter integration might prove to be fateful. A tighter integration means in particular a social regulation of the free market for labour, commodities and capital. In the wake of threats, real or not, of cheap labour from the new member states invading the Western parts of EU, or jobcreating production leaving the old member states to where labour is cheap, protectionist politics and social dumping seem to be the alternatives in a debate that becomes ever more polarised. The debate in France and Germany are clear signs of such a development. It goes without saying that the social Europe is much more difficult to establish in response to these recent developments than it had been before the enlargement.

Perspectives

One thing seems to be clear. The old teleology of the European project as a progressive enterprise towards ever higher stages of integration is not very credible any more. There is little utopian energy in EU, which is historically new. The peace vision after 1945, the image of functional developments towards a federation in the 1950s, the identity discourse in the 1970s and the market regulation project under the architecture of Jaques Delors in the 1980s had all one thing in common: a clear goal and the feeling of being on march towards that goal. The expectations invested in the constitution seem in that respect to have evaporated even before it has come into force. We do not even know if it ever will come into force.

The evaporation of utopian energy can be related to what German history philosopher Reinhart Koselleck has said about the permanently declining scope between the experiences and the expectations. This is the essence of modernity in his pessimistic scenario (Koselleck 1992 [1954]). The experiences are in the information society so overwhelming that we cannot overview them and use them as a point of departure for the outlining of future horizons of political visions and imaginations. The narrowing scope between experiences and expectations, he describes as the acceleration of time. The idea of political control and mastery of the economy which was at the core of the development of the nation-states and of the first fifty years or so of the European Community in the modernisation narrative has been replaced by the idea of the self-healing forces of the market in the globalisation narrative. This narrative hardly contributes to the rise of future horizons and expectations anymore.

The question is whether EU somehow can reverse this development and re-introduce the political and social dimension in the economy where the European markets for capital, labour and commodities get a distinctive social profile through common standards and rules. This question is an open question but it is no doubt the crucial question in any estimation of the future of Europe.

Reinhart Koselleck's methodology of conceptual history provides us with an instrument to understand the development of the European project in terms that are not teleological and where the futures are always open, in the past as well as in the present. There is in his view no point from which concepts like integration, identity and constitution can be defined and made into essential categories. The outcomes of conceptual struggles are always uncertain. The outcome of the battle among social forces about the interpretation of a concept is a highly contingent affair, the outcome of which is emergent not causative. The ability to launch new concepts with convincing capacity, and the ability to, so to speak, appropriate key concepts and positions of priority or even monopoly of interpretation of them, is of critical importance in the historical process. However, concepts do not in themselves cause change, rather they establish a particular horizon for potential action. They make change possible, on the one hand, and they set limits for possible change, on the other. These are the framework conditions under which the European project takes form (Koselleck 1985 [1979]).

Reinhart Koselleck's article on *Bund* in *Geschichtliche Grundbegriffe* does not deal with the issue of a European federation but analyses in a long historical perspective the preconditions of federal politics in more general terms with a special reference to the German experiences (Koselleck 1979). His text can nevertheless be read as a serious warning that the European project is close to overstretching. 25 member states are too much for a federal structure *if the social differences are as big as they are.* USA have 50 member states but the social differences are smaller and the adjustment to a federal labour market began in a different historical situation. Without a clear power centre with redistributive capacity social equality is difficult to achieve if the alternative is not social dumping. Few believe still that the market forces will provide equality.[1] Europe is looking for a political re-embedding force, which is difficult to find, however.

One thing seems clear, however. The risk of overstretching does not have to do with a lack of cultural cohesion – read Turkey and Islam – but with the difficulty to establish a social Europe. This conclusion does not exclude that the lack of cultural cohesion is made the scapegoat for a disintegrating Europe. The prescription in order to avoid a negative development must therefore be a political concentration to produce social cohesion. This is the point where the experiences from the nineteenth and twentieth century nation-state building in Europe are particularly valid. The crucial question is whether the open method of coordination provides sufficient institutional strength for such political concentration.

Alain Supiot (2004) has investigated the legal embedding of the conceptual topography of labour markets in Europe. With eloquence he demonstrates that law is not an instrument to use rashly. As opposed to economic perspectives, which are nothing but implicit ideological and normative views with universal pretensions, legal perspectives explicitly pronounce norms and values, which are closely connected to the history and the culture of the societies they regulate. From this point of departure Supiot analyses the legal conceptualisation of labour and work relations as it emerged through two legal traditions, the Roman and the German, and in a third version the British Common Law as a special descendant of Roman Law. The two or three versions exist nowhere in their pure forms. In historical processes of nation building and responses to industrial capitalism they absorbed dimensions of each other. The belief that it would be possible to merge this plurality of historical mergers into a European 'ecumenical' model is naïve in the estimation of Supiot. Instead of a European social model he prefers to talk about Europe as a social forum where the aim would be to create connections between the national models rather than to unify those models into one bigger entity. The test case of Supiot's thesis is obviously the open method of cooperation.

On the other hand, and problematising Supiot's perspective, it could be argued that the European integration with EMU has achieved such intensity that it requires a federal structure to keep together. The political merger of the economic and the social, the monetary and the financial requires a centralised power. If not the risk of overstretching is obvious. This is the problem the EU is facing. The diffculty with a federal solution is that the EU has got so many members that it is hard to unify them into that centralised power. The EU wants with the open method of coordination to describe itself as a learning organisation. It is unclear what that catch word really means in practical as well as theoretical terms. On what grounds do we learn what and what are the conclusions of what we learn? Is it possible to get a unanimous answer to that question? More than a learning organisation, the EU is, ever since its beginning, a negotiating organisation. The success on this point can be seen as the historical *sui generic* of the EU. However, the combination of cohesion and negotiation is easier with six than with twenty-five or more members. This is what the risk of overstretching is about.

Jürgen Habermas has shifted ground from his earlier connection of the public sphere to the nation-state to the conditions of a European public sphere (Habermas 1989, 1997 and 2001). The constitutional framework is supposed to structure and embody a common political identity. A public sphere emerges as a smooth invisible hand over Europe providing cohesion and community. Democratic societies in Europe never emerged in that way. There is no historical analogy to build on in this respect, only historical ideal types. Public spheres in democratising societies emerged through political strife, contention and struggles where the social issue was at the focus. The future of Europe is very much related to a construction as bottom-up rather than top-down. One tool in such a development could be to take up the social issue at the European level, a parliamentarisation of the social issue through various contested outlines from both the left and the right spectrums of politics. The very contention and the disagreement after all mean the social work on something in common. Only in the nation states so emerged feelings of belonging in the long run. If this is a feasible European development is another matter.

Note

1. Equality is, of course, a contested concept. For a discussion of its use in the neoliberal language under connection to the concept of freedom, not less contested, see Schmid 2004.

References

Af Malmborg, Mikael. 1994 *Den ståndaktiga nationalstaten*. PhD Diss. Lund: Lund UP.

Bauböck, Rainer, Mokre, Monika and Weiss, Gilbert (eds). 2003. *Europas Identitäten: Mythen, Konflikte, Konstruktionen*. Frankfurt: Campus.

Bottici, Chiara 2004. *A Philosophy of Political Myth*. PhD Thesis. Florence: European University Institute.

Didry, C., Wagner, Peter and Zimmermann, Bénédicte (eds). 1999. *Le travail et la nation. Histoire compare de la France et l'Allemagne à l'horizon européen*. Paris: Éditions de la Maison des Sciences de l'Homme.

EMU after five Years. 2004. Brussels: the European Commission DG Economic and Financial Affairs Special Report No 1.

European Central Bank, Frankfurt/Main. 2005. Papers for the Conferencce on "What Effects is EMU Having on the Euro Area and its Member Countries?" in Frankfurt/Main 16–17 June.

Fischer, Joschka. 2005. From confederacy to federation – Thoughts on the finality of European integration. Speech at the Humboldt University in Berlin, 12 May 2000. www.auswaertiges-amt.de

Fukuyama, F. 1992. *The End of History and the Last Man*. New York: Free Press.

Koselleck, Reinhart. 1979[1972]. Bund. In: Otto Brunner, Werner Conze, Reinhart Koselleck (eds). *Geschichtliche Grundbegriffe: historisches Lexikon zur politisch-sozialen Sprache in Deutschland*.Bd 1. Stuttgart Klett-Cotta.

Koselleck, Reinhart. 1985[1979]. *Futures Past: On the Semantics of Historical Time*. Cambridge (MA)-London: MIT Press.

Koselleck, Reinhart. 1992[1954]. *Kritik und Krise : Eine Studie zur Pathogenese der bürgerlichen Welt*. Frankfurt/Main: Suhrkamp. (English edition *Critique and Crisis: Enlightenment and the Pathogenesis of Modern Societ*. Oxford: Berg, 1988)

Milward, Alan S. 1994. *The European Rescue of the Nation State*. London: Routledge.

Muntigl, Peter, Weiss, Gilbert and Wodak, Ruth. 2000. European Union Discourses on Un/ employment. An Interdisciplinary Approach to Employment Policy-Making and Organizational Change. Amsterdam: John Benjamins.

Niethammer, Lutz. 2000. A European identity?. In: Bo Stråth (ed.). *Europe and the Other and Europe as the Other*. Brussels: PIE-Peter Lang 2000.

Passerini, Luisa. 1998. *Identità culturale Europea. Idee, sentimenti, relazioni*. Firenze: La Nuova Italia.

Passerini, Luisa. 2000. Why some of us would like to call ourselves Europeans and what we mean by this. In: Bo Stråth (ed.). *Europe and the Other and Europe as the Other*. Brussels: PIE-Peter Lang.

Polanyi, Karl. 2001. *The Great Transformation: the political and economic origins of our time*. Foreword by Joseph E. Stiglitz; Introduction by Fred Block. Boston, MA: Beacon Press [New York 1944].

Sabel, Charles.1989. The reemergence of regional economies. In: Paul Hirst and Jonathan Zeitlin (eds). *Reversing Industrial Decline?* Oxford: Berg.

Sabel, Charles and Zeitlin, Jonathan (eds). 1997. *World of Possibilities. Flexibility and Mass Production in Western Industrialisation*. Cambridge: Cambridge UP.

Schlesinger, Philip and Foret, François. 2006. Political roof and sacred canopy? Religion and the EU constitution. *European Journal of Social Theory* 9.

Schmid, Günther. 2004. Risikomanagement im europäischen Sozialmodell. Arbeitsmarktpolitische und normative Aspekte eines Paradigmenwechsels. In: Hartmut Kaelble and Günther Schmid (eds). *Das europäische Sozialmodell. Auf dem Weg zum transnationalen Sozialstaat*. Berlin: Wissenschaftskolleg Jahrbuch.

Schmitter, Ph. 1996. *Is it really Possible to Democratize the Europolity?* Oslo: Arena Working Papers No 10.

Stråth, Bo. 2000a. The concept of work in the construction of community. In: Bo Stråth (ed.). *After Full Employment. European Discourses on Work and Flexibility*. Brussels: PIE-Peter Lang.

Stråth, Bo, 200b. From the Werner Plan to the EMU. In: Bo Stråth (ed.). *After Full Employment. European Discourses on Work and Flexibility*. Brussels: PIE-Peter Lang.

Stråth, Bo. 2000c. Multiple Europes: Integration, identity and demarcation to the other. In: Bo Stråth (ed.). *Europe and the Other and Europe as the Other*. Brussels: PIE-Peter Lang 2000.

Stråth, Bo and Triandafyllidou, Anna (eds). forthcoming. *Media, Elites and Citizens: European and National Allegiances*. Report from the EURONAT Project.

Supiot, Alain. 2004. Was ist ein Arbeitnehmer? Untersuchung über die Vielfalt der Sozialmodelle in Europa. In: Hartmut Kaelble and Günther Schmid (eds). *Das europäische Sozialmodell. Auf dem Weg zum transnationalen Sozialstaat*. Berlin: Wissenschaftskolleg Jahrbuch.

Topalov, C. 1994. *Naissance du chômeur 1890–1940*. Paris: Albin Michel.

Wagner, Peter. 1990. *Sozialwissenschaften und Staat. Frankreich, Italien, Deutschland 1870–1980*. Frankfurt/Main: Campus.

Wodak, R. and Wright, S. 2005. The European Union in cyberspace: Democratic participation via online multilingual discussion boards? In B. Danet and S. C. Herring (eds). *The Multilingual Internet: Language, Culture and Communication in Instant Messaging, Email and Chat*.

Wright, S. 2004. *A Comparative Analysis of Government-run Discussion Boards at the Local, National and European Union levels*. PhD. Thesis, University of East Anglia.

Zimmermann, Bénédicte. 1996. *La constitution du chômage en Allemagne*. Paris: Thèse de l'Institut d'Études Politiques.

Zimmermann, Bénédicte. 2000. *La constitution du chômage en Allemagne*. Paris: Éditions de la Maison des Sciences de l'Homme.

65

Discourse and Manipulation

Teun A. Van Dijk

Introduction

There are a number of crucial notions in Critical Discourse Analysis (CDA) that require special attention because they imply discursive power abuse. Manipulation is one of these notions. Yet, although this notion is often used in a more impressionistic way, there is no systematic theory of the structures and processes involved in manipulation.

In this article, I examine some of these properties of manipulation, and do so within the 'triangulation' framework that explicitly links discourse, cognition and society (Van Dijk, 2001). A discourse analytical approach is warranted because most manipulation, as we understand this notion, takes place by text and talk. Secondly, those being manipulated are human beings, and this typically occurs through the manipulation of their 'minds', so that a cognitive account is also able to shed light on the processes of manipulation. Thirdly, manipulation is a form of talk-in-interaction, and since it implies power and power abuse, a social approach is also important.

I have advocated many times that these approaches cannot be reduced to one or two of them (see, e.g., Van Dijk, 1998, 2001). Although social, interactional and discursive approaches are crucial, I aim to show that a cognitive dimension is important as well because manipulation always involves a form of mental manipulation.

In this article I do not deal with the form of 'manipulation' used in physics, computer science, medicine or therapy, among other uses, more or less directly derived from the etymological meaning of 'manipulation' as moving

Source: *Discourse & Society*, 17(3) (2006): 359–383.

things by one's hands. Rather, I deal with 'communicative' or 'symbolic' forms of manipulation as a form of interaction, such as politicians or the media manipulating voters or readers, that is, through some kind of discursive influence.

Conceptual Analysis

Before we embark on a more theoretical account and the analysis of some data, we need to be more explicit on the kind of manipulation we want to study. As suggested, manipulation as intended here is a communicative and interactional practice, in which a manipulator exercises control over other people, usually against their will or against their best interests. In everyday usage, the concept of manipulation has negative associations – manipulation is *bad* – because such a practice violates social norms.

It should therefore be borne in mind in the rest of this article that 'manipulation' is a typical observer's category, e.g. of critical analysts, and not necessarily a participant category; few language users would call their own discourse 'manipulative'. As is also the case for racist discourse, this shows that the well-known principle of some forms of ethnomethodology and Conversation Analysis (CA), namely to make explicit members' categories, is not always a useful method in more critical approaches. Indeed, this would make the (critical) study of sexist or racist discursive practices impossible.

Manipulation not only involves power, but specifically *abuse* of power, that is, *domination*. That is, manipulation implies the exercise of a form of *illegitimate* influence by means of discourse: manipulators make others believe or do things that are in the interest of the manipulator, and against the best interests of the manipulated (of the many studies on discourse and legitimation, see, e.g., Chouliaraki, 2005; Martín Rojo and Van Dijk, 1997).

In a broader, semiotic sense of manipulation, such illegitimate influence may also be exercised with pictures, photos, movies or other media (Van Leeuwen, 2005). Indeed, many forms of contemporary communicative manipulation, e.g. by the mass media, are multimodal, as is typically the case in advertising (Day, 1999; Messaris, 1997).

Without the negative associations, manipulation could be a form of (legitimate) persuasion (see, e.g., Dillard and Pfau, 2002; O'Keefe, 2002). The crucial difference in this case is that in persuasion the interlocutors are free to believe or act as they please, depending on whether or not they accept the arguments of the persuader, whereas in manipulation recipients are typically assigned a more passive role: they are *victims* of manipulation. This negative consequence of manipulative discourse typically occurs when the recipients are unable to understand the real intentions or to see the full consequences of the beliefs or actions advocated by the manipulator. This may be the case especially when the recipients lack the specific knowledge that might be used to resist manipulation (Wodak, 1987). A well-known example is governmental and/or media discourse about immigration and immigrants, so that ordinary citizens blame the bad state of the economy, such as unemployment, on immigrants and not on government policies (Van Dijk, 1993).

Obviously, the boundary between (illegitimate) manipulation and (legitimate) persuasion is fuzzy, and context dependent: some recipients may be manipulated by a message that is unable to manipulate others. Also the same recipients may be more or less manipulable in different circumstances, states of mind, and so on. Many forms of commercial, political or religious persuasion may formally be ethically legitimate but people may still feel manipulated by it, or critical analysts may judge such communication to be manipulating people. Provisionally, then, I shall assume that the crucial criteria are that people are being acted upon against their fully conscious will and interests, and that manipulation is in the best interests of the manipulator.

In the following theoretical account of discursive manipulation, I follow the overall multidisciplinary framework I have advocated in the last decade, triangulating a social, cognitive and discursive approach (see, e.g., Van Dijk, 1998, 2001). That is, manipulation is a social phenomenon – especially because it involves interaction and power abuse between groups and social actors – a cognitive phenomenon because manipulation always implies the manipulation of the minds of participants, and a discursive–semiotic phenomenon, because manipulation is being exercised through text, talk and visual messages. As claimed earlier, none of these approaches can be reduced to the other and all three of them are needed in an integrated theory that also establishes explicit links between the different dimensions of manipulation.

Manipulation and Society

To understand and analyse manipulative discourse, it is crucial to first examine its social environment. We have already assumed that one of the characteristics of manipulation, for instance as distinct from persuasion, is that it involves power and domination. An analysis of this power dimension involves an account of the kind of control that some social actors or groups exercise over others (Clegg, 1975; Luke, 1989; Van Dijk, 1989; Wartenberg, 1990). We also have assumed that such control is first of all a control of the mind, that is, of the beliefs of recipients, and indirectly a control of the actions of recipients based on such manipulated beliefs.

In order to be able to exercise such social control of others, however, social actors need to satisfy personal and social criteria that enable them to influence others in the first place. In this article, I limit my analysis to social criteria, and ignore the influence of psychological factors, such as character traits, intelligence, learning, etc. In other words, I am not interested here in what might be a 'manipulating personality', or in the specific personal way by which people manipulate others.

Social conditions of manipulative control hence need to be formulated – at least at the macro level of analysis – in terms of group membership, institutional position, profession, material or symbolic resources and other factors that define the power of groups and their members. Thus, parents can manipulate their children because of their position of power and authority in the family, professors can manipulate their students because of their institutional position or profession and because of their knowledge, and the same is true for politicians manipulating voters, journalists manipulating the recipients of media discourse or religious leaders manipulating their followers. This does not mean that children cannot manipulate their parents, or students their teachers, but this is not because of their position of power, but as a form of opposition or dissent, or ad hoc, on the basis of personal characteristics.

Thus, the kind of social manipulation we are studying here is defined in terms of social domination and its reproduction in everyday practices, including discourse. In this sense, we are more interested in manipulation between groups and their members than in the personal manipulation of individual social actors.

A further analysis of domination, defined as power abuse, requires special access to, or control over, scarce social resources. One of these resources is preferential access to the mass media and public discourse, a resource shared by members of 'symbolic' elites, such as politicians, journalists, scholars, writers, teachers, and so on (Van Dijk, 1996). Obviously, in order to be able to manipulate many others through text and talk, one needs to have access to some form of public discourse, such as parliamentary debates, news, opinion articles, textbooks, scientific articles, novels, TV shows, advertising, the internet, and so on. And since such access and control in turn depend on, as well as constitute, the power of a group (institution, profession, etc.), public discourse is at the same time a means of the social reproduction of such power. For instance, politicians can also exercise their political power through public discourse, and through such public discourse they at the same time confirm and reproduce their political power. The same is true for journalists and professors, and their respective institutions – the media, the universities, etc.

We see that manipulation is one of the discursive social practices of dominant groups geared towards the reproduction of their power. Such dominant groups may do so in many (other) ways as well, e.g. through persuasion, providing information, education, instruction and other social practices that are aimed at influencing the knowledge, beliefs and (indirectly) the actions of the recipients.

We have seen that some of these social practices may of course be quite legitimate, e.g. when journalists or teachers provide information for their audiences. This means that manipulation, also in accordance with what has been said before about its negative characteristics, is characterized as an illegitimate social practice because it violates general social rules or norms. We define as illegitimate all forms of interaction, communication or other social practices that are only in the interests of one party, and against the best interests of the recipients.

We here touch upon the very social, legal and philosophical foundations of a just or democratic society, and of the ethical principles of discourse, interaction and communication (see, e.g., Habermas, 1984). A further discussion of these principles, and hence an explanation of why manipulation is illegitimate, is outside the scope of this article. We assumed that manipulation is illegitimate because it violates the human or social rights of those who are manipulated, but it is not easy to formulate the exact norms or values that are violated here.

One might venture as a norm that recipients are always duly informed about the goals or intentions of the speaker. However, this would be much too strict a criterion because in many forms of communication and interaction such intentions and goals are not made explicit, but contextually attributed to speakers by recipients (or analysts) on the basis of general rules of discourse and interaction. Indeed, one might even postulate a social egoism principle, saying that (nearly) all forms of interaction or discourse tend to be in the best interests of the speakers. This means that the criteria of legitimacy must be formulated in other terms, as suggested, namely that manipulation is illegitimate because it violates the rights of recipients. This need not imply the norm that all forms of communication should be in the best interests of the recipients. Many types of communication or speech act are not, as is the case for accusations, requests, commands, and so on.

A more pragmatic approach to such norms and principles are the conversational maxims formulated by Grice (1975), which require contributions to conversations to be truthful, relevant, relatively complete, and so on. In actual forms of talk and text, however, such maxims are often hard to apply: People lie, which may not always be the wrong thing to do; people tell only half of a story for all kinds of, sometimes legitimate, reasons and irrelevant talk is one of the most common forms of everyday interaction.

In other words, manipulation is not (only) 'wrong' because it violates conversational maxims or other norms and rules of conversation, although this may be one dimension of manipulative talk and text. We therefore will accept without further analysis that *manipulation is illegitimate in a democratic society, because it (re)produces, or may reproduce, inequality*: it is in the best interests of powerful groups and speakers, and hurts the interests of less powerful groups and speakers. This means that the definition is not based on the intentions of the manipulators, nor on the more or less conscious awareness of manipulation by the recipients, but in terms of its societal consequences (see also Etzioni-Halevy, 1989).

For each communicative event, it then needs to be spelled out how such respective interests are managed by manipulative discourse. For instance, if the mass media provide incomplete or otherwise biased information about a specific politician during an election campaign so as to influence the votes of the readers, we would have a case of manipulation if we further assume that the readers have a right to be 'duly' informed about the candidates in an election. 'Due' information in this case may then further be specified as balanced, relatively complete, unbiased, relevant, and so on. This does not mean that a newspaper may not support or favour its own candidate, but it should do so with arguments, facts, etc., that is through adequate information and persuasion, and not through manipulation, for instance by omitting very important information, by lying or distorting the facts, and so on. All these normative principles, as they are also laid down in the professional codes of ethics of journalism, are part of the specific implementation of what counts as 'legitimate' forms of interaction and communication. Each of them, however, is quite vague, and in need of detailed further analysis. Again, as suggested earlier, the issues involved here belong to the *ethics of discourse*, and hence are part of the *foundations of CDA*.

This informal analysis of the social properties of manipulation also shows that if manipulation is a form of domination or power abuse, it needs to be defined in terms of *social groups, institutions* or *organizations*, and not at the individual level of personal interaction. This means that it only makes sense to speak of manipulation, as defined, when speakers or writers are manipulating others in their role as a member of a dominant collectivity. In contemporary information societies, this is especially the case for the symbolic elites in politics, the media, education, scholarship, the bureaucracy, as well as in business enterprises, on the one hand, and their various kinds of 'clients' (voters, readers, students, customers, the general public, etc.) on the other. Thus, manipulation, socially speaking, is a discursive form of elite power reproduction that is against the best interests of dominated groups and (re) produces social inequality.

Obviously, this formulation is in terms of traditional macro-level categories, such as the power of groups, organizations and institutions. Especially relevant for discourse analysis is of course also the more local, situated micro-level of social structure, that of *interaction*. Manipulation is also very fundamentally a form of social practice and interaction, and we shall therefore pay more attention to those local forms of manipulation when we discuss discursive manipulation later in this article.

Manipulation and Cognition

Manipulating people involves manipulating their minds, that is, people's beliefs, such as the knowledge, opinions and ideologies which in turn control their actions. We have seen, however, that there are many forms of discourse-based mental influence, such as informing, teaching and persuasion, that also shape or change people's knowledge and opinions. This means that manipulation needs to be distinguished from these other forms of mind management, as we have done earlier in social terms, that is, in terms of the context of discourse. In order to be able to distinguish between legitimate and illegitimate mind control, we first need to be more explicit about how discourse can 'affect' the mind in the first place.

Since the mind is extraordinarily complex, the way discourse may influence it inevitably involves intricate processes that can only be managed in real time by applying efficient strategies. For our purposes in this article, such an account will be simplified to a few basic principles and categories of cognitive analysis. There are a vast number of cognitive (laboratory) studies that show how understanding can be influenced by various contextual or textual 'manipulations', but it is beyond the scope of this article to review these (for general accounts of discourse processing, see Britton and Graesser, 1996; Kintsch, 1998; Van Dijk and Kintsch, 1983: Van Oostendorp and Goldman, 1999).

Manipulating Short Term Memory (STM)-based Discourse Understanding

First of all, discourse in general, and manipulative discourse in particular, involve processing information in the short term memory (STM), basically resulting in 'understanding' (of words, clauses, sentences, utterances and non-verbal signals) for instance in terms of propositional 'meanings' or 'actions'. Such processing is strategic in the sense of being online, goal-directed, operating at various levels of discourse structure, and hypothetical: fast and efficient guesses and shortcuts are made instead of complete analyses.

One form of manipulation consists of controlling some of this, partly automatized, strategy of discourse understanding. For instance, by printing part of the text in a salient position (e.g. on top), and in larger or bold fonts; these devices will attract more attention, and hence will be processed with extra time or memory resources, as is the case for headlines, titles or publicity slogans – thus contributing to more detailed processing and to better representation and recall. Headlines and titles also function as the conventional text category for the expression of semantic macro-structures, or topics, which organize local semantic structures; for this reason, such topics are better represented and recalled. Our point here is that specific features of text and talk – such as its visual representation – may specifically affect the management of strategic understanding in STM, so that readers pay more attention to some pieces of information than others.

Of course, this occurs not only in manipulation, but also in legitimate forms of communication, such as news reports, textbooks and a host of other genres. *This suggests that, cognitively speaking, manipulation is nothing special: it makes use of very general properties of discourse processing.* So, as was the case for the social analysis of manipulation, we need further criteria that distinguish between legitimate and illegitimate influence on the processing of discourse. Manipulation in such a case may reside in the fact that by drawing attention to information A rather than B, the resulting understanding may be partial or biased, for instance when headlines emphasize irrelevant details, rather than expressing the most important topics of a discourse – thus impairing understanding of details through top-down influence of topics. The further social condition that should be added in this case, as we have done earlier, is that such partial or incomplete understanding is in the best interests of a powerful group or institution, and against the best interests of a dominated group. Obviously, this is not a cognitive or textual condition, but a normative social and contextual one: the rights of recipients to be adequately informed. Our cognitive analysis merely spells out how people are manipulated by controlling their minds, but cannot formulate why this is *wrong*. Similar processes are at play with many forms of non-verbal expressions, such as general layout, use of colour, photos, or drawings in written conversation, or gestures, facework and other non-verbal activity in oral discourse.

Since discourse processing in STM involves such different forms of analysis as phonetic, phonological, morphological, syntactic and lexical operations, all geared towards efficient understanding, each and any of these processes of STM may be influenced by various means. For instance, more distinct, slower pronunciation, less complex syntax and the use of basic lexical items, a clear topic on a subject the recipients know well, among many other conditions, will generally tend to favour understanding.

This also means that if speakers wish to hinder understanding, they will tend to do the opposite, that is, speak faster and less distinctly, with more complex sentences and abstruse words, on a confused topic or a subject less familiar to the recipients – as may be the case, for instance, in legal or medical discourse that is not primarily geared towards better understanding by clients, and hence may assume manipulative forms when understanding is intentionally impaired.

In other words, if dominant groups or institutions want to facilitate the understanding of the information that is consistent with their interests, and hinder the comprehension of the information that is not in their best interests (and vice versa for their recipients), then they may typically engage in these forms of STM-based manipulation of discourse understanding. We see that cognitive, social, discursive and ethical dimensions are involved in this case of illegitimate hindering or biasing of the process of discourse comprehension. The ethical dimension also may involve the further (cognitive) criterion whether such control of comprehension is *intentional* or not – as is the case for the distinction between murder and manslaughter. This means that in the context models of the speakers or writers there is an explicit plan to impair or bias understanding.

Episodic Manipulation

STM-based manipulation takes place online and affects strategic processes of the understanding of specific discourses. However, most manipulation is geared to more stable results, and hence focuses on long term memory (LTM), that is, knowledge, attitudes and ideologies, as we shall see in a moment. Also forming part of LTM, however, are the personal memories that define our life history and experiences (Neisser and Fivush, 1994), representations that are traditionally associated with 'episodic' memory (Tulving, 1983). That is, our memory of communicative events – which are among our everyday experiences – is stored in episodic memory, namely as specific mental models with their own schematic structures. Telling a story means formulating the personal, subjective mental model we have of some experience. And understanding a news report or a story involves the construction of such a (subjective) mental model by the recipients.

In episodic memory, the understanding of situated text and talk is thus related to more complete models of experiences. Understanding is not merely associating meanings to words, sentences or discourses, but constructing mental models in episodic memory, including our own personal opinions and emotions associated with an event we hear or read about. It is this mental model that is the basis of our future memories, as well as the basis of further learning, such as the acquisition of experience-based knowledge, attitudes and ideologies.

Note that mental models are unique, ad hoc and personal: it is *my* individual interpretation of this particular discourse in this specific situation. Of course, such personal models also involve the 'instantiation' of general, socially shared knowledge or beliefs – so that we can actually understand other people and communication and interaction is possible in the first place – but the mental model as a whole is unique and personal. There are other notions of (mental, cognitive) models that are used to represent socially shared, cultural knowledge (see, e.g., Shore, 1996), but that is not the kind of model I am referring to here.

Mental models not only define our understanding of talk and text itself (by representing what a discourse is about), but also the understanding of the whole communicative event. Such understandings are represented in 'context models', which at the same time, for the speakers, operate as their – dynamically changing – plans for speaking (Van Dijk, 1999).

Given the fundamental role of mental models in speaking and understanding, manipulation may be expected to especially target the formation, activation and uses of mental models in episodic memory. If manipulators are aiming for recipients to understand a discourse as *they* see it, it is crucial that the recipients form the mental models the manipulators want them to form, thus restricting their freedom of interpretation or at least the probability that they will understand the discourse against the best interests of the manipulators.

We shall later examine some of the discourse strategies that are geared in this way towards the formation or activation of 'preferred' models. More generally the strategy is to discursively emphasize those properties of models that are consistent with our interests (e.g. details of our good deeds), and discursively de-emphasize those properties that are inconsistent with our interests (e.g. details of our bad deeds). Blaming the victim is one of the forms of manipulation in which dominant groups or institutions discursively influence the mental models of recipients, for instance by the re-attribution of responsibility of actions in their own interests. Any discursive strategy that may contribute to the formation or reactivation of preferred models may thus be used in manipulative discourse use. As is the case for STM processing, much model formation and activation tend to be automatized, and subtle control of mental models is often not even noticed by language users, thus contributing to manipulation.

Manipulating Social Cognition

Discursively manipulating how recipients understand one event, action or discourse is at times quite important, especially for such monumental events as the attack on the World Trade Center in New York on 11 September, 2001, or the bomb attack on Spanish commuter trains on 11 March, 2004. Indeed, in the latter case, the conservative Spanish government led by José María Aznar tried to manipulate the press and citizens into believing that the attack was committed by ETA instead of by Islamist terrorists. In other words, through his declarations as well as those of his Minister of the Interior, Acebes, Aznar wanted to influence the structure of the mental model of the event by emphasizing the preferred agent of the attack – a model that would be consistent with the government's own anti-ETA policies. Since it soon became clear that this time it was not ETA but Al Qaida that was responsible for the attack, the voters in the upcoming elections felt manipulated and voted Aznar and the government of the Partido Popular out of office.

Although these and similar events, as well as the many discourses accompanying, describing and explaining them give rise to mental models that may have a special place in episodic memory so that they are well recalled even much later, the most influential form of manipulation does not focus on the creation of specific preferred mental models, but on more general and abstract beliefs such as knowledge, attitudes and ideologies. Thus, if a political party wants to increase its popularity with the voters, it will typically try to positively change voters' attitudes towards such a party, because a general, socially shared attitude is far more stable than the specific mental models (and opinions) of individual language users. Influencing attitudes implies influencing whole groups, and on many occasions. Thus, if governments want to restrict immigration, they will try to form or modify the attitudes of citizens (including other elites) about immigration (Van Dijk, 1993; Wodak and Van Dijk, 2000). In this case, they need not engage in multiple persuasion attempts every time immigrants want to enter the country. Manipulation thus focuses on the formation or modification of more general, socially shared representations – such as attitudes or ideologies – about important social issues. For instance, governments may do so for the issue of immigration by associating increased immigration with (fears of) increasing delinquency, as former Prime Minister Aznar – as well as other European leaders – did in the past decade.

We see that the cognitive processes of manipulation assume that LTM not only stores subjectively interpreted personal experiences as mental models, but also more stable, more permanent, general and socially shared beliefs, sometimes called 'social representations' (Augoustinos and Walker, 1995; Moscovici, 2001). Our sociocultural knowledge forms the core of these beliefs, and allows us to meaningfully act, interact and communicate with other members of the same culture. The same is true for the many social attitudes and ideologies shared with other members of the same social group, e.g. pacifists, socialists and feminists, on the one hand, or racists and male chauvinists on the other (Van Dijk, 1999). These social representations are gradually acquired throughout our life time, and although they can be changed, they do not typically change overnight. They also influence the formation and activation of the personal mental models of group members. For instance, a pacifist will interpret events such as the US-led attack on Iraq, or news reports about them, in a different way from a militarist, and hence form a different mental model of such an event or sequence of events.

We have assumed that mental models on the one hand embody the personal history, experiences and opinions of individual persons, but on the other hand also feature a specific instantiation of socially shared beliefs. Most interaction and discourse is thus produced and understood in terms of mental models that combine personal and social beliefs – in a way that *both* explains the uniqueness of all discourse production and understanding, *and* the similarity of our understanding of the same text. Despite the general constraints of social representations on the formation of mental models and hence on discourse production and understanding, no two members of the same social group, class or institution, not even in the same communicative situation, will produce the same discourse or interpret a given discourse in the same way. In other words, mental models of events or communicative situations (context models) are the necessary interface between the social, the shared and the general, as well as the personal, the unique and the specific in discourse and communication.

Whereas manipulation may concretely affect the formation or change of unique personal mental models, the general goals of manipulative discourse are the control of the shared social representations of groups of people because these social beliefs in turn control what people do and say in many situations and over a relatively long period. Once people's attitudes are influenced, for instance on terrorism, little or no further manipulation attempts may be necessary in order for people to act according to these attitudes, for instance to vote in favor of antiterrorism policies (Chomsky, 2004; Sidel, 2004).

It comes as no surprise that, given the vital importance of social representations for interaction and discourse, manipulation will generally focus on social cognition, and hence on groups of people, rather than on individuals and their unique personal models. It is also in this sense that manipulation is a discursive practice that involves both cognitive and social dimensions. We should therefore pay special attention to those discourse strategies that typically influence socially shared beliefs.

One of these strategies is generalization, in which case a concrete specific example that has made an impact on people's mental models is generalized to more general knowledge or attitudes, or even fundamental ideologies. The most striking recent example is the manipulation of US and world opinion about terrorism after 9/11, in which very emotional and strongly opinionated mental models held by citizens about this event were generalized to more abstract, shared fears, attitudes and ideologies about terrorism and related issues. This is also a genuine example of massive manipulation, because the resulting social representations are not in the best interests of the citizens when such attitudes are being manipulated in order to dramatically raise military spending, legitimate military intervention and pass legislation that imposes severe restrictions on civil rights and freedoms (such as the Patriot Act). Manipulation in this case is an abuse of power because citizens are manipulated into believing that such measures are taken in order to protect them (of the many books on manipulating public opinion after the September 11 attacks in the USA, see, e.g., Ahmed, 2005; Chomsky, 2004; Greenberg, 2002; Halliday, 2002; Palmer, 2003; Sidel, 2004; Žižek, 2002).

This notorious example of national and international manipulation by the US government, partly supported and carried out by the mass media, also shows some of the cognitive mechanisms of manipulation. Thus, first of all a very emotional event with a strong impact on people's mental models is being used in order to influence these mental models as desired – for instance in terms of a strong polarization between Us (good, innocent) and Them (evil, guilty). Secondly, through repeated messages and the exploitation of related events (e.g. other terrorist attacks), such a preferred model may be generalized to a more complex and stable social representation about terrorist attacks, or even an antiterrorist ideology. Of importance in such a case is that the (real) interests and benefits of those in control of the manipulation process are hidden, obscured or denied, whereas the alleged benefits for 'all of us', for the 'nation', etc. are emphasized, for instance in terms of increased feelings of safety and security. That through anti-terrorist actions and military intervention not only the military and business corporations who produce arms and security outfits may profit, but more terrorism may actually be promoted, and hence security of the citizens further endangered, is obviously not part of the preferred attitudes that are the goals of such manipulation. Thus, one crucial cognitive condition of manipulation is that the targets (persons, groups, etc.) of manipulation are made to believe that some actions or policies are in their own interests, whereas in fact they are in the interests of the manipulators and their associates.

The examples of immigration, political violence and anti-terrorist ideologies involve strong opinions, attitudes and ideologies, and are textbook examples of governments and media manipulating the population at large, as they also were manipulated, for instance, during the 'Red scare' of anticommunist ideologies and manipulation in the Cold War and McCarthyism in the USA (Caute, 1978).

However, manipulation of social cognition may also involve the very basis of all social cognition: general, socioculturally shared *knowledge*. Indeed, one of the best ways to detect and resist manipulation attempts is specific knowledge (e.g. about the current interests of the manipulators) as well as general knowledge (e.g. about the strategies of maintaining the military budget at a high level). It will thus be in the best interests of dominant groups to make sure that relevant and potentially critical general knowledge is *not* acquired, or that only partial, misguided or biased knowledge is allowed distribution.

A well-known example of the latter strategy was the claim with which the US and its allies legitimized the attack on Iraq in 2003: 'knowledge' about weapons of mass destruction, knowledge that later turned out to be false. Information that may lead to knowledge that may be used critically to resist manipulation, for instance about the real costs of the war, the number of deaths, the nature of the 'collateral damage' (e.g. civilians killed in massive bombing and other military action), and so on, will typically be hidden, limited or otherwise made less risky, and hence discursively de-emphasized, for instance by euphemisms, vague expressions, implicitness, and so on.

Manipulation may affect social representations in many ways, both as to their contents as well as to their structures. Although as yet we know little about the internal organization of social representations, they are likely to feature schematic categories for participants and their properties as well as the typical (inter)actions they (are thought to) perform, how, when and where. Thus, attitudes about terrorist attacks may feature a script-like structure, with terrorists as main actors, associated with a number of prototypical attributes (cruel, radical, fundamentalist, etc.), using violent means (e.g. bombs) to kill innocent civilians as their victims, and so on.

Such attitudes are gradually acquired by generalization and abstraction from mental models formed by specific news stories, government declarations as well as films, among other discourses. It is important in this case that 'our' forms of political violence, such as military intervention or the actions of the police, are spoken and written about in such a way that they do not give rise to mental models that can be generalized as terrorist attacks, but as legitimate forms of (armed) resistance or punishment. And, vice versa, terrorist attacks need to be represented in such a way that no legitimation of such political violence may be construed in mental models and attitudes. The very notion of 'state terrorism' for this reason is controversial and used largely by dissidents, while blurring the distinction between illegitimate terrorist action and legitimate government and military action (Gareau, 2004). Mainstream media therefore consequently avoid describing state violence in terms of 'terrorism', not even when they are critical of the foreign policy of a country, as was the case for many European media in regard to the US attack against Iraq in 2003.

Finally, the manipulation of social cognition may affect the very norms and values used to evaluate events and people and to condemn or legitimate actions. For instance, in the manipulation of globalized world opinion, those who advocate neoliberal market ideologies will typically emphasize and try to get adopted the primary value of 'freedom', a very positive value, but in such a case specifically interpreted as the freedom of enterprise, the freedom of the market, or the freedom from government interference with the market. In the case of terrorist threats and actions, anti-terrorist discourse celebrates the value of security, assigning it a higher priority than, for instance, the value of civil rights, or the value of equality (Doherty and McClintock, 2002).

We see how the cognitive dimension of manipulation involves strategic understanding processes that affect processing in STM, the formation of preferred mental models in episodic memory, and finally and most fundamentally, the formation or change of social representations, such as knowledge, attitudes, ideologies, norms and values. Groups of people who thus adopt the social representations preferred by dominant groups or institutions henceforth barely need further manipulation: they will tend to believe and act in accordance with these – manipulated – social cognitions anyway, because they have accepted them as their own. Thus, as we have seen, racist or xenophobic ideologies, manipulated in this way by the elites, will serve as a permanent basis for the discrimination (such as blaming the victim) of immigrants: a very effective strategy for steering critical attention away from the policies of the government or other elites (Van Dijk, 1993).

Discourse

Manipulation as defined here takes place through discourse in a broad sense, that is, including non-verbal characteristics, such as gestures, facework, text layout, pictures, sounds, music, and so on. Note though that, as such, discourse structures are not manipulative; they only have such functions or effects in specific communicative situations and the way in which these are interpreted by participants in their context models. For instance, as stipulated, manipulation is a social practice of power abuse, involving dominant and dominated groups, or institutions and their clients. This means that in principle the 'same' discourse (or discourse fragment) may be manipulative in one situation, but not in another situation. That is, the manipulative meaning (or critical evaluation) of text and talk depends on the context models of the recipients – including their models of the speakers or writers, and their attributed goals and intentions. Manipulative discourse typically occurs in public communication controlled by dominant political, bureaucratic, media, academic or corporate elites. This means that further contextual constraints prevail, namely on participants, their roles, their relations and their typical actions and cognitions (knowledge, goals). In other words, *discourse is defined to be manipulative first of all in terms of the context models of the participants.* That is, as critical analysts, we evaluate discourse as manipulative first of all in terms of their context categories, rather than in terms of their textual structures.

And yet, although discourse structures per se need not be manipulative, some of these structures may be more efficient than others in the process of influencing the minds of recipients in the speaker's or writer's own interests. For instance, as suggested earlier, headlines are typically used to express topics and to signal the most important information of a text, and may thus be used to assign (extra) weight to events that in themselves would not be so important. And, vice versa, discourse about events or states of affairs that are very relevant for citizens or clients may eschew headlines that emphasize the negative characteristics of dominant groups and institutions. To wit, the press *never* publishes stories about racism in the press, let alone emphasizes such information by prominent headlines on the front page (Van Dijk, 1991).

The overall strategy of positive self-presentation and negative other-presentation is very typical in this biased account of the facts in favour of the speaker's or writer's own interests, while blaming negative situations and events on opponents or on the Others (immigrants, terrorists, youths, etc.). This strategy can be applied to the structures of many discourse levels in the usual way (for examples and detail, see, e.g., Van Dijk, 2003):

- Overall interaction strategies
  - Positive self-presentation
  - Negative other-presentation
- Macro speech act implying Our 'good' acts and Their 'bad' acts, e.g. accusation, defence
- Semantic macrostructures: topic selection
  - (De-)emphasize negative/positive topics about Us/Them

- Local speech acts implementing and sustaining the global ones, e.g. statements that prove accusations.
- Local meanings Our/Their positive/negative actions
  - Give many/few details
  - Be general/specific
  - Be vague/precise
  - Be explicit/implicit
  - Etc.
- Lexicon: Select positive words for Us, negative words for Them
- Local syntax
  - Active vs passive sentences, nominalizations: (de)emphasize Our/Their positive/negative agency, responsibility
- Rhetorical figures
  - Hyperboles vs euphemisms for positive/negative meanings
  - Metonymies and metaphors emphasizing Our/Their positive/negative properties
- Expressions: sounds and visuals
  - Emphasize (loud, etc.; large, bold, etc.) positive/negative meanings
  - Order (first, last; top, bottom, etc.) positive/negative meanings

These strategies and moves at various levels of discourse are hardly surprising because they implement the usual ideological square of discursive group polarization (de/emphasize good/bad things of Us/Them) one finds in all ideological discourse (Van Dijk, 1998, 2003). Since social–political manipulation as discussed here also involves domination (power abuse), it is likely that such manipulation is also ideological. Thus, in the manipulative discourses that followed the September 11 and March 11 terrorist attacks in New York and Madrid, nationalist, anti-terrorist, anti-Islam, anti-Arab and racist ideologies were rife, emphasizing the evil nature of terrorists, and the freedom and democratic principles of the 'civilized' nations. Thus, if Bush & Co. want to manipulate the politicians and/or the citizens in the USA into accepting going to war in Iraq, engaging in world-wide actions against terrorists and their protectors (beginning with Afghanistan), and adopting a bill that severely limits the civil rights of the citizens, such discourse would be massively ideological. That is, they do this by emphasizing 'Our' fundamental values (freedom, democracy, etc.) and contrast these with the 'evil' ones attributed to Others. They thus make the citizens, traumatized by the attack on the Twin Towers, believe that the country is under attack, and that only a "war on terrorism" can avert a catastrophe. And those who do not accept such an argument may thus be accused of being unpatriotic.

Much more detailed analyses of these discourses have shown that they are fundamentally ideological in this way, and it is likely that social–political manipulation always involves ideologies, ideological attitudes and ideological discourse structures (see the special double issue of *Discourse & Society*

15(2–3), 2004, on the discourses of September 11, edited by Jim Martin and John Edwards). If many Western European leaders, including former Prime Minister Aznar, and more recently also Tony Blair, want to limit immigration so as to increase support from the voters, then such manipulative policies and discourses are also very ideological, involving nationalist feelings, Us/ Them polarization, and a systematic negative representation of the Others in terms of negative values, characteristics and actions (delinquency, illegal entry, violence, etc.).

Although socio-political manipulation is usually ideological, and manipulative discourses often feature the usual ideological polarization patterns at all levels of analysis, the discursive structures and strategies of manipulation cannot simply be reduced to those of any other ideological discourse. Indeed, we may have social–political discourses that are persuasive but not manipulative, such as persuasive parliamentary debates or a discussion in a newspaper or on television. That is, given our analysis of the social and cognitive contexts of manipulative discourse, we need to examine the specific constraints formulated earlier, such as the dominant position of the manipulator (for instance), the lack of relevant knowledge of the recipients, and the condition that the likely consequences of the acts of manipulation are in the interest of the dominant group and against the best interests of the dominated group, thus contributing to (illegitimate) social inequality.

As suggested earlier, it is not likely that there are discursive strategies that are only used in manipulation. Language is seldom that specific – it is used in many different situations and by many different people, also by people of different ideological persuasions. That is, the same discourse structures are used in persuasion, information, education and other legitimate forms of communication, as well as in various forms of dissent.

However, given the specific social situation, there may be distinctive strategies preferred in manipulation, that is, 'manipulative prototypes'. Specific kinds of fallacies might be used to persuade people to believe or do something, for instance those that are hard to resist, such as the Authority fallacy consisting of presenting devote Catholics with the argument that the Pope believes or recommends a certain action, or addressing Muslims and pointing out that a certain action is recommended by the Koran.

We thus introduce a contextual criterion that recipients of manipulation – as a form of power abuse – may be defined as victims, and this means that somehow they need to be defined as lacking crucial resources to resist, detect or avoid manipulation. Crucially, this may involve:

(a) Incomplete or lack of relevant knowledge – so that no counter-arguments can be formulated against false, incomplete or biased assertions.
(b) Fundamental norms, values and ideologies that cannot be denied or ignored.
(c) Strong emotions, traumas, etc. that make people vulnerable.

(d) Social positions, professions, status, etc. that induce people into tending to accept the discourses, arguments, etc. of elite persons, groups or organizations.

These are typical conditions of the cognitive, emotional or social situation of the communicative event, and also part of the context models of the participants, i.e. controlling their interactions and discourses. For instance, if recipients of manipulative discourse feel afraid of a speaker, then this will be represented in their context models, and the same is true for their relative position and the power relation between them and the speaker. Conversely, in order for manipulation to be successful, speakers need to have a mental model of the recipients and their (lack of) knowledge, their ideologies, emotions, earlier experiences, and so on.

Obviously, it is not necessary for all recipients to have the ideal properties of the target of manipulation. It may be sufficient that a large group or a majority has such properties. Thus, in most real-life situations there will be critical, sceptical, cynical, incredulous or dissident people who are impervious to manipulation. But as long as these people do not dominate the mainstream means of communication, or the elite institutions and organizations, the problem of counter-discourses is less serious for the manipulators.

Again, the most typical recent example has been the US-led war against Iraq, in which the majority of the mainstream media supported the government and congress, and critical voices were effectively marginalized, especially in the USA. As soon as such dissident voices become more powerful (for instance, when part of the mainstream media supports them) and more widespread, as was the case during the war against Vietnam, manipulation functions less efficiently and finally may become useless, because the citizens have enough counter-information and arguments to resist manipulative discourse. Indeed, as was the case after the terrorist bomb attack in Madrid, citizens may resent manipulation so much that it will turn against the manipulators – and vote them out of office.

Given these contextual constraints, we may focus on those discourse structures that specifically presuppose such constraints:

(a) Emphasize the position, power, authority or moral superiority of the speaker(s) or their sources – and, where relevant, the inferior position, lack of knowledge, etc. of the recipients.
(b) Focus on the (new) beliefs that the manipulator wants the recipients to accept as knowledge, as well as on the arguments, proofs, etc. that make such beliefs more acceptable.
(c) Discredit alternative (dissident, etc.) sources and beliefs.
(d) Appeal to the relevant ideologies, attitudes and emotions of the recipients.

In sum, and in quite informal terms, the overall strategy of manipulative discourse is to focus on those cognitive and social characteristics of the recipient that make them more vulnerable and less resistant to manipulation, that make them credulous or willing victims to accept beliefs and do things they otherwise would not do. It is here that the essential condition of domination and inequality plays a role.

As formulated earlier, these general strategies of manipulative discourse appear to be largely semantic, i.e. focused on manipulating the 'content' of text and talk. However, as is the case for the implementation of ideologies, these preferred meanings may also be emphasized and de-emphasized in the usual ways, as explained: by (de-)topicalization of meanings, by specific speech acts, more or less precise or specific local meanings, manipulating explicit vs implicit information, lexicalization, metaphors and other rhetorical figures, as well as specific expression and realization (intonation, volume, speed; text layout, letter type, photos, etc.). Thus, the powerful position of the speaker may be emphasized by a very formal setting, attire, tone of voice, lexical choice, and so on, such as an official discourse of the president addressing the nation or Congress. The reliability of sources may be further enhanced by mentioning authoritative sources, using photographs, and so on – for example, the demonstration of the presence of weapons of mass destruction in Iraq. People's emotions may be roused and appealed to by specially selected words, dramatic rhetoric (hyperboles, etc.), photographs, and so on. Opponents and dissidents may be discredited by the usual display of Us/Them polarization mentioned earlier. All these discourse features of manipulation need to be examined in closer detail to see how they are formulated, how they function in text and talk and how they achieve their contextual functions and effects.

An Example: Tony Blair Legitimating the War against Iraq

Instead of continuing to theorize about these properties, however, let us examine an example of well-known manipulative discourse, e.g. when the UK Prime Minister (PM) Tony Blair in March 2003 legitimated his government's decision, in line with that of US President George W. Bush, to go to war and invade Iraq. This is a classic example that has attracted much attention in the press as well as from academic analysts from different disciplines. The case is important because until the following general elections in May 2005, Tony Blair was permanently accused of having misled UK citizens about this decision.

Examine the following initial fragment of this debate:

Extract 1

1   At the outset, I say that it is right that the House debate this issue and
    pass judgment. That is the

2 democracy that is our right, but that others struggle for in vain. Again,
  I say that I do not disrespect the
3 views in opposition to mine. This is a tough choice indeed, but it is
  also a stark one: to stand British
4 troops down now and turn back, or to hold firm to the course that we
  have set. I believe passionately
5 that we must hold firm to that course. The question most often posed
  is not "Why does it matter?" but
6 "Why does it matter so much?" Here we are, the Government, with
  their most serious test, their
7 majority at risk, the first Cabinet resignation over an issue of policy,
  the main parties internally
8 divided, people who agree on everything else –
9
10 [Hon. Members: "The main parties?"]
11
12 Ah, yes, of course. The Liberal Democrats – unified, as ever, in opportunism and error.
13

14 [Interruption.]

Tony Blair begins his speech with a well-known *captatio benevolentiae*, which at the same time is a specific move in the overall strategy of positive self-presentation, by emphasizing his democratic credentials: respect for the House and other opinions, as well as recognizing the difficulty of the choice about whether or not to go to war. The manipulative effect here consists of suggesting that the UK Parliament (still) had the right to decide about going to war, although it later became clear that this decision had already been made the previous year. In the following sentences, Blair also insists that he/we/they must 'hold firm', which is also a strategic move of positive self-presentation. And when he finally refers to his 'passionate beliefs', we see that, in addition to the rational arguments, Blair is also presenting his emotional (and hence vulnerable) side, thus emphasizing the strength of his beliefs.

He even concedes that the matter is so serious that for the first time – due to the opinions and votes, even in his own party, against the war in Iraq – his government majority is at risk. Secondly, he construes the well-known polarized opposition between Us (democracies) and Them (dictatorship), thereby politically implying that those who are opposed to the war might be accused of supporting Saddam Hussein – trying, in this way, to silence opposition. Going to war, thus, is a way of defending democracy, an implicit – fallacious – argument that is quite common in manipulation, namely by associating recipients with the enemy and hence possibly as traitors. This move is further sustained by another – ideological – move, namely that of nationalism when he refers to 'British troops' that cannot be stood down, which also politically implicates that not supporting British troops is disloyal and also a threat to the UK, democracy, and so on.

Finally, after protests from the House about mentioning only the major parties (Labour and Conservatives), he discredits the opposition of the Liberal Democrats by ridiculing them and calling them opportunistic.

We see that even in these few lines all aspects of manipulation are evident:

(a) ideological polarization (Us/Democracies vs Them/Dictatorships, nationalism, supporting the troops);
(b) positive self-presentation by moral superiority (allowing debate, respect for other opinions, struggling for democracy, holding firm, etc.);
(c) emphasizing his power, despite the opposition;
(d) discrediting the opponents, the Liberal Democrats, as being opportunistic; and
(e) emotionalizing the argument (passionate beliefs).

In sum, those who oppose the decision to go to war are implicitly being accused (and once explicitly, such as the Liberal Democrats) as being less patriotic, as being unwilling to resist dictatorship, etc.

Consider the next paragraph of Blair's speech:

Extract 2

1 The country and the Parliament reflect each other. This is a debate that, as time has gone on, has
2 become less bitter but no less grave. So why does it matter so much? Because the outcome of this issue
3 will now determine more than the fate of the Iraqi regime and more than the future of the Iraqi people
4 who have been brutalized by Saddam for so long, important though those issues are. It will determine
5 the way in which Britain and the world confront the central security threat of the 21st century, the
6 development of the United Nations, the relationship between Europe and the United States, the
7 relations within the European Union and the way in which the United States engages with the rest of
8 the world. So it could hardly be more important. It will determine the pattern of international politics
9 for the next generation.

Manipulation in this fragment becomes even more explicit. First, Blair continues his positive self-presentation by emphasizing his generosity and democratic credentials (recognizing opposition in parliament and the country).

Secondly, he rhetorically enhances the seriousness of the matter (with the litotes 'no less grave'). Thirdly, he continues the ideological polarization strategy (We/Democracy vs Them/Dictatorship). Fourthly, he uses hyperboles ('brutalized') to enhance that the Other is evil. And finally and crucially, he extends the ideological opposition between Us and Them, to an in-group of Us, Europe, the United States and the rest of the world, facing its major security threat. To summarize, what in reality is (among many other things) getting control with the USA of a key (oil) country in the Middle East, using as an excuse weapons of mass destruction and the support of terrorism, is now presented as defending the whole 'free' world against its major threat. Besides the extension of the in-group from 'Us' in the UK to the rest of the 'free' world (a move one might call 'ideological globalization'), we also witness several other hyperbolic moves to emphasize the seriousness of the situation, e.g. the extension of time: 'for the next generation'.

Thus we see that manipulative discourse focuses on several crucial and fundamental issues: the international struggle between Good and Evil, national and international solidarity, the seriousness of the situation as an international conflict, positive self-presentation as a strong ('firm') and morally superior leader, and negative other-presentation (e.g. of the opposition) as opportunistic.

In the rest of his speech, not analysed here, Blair engages in the following manipulative moves:

(a) History of the aftermath of the previous war with Iraq, the importance of the issue of the WMD, Saddam Hussein's bad intentions, and misleading UN weapons inspections, etc.
(b) Description of the WMD: anthrax, etc.
(c) Repeated expressions of doubts about Saddam Hussein's credibility.
(d) Repeated positive self-presentation: details of willingness to compromise, as being reasonable ('Again, I defy anyone to describe that as an unreasonable proposition'.)

In other words, this part is essentially what was missing in the earlier part: a detailed account of the 'historical facts', up to Resolution 1441 of the Security Council, as a legitimation to go to war.

Although this single example obviously does not present all the relevant strategies of manipulative discourse, we have found some classic examples of manipulative strategies, such as emphasizing one's own power and moral superiority, discrediting one's opponents, providing details of the 'facts', polarization between Us and Them, negative Other-presentation, ideological alignment (democracy, nationalism), emotional appeals, and so on.

Members of parliament are not exactly stupid people, and there is little doubt that they would perfectly understand many of Blair's moves of legitimation and manipulation. This means that if they are not powerless victims, and there is no consequential political inequality, we may have a form of political persuasion but not of manipulation, as stipulated earlier.

Yet, there is a crucial point where parliament and the opposition are less powerful than the government: they lack the crucial information, e.g. of the secret services, about the WMD, in order to be able to accept the legitimacy of the invasion of Iraq. Secondly, the Labour majority in the House, even when many of them opposed the invasion of Iraq – as did the majority of the British people – can hardly reject Blair's motion without putting the Labour government at risk. We know that only a few Labour politicians openly defied the party leadership, and thus were willing to risk losing their jobs. Thirdly, such a rejection would also mean defying the USA and damaging the friendship between the UK and the USA. Fourthly, no one in the House can morally defend showing any lack of solidarity with British troops abroad – and hope to get re-elected. Finally, withholding support for this motion could indeed be (and has been) explained as defending Saddam Hussein: a double bind or Catch 22 situation in which those on the left wing in particular, who are most explicitly engaged in the struggle against dictatorships, can hardly disagree with the manipulative argument.

In this specific case, we see that some relevant context properties of this speech help us to distinguish between manipulation and legitimate persuasion, although in real life the two kinds of mind control overlap. That is, many of the strategies used may also be applied in perfectly legitimate political rhetoric in parliament. However, in this case of what is defined as a national and international emergency, even a powerful parliament like that of the UK may be manipulated into accepting the Prime Minister's policy of joining the USA in what is presented as a war against tyranny and terrorism. Both contextually (the speaker as leader of the Labour party and PM, the recipients as MPs and British, etc.) as well as textually, Blair defines the situation in such a way that few MPs *can* refuse, even when they know they are being manipulated and probably lied to.

In sum, the MPs are 'victims' of the political situation in several ways, and can thus be manipulated, as happened in the USA and Spain, by those in power. By accepting the reasons provided by Blair in his speech legitimating the war, they are manipulated not only into accepting specific beliefs, e.g. on international security, but also into the concrete act of accepting the motion and thereby sending troops to Iraq.

Final Remark

In this article, we have taken a multidisciplinary approach to an account of discursive manipulation. In order to distinguish such discourse from other forms of influence, we first *socially* defined it as a form of power abuse or domination. Secondly, we focused on the *cognitive* dimensions of manipulation by identifying what exactly the 'mind control' dimension of manipulation means. And finally, we analysed the various *discursive* dimensions of manipulation by focusing on the usual polarized structures of positive self-presentation and negative other presentation expressing ideological conflict. In addition, we found that manipulation involves: enhancing the power, moral superiority and credibility of the speaker(s), and discrediting dissidents, while vilifying the Others, the enemy; the use of emotional appeals; and adducing seemingly irrefutable proofs of one's beliefs and reasons. Future work will need to provide much more detail about the discursive, cognitive and social aspects of manipulation.

References

Ahmed, N.M. (2005) *The War on Truth: 9/11: Disinformation, and the Anatomy of Terrorism*. New York: Olive Branch Press.

Augoustinos, M. and Walker, I. (1995) *Social Cognition: An Integrated Introduction*. London: Sage.

Britton, B.K. and Graesser, A.C. (eds) (1996) *Models of Understanding Text*. Mahwah, NJ: Erlbaum.

Caute, D. (1978) *The Great Fear: The Anti-Communist Purge under Truman and Eisenhower*. London: Secker and Warburg.

Chomsky, N. (2004) *Hegemony or Survival: America's Quest for Global Dominance*. New York: Henry Holt.

Chouliaraki, L. (2005) 'The Soft Power of War: Legitimacy and Community in Iraq War Discourses', special issue of *Journal of Language and Politics* 4(1).

Clegg, S. (1975) *Power, Rule, and Domination: A Critical and Empirical Understanding of Power in Sociological Theory and Organizational Life*. London: Routledge & Kegan Paul.

Day, N. (1999) *Advertising: Information or Manipulation?* Springfield, NJ: Enslow.

Dillard, J.P. and Pfau, M. (2002) *The Persuasion Handbook: Developments in Theory and Practice*. Thousand Oaks, CA: Sage.

Doherty, F. and McClintock, M. (2002) *A Year of Loss: Reexamining Civil Liberties since September 11*. New York: Lawyers Committee for Human Rights.

Edwards, J. and Martin, J.R. (eds) (2004) Interpreting tragedy: the language of 11 September 2001. Special issue. *Discourse & Society* 15(2–3).

Etzioni-Halevy, E. (1989) *Fragile Democracy: The Use and Abuse of Power in Western Societies*. New Brunswick, NJ: Transaction.

Gareau, F.H. (2004) *State Terrorism and the United States: From Counterinsurgency to the War on Terrorism*. Atlanta, GA: Clarity Press.

Greenberg, B.S. (ed.) (2002) *Communication and Terrorism: Public and Media Responses to 9/11*. Cresskill, NJ: Hampton Press.

Grice, H. (1975) 'Logic and Conversation', in P. Cole and J. Morgan (eds) *Syntax and Semantics*, Vol. 3: *Speech Acts*, pp. 68–134. New York: Academic Press.

Habermas, J. (1984) *The Theory of Communicative Action*. Boston, MA: Beacon Press.

Halliday, F. (2002) *Two Hours that Shook the World: September 11, 2001: Causes and Consequences*. London: Saqi.

Kintsch, W. (1998) *Comprehension: A Paradigm for Cognition*. Cambridge: Cambridge University Press.

Luke, T.W. (1989) *Screens of Power: Ideology, Domination, and Resistance in Informational Society*. Urbana: University of Illinois Press.

Martín Rojo, L.M. and Van Dijk, T.A. (1997) 'There Was a Problem, and It Was Solved: Legitimating the Expulsion of Illegal Migrants in Spanish Parliamentary Discourse', *Discourse & Society* 8(4): 523–66.

Messaris, P. (1997) *Visual Persuasion: The Role of Images in Advertising*. Thousand Oaks, CA: Sage.

Moscovici, S. (2001) *Social Representations: Explorations in Social Psychology*. New York: New York University Press.

Neisser, U. and Fivush, R. (eds) (1994) *The Remembering Self: Construction and Accuracy in the Self-Narrative*. Cambridge: Cambridge University Press.

O'Keefe, D.J. (2002) *Persuasion: Theory & Research*. Thousand Oaks, CA: Sage.

Palmer, N. (ed.) (2003) *Terrorism, War, and the Press*. Teddington, Middlesex: Hollis.

Shore, B. (1996) *Culture in Mind: Cognition, Culture, and the Problem of Meaning*. New York: Oxford University Press.

Sidel, M. (2004) *More Secure, Less Free? Antiterrorism Policy & Civil Liberties after September 11*. Ann Arbor: University of Michigan Press.

Tulving, E. (1983) *Elements of Episodic Memory*. Oxford: Oxford University Press.

Van Dijk, T.A. (1989) 'Structures of Discourse and Structures of Power', in J.A. Anderson (ed.) *Communication Yearbook* 12, pp. 18–59. Newbury Park, CA: Sage.

Van Dijk, T.A. (1991) *Racism and the Press*. London: Routledge.

Van Dijk, T.A. (1993) *Elite Discourse and Racism*. Newbury Park, CA: Sage.

Van Dijk, T.A. (1996) 'Discourse, Power and Access', in C.R. Caldas-Coulthard and M. Coulthard (eds) *Texts and Practices: Readings in Critical Discourse Analysis*, pp. 84–104. London: Routledge.

Van Dijk, T.A. (1998) *Ideology: A Multidisciplinary Approach*. London: Sage.

Van Dijk, T.A. (1999) 'Context Models in Discourse Processing', in H. van Oostendorp and S.R. Goldman (eds) *The Construction of Mental Representations during Reading*, pp. 123–48. Mahwah, NJ: Erlbaum.

Van Dijk, T.A. (2001) 'Multidisciplinary CDA: A Plea for Diversity', in Ruth Wodak and Michael Meyer (eds) *Methods of Critical Discourse Analysis,* pp. 95–120. London: Sage.

Van Dijk, T.A. (2003) *Ideología y discurso*. Barcelona: Ariel.

Van Dijk, T.A. and Kintsch, W. (1983) *Strategies of Discourse Comprehension*. New York: Academic Press.

Van Leeuwen, T. (2005) *Introducing Social Semiotics*. London: Routledge.

Van Oostendorp and S.R. Goldman (eds) (1999) *The Construction of Mental Representations during Reading*. Mahwah, NJ: Erlbaum.

Wartenberg, T.E. (1990) *The Forms of Power: From Domination to Transformation*. Philadelphia, PA: Temple University Press.

Wodak, R. (1987) '"And Where Is the Lebanon?" A Socio-Psycholinguistic Investigation of Comprehension and Intelligibility of News', *Text* 7(4): 377–410.

Wodak, R. and Van Dijk, T.A. (eds) (2000) *Racism at the Top: Parliamentary Discourses on Ethnic Issues in Six European States*. Klagenfurt: Drava Verlag.

Žižek, S. (2002) *Welcome to the Desert of the Real! Five Essays on 11 September and Related Dates*. London: Verso.

66

Performing Success: Identifying Strategies of Self-Presentation in Women's Biographical Narratives

Ina Wagner and Ruth Wodak

Introduction

Twenty-five years ago Georgia Sassen examined the notion of women's presumed success anxiety. Building on the work of Carol Gilligan and others she argued that women 'are unable to take competitive success and construct around it a vision, a new way of making sense, to which they can feel personally committed' (Sassen, 1980: 18). According to Sassen, there is an incompatibility between competitive, isolated success, achieved without the cooperation of others, and meaning structures that are particular to women. She also asserts that in institutions that build upon these kinds of success, women tend to experience frustration and anxiety.

Analysing biographical material collected in several research projects,[1] we asked ourselves what has changed since feminist researchers discussed the difficulties women face in thinking about themselves/perceiving themselves as successful professionals. Our approach is resonant with what Kellner (1995) and Fenwick (2002) among others have stated 'that one must study the complex and sometimes contradictory interweaving of people's shifting desires and identities, the texts and activities in which they participate, and their own representations and understandings of these relations' (Fenwick, 2002: 166).

Source: *Discourse & Society*, 17(3) (2006): 385–411

We selected eight biographies for our analysis. In four cases we also observed the women at work over several weeks (Wagner, 2003; Wagner and Birbaumer, 2005). These biographies represent different life story patterns of highly professional women in different stages of their lives and different discursive strategies of self-representation. The focus on self-presentation is important to emphasize as, in some cases, we will point to salient contrasts between the images these women project and perform and their actual behaviour when observed. All the women are between 35 and 45 years old, hence not at the beginning of their careers. Three of the women work in the IT sector (small multimedia companies, a partner in a small software company), two in the financial sector (a senior manager in a specialized bank, the owner of a small accounting firm), and three are architects and partners in small architectural firms (see Table 1).

This choice of women and areas of work was also motivated by our interest in diversity and change – of professional roles, competences, organizational forms, and (gendered) cultures. Multimedia production and architecture represent two design disciplines. Multimedia is considered a new-economy type of workplace in search of a specific identity and profile while architecture is a classical male profession which is in transition, due to the increasing complexity of requirements and the erosion of what has often been seen as the universalist role of the architect (Winch and Schneider, 1993). In financial services (in our case, mergers and acquisitions transactions), specialization as a strategy attracts a new type of professional who combines domain knowledge with competence in coaching and counselling. Accounting firms also need to define new territories and legitimize their special role, with clients having more and more access to accounting software and knowledge. Despite being diverse, these areas of work share certain features, among them the increasing complexity of work, a focus on distinctive expertise and creative solutions, the importance of client relationships, and the turbulent and highly competitive character of their environment (Jones et al., 1998). All three areas are considered to be male dominated, although we tend to find an increasing share of women in responsible positions.

As we will show, the women selected for our analysis represent and reflect relevant aspects of these characteristics. They are neither separable from nor neutral towards the organizational cultures which they find in their field. We analyse the women's narratives and self-images against the background of these cultures, trying to understand why and how they absorb and reflect, critically examine, fight against or rewrite them, or why they want to be seen and perceived in certain ways.[2] Moreover, as our interviewees are all integrated in specific organizational contexts, we attempt to illustrate how these contexts and their latent or explicit values and ideologies intrude interdiscursively into their performances.

Table 1: The women selected for the study – an overview

Name/ Field Organization/position, background (Previous jobs)	Biographical note
Maria Project manager (PM), multimedia company BA Economics & Liberal Arts, Training PM, MBA in technology (advertising & marketing company)	*Maria comes from India, works in a highly successful design-oriented multi-media company, under considerable pressure, where work is often enacted as 'drama'. Coaching is a central aspect of Maria's work as a PM – she defines herself as an 'enabler'. She frequently complains that she is not able to meet her standards of quality in a constraining, hectic environment with a premium on speed.*
Susi Partner in small software company MA in Computer Science (research assistant at university)	*Susi is one of the four self-employed women in our sample. She is one of two directors of a small software company and responsible for financial planning – budgeting, controlling – and software development, with her male co-director focusing on project acquisition.*
Sissy Director's assistant in small multimedia company Theatre and journalism without degree (theatre companies, production manager and assistant to director, PR agency)	*Sissy comes from the free art scene, having studied but never completed a degree in journalism and performing arts. She tells the story of her career as having been driven by chance encounters and offers. She currently works as the 'right hand' of the owner of a highly successful multimedia company specializing in film and CD production. Writing is a hobby and an outlet for Sissy, it may even offer an alternative future.*
Chris Director/owner of small accounting firm MA in Business Administration, additional training in transaction analysis, business mediation, therapies, etc. (accounting firm)	*The Human Money Company – this is the name that Chris chose for her company, a small accounting office. Chris talks of her company as being 'unconventional'. She sees herself as a member of a team which takes decisions cooperatively. In the meantime she herself only does consulting and has no fixed working times in the office. Another unusual factor is the friendly, almost family-like atmosphere in the company.*
Claire Department leader in specialized bank MA and PhD in Business Administration ((political) adviser/member of cabinet in Ministry)	*Claire entered a bank specializing in acquisition and merger activities in 1983, after having completed her doctorate in business studies and only left it for a short episode in politics – 'a wonderful experience'. When she returned, she was asked to merge three departments into one, re-define responsibilities, unify processes, and shape 'the culture and people's attitudes'.*
Mary Architect, partner in architectural firm MA in Architecture, Civil Engineer	*Mary runs a very successful office with her partner. It took them 10 years of hard work in a small flat with hardly any projects and little encouragement to get to where they are now. Mary is a dedicated architect and when she talks about herself, she talks architecture.*
Eva Architect, partner in architectural firm MA in Architecture	*Eva is the co-founder of one of the highly successful young practices in Vienna. The group also assures her future with a child. She trusts that she will be able to combine work and caring for her child, to work a bit less without endangering the quality of the group's projects.*
Jane Architect, partner in architectural firm MA Architecture (assistant in architectural firm)	*Jane is one of four partners in a successful architectural firm. This is a company that relies on teamwork, has developed a strong meeting culture and dedicates a lot of resources to building organizational structures and planning competence, on all levels. This is to a great extent due to Jane, who took over responsibility for the company's organizational development and finances.*

Theoretical Background

(Linguistic) Gender Studies has focused primarily on differences between the biological sexes for a long time; much research was (and still is) devoted to illustrating the domination of women by men in organizations, conversations, media, education, and so forth.[3] However, more recently, the focus of research has shifted to investigating the range of constructions/performances of female gender identities and female leadership in various professions and social fields. Sunderland (2004) states that 'gender can be *constructed, performed, represented* and *indexed*' (p. 22, emphasis in original). Later, she continues: 'Associated with social constructionism and poststructuralism, *construction* and *performance* are members of the same field. Lexical variations include *accomplish, achieve* and *enact*' (p. 23). Buchholtz (1999) describes language as '*effecting* gender' . . . "*Performance*" – which goes beyond language – de-privileges the idea of *identity*' (Sunderland, 2004: 23); see also Butler (1999[1990]).

In recent years research has changed focus, from analysing the representation of women in the media and elsewhere and their impact (in conversations) on forms of gendered discourses and on ways in which gender is constructed discursively or visually, and performed (for example, on stage and in conversations). This shift implies a different approach to gender and sex, both of which are seen by Judith Butler as inherent to interaction and not as given by nature. This approach rejects essentialism and claims that women and men alike have a choice of how to express themselves in discourses and how to perform the gender roles in which they would like to be perceived (see also Cammack and Kalmbach Phillips, 2002). However, agency can also be backgrounded, neglected or even absent fron the text (these are terms used by Van Leeuwen, 1996).

In our opinion, this approach grasps relevant issues which become apparent from research into female leadership and successful women. In positions of power, there are fewer constraints regulating behaviour, and the space for enactment becomes larger. However, in less powerful positions, constraints prevail. The notions of performance and of 'doing gender' tend to reflect the living conditions of the privileged elites (see also Kotthoff and Wodak, 1997; Wodak, 1997a). This is why, in our analysis, we strongly emphasize the *material dimension* of women's lives. Moreover, we make clear that the local, individual performance of biography and identity that we observe and analyse always reflects and presupposes more general cultural, professional and structural patterns.

The richness of empirical studies on women in different professions is impressive. We find studies on women working in schools (Wodak, 1997b), administrative workplaces (Kendall and Tannen, 1997), large companies (Martín Rojo and Esteban, 2003), management (Tomlinson et al., 1997; Liff and Ward, 2001), medical professions and hospitals (Nonnemaker, 2004;

Smulyan, 2004), universities (Diem-Wille, 1996), computing (Valenduc et al., 2004, Birbaumer et al., 2006), construction industries (Greed, 2000), engineering and manufacturing (Greene et al., 2002; Miller, 2002), legal professions (Coontz, 1995), and politics (Moosmüller, 1997; Wodak, 2003a, 2005a). The multimodal analysis of representation of women in the media illustrates the ideal gender types in different cultures and societies (Machin and Van Leeuwen, 2003). Although we cannot review the extensive literature in this article, it is necessary to summarize a few relevant issues which have a bearing on our research.

First, research points to a variety of gendered aspects of professional roles. One example is leadership roles. A study of school principals identified three different models of leadership when analysing tape-recorded meetings in various high schools in Vienna, Austria: a 'caring motherly role', an 'authoritarian hierarchical role', and an 'efficient managerial role' (Wodak, 1997b). Moreover, as Diem-Wille (1996) shows, women university professors and managers believed their careers to have been shaped by accident and coincidence, while men seemed to have ambitiously set themselves clear goals (see also Licht and Dweck, 1984). Men reported and narrated in an active way, women more passively. In the field of politics, for example in the European Parliament, female MEPs told exciting anecdotes about their successful interventions but there were marked national/cultural differences between MEPs from Scandinavia and the Mediterranean countries. Some of them emphasized that only finding a niche ('being an exotic bird') allowed them to carry out their work successfully because they would not threaten male colleagues (Wodak, 2003a).

In other fields, for example computing, the diversity of professional trajectories and 'life-story patterns' stands out. Some women follow a clear career model, striving to reach the top, accepting the conditions for success in ICT, including long hours, stressful working conditions, a competitive environment, and hierarchical structures. Some informants' stories show a strong will and skill at shaping their own environment so that it fits their idea of good work and a good life. These women define themselves through the content of their work (Birbaumer et al., 2006). Some of the women describe a crisis and how it shaped their decision to change something in their life. The notion of crisis is close to fate, to some predetermined event. However, the women portray their decisions as having been made voluntarily.

Second, we find a 'double discourse', which, on the one hand, promotes democratic models of management, consistent with prevalent democratic and egalitarian ideologies but, on the other hand, masks the permanence of traditional models, which have been only partially and superficially updated (see also Baxter, 2003). An example of 'double voicing' is given by (Martín Rojo and Gomez-Esteban, 2003). If the women managers they studied were caring and flexible, they were perceived as weak; if they were more efficient and hierarchical, they were viewed as tough and male. In both cases, women were not respected.

Third, when new regulations of gender mainstreaming are implemented, organizations may develop subtle ways of avoiding these guidelines. In comparing reference letters written for female and male applicants for high positions in medical faculties, Trix and Psenka (2003) were able to illustrate the different ways that prominent professors formulated their letters which highlighted research in the case of male applicants and teaching in the case of female applicants (research is usually valued more highly).

Fourth, research into media representations of successful women, such as the ones to be found in the magazine *Cosmopolitan* reveals a narrow set of *topoi* across languages and cultures: the adoration of youth; values related to beauty; values related to success as being efficient but also feminine; an image of a self-assured, but also non-threatening leadership role. Koller (2005), in her analysis of business magazines (e.g. *Business Week*), which portray representations of female executives was able to illustrate how conventional conceptual frames ('playing the game', 'being at war', 'market as conversation' and so forth) construct forms of a new hegemonic masculinity ('executives' are 'soldiers', for example). The magazines described women, relatively more often than men, in terms of a war metaphor.

Finally we see a strong connection between women's careers, their strategies of self-presentation and the culture of the organizations or professional fields in which they work. Davies (1996) argues that professions exhibit a 'gendered substructure' in the same way as work organizations do. Acker (1992) introduced this notion to describe the dynamic of gender relations in organizations, as something that mirrors the gender relations within society but at the same time is in flux, changing with the mix of people, skills, and tasks. Gherardi (1996) studied women pioneers in male occupations, inviting them to perform their identity through telling their stories. She identifies different ways in which the host culture and the women position themselves in relation to each other. A woman-friendly culture, she argues, 'extends an invitation which: (a) may be gratefully accepted – a cooperative position; (b) may not be understood – a mismatched position; (c) may be forced but open-ended' (p. 199). In a woman-hostile culture, women may hold a stigmatized, contested or a unilaterally enforced position. In her study of women in the oil industry, Miller (2002) emphasizes myths (the frontier, the cowboy hero) that are deeply embedded in the industry's cultural assumptions and that have powerful effects on people's everyday behaviour. Conditions seem to be similar in the construction industry, in particular the tougher site-related jobs, which Greed (2000) characterizes as 'fortress-like settings' that are occupied by 'male-dominated tribes'. But even in the legal professions where the number of women has increased dramatically over the last 20 years or so, gender enters into day-to-day interactions. Not only are the prototypes of lawyers predominantly male but the schemas that explain success in the professions are associated with male attributes and so are the scripts that set the norms of professional interaction. Coontz (1995) found that female characteristics such as 'being pregnant' or 'a shrill voice' eclipse women's competence in court, their 'good looks' being translated into 'distraction' by the opposing attorney, and judges being impatient with female attorneys, interrupting them, looking bored, or cutting short an argument.

In view of all this recent research, we claim that Gender Studies needs an interdisciplinary framework to be able to grasp this complexity of phenomena just outlined: issues of organizational studies, gender studies, linguistics, cultural studies, media studies, discourse studies and political sciences overlap and influence each other. Several research questions are generated by these findings:

- How do the women define success? What are their criteria of success, which aspects of their work and which particular events do they experience as contributing to being successful? How do successful women perform their achievements in their stories and in relationship to the interviewer?
- What are women's strategies for presenting themselves, their career decisions, their personal relationship with work and colleagues, crises at work or in their personal lives, and how do they respond to them? How do the discursively constructed and performed self-presentations relate to their own definitions of success as well as to widespread social stereotypes about successful/career women?
- Although more women have achieved higher status in their professions, do subtle (and also manifest) procedures of discrimination still exist? Are their biographies shaped by the 'gendered substructures' of the professions and/or organizations in which they work? Are these substructures visible in how successful women relate their stories?
- Since even in leading positions women are confronted with 'double discourses', do they still have to justify their presence and their achievements constantly and are they still measured against different norms? Do women relate similar experiences?

Methodology

The aim of a biographical interview is to develop an understanding of a person's biography or trajectory – her development as based on opportunities, choices, and individual coping strategies. Biographical research was emphasized in particular by the Chicago school of qualitative sociology (e.g. Glaser and Strauss, 1971). It was and is mostly used to understand people's sometimes life-long struggles with particular problems (e.g. a disability, being an outsider) or crises (e.g. unemployment, migration) or to understand historical events – how they were experienced, have shaped people's lives and are remembered. A more recent notion that stimulated the examination of biographical forms is that of the self as a 'reflexive project' (Lash and Urry, 1994; Beck and Beck-Gernsheim, 2002). We use it here as a method for learning more about the still fairly rare situation of women in a particular field or profession, to dig through the maze of assumptions and prejudices surrounding such a situation, and to do this from the perspective of the women themselves.

The most common method for unravelling biographical information is the narrative interview. Although parts of the interview may be pre-structured, particularly the parts that relate to the main facts of a person's biography, most of the interview is conducted in an open way. They are what Flick (1995) calls 'episodic interviews' with a strong narrative character. The main idea is to stimulate a person to tell stories – significant episodes in her life that illustrate why and how certain events are significant in her biography, and the role of relevant others in these events. Normally the interviewee covers several topics in her narration in her own order. A good narrative interview also allows for a certain amount of reflection, supporting a person in remembering, making connections, evaluating, regretting or rejoicing. From the perspective of discourse analysis, these stories are analysed for their narrative structure, the roles of social actors, and the argumentative strategies deployed to establish a certain coherence which the interviewee consciously constructs as *the image* which they want to transfer to the audience (the interviewer) – the enacted performance. Bourdieu (1994) even talks of the 'biographical illusion' which describes life as a coherent path according to culturally available interpretive patterns and images. This is precisely what we sought to avoid. It was our explicit aim to dig up the detours, confusions, and contradictions in the women's seemingly coherent biographies.

Moreover, the situative context has to be taken into account: Biographical interviews are constructed from the interviewee's present social position and life situation and coloured by it, as well as by the interview situation itself and the interpretive frameworks that are operative: 'When interviewees report on experience, they do so from different social positions and in greater or lesser agreement with recognizable cultural scripts' (Järvinen, 2000: 386).

In our analysis of the biographical material we pursued a variety of methods.

On the one hand, we identified *macro-topics* related to success which became apparent in all interviews, albeit in different phases of the narratives (see Van Dijk, 2001). The macro-topics were used to structure the narratives, either in a temporal/chronological way, or in an event-related way. We illustrate these topics with relevant sequences from the interviews. On the other hand, we were interested in the discursive strategies of positive self-presentation (Reisigl and Wodak, 2001),[4] focusing primarily on the use of metaphors, the role of social actors, argumentative strategies, cohesion devices, and transitivity, amongst other indicators. By 'strategy', we generally mean

> a more or less accurate and more or less intentional plan of practices (including discursive practices) adopted to achieve a particular social, political, psychological or linguistic aim. As far as the discursive strategies are concerned, that is to say, systematic ways of using language, we locate them at different levels of linguistic organization and complexity. (Wodak, 2003b: 139)

We define *topoi* as 'parts of argumentation that belong to the obligatory premises. They are content-related warrants or "conclusion rules" that connect the argument with the conclusion' (Reisigl and Wodak, 2001: 74–5).

Discursive strategies of positive self-presentation relate to five dimensions of textual realizations:

1. How do the interviewees label themselves?
2. Which characteristics do they attribute to success in general and to their own success?
3. Which arguments are positioned and constructed to justify these views? Which *topoi* are used consistently? Do their descriptions match public images? Are stereotypes used? Are traditional metaphors used or even new ones created?
4. From which perspective do our interviewees narrate their experiences?
5. Are these self-presentations intensified or mitigated?

One important aspect of our analysis, apart from metaphors, *topoi* and genres, is the representation of 'social actors'. Van Leeuwen (1996) offers an elaborate and powerful framework for analysing the representations of social actors in discourses – a hierarchically arranged set of abstract categories which are in part social and in part discursive (p. 32). Agency is a sociological category which is not always realized by linguistic agency, argues Van Leeuwen. There is no one-to-one relation between social and linguistic categories – a lack of bi-uniqueness (p. 35). We focus primarily on which social actors are represented (included) and which are excluded; moreover, how concrete or abstract actors are realized. Both dimensions are salient because suppressed, absent or excluded agency usually indicates some problematic positioning of the speaker. Similarly, personal or general, concrete or abstract agencies – for example the use of personal or impersonal pronouns – point to degrees of identification.

Van Leeuwen lists linguistic features which are indicative of suppression or backgrounding of social actors; we use some of these in our own analysis. The most common backgrounding features we found in our interviews are use of nominal/nominalization and passive agent deletion.

When analysing macro-topics related to success and women's discursive strategies we tried to preserve the narrative flow and to interweave it with contextual information (which was captured through the interviews and observations) rather than presenting the analysis step by step for each woman or even textual sequence. (Such a systematic analysis was, of course, the pre-requisite for the following summary and interdisciplinary approach.) Quotes are mainly used as illustrations of particular *topoi*, metaphors, social actors, narrative structures, and argumentative strategies, and for conveying some of the richness and vividness of the women's accounts.

Success: Multiple Understandings

In the following section, we combine content-oriented and discourse-analytical approaches in applying the two methodologies (i.e. re-constructing the narrative flow and de-constructing strategies of self-presentation) out-lined earlier, while using the clustered macro-topics (themes) of 'defining success' to organize sequences from our interviews.

Theme 1: Building and 'Place-Making' – Creativity

All women define themselves as 'builders' – of spaces, competences, organiza-tions (in some cases with an emphasis on entrepreneurship) or high-quality products. The metaphors of 'building' and 'defining and constructing their own space' are closely connected with what they describe as their passion. For the architects among our interviewees, 'building' is strongly related to their profession. They talk about their success through descriptions of their buildings – the spaces they design – and success is when their designs have achieved a particular spatial quality ('topic-triggered metaphor'). Mary designs spaces that have a clear geometry, create transitions between inside and outside, and reflect the environment. She says:

> . . . I'm interested in complexity, and the essence of complexity translated into a simple form, thus superimposing things, shifting them. Well I'm sure we're not that expressive and all that. We do look for clear geometry, and have a certain way of understanding space . . . It's about spatiality, it's about outside space, inside space, the relationship between them, about transitions, about sort of public–private, urbanity, ambivalence, these are things that interest us.

In her definition of 'complexity', Mary lays out a whole semantic space in deictic terms ('inside–outside', 'clear–complex') as well as in structural dichotomies ('public–private'). Even in this very short sequence there is a shift in narrative perspective in two directions: from personal to general and from the content-level to a meta-level. Mary deconstructs the meaning of complexity for her and them ('we'). She addresses the ambivalence created by the dichotomies of inside/outside, public/private by emphasizing fluidity ('transitions'). A short declarative statement denying 'expressivity and all that' serves rhetorically and argumentatively to reject any stereotypes about architects and their suggested intuitivism. Mary uses material verbs (verbs of doing), with strong explicit evaluations of taking pride in their work ('super'), the verbs producing a sense of activeness. The way in which she describes transitions between (architectural) spaces may be read as a metaphor for the individual (body) space.

As can be seen in another short extract from Mary's narrative, implementing a building and seeing how it is appropriated and inhabited is an 'incredible' experience:

> And that gets superimposed on things that you only see when the building has been erected, or when the space, that actually brings another level to it. And I think this is actually the interesting thing and there are always new ways of seeing it . . . But that is very interesting for us . . . whether it is the use, whether these rooms will be accepted in the way that we expected. That is of course the great thing about the X project, that we were able to enliven a whole part of a city. It simply worked . . . And there was nothing there before, it was dead. And that this worked, I mean that's really, that is simply incredible.

Mary uses vivid images and metaphors ('enliven a whole part of a city', 'it was dead'), as well as positive, evaluative adjectives. The dialogic explanation of what it means to build suggests enormous power – the power of transforming something dead into something which is alive. Moreover, she suggests risk and adventure in a scenic form, using questions addressed to the interviewer and a wider, anonymous audience. The coda of the story – 'it simply worked' – is realized impersonally and agent-less, as if there were no actors and no stressful and long planning involved, both of which can only be contextually inferred. The performance makes the audience believe that building 'simply works' is unpredictable and 'incredible'. This story is a good example of the attempt to construct an 'event model' (a cognitive script of an event, process, occasion; see later) which contradicts the everyday knowledge of the difficulties of building processes and suppresses social actors.

The younger Eva compares creating architecture to 'giving birth' (she was close to giving birth at the time of the interview). She also alludes to the grandiose experience of getting something built, of getting things moving, getting them into a three-dimensional space. This resonates with another aspect in women's descriptions of success. It has to do with 'place-making'. Place-making is a material process; it is to do with shaping one's environment for particular projects, activities, and interactions; it also means colonizing space, making it one's own. It also implies 'being independent'.

Place-making – transforming perceptions and ideas (designs) into materiality (Iedema, 2003) – is an example of re-semiotization.

Chris expresses her identity through place-making. Her accounting office resembles a living space, with every minor detail designed by her. Each room has its own character, its own colour, lighting, the colour of the folders, the paintings on the walls (many of her clients are artists and sometimes they pay with their own work), a sofa, plants creating a particular atmosphere. All materials carry the firm's logo and web address. The office not only reflects her idea of how to make people (co-workers, clients) feel comfortable but it also strongly signals her identity – a place that combines comfort and aesthetic values with a concern for money; it also speaks of her power to design at will.

Chris's carefully designed office spaces illustrate that place-making is also about creating the conditions for success and this is strongly connected to entrepreneurship. Place-making may be practised on different levels – from literally furnishing a place to organization building and finally to nourishing what Hedman (2003) calls 'incorporeal places'. In the women's accounts, place-making (furnishing) and building become a form of discursive self-presentation. This relates well with cognitive semantics which argues that spatial metaphors are the most basic ones we have and that they are embodied, i.e. expressed by humans experiencing their bodies moving through space (Lakoff and Johnson, 1998).

Theme 2: The Right Emotional Environment

Denise Scott Brown (1989) describes the most outrageous forms of discrimination she was exposed to when she was getting married to Robert Venturi:

> These experiences have caused me to fight, suffer doubt and confusion, and expend too much energy. 'I would be *pleased* if my work were attributed to my husband', says the wife of an architect. And a colleague asked, 'Why do you worry about these things? We know you're good. You know your real role in your office and in teaching. Isn't that enough?' I doubt whether it would be enough for my male colleagues. (p. 239)

With the younger generations of architects we found strong notions of success as being shared (rather than individual), of depending on building emotional bonds with and trust in partners and colleagues, and, more generally, linked to the explicit expression of positive emotions and having fun. Being a successful architect is no longer defined as individual stardom but as being part of a successful group. This resonates with, among others, findings by Schlosser (2001) who reports that the eminent Finnish women she interviewed all emphasized their strong connections with a group.

This theme is most pronounced in Eva's account of her work as having been, from the very beginning, closely tied to her three male architect partners, whom she describes as her 'friends', the 'nest', the 'boys', the 'team'. To Eva, her 'boys' represent home, professional partners, the centre of her life, the stable and secure grounds on which she can move and live ('the nest'). She does not distinguish herself in any dichotomized way from the 'others' but presents herself and her life as part of a team ('personification' and backgrounding of self). The coherence of her narrative is constructed through the description of events holding the team together, each clause starting with 'we'. She has sacrificed her autonomous self for the team.

> And then, it will surely get to the point that I had the good luck to get to know my friends here, where we actually were so impressed by this job that we really spent our lives doing nothing else. Well we really worked from morning to evening and had hardly any time for holidays or whatnot. And then you actually get into this whole spectrum. We also had the good luck, well that we all worked together in the office. So this group, our group of four people. That was actually in some ways the centre of our lives for all four of us, because we just spend so many years together. And that is, well, actually, our nest or something, yes, our centre.

In Eva's account, the *topos* of luck occurs twice. We may understand this as Eva being proud to be part of the team and viewing this as being lucky. We may also read it as Eva downplaying the active work that success requires. Luck always implies coincidence. Her story does not give voice to her own ambitions nor does it express the energy needed to establish such a 'nest' and team and to keep it working.

Going back to the experience of Denise Scott Brown, Jane successfully managed the transition of their architectural firm from a small, chaotic practice with frequent 'hysterical situations' to an entrepreneurial office. Although she has housekeeping and caring roles, she does not feel diminished or as if she has been pushed into the second row. This may have to do with her more modest ambitions as an architect (none of these young architects is famous). But it also seems to indicate that understanding herself as the member of a successful team allows her to identify with the firm's successful design activities. The following sequence presents the total identification with 'we' as a team, arguing and justifying such a collective view with almost absurd and exaggerated sarcastic examples, in an argumentative contrast which is displayed in a scenic performance and confronts the human environment with people working like machines or parts of machines.

> And if someone says 'You're a fantastic office, and this is a great project' or something, then I have no problem at all. I immediately accept the accolade. Yes, because otherwise everyone would have to start: 'I am the bolt', and 'I am this', it's only possible as a communal success, so that it

sort of looks like actually, when there's always a trend, that so to speak some brilliant idea gets over-rated.

In the two accounts, two metaphors and two conceptual frames are thus presented as two poles, as two life styles of work: the nest and the machine (see also Morgan, 1997, for a discussion of organizational metaphors).

Apart from being part of the 'right team' in terms of people you like, with whom you have a shared understanding, there is a strong emotional aspect to how the women define success. This is the case for the banker Claire who strongly believes in tension/energy as a source of creativity. She has a motto, realized as metaphor, for her life – 'to plant the seeds, take care, harvest, and celebrate thanksgiving'. She firmly believes in 'positive thinking' and employs many superlatives in her description. Her self-definition comes close to persuasive discourse, to the genre of a mission statement, employing the catchwords (future, passion, motivation, personality, emotional environment), phrased in an elliptic evocation, and generalizing her belief through the *topos* of necessity (Muntigl and Gruber, 2005). Implied indirectly is her achievement: she has found the right people with the right personality and she is able to lead them:

> With future, with bringing things into the world, with motivation, with enthusiasm. So I have a lot to do with people who are positively motivated. Now, that's really not the case everywhere, in every department of the bank . . . I think it takes a certain personality. And so every firm in various phases, but also every task, I think, also has its emotional environment. And you somehow have to be lucky enough to be the person in the right place. That has to match, otherwise it doesn't work.

A few sentences later Claire mentions the role of significant others in her career

> So I think that one then also always needs different people to relate to, yes. You know on one's own you can't do anything, yes. So I've been lucky that I . . .

Like Eva, Claire refers to luck, belittling the immense work behind the construction of a good, functioning team, and she suggests coincidence, which also implies passiveness, in contrast to the material verbs which characterized our first examples. The impersonal 'one' emphasizes such a passive and generalizing perspective (backgounding of self). Her definitions are dogmatic because they are justified with the *topos* of necessity. Observing Claire in her work, however, gives a somewhat different impression, that of a strong-willed almost charismatic person who has the gift to motivate, challenge and support others.

Being successful also has connotations of having fun, being motivated, and enthusiastic, moving things. The women refer to the fascination of mathematics, the enthusiasm their architectural projects inspire, and the art of fascinating others through the spoken word. Software developer Susi talks about her passion for structuring and solving problems – mathematical riddles – and about the privilege of being autonomous in her work ('*Selbst-bestimmen-können*'), adding that she has fun in her work. She oscillates between a personal, a dialogic and an impersonal perspective. This time, the impersonal perspective implies a generalizing tendency:

> And I also think that fun . . . well you can stand a lot of stress if work makes you happy. And it is just exciting to be able to join in making decisions, being able to share in taking responsibility for them.

Susi perceives herself as a person who shapes or designs her own environment, albeit in a hesitating/mitigating way, introduced by mental verbs ('I think'):

> Let's put it like this, I have . . . I'd rather say, I think, I have shaped my environment in the way I like it to be.

At the same time she expresses ambivalence. Work is no game anymore, but hard, tiring, and difficult. Once having taken the decision to create her software company by herself, there is no easy way of going back. Her statement uses the impersonal 'one' and the generalizing, short and dense description in the past tense through which she summarizes and essentializes a certain career trajectory (a path which is followed without any other options symbolizes a specific cognitive frame and event model) as an example of many women with similar problems and stress:

> And it's like that, after founding the company, after expansion and so on, there are lots of things, well, there were decisions made, and there are lots of things pretty clearly specified. One can change it, after all, but one doesn't get out too easily. One has forged a path, and one just follows it. Well that is clear. One has made this decision and then one has a business and responsibility. And somehow it does work.

For Chris, being herself, living her own life is at the core of having a successful career. The name she chose for her firm – Human Money Company – reflects the mixture of trust, personalized relationships and high professionalism that Chris sees as the cornerstones of her success. A part of this is her dream of connecting all the things she values in her life in the form of a service centre (combined with a fitness centre and options of luxury). She explains this fantasy of the utopian office as a trajectory, very personal in the mode (through direct address), discursively constructing a scenic narrative where the coherence is created dynamically – the story of somebody passing from one room to the next and experiencing the unique combination of work and leisure. In Fairclough's (1992) terms, we find interdiscursivity, a combination of consumerism and marketization, in a rhetorically persuasive and strategic hybrid genre, mixing a promotional advertisement with a personal wish

> . . . where fashion, health treatments and business services are offered. So you come in and go down a corridor and see clothes and jewellery to the left and right. And when you have done the whole house, you go out and have everything on and you're feeling well and you're smiling and you have your tax return, you have your lawyer, business consultant or treatment. And while you're waiting for the profit–loss account you can decide whether you want to watch a film or go to a health practitioner, to a Feng-Shui advisor or to the tailor and so on, or into the café that they also have there.

There is also a streak of ambivalence in Chris, depite being so visibly successful in her accounting business: Chris accumulates certificates in various therapeutic techniques or courses about transaction analysis, which indicates a familiar female dilemma – having to know more (than men) and being perfect! And asked about her notion of success, she replies:

> Depends on which hat I've got on when you ask me, so to speak as a woman or as a human. As a woman I say: Success? What success? I haven't had any success. And as a human I say: most of the time I just really almost live the life I want to live. That's enough. That is success for me that I can do what I want, and it also works out financially.

First she negates that she has success at all: what she is doing is 'normal'. She downplays her visible ambition and success through repeating a rhetorical question 'Success?' twice. She also rejects her female identity by substituting 'woman' through 'human' (*topos* of definition). This sequence indicates strong ambivalence with *female* success, even though Chris knows what she wants, and she has most probably experienced her limitations.

Theme 3: Being Powerful – Climbing onto the Stage

Maybe the most marked contrast to Sassen's (1980) account of 'success anxiety' is the explicitly expressed positive relationship of our interviewees to power and fame, our third macro-cluster of topics, where entrepreneurial ideologies clearly manifest themselves. Maria, project manager in a glamorous, fast-moving multimedia company has a clear notion of what being successful means. She describes a feeling she experienced the evening before one of the interviews we conducted with her in the following narrative:

> Yesterday, what did I achieve? There was this schedule, that I taught those two something, and that we had worked out something bigger and sent it to the client and that I had a meal for half an hour. That was a greater

achievement for me than the 50 deliveries that we sent out . . . I measure my success differently from how I am measured. But I see that just as – for me it's a liberation. I see it not as a duty, instead I feel I'm not dependent on another's evaluation or on their, let's say praise or criticism, because I know I have other priorities.

Starting out with a quasi rhetorical question which she immediately answers herself, she gives an example of her definition of success, as argumentative strategy: interacting and teaching others something which she finds important. She has a wider notion of success than 'those 50 deliverables' and she stresses her independence, always very much involved in her professional jargon which indicates her identification with the job. Maria performs her own – different – success story. She also justifies her opinion by being independent of praise or criticism (*topos* of definition). The fact that she emphasizes her opinion indicates that she needs to defend her position against an anonymous other position which is described as contrast but without actors and subjects ('suppression of actors'). It is not clear if she promotes her role against existing stereotypes or against colleagues in her firm. In contradicting herself immediately in the following clauses, she tells a long story (one of many in the interview) about how much she enjoys being on the stage, in the media, receiving praise, being publicly acknowledged:

> . . . and now he has my face on the cover, just as I was starting, as a cartoon, as an illustration. That's called *Global Citizen*. And I really had to laugh, because like Andy Warhol everyone has to be famous for five minutes or ten minutes. And now I have my face on a cover, and that's enough. That is enough now, yes, it says *Global Citizen* and a stupid article. And it is off-key . . . And we're like that, for me, I observe that, and I think, yes, and what do you want now? It's like Ticks now. I never wished for or wanted this, but it's more or less okay like that, it's your exam paper, so to speak. Carry on. Carry on.

Maria simultaneously enjoys the fame and downplays it with irony ('stupid article') and with reference to famous people like Andy Warhol, stressing at the same time: 'I never wished for or wanted this'. On the other hand, she describes and repeats precisely in which magazine she had been put on the front page. She also repeats that this is 'enough', indicating her irony once more. Finally, she simultaneously downplays her ambition and her active search for fame and success, by using a rhetorical question 'what do you want now?' The obvious and explicit contradictions are a good example of the existence of ideological dilemmas, as proposed by Michael Billig (1991), see later. This narrative is performed like a dialogue, as if Maria is interacting with somebody with a different and contradictory opinion, somebody she wants to persuade and impress. This ambivalence could also be interpreted as being a bit arrogant or even coquettish, playing the game of the famous and beautiful, but in a reflected and conscious way.

Claire is equally direct in her account of her glorious moments, when she talks about striving for more than solid work as senior manager in a bank. She wants to be visible and a way for her to achieve this is through her lectures and publications. She oscillates between the impersonal 'one' in the present and the personal 'I' in the past tense, as a narrative and anecdote. The anecdotes serve argumentatively to illustrate the discursive construction of her identity and identification patterns by stressing her name as unique ('a name in the field') and by being identified by her name on the top. This is the third explicit event model encountered in our interviews which contrasts clearly with the model of being symbiotic with the team:

> . . . where one can hold lectures, so where one can also make a bit of one's career, so just making oneself a name in a field. And that was always strongly intertwined, because it was always a personal wish, also with regard to economic policies. For me it is always a piece of identity, yes. Also not to drown in being-a-co-worker-with, but 'Claire X in'. Creating a set, but then also being up there at the top. I do want that.

Interestingly, when asked about possible career steps, her answer is:

> Well, one could say, when one looks at it from a career point of view, one step would be the board of directors. So if you ask me, would I do that, I would say 'of course'. Yes. But it isn't something where I would say I'm in a deep depression because I'm not in it, yes.

Stepping back from being on the top of the bank's hierarchy as a relevant stage seems to indicate that there is also a moment of ambivalence in Claire's ambitions.

Sissy is on the stage, as the right hand of an internationally successful owner of a multimedia company. Like Maria, she works in a chaotic and completely designed environment, everything communicating style and accomplishment. She has always been, as part of her work, in the theatre and in film-making, where personalities (and conflicts between them) and the media matter so much. Sissy is a story teller, using a lot of casual in-sider jargon which is very common in this profession:

> . . . in these past ten years in the theatre I have learnt unbelievably much, just for organization, for how to handle people, how do I handle conflicts, how do all the power games run, how does the press run and so on. Nobody ever taught me, so it was always learning by doing.

The story she tells is one of almost continuous and entirely self-made success – of her acquiring skills 'by doing', discovering abilities she was not aware of, mastering challenge after challenge, each ending with a special achievement and recognition – 'phenomenal feedback'. Things happened; she obviously did not look for them. The coincidental factor is emphasized here.

The interdiscursivity between persuasive, promotional, advertising, organizational, and professional discourses is apparent in many of our examples of the more entrepreneurial women. The socialization into the business world leaves its traces in the habitus of our interviewees. One might even go as far as to detect influences of neo-liberal ideologies, such as flexibility, individualism ('self-made woman') and efficiency combined with leisure and consumerism. Moreover, the attempt to relate leisure to work, luxury to efficiency, and public to private indicates the colonization of the private through the hard work expected in such positions, as well as the intrusion of traditionally female discourses into formerly male environments.

Discussion

Self-Presentation: Desires, Identities, Values – Self-Presentation through (Metaphoric) Conceptual Frames

The images and messages in the women's stories reveal a diversity of strategies in balancing existing discourses of success with their own ideas of what constitutes achievement and their own constructed self-presentation. Their statements combine elements of active shaping with streaks of passivity and ambivalence, in the use of pronouns, deictic devices, argumentative and rhetorical strategies, and the mixing of different organizational and promotional genres.

Many rhetorical and argumentative strategies of self-presentation can be summarized by focusing on one of the most fore-grounded linguistic devices: the use of metaphors. Metaphors define the conceptual and perceptual frames of our interviewees.

> Metaphor . . . is not a mere reflection of a pre-existing objective reality but a construction of reality, through a categorisation entailing the selection of some features as critical and others as non-critical . . . metaphors can consciously be used to construct . . . reality. (Goatly, 1997: 5)

This crucial aspect of the use of metaphors – discursively and cognitively constructing one's own subjective realities – is present throughout our interviews. Moreover, the abundance of evaluative adjectives intensifies such metaphors and complements the cognitive, conceptual frames with emotions and values. Without being able to present all the details of the ongoing debate of theories and analysis of metaphors, we would like to stress the function of conceptual frames, realized in metaphorical expressions, for the women's self-presentations. Metaphors form a constitutive part of 'performing gender' and 'performing success'.[5] Metaphors support the construction of specific 'event models', which serve to establish a coherent self-presentation and an explanation of unique life trajectories.

'Event models' integrate and update every new experience in specific stereotypical and/or prejudiced ways even if these events might mean something totally different. Event models store experiences in specific schemas and scripts, and offer models for updating and explaining new experiences. In our case, they are used to reduce complexity and offer coherence for otherwise fragmented or conflicting life stories (Linde, 1993). They are automatically processed as either masculine or feminine, as successful or non-successful, as good or bad. They get distorted, adapted and integrated with previously stored event models.

Self-presentations, perceptions, stereotypes, opinions, and beliefs are enforced and manifested inter alia by metaphors, analogies and insinuations as well as stories (Van Dijk, 1984). They are cognitively and emotionally deeply embedded and also have historical roots. A change of frames, in our case, of belief systems and ideologies related to success and successful women – should this be more then a superficial change of language – would turn out to be very difficult. Such changes (if at all possible) would take a long time and would need to produce some kind of deep insight ('catharsis') which would allow the substitution of certain mental representations and long-stored event models with new ones (Wodak, 2005b). This fact might explain the emphasis some of our interviewees placed on a crisis, its meaning for their lives, and of how the crisis affected the way they re-directed their lives.

In our analysis we found the following clusters of metaphorical frames dominating the self-presentations as successful women, or put differently, as describing success:

- *Self-presentation as creating space:* success consists of defining one's space, transforming space, building space formations (inside space and outside space), and creating space. These metaphors are, on the one hand, sometimes related to the profession of architecture and thus not surprising. These women identify with this dimension of the profession and find it very empowering. However, on the other hand, these metaphors and frames also appear in other professions where the creation of autonomy is meant which links to creating one's own surrounding and environment as somewhere pleasant – a space in which one feels comfortable.
- *Self-presentation as a team:* success consists of creating a team and being part of a team. This conceptual frame, often realized in metaphors, such as 'nest', 'family' or 'team', corresponds to the stereotypical female capability of caring for others and being involved in interpersonal relationships. This frame extends to the point where one of our interviewees even mentioned giving birth as a metaphor for constructing both one's space as well as one's environment. The conceptual frame, however, can also be expressed mechanistically as a contrast: being the relevant part or bolt of a machine without which the machine would not work.
- *Self-presentation as creating life:* giving birth which traditionally characterizes the greatest female power is also linked strongly to emotional

metaphors, such as being totally engaged/involved/obsessed with one's profession, even '*beseelt* (enlivened)'. Creating in this motherly sense relates to planting seeds or trees, thus creating something for eternity or posteriority.

- *Self-presentation as main actor on the stage:* success is linked to conceptual frames of performance, of being on stage, of playing the game. This self-presentation is conscious of power, of the power of working hard, of impressing, of being different from others, and finally, of being publicly acknowledged and a prominent figure. Such narratives indicate pride, quite unmitigated, with a great deal of emotional involvement, and sometimes, with a bit of irony and ambivalence.
- *Self-presentation as mover:* success is defined as an achievement of moving things, getting designs materialized, moving others in the right direction, taking the right train. Space is combined here with time and activity, in a quasi teleological way: in the direction of achievement and success, planned by the women themselves. These women do not carry out orders from others; they define the direction they want to take.
- *Self-presentation as enjoying a good life:* success is defined as pleasure, as enjoying a good life-style, as working together with the right people; basically as leading a comfortable life. This frame mystifies the hard work involved. Ambition is down-played, stress not mentioned.
- *Self-presentation as being at the right place at the right time:* this form of self-presentation takes us to more traditional female roles. Success and achievement are defined as luck and coincidence; these women emphasize that they never thought that they would be able to succeed, they were helped, depended on a mentor, or were just lucky. They portray themselves as passive, as having fallen into success. Their own efforts are mitigated.

Ambivalence becomes apparent when several of these conceptual frames are mixed in one narrative. Such stories or descriptions remind us of the concept of ideological dilemmas (Billig et al., 1991), which explains the appearance of totally contradictory claims in the same narrative. These dilemmas, however, illustrate the spontaneity of many narratives in the interviews; the interviewees have not planned their answers, they become emotionally involved, and thus *perform* their success and life stories for the interviewer, sometimes even in fictive scenes, interacting with the interviewer and an anonymous audience.

Re-Embedding the Life Stories – Sources of Ambivalence, Activeness, and Passiveness

Additional aspects of women's success come to the fore when we re-embed our findings in the context of their life stories. In more general terms, we can identify a variety of sources in the women's biographies that give them strength, create ambivalence or evoke moments of passivity:

- *Events that let women experience the problems of finding a balance* – between having a career in a demanding environment and being a mother or finding time for personal relationships.
- *Significant others who accompany the women through transitory and/or dilemmatic life situations*: this may be a mentor (Claire), a strong and caring parent, the right team (the 'boys' that help Eva continue work as an architect and be a mother). Experiences such as these are reported again and again in women's biographies (e.g. Schlosser, 2001).
- *Experiences that help form a strong sense of self*: for example, the privilege of living in two cultures (Maria, who seeks to combine a philosophy shaped by the notion of 'having time' and 'looking inward' with a more European way of running a business), becoming engaged in environments in which she could feel herself (for Susi, the women's movement) or the experience of 'mastering' tasks she has never performed before (film making in the case of Sissy) or a severe financial crisis (Jane's architectural firm).
- *Experiences of anxiety and defeat* which may have roots far back in a woman's childhood and youth. Chris, for example, talks about her fits of anxiety as a student, for instance, being afraid of opening the door of the lecture hall, starting to cry when someone addressed her in public – she still seeks to perfect herself.

Related to these differing experiences, we encountered four event models throughout our data which are employed to systematize the narratives, organizing them coherently, and thus providing a rational order for the life trajectories (Linde, 1993).

(a) Symbiosis – work is experienced together, the women's own identities merge with the identities of the other team members, the team is more important than each part. This model manifests itself inter alia in the repeated use of the personal pronoun 'we' and of the active voice.
(b) Self-made woman: individualism is foregrounded. Life stories are structured around constructing the self through making one's name and being famous. 'I' is used throughout; some of the accounts come close to persuasive mission statements.
(c) Creating one's space and work, being autonomous is seen as the most important part of one's identity and life story (and work); work achievements define the identity. Space metaphors construct this model, as do abstract actors and nominalizations.
(d) Coincidence and luck – 'it simply works': achievements are presented almost as unpredictable miracles; the hard work involved is denied.

In this case, social actors are suppressed or backgrounded, the passive voice is salient. A more descriptive genre substitutes narrative structure, the reports are usually in the present tense.

These event-models are also somewhat related to the professions of the women we interviewed: for example, the entrepreneurial women are more individualistic, the architects more team-oriented. We interpret these differences as related to pressures in the respective field as well as to different forms of organizational structures and also to creativity.

New Forms of Success – Performing Differently?

Do these women 'search for a different language from which to construct the meaning of success' (Smulyan, 2004), challenging male-dominated constructs? Do they use pre-existing narratives of stereotyped gender relations to reinvent themselves (Gherardi, 1996)? The women's stories are clearly interwoven with professional commitments and expectations, which are more generally shared by members of these communities. Some, but not all of them try to rewrite the conditions for success.

The company in which Maria works presents itself as a 'magical place' but the reality is different. Dealing with competitors and formulating strategies requires a lot of toughness – we observed men in the company describe their work and their competitors in rather aggressive metaphors. This toughness translates into the rhythm of everyday work and burnout is a widespread phenomenon (Moore, 2000). As we have shown, Maria has absorbed the professional jargon and she evidently shares some of the success criteria of the field. Like software specialist Susi, Maria defies the traditional role patterns, seeking to create an environment that is inclusive and supportive of women, fighting the male schemas and scripts that typically see toughness and dominance as 'a bit choleric' when exhibited by men and 'hysterical' when shown by women.

'The manly architect' is 'the authoritative administrator', the designer of large building complexes, and the 'orchestrator of the work of others' (Adams and Tancred, 2000). Exceedingly long working hours make having a private life difficult, as a female architect explains: 'Things are changing slowly. While the stars among architects are still mostly men, young groups often have women in leading positions. The architects among our informants don't question this "crazy profession".' Their identity is shaped by and expressed in what they design and ultimately gets built. Their issue is the aesthetic and the quality of use of the spaces they design, and not to design differently, being women. Jane is refreshing in how she values her 'housekeeping' role, seeing it as no less important then the design role of her (male and female) colleagues in the office.

The general trend within the financial services towards specialization and offering more integrated services is reflected in the narratives of both women in this field. Claire combines banking knowledge with skills in consulting, supervision, and coaching. She strongly believes in the open, intense, and result-oriented communication structure of the bank. Chris's enormous success lies in her 'holistic' approach to accounting, her ability to take care of details, to combine technical expertise with a view of her clients as a whole.

When looking at Gherardi's (1996) patterns of reciprocal positioning (of women vis à vis the organizational/professional cultures they find), most of our informants are in the cooperative position of 'the guest'. None of them is in a marginal, stigmatized position, appears as a mere 'holiday maker' let alone 'a snake in the grass' or 'intruder'. Does this mean that they follow the male patterns that are dominant in their fields? We have tried to show that this is not the case and that the cooperating, non-antagonistic positioning that the women practise offers space for them to build their own success stories in many small but important ways. In some cases, however, there is a significant gap between performances and organizational realities.

Notes

1. Women in Innovative Firms – Case Studies on Environment, Work Practice, Qualifications and Coping Strategies, in cooperation with the University of Technology in Cottbus, Germany, funded by the Deutsche Forschungsgemeinschaft (2000–2002); IST-2001-34520 Project WWW-ICT Widening Women's Work in Information and Communication Technology, funded by the European Commission (2002–2004); The Discursive Construction of European Identities; funded through the Wittgenstein Prize awarded to Ruth Wodak in 1996, see <http://www.univie.ac.at/discourse-politics-identity>.
2. In our analysis, we cannot present the huge amount of data (the whole life stories) due to space restrictions. We focus on sequences from our interviews where the interviewees explicitly narrate stories about their success, their career trajectories or define what they mean by 'success'. The entire analysis and projects are published elsewhere (see earlier).
3. See Holmes and Meyerhoff (2003), Sunderland (2004), Lazar (2005), Wodak (1997a), and Kotthoff and Wodak (1997), for recent overviews and introductions to the field of linguistic Gender Studies.
4. In Reisigl and Wodak (2001: 70ff), the main linguistic units are defined and illustrated extensively. Thus, we refer to argumentation theory (Van Eemeren and Grootendorst, 1994) as well as to Functional Systemic Linguistics (Halliday, 1994) and to Theo van Leeuwen's Actor's Analysis (Van Leeuwen, 1996) (see later).
5. Koller (2004: 42) presents an interesting approach to metaphor research, integrating research on ideology with socio-cognition and critical discourse analysis (CDA). In contrast to Lakoff and Johnson (1998), she emphasizes the possibility of also inten- tionally choosing one's own frames, thus distancing herself from an over-deterministic position.

References

Acker, J. (1992) 'Gendering Organizational Theory', in A. Mills and P. Tancred (eds) *Gendering Organizational Analysis*, pp. 248–60. Newbury Park, CA: Sage:

Adams, A. and Tancred, P. (2000) *'Designing Women': Gender and the Architectural Profession*. Toronto: University of Toronto Press.

Baxter, J. (2003) *Positioning Gender in Discourse: A Feminist Methodology*. Basingstoke: Palgrave.

Berg, N. and Lien, D. (2002) 'Measuring the Effect of Sexual Orientation on Income: Evidence of Discrimination?', *Contemporary Economic Policy* 20(4): 394–414.

Billig, M. et al. (1991) *Ideological Dilemmas*. London: Sage.

Birbaumer, A., Tolar, M. and Wagner, I. (2006, forthcoming) 'Working Women in ICT – Approach and Findings of a European Project', in E.M. Trauth (ed.) *Encyclopedia of Gender and Information Technology*. Hershey, PA: Idea Group Publishing.

Bourdieu, P. (1994) *Raisons pratiques. Sur la théorie de l'action*. Paris: éditions du Seuil.

Brown, D. S. (1989) 'Sexism and the Star System in Architecture', in E.P. Berkeley (ed.) *Architecture: A Place for Women*, pp. 237–46. Washington, DC: Smithsonian Institute.

Buchholtz, M. (1999) 'Bad Examples: Transgression and Progress in Language and Gender Studies', in M. Buchholtz, A.C. Liang and L.A. Sutton (eds) *Reinventing Identities: The Gendered Self in Discourse*, pp. 3–24. New York: Oxford University Press.

Butler, J. (1999 [1990]) *Gender Trouble: Feminism and the Subversion of Identity*. New York: Routledge.

Cammack, J.C. and Kalmbach Phillips, D. (2002) 'Discourses and Subjectivities of the Gendered Teacher', *Gender and Education* 14(2): 123–33.

Coontz, P.D. (1995) 'Gender Bias in the Legal Profession: Women "See" It, Men Don't', *Women and Politics* 15(2): 1–22.

Davies, C. (1996) 'The Sociology of Professions and the Profession of Gender', *Sociology* 30(4): 661–78.

Diem-Wille, G. (1996) *Karrierefrauen und Karrieremänner. Eine psychoanalytisch orientierte Untersuchung ihrer Lebensgeschichte und Familiendynamik*. Opladen/Stuttgart: WDV.

Fairclough, N. (1992) *Discourse and Social Change*. London: Polity.

Fenwick, T.J. (2002) 'Lady, Inc.: Women Learning, Negotiating Subjectivity in Entrepreneurial Discourses', *International Journal of Lifelong Education* 22(2): 162–77.

Flick, U. (1995) *Qualitative Forschung: Theorie, Methoden, Anwendung in Psychologie und Sozialwissenschaften*. Reinbek bei Hamburg: Rowohlt.

Gherardi, S. (1996) 'Gendered Organizational Cultures: Narratives of Women Travellers in a Male World', *Gender, Work and Organization* 3(4): 187–201.

Gilligan, C. (1982) *In a Different Voice. Psychological Theory and Women's Development*. Cambridge, MA: Harvard University Press.

Glaser, B. and Strauss, A.L. (1967) *The Discovery of Grounded Theory*. Chicago: Aldine.

Goatly, A. (1997) *The Language of Metaphors*. London: Routledge.

Greed, C. (2000) 'Women in the Construction Professions: Achieving Critical Mass', *Gender, Work and Organization* 7(3): 181–96.

Greene, A., Ackers, P. and Black, J. (2002) 'Going Against the Historical Grain: Perspectives on Gendered Occupational Identity and Resistance to the Breakdown of Occupational Segregation in Two Manufacturing Firms', *Gender, Work and Organization* 9(3): 266–85.

Halliday, M.A.K. (1994) *An Introduction to Functional Grammar*. London: Arnold.

Hedman, A. (2003) *Visitor Orientation in Context: The Historically Rooted Production of Soft Places*. Stockholm: Royal Institute of Technology.

Holmes, J. and Meyerhoff, M. (eds) (2003) *Handbook of Discourse and Gender*. Oxford: Oxford University Press.

Iedema, R. (2003) *Discourse in Post Bureaucratic Organizations*. Amsterdam: Benjamins.

Järvinen, M. (2000) 'The Biographical Illusion: Constructing Meaning in Qualitative Interviews', *Qualitative Inquiry* 6(3): 370–91.

Jones, C. et al. (1998) 'Professional Service Constellations: How Strategies and Capabilities Influence Collaborative Stability and Change', *Organization Science* 9(3): 396–410.

Kellner, D. (1995) *Media Culture*. London: Routledge.

Kendall, S. and Tannen, D. (1997) 'Gender and Language in the Workplace', in H. Kotthoff and R. Wodak (eds) *Communicating Gender in Context*. Amsterdam: Benjamins.

Koller, V. (2005) 'Critical Discourse Analysis and Social Cognition: Evidence from Business Media Discourse', *Discourse & Society* 16: 199–224.

Kotthoff, H. and Wodak, R. (eds) (1997) *Communicating Gender in Context*. Amsterdam: Benjamins.

Lakoff, G. and Johnson, M. (1998). *Leben in Metaphern*. Heidelberg: Carl-Auer-Systeme.

Lash, S. and Urry, J. (1994) *Economics of Signs and Space*. London: Sage.

Lazar, M. (ed.) (2005) *Feminist Critical Discourse Analysis*. London: Palgrave.

Licht, B.G. and Dweck, C.S. (1984) 'Determinants of Academic Achievement: The Interaction of Children's Achievement Orientations with Skill Area', *Developmental Psychology* 20: 628–36.

Liff, S. and Ward, K. (2001) 'Distorted Views through the Glass Ceiling: The Construction of Women's Understandings of Promotion and Senior Management Positions', *Gender, Work and Organization* 8(1): 19–36.

Linde, C. (1993) *Life Stories: The Creation of Coherence*. Oxford: Oxford University Press.

Machin, D. and Van Leeuwen, T. (2003). 'Global Schemas and Local Discourses in Cosmopolitan', *Journal of Sociolinguistics* 7(4): 493–512.

Martín Rojo, M.L. and Gomez-Esteban, C. (2003) 'Discourse at Work: When Women Take on the Role of Managers', in G. Weiss and R. Wodak (eds) *Critical Discourse Analysis. Theory and Interdisciplinarity*, pp. 241–171. London: Palgrave/Macmillan.

Miller, G.E. (2002) 'The Frontier, Entrepreneurialism, and Engineers: Women Coping with a Web of Masculinities in an Organizational Culture', *Culture and Organization* 8(2): 145–60.

Moore, J.E. (2000) 'One Road to Turnover: An Examination of Work Exhaustion in Technology Professionals', *MIS Quarterly* 24(1): 141–68.

Moosmüller, S. (1997) 'The Relevance of Fundamental Frequency Contour for Interruptions: A Case Study of Political Discussion in Austria', in H. Kotthoff and R. Wodak (eds) *Communicating Gender in Context*, pp. 401–21. Amsterdam: Benjamins.

Morgan, G. (1997) *Images of Organization*. London: Sage.

Muntigl, P. and Gruber, H. (2005) 'Introduction: Approaches to Genres', *Folia Linguistica* XXXIX/1–2: 1–19.

Nonnemaker, L. (2005) 'Women Physicians in Academic Medicine', *The New England Journal of Medicine* 342(6): 399–405.

Reisigl, M. and Wodak, R. (2001) *Discourse and Discrimination*. London: Routledge.

Sassen, G. (1980) 'Success Anxiety in Women: A Constructivist Interpretation of its Source and Significance', *Harvard Educational Review* 50(1): 13–24.

Schlosser, G.A. (2001) 'Stories of Success from Eminent Finnish Women: A Narrative Study', *High Ability Studies* 12(1): 61–87.

Smulyan, L. (2004) 'Redefining Self and Success: Becoming Teachers and Doctors', *Gender and Education* 16(2): 225–45.

Sunderland, J. (2004) *Gendered Discourses*. London: Palgrave.

Tomlinson, F., Brockbank, A. and Traves, J. (1997) 'The "Feminization" of Management? Issues of "Sameness" and "Difference" in the Roles and Experiences of Female and Male Retail Managers', *Gender, Work and Organization* 4(4): 218–29.

Trix, F. and Psenka, C. (2003) 'Exploring the Colour of Glass: Letters of Recommendation for Female and Medical Faculty', *Discourse & Society* 14(2): 191–220.

Valenduc, G. et al. (2004: *Widening Women's Work in Information and Communication Technology*. Synthesis Report of The European Project 2002–2004. Namur, Belgium, European Commission.

Van Dijk, Teun A. (1984) *Prejudice in Discourse*. Amsterdam: Benjamins.

Van Dijk, Teun A. (2001) 'Critical Discourse Analysis', in D. Tannen, D. Schiffrin and H. Hamilton (eds) *Handbook of Discourse Analysis*. Oxford: Blackwell.

Van Eemeren, F. and Grootendorst, B. (eds) (1994) *Studies in Pragma-Dialectics*. Amsterdam: International Centre for the Study of Argumentation, Sic Sat.

Van Leeuwen, T. (1996) 'The Analysis of Social Actors', in C.R. Caldas-Coulthard and M. Coulthard (eds) *Texts and Practices: Readings in Critical Discourse Analysis*, pp. 32–70. London: Routledge.

Wagner, I. (2003) 'Women in Innovative Companies – Issues of Work Practice, Gender and Technology', in C. Mörtberg, P. Elovaara and A. Lundgren (eds) *How Do We Make a Difference? Information Technology, Transnational Democracy and Gender*, pp. 113–33. Lulea: Lulea University.

Wagner, I. and Birbaumer, A. (2005) 'Les femmes cadres dans les entreprises innovantes', *Travail, genre et sociétés, la revue du MAGE* (Fall).

Winch, G. and Schneider, E. (1993) 'Managing the Knowledge-Based Organization: The Case of Architectural Practice', *Journal of Management Studies* 30(6): 923–37.

Wodak, R. (ed.) (1997a) *Gender and Discourse*. London: Sage.

Wodak, R. (1997b) '"I Know, We Won't Revolutionize the World with It, But . . .": Styles of Female Leadership in Institutions', in H. Kotthoff and R. Wodak (eds) *Communicating Gender in Context*, pp. 335–70. Amsterdam: Benjamins.

Wodak, R. (2003a) 'Multiple Identities: The Roles of Female Parliamentarians in the EU Parliament', in J. Holmes and M. Meyerhoff (eds) *Handbook of Discourse and Gender*, pp. 671–98. Oxford: Oxford University Press.

Wodak, R. (2003b) 'Populist Discourses: The Rhetoric of Exclusion in Written Genres', *Document Design* 4(2): 133–48.

Wodak, R. (2005a) 'Gender Mainstreaming and the European Union: Interdisciplinarity, Gender Studies and CDA', in M. Lazar (ed.) *Feminist Critical Discourse Analysis*, pp. 61–89. Basingstoke: Palgrave.

Wodak, R. (2005b) 'Mediation between Discourse and Society – Assessing Cognitive Approaches', *Discourse Studies* 8(1): 179–90.